The New Internet Business Book

The New Internet Business Book

Jill H. Ellsworth, Ph.D.
Matthew V. Ellsworth

JOHN WILEY & SONS, INC.

New York • Chichester • Brisbane • Toronto • Singapore

Publisher: Katherine Schowalter

Editor: Tim Ryan

Managing Editor: Mark Hayden

Text Design & Composition: SunCliff Graphic Productions

This text is printed on acid-free paper.

This publication is designed to provide accurate and authoritative information in regard to the subject matter covered. It is sold with the understanding that the publisher is not engaged in rendering legal, accounting, or other professional service. If legal advice or other expert assistance is required, the services of a competent professional person should be sought.

Library of Congress Cataloging-in-Publication Data

Ellsworth, Jill H., 1949–
    The New Internet business book / Jill H. Ellsworth, Matthew V. Ellsworth
        p.   cm
    Rev. ed of: The Internet business book / Jill H. Ellsworth, Matthew V. Ellsworth. c1994
    Includes bibliographical references and index.
    ISBN 0-471-14160-7
    1. Industrial management—Computer network resources.   2. Business enterprises—Communication systems.   3. Internet (Computer network)   4. Information networks.   I. Ellsworth, Mathew V.   II. Ellsworth, Jill H., 1949-   Internet business book.   III. Title.
HD30.37.E44   1996
650'.0285'467—dc20   95-25740
                                                                                                              CIP

Printed in the United States of America

10 9 8 7 6 5 4 3 2 1

Dedicated to the memory of
John V. Ellsworth and Doris E. Ellsworth

Contents

Chapter 16   Online Resources, Databases, and Libraries of General Interest   337

Acknowledgments

We want to thank all of the readers of *The Internet Business Book* who wrote to us with such enthusiasm and passion about their success stories, ideas, and helpful suggestions. We continue to be amazed by the rich variety of ways you are using the Internet for business, and we hope that readers will continue to be in touch with us about their projects.

We would especially like to thank several individuals among the many helpful people at John Wiley & Sons: our editor, Tim Ryan, for his ongoing assistance in this project, and Bob Ipsen and Susan Straub.

In addition, we would like to thank Jodie Beder and Cliff Fischbach for their contributions to the clarity and appearance of this book.

Introduction to The New Internet Business Book

News coverage of the Internet is intense. There are stories about the Information Superhighway, the National Information Infrastructure, the World Wide Web, and businesses on the Internet. News reporters often seek to develop stories about things that are shocking, or diverge from the norm. These stories have made it difficult for those not on the Internet to understand what is happening on the Internet, and to separate the hype from the reality. But that's exactly what this book can do for you. In this book, you'll get clear answers to the following questions:

- WHO is using the Internet?
- WHAT are businesses and organizations doing on the Internet and the World Wide Web?
- WHY are so many businesses, from one person start-ups to large corporations, getting connected to the Internet?
- WHERE can you get Internet access?
- HOW do you actually use the Internet for business?

This is not a false alarm or a passing fad. This is not CB, or baby vegetables, or 8-track tapes. As the telephone system did before it, the Internet is becoming a major, multibillion-dollar, integral part of international business. And with an estimated 40 million potential customers online now and a predicted 100 million by 1998, this is not a marketplace to ignore.

It is this incredible growth and resulting change that lead to *The New Internet Business Book*. Seventy-five percent of the original *Internet Business Book*, written just over a year ago, was rewritten and updated for this edition.

While this book covers what the Internet is, how to get access to it, and how to use the it, there is much more to doing business on the Internet than just getting online. Businesses must develop new strategies to utilize the Internet. Unlike the broadcast and print media, the Internet is an interactive, two-way communication system. It crosses time zones and country borders in such a seamless way that discussions and information exchanges may go on among individuals in different countries without the participants necessarily being aware of the locations of the others. Also, discussions can take place in open, multiperson configurations unlike anything that is available via the normal telephone system. And, unlike the telephone system, the Internet allows information to be stored, searched, and retrieved worldwide, inexpensively and with ease. These characteristics of the Internet can provide real power and extended reach to businesses. Much of this book deals with techniques to leverage these characteristics to improve your business and marketing efforts.

Until fairly recently, the Internet was primarily for research, government, and education institutions. Now, subject to abiding by the rules of the road, the Internet is open to individuals and businesses. These rules of the road or "netiquette" are extremely important—businesses have severely damaged their reputations literally overnight, because they didn't understand the Internet's rules and guidelines. This book will show you how to do business on the Internet safely and successfully in this new, business-friendly Internet.

In a recent speech about the National Information Infrastructure, Vice President Al Gore spoke of the changes that increased networking will bring to businesses: "The impact on America's businesses will not be limited just to those who are in the information business, either. Virtually every business will find it possible to use these new tools to become more competitive. And by taking the lead in quickly employing these new information technologies, America's businesses will gain enormous advantages in the worldwide marketplace."

Currently, a company known to be on the Internet stands out as being a sophisticated, up-to-date company. With the current growth of businesses on the Internet, it may not be too long before *not* being on the Internet will be considered a sign of a hopelessly outdated company. And obviously, if the Internet is where business is happening, then, that is where businesses must be. The Internet tools and resources described in this book can open the door wide for both you and your business to enter the Internet.

What kinds of businesses are using the Internet? Here is a tiny sampling of the many thousands of businesses on the Internet:

- Restaurants and grocery stores

  Monti's La Casa Vieja: *http://www.primenet.com/~montis/*
  Whole Foods: *http://www.wholefoods.com/wf.html*

- Car dealers and travel agents

  DealerNet: *http://www.dealernet.com*
  Bolack Total Travel's CyberConnection: *http://www.bolack.com/index.htm*

- Investment companies and bankers

  Quote.Com: *http://www.quote.com*
  Wells Fargo Bank: *http://www.wellsfargo.com/index.html*

- Artists and musicians

  Kaleidospace Internet Artists: *http://kspace.com*
  CDnow: *http://cdnow.com/*

- Doctors and lawyers

  Center for Arthroscopic Surgery: *http://mmink.cts.com/mmink/dossiers.cas.html*
  Arent Fox Kintner Plotkin & Kahn: *http://www.arentfox.com/*

- Chocolatiers and florists

  Godiva Chocolates: *http://www.godiva.com*
  Grants Flowers: *http://branch.com/flowers*

- Booksellers and publishers

  Book Stacks Unlimited: *http://www.books.com*
  John Wiley & Sons: *http://www.wiley.com*

- And some toys:

  Sharper Image Gadgets: *http://www.pathfinder.com/@@NkZVf7BbpAEAQMcs/Catalog1/Sharper.index.html*

  Duncan & Boyd Fine Jewelry: *http://dbaadv.arn.net/duncan-boyd/*

  Crailville Limited Complete Coach Building Service: *http://www.gold. net/users/eo95/*

  Lear Jets: *http://www.learjet.com*

  Yachts: *http://www.vossnet.co.uk/yacht/*

And what are business people saying about the Internet as a place to do business?

"We feel that we are able to show more of our products to the consumer than with any other medium. We are more on target with our market. We can show more online than they would find going to 5–6 suppliers." Dan Sullivan, Faucet Outlet Online

"E-mail is the holy grail of customer service. Our Web site offers the greatest marketing bang for the buck around anywhere these days." Michael Monti, Monti's La Casa Vieja restaurant

"After only 5 weeks, our Web site has paid for itself. It has been the best advertising we have ever done. We usually get a 3% return on our direct mail pieces, but we are experiencing a 10–12% return rate on the Web site." Jim Doyle of SDG Insurance

How to Use This Book

This book is divided into seven main parts:

Part I. The Internet: What It Is and How to Get Started Using It

Chapters 1 and 2 explain what the Internet and the World Wide Web are. Chapters 3 and 4 explain how to get access to the Internet, and how to get and use the software for the most important business resource on the Internet—the World Wide Web. By the end of this part of the book, you will be ready to go online on the Internet.

Part II. Business on the Internet

Chapters 5 and 6 reveal why and how businesses are using the Internet, and what techniques are acceptable—and unacceptable. Chapter 7 examines the important issues surrounding security, authentication, and on-line transactions.

Part III. Creating a Business Presence on the Internet

Chapters 8 and 9 reveal why it is important to create a business presence on the Internet and the World Wide Web, and what techniques can be used to do so.

Part IV. The World Wide Web

Chapters 10 and 11 deal with software and tools for creating a World Wide Web site, and general resources for anyone using the World Wide Web.

Part V. The Other Internet Tools

Chapters 12–14 explain how to use the most popular and broadly available Internet tool—e-mail (electronic mail)—and how e-mail can be used with discussion groups and for posting Usenet messages. This section also describes how to use several widely available Internet search and navigation systems.

Part VI. Business and Professional Resources on the Internet

In Chapters 15–17 Internet resources, categorized by their value for various professions and business functions, are listed, evaluated, and discussed.

Part VII. Your Business Online—Now and in the Future

Chapter 18 outlines how all of these Internet tools and resources can be brought together to create an integrated Internet business and marketing plan. Chapter 19, the final chapter, discusses the future of business on the Internet.

Glossary.

The glossary explains some of those pesky acronyms and strange terms that are part of the Internet jargon.

Appendixes.

Appendixes A, B, and C are designed for those new to any kind of online computing, providing information on hardware and software requirements and sources, explanation of how to upload and download files, and some basic UNIX commands needed for some types of access to the Internet. The remaining appendixes explain the use of FTP to transfer files, and the use of Telnet to log in to remote computers.

As you go through this book, remember that just as we operate and derive great value from cars, computers, and TV sets that most of us do not fully understand—so, too, we can use the Internet successfully without completely understanding all of its technical aspects. Get online as soon as you can (after finishing Part I) and interact with the Internet, and expect understanding and insights to continue coming for a long time.

A system like the Internet that is growing like gangbusters is obviously going through a lot of changes. Sites where resources are stored and ways of using the Internet tools are changing. If a resource is not where it is currently shown in this book, use one of the Internet search tools (such as discussed in Chapters 11 and 14) to relocate the information. This book is a starting point—to really benefit from the Internet you will need to stay with it, learning more about it and keeping up with it as it changes and grows.

Bon voyage!

PART I

The Internet: What It Is and How to Get Started Using It

CHAPTER 1

What Is the Internet?

What is the Internet? There are more opinions on that than there are people on the Internet. There is no one "location," no exact idea of how large it is, and no agreement on who is actually on the Internet. That's okay, though, because the Internet works, and works well. Here's some background that will help you develop your own working definition of what the Internet is.

Where the Internet Came From

Understanding the history of the Internet is vital to understanding what is happening today on the Internet. Rules, customs, and many layers of technical protocols were designed with the goals and objectives of the sponsors and inhabitants of the original networks. While the Internet is changing very rapidly now, it is still very much a product of this history.

What is known today as the Internet has its roots in a network set up by the U.S. Department of Defense in the early 1970s. This network (ARPAnet), established by the Advanced Research Projects Agency (ARPA), connected various military and research sites and was itself a research project on how to build reliable networks. The methods ARPA developed included a "protocol" allowing dissimilar computer systems to communicate, and a method that could route data through multiple communications paths using groups of data with their own destination addresses built in (packets). These methods were so successful that many other networks adopted the standards they used, known today as TCP/IP.

Beginning in the late 1980s the National Science Foundation (NSF), a federal agency, started expanding its own NSFNET, using the technology developed by ARPAnet, and a high-speed backbone network. This was done at first to allow campuses and research centers to use NSF's super-computers, but increasingly the connections were used for e-mail and for transferring data and information files between sites. With this growth of what came to be called the Internet, and the subsequent upgrading of the system, came broader goals for the Internet and inclusion of more diverse groups.

The National Science Foundation backbone provided very high-speed links. Though the NSF has been phased out as the backbone provider of the Internet and replaced by private National Access Providers (NAPs), its influence is still felt in the structure and customs of the Internet.

Other networks communicating among themselves and through the Internet have, in the last three years, brought a large commercial presence to the Internet and much easier access for individuals who are not part of government or educational institutions.

The Internet Today

Because the Internet is made up of over 60,000 networks that can each transfer data via many routes, it is nearly impossible to pin down any exact numbers concerning its size. Here are some highlights of the Internet's growth and estimated size (Figure 1.1 shows network growth graphically):

- Growth is close to 10 percent per *month*!
- There are currently more than 7 million host computer systems connected to the Internet.
- There are estimates that 50 million people worldwide have e-mail access to the Internet.
- Use of one Internet file search and retrieving tool is currently growing at 1,000 percent annually.

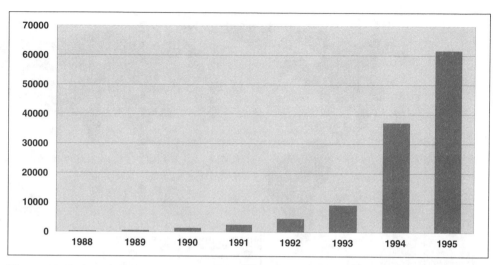

Figure 1.1 Growth in the number of networks connected to the Internet. Statistics from Merit Network Information Center (*http://nic.merit.edu/*) and Network Wizards (*http://www.nw.com/*).

- Dr. Vinton Cerf, one of the developers of the Internet's data transfer protocols, testified to the U.S. House of Representatives that "there is reason to expect that the user population will exceed 100 million by 1998."

- The news media have discovered the Internet as well. Three years ago, U.S. newspapers carried an average of three articles about the Internet per month; now there are over 1,200 per month. Internet reporting and stories are now common in major news and other popular magazines, and on network radio and TV, not to mention being the focus of major movies.

Who Is Part of the Internet?

In the broadest sense of Internet connectivity, individuals, organizations, companies, governments, colleges, schools, and *ad hoc* groups are part of the Internet. In a more limited definition, approximately 60,000 networks are part of the Internet.

An individual does not "sign up for an Internet account." Instead, an individual gets an account on an organization's host computer that is connected in some way to the Internet. The organization may be for-profit

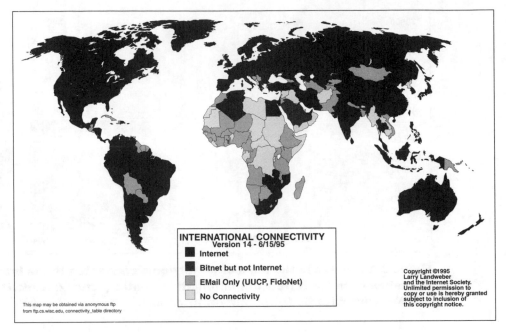

Figure 1.2 World map showing countries with Internet access.

or not-for-profit. The individual's connection to this organization's computer can be via one of the host computer's hard-wired terminals or via phone lines (using a modem and a personal computer). Chapter 3 explains the details of getting access to the Internet.

Networks in countries around the world are continuing to join the Internet (often first with e-mail connections and then later with full access to Internet services). Countries with at least some Internet access are shown in Figure 1.2, and countries with many networks connected are shown in Figure 1.3.

The majority of networks that make up the Internet are from the English-speaking world, and while all languages can be, and are, used, many sites in non-English-speaking countries provide services and resources in English. Many services in Europe, for example, have menus in English, and give other language options.

As you can see in Table 1.1, the last few years have seen a dramatic increase in the number of countries obtaining their initial connection to the Internet. Even Antarctica has Internet networks.

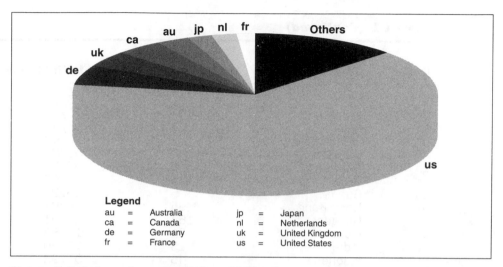

Figure 1.3 Internet connectivity of the major countries on the Internet.

Table 1.1 Network distribution by countries/political entities.

Code	Country	Number of Networks	Initial Connection
dz	Algeria	3	04/94
ar	Argentina	27	10/90
am	Armenia	3	06/94
au	Australia	1875	05/89
at	Austria	408	06/90
by	Belarus	1	02/95
be	Belgium	138	05/90
br	Brazil	165	06/90
bg	Bulgaria	9	04/93
bf	Burkina Faso	2	10/94
cm	Cameroon	1	12/92
ca	Canada	4795	07/88
cl	Chile	102	04/90
cn	China	8	04/94
co	Columbia	5	04/90
cr	Costa Rica	6	01/93
hr	Croatia	31	11/91
cy	Cyprus	25	12/92
cz	Czech Republic	459	11/91
dk	Denmark	48	11/88
do	Dominican Republic	1	04/95
ec	Ecuador	85	07/92
eg	Egypt	7	11/93
ee	Estonia	49	07/92

Table 1.1 (*Continued*)

Code	Country	Number of Networks	Initial Connection
fj	Fiji	1	06/93
fi	Finland	643	11/88
fr	France	2003	07/88
pf	French Polynesia	1	10/94
de	Germany	1750	09/89
gh	Ghana	1	05/93
gr	Greece	105	07/90
gu	Guam	5	10/93
hk	Hong Kong	95	09/91
hu	Hungary	164	11/91
is	Iceland	31	11/88
in	India	13	11/90
id	Indonesia	46	07/93
ie	Ireland	160	07/90
il	Israel	217	08/89
it	Italy	506	08/89
jm	Jamaica	16	05/94
jp	Japan	1847	08/89
kz	Kazakhstan	2	11/93
ke	Kenya	1	11/93
kr	South Korea	476	04/90
kw	Kuwait	8	12/92
lv	Latvia	22	11/92
lb	Lebanon	1	06/94
li	Liechtenstein	3	06/93
lt	Lithuania	1	04/94
lu	Luxembourg	59	04/92
mo	Macau	1	04/94
my	Malaysia	6	11/92
mx	Mexico	126	02/89
ma	Morocco	1	10/94
mz	Mozambique	6	03/95
nl	Netherlands	406	01/89
nc	New Caledonia	1	10/94
nz	New Zealand	356	04/89
ni	Nicaragua	1	02/94
ne	Niger	1	10/94
no	Norway	214	11/88
pa	Panama	1	06/94
pe	Peru	44	11/93
ph	Philippines	46	04/94
pl	Poland	131	11/91
pt	Portugal	92	10/91
pr	Puerto Rico	9	10/89
ro	Romania	26	04/93

Table 1.1 (*Continued*)

Code	Country	Number of Networks	Initial Connection
ru	Russian Federation	405	06/93
sn	Senegal	11	10/94
sg	Singapore	107	05/91
sk	Slovakia	69	03/92
si	Slovenia	46	02/92
za	South Africa	419	12/91
es	Spain	257	07/90
sz	Swaziland	1	05/94
se	Sweden	415	11/88
ch	Switzerland	324	03/90
tw	Taiwan	575	12/91
th	Thailand	107	07/92
tn	Tunisia	19	05/91
tr	Turkey	97	01/93
ua	Ukraine	60	08/93
ae	United Arab Emirate	3	11/93
uk	United Kingdom	1436	04/89
us	United States	28470	07/88
uy	Uruguay	1	04/94
uz	Uzbekistan	1	12/94
ve	Venezuela	11	02/92
vn	Vietnam	1	04/95
vi	Virgin Islands	4	03/93

Data from *nic.merit.edu*, 01-05-95.

Within the United States, the number of networks per state generally reflects relative state population. Rural areas, while having dial-up access to the Internet, have much higher communications charges. Table 1.2 shows how many networks each state has currently hooked up to the Internet.

Table 1.2 Networks connected to the Internet by U.S. state.

Code	State	Number of Nets
AL	Alabama	260
AK	Alaska	26
AZ	Arizona	186
AR	Arkansas	70
CA	California	4832
CO	Colorado	696

Table 1.2 (*Continued*)

Code	State	Number of Nets
CT	Connecticut	463
DE	Delaware	23
FL	Florida	770
GA	Georgia	445
HI	Hawaii	127
ID	Idaho	56
IL	Illinois	577
IN	Indiana	347
IA	Iowa	147
KS	Kansas	70
KY	Kentucky	82
LA	Louisiana	198
ME	Maine	103
MD	Maryland	1178
MA	Massachusetts	2005
MI	Michigan	540
MN	Minnesota	867
MS	Mississippi	109
MO	Missouri	303
MT	Montana	37
NE	Nebraska	156
NV	Nevada	40
NH	New Hampshire	175
NJ	New Jersey	1208
NM	New Mexico	142
NY	New York	2152
NC	North Carolina	677
ND	North Dakota	21
OH	Ohio	1233
OK	Oklahoma	136
OR	Oregon	593
PA	Pennsylvania	919
RI	Rhode Island	147
SC	South Carolina	240
SD	South Dakota	15
TN	Tennessee	353
TX	Texas	1341
UT	Utah	141
VT	Vermont	68
VA	Virginia	1964
WA	Washington	972
DC	Washington, D.C.	744
WV	West Virginia	46
WI	Wisconsin	280
WY	Wyoming	28

Data from *nic.merit.edu*, 01-05-95.

Who Is in Charge?

Who's in charge? Nobody, and at least 60,000 groups.

Nobody is in charge, because no one individual, network, or organization owns the entire network, or any absolutely necessary part of the network. Certainly the backbone links are very important, but networks often have alternate paths for linking to the Internet.

One could say equally well that since there are 60,000 networks connected, there are at least 60,000 groups in charge; or that since the networks are made up of organizations that own their own host computers, more than 7 million groups are in charge, or....

The important point is that the Internet is a voluntary, cooperative undertaking. The networks have agreed on common communications protocols, addressing methods, and rules. Groups such as the Internet Society, Internet Engineering Task Force, the Internet Assigned Number Authority, the Federal Networking Council, Network Information Centers, and the Internet Architecture Board provide an organized means for deriving these rules and protocols. To be part of the Internet, the businessperson should be aware of the nature of this Internet "organization" and of the resulting acceptable use policies for different networks. (Chapter 6 discusses acceptable and unacceptable uses of the Internet.)

What Do You Do When You Get There?

Okay, once you've gotten there, what can you do? Here are a few ideas:

- Search for, retrieve, and read literally millions of documents stored on computers throughout the world.
- Exchange e-mail with any of tens of millions people with e-mail accounts (by some estimates there are 50 million people worldwide with e-mail access to the Internet).
- Search for and retrieve shareware, freeware, and commercial software.
- Search databases of organizations, individuals, and government sources for files on thousands of topics.
- Read messages from and respond to subject-oriented discussion groups and newsgroups (more than 30,000 different topics).

- Send and receive program data files such as spreadsheets, CAD files, and desktop publishing files.
- Send and receive picture, movie, and sound files.
- Set up temporary or permanent discussion/work groups.
- Browse through resources of public and private information services.
- Communicate in real time, via the keyboard, with others, anywhere in the world, while connected to the Internet.
- Browse and search catalogs of goods and services, and purchase many of the items via the Internet.
- Set up a site with information about your company and its products.
- Conduct test marketing.
- Distribute electronic publications.
- Sell products and services.

These activities can be combined to provide a business presence on the Internet with marketing, sales, research, and customer support components.

Now that you've read a brief sketch of the nature of this mammoth Internet, you can learn from the rest of this book specifically what you can do on the Internet and how your business can profit from it. The Internet offers your business an incredible variety of marketing and research opportunities.

And On to the Web...

This overview of the Internet hasn't covered the fastest growing, most interesting, easiest to use, most colorful, and best business resource on the Internet—the World Wide Web. The next chapter is an overview of this very important segment of the Internet.

CHAPTER 2

World Wide Web—The Overview

The World Wide Web is the multimedia part of the Internet. It is just one of the many systems used on the Internet to find and transfer information. It has, however, become (with the exception of e-mail) the most popular system, and the most promising and active for business use.

> **Note:**
>
> The World Wide Web is also called the WorldWideWeb, the Web, WWW, and W3.

The Web is made up of documents on computers throughout the world. These documents have special codes written into them that provide links to other documents on the Internet, and that dictate how the documents are to be displayed. Computers holding these Web documents use software called Web servers to communicate via the Internet with client programs called browsers. Browsers are used by individuals on their own computers to find and view Web documents and other documents linked to them.

What this means in practice will be made clearer by looking at some of the components of the Web and how they work.

How the Web Works

To start with we'll look at the Web from the standpoint of the individual visiting the Web using a browser. Later in this chapter we'll look at it from the view of someone wanting to offer information to others on the Web.

Browsers

To use the Web, you need Web browser software. (See Chapter 4 for information about various browsers.) This software is installed on your own personal computer, or on you organization's mainframe or server computer.

The browser software communicates via the Internet with Web servers on remote computers using a standardized set of rules called the HyperText Transfer Protocol (HTTP). When the browser retrieves a Web document from a Web server, it interprets instructions in the HyperText Markup Language (HTML) within the document in order to properly display the document.

The HTML commands affect text size, boldness, italics, underlining, positioning on the screen, and so on. HTML also has commands that allow pictures and other graphics to be displayed on the screen along with the text.

> **Note:**
>
> A Web document is called a *page*. It is considered one page even if you need to scroll down several screens to view it all. A *homepage* is the "top," index, or Welcome page at a site—that is, the page designed to be viewed first. It will provide links to the other pages at the site.

HTML commands also allow the author of the Web document to designate any of the words or pictures on the page as links to other documents. These are displayed by browsers as highlighted, underlined, or boxed text or pictures (see Figure 2.1). The user of the browser software just needs to move the mouse cursor over this highlighted text and press

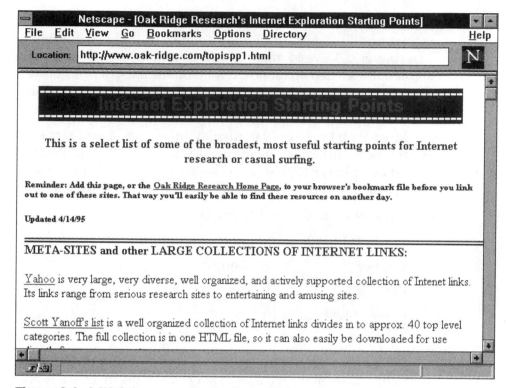

Figure 2.1 A Web browser displaying a Web page.

the mouse button. The browser will then send a request to whatever Web server has the linked document, and the browser will then automatically display the received document. This new document may also have highlight links that can be clicked on, and so on and so forth. This jumping from document to document on the Web is called "surfing."

URLs

There is another way, in addition to clicking on highlighted links, to retrieve a Web page: by using its unique address. Web page addresses are written in a standardized Uniform Resource Locator (URL) format. Browsers can be directed, or pointed, to a particular Web page by typing in the page's URL.

The URL of the Web page shown in Figure 2.1 is *http://www.oak-ridge. com/topispp1.html*.

This book lists many other Web page URLs related to business. There is an increasing number of other sources of URLs, including magazines, newspapers, TV and radio stations, and business cards. We've even sighted ones listed on billboards and on the back of a motorcycle. Chapter 11 provides URLs for sites that contain large categorized lists of URLs and sites that have searchable databases of Web page URLs.

Most Web browsers can display information and retrieve files from several other Internet systems in addition to the World Wide Web. These include Gopher, FTP, Usenet news, and Telnet (all described later in this book). Each of these systems has a characteristic URL prefix.

Internet system	*URL prefix*
World Wide Web	http://
Gopher	gopher://
FTP	ftp://
Usenet news	news:
Telnet	telnet://

While you can easily use URLs without knowing how they are formed, it does make it easier to spot problems in a URL if you know the structure.

As an example, we'll disassemble this URL:

ftp://ftp.std.com/pub/oakridge/information.txt

ftp:// = Internet system/protocol (in this case, FTP)

ftp.std.com = Name and address of the remote computer

/pub/oakridge/ = Subdirectory path on the remote computer

information.txt = File name on the remote computer

Offering Your Own Web Pages

If you are interested in putting your own information on the Web, you will need to write, or have someone else prepare HTML documents (see Chapter 10, "Preparing World Wide Web Pages"), and you will need to have these documents placed at an Internet site with a Web server (further information on this is given in several chapters, including Chapters 3 and 10).

While Chapter 10 will discuss HTML more fully, here's a quick look at an HTML document. It is the same document displayed by the Web browser in Figure 2.1. (Approximately the top quarter of the full HTML document is displayed on the browser screen in this figure.)

```
<HTML>
<HEAD>
<!-- HTML document prepared by Oak Ridge Research
oakridge@world.std.com  -->
<TITLE>Oak Ridge Research's Internet Exploration Starting
Points </TITLE>

</HEAD>
<BODY>
<CENTER><IMG ALIGN=bottom SRC="isp.gif"></CENTER><BR>

<CENTER><B>This is a select list of some of the broadest, most
useful starting points for Internet research or casual
surfing.</B></CENTER><P><P>

<H6>Reminder: Add this page, or the <A HREF="orr.html">Oak
Ridge Research Home Page</A>, to your browser's bookmark file
before you link out to one of these sites. That way you'll
easily be able to find these resources on another day.</H6>
<H6>Updated 4/14/95</H6>

<IMG ALIGN=bottom SRC="rwb6line.gif"><BR>
<B>META-SITES and other LARGE COLLECTIONS OF INTERNET
LINKS:</B><P>

<A HREF="http://www.yahoo.com/">Yahoo</A> is a very large, very
diverse, well organized, and actively supported collection of
Internet links. Its links range from serious research sites to
entertaining and amusing sites.<P>

<A HREF="http://www.uwm.edu/Mirror/inet.services.html">Scott
Yanoff's list</A> is a well organized collection of Internet
links divided into approx. 40 top level categories. The full
collection is in one HTML file, so it can also easily be
downloaded for use directly from your computer.<P>

<a href="http://nearnet.gnn.com/gnn/wic/index.html">The Whole
Internet Catalog</a> is a well organized and well maintained
list of Internet resources that includes over 160 categories.<P>
```

<A HREF="http://www.rpi.edu/Internet/Guides/decemj/icmc/toc3.
html">John December's list</A> is a uniquely organized, well
selected group of links to many types of Internet resources,
with an emphasis on Computer Mediated Communication (CMC), and
the Internet itself.<P>

<a href="http://www.einet.net/galaxy.html">EINet Galaxy</a> is
another varied, and interesting assortment of Internet links.
You can browse through the list, or search using any word you
specify.<P>

A large list of links to Internet resources, divided into
approximately 70 categories, is available from the
<a href="http://honor.uc.wlu.edu:1020/-su">W&L Subject
Menu</a>. These lists can be searched by keyword and sorted by
subject, date, geographic origin, and type of Internet
protocol.<P>

<a href="http://www.ncsa.uiuc.edu/SDG/Software/Mosaic/
MetaIndex.html">Internet Resources Meta-Index</a> is an
excellent starting point for surfing the Web.<P>

<A HREF="http://ice.ucdavis.edu/Cyberspace_Jump_Station/">
Harvey's Cyberspace Jump Station</A> provides a unique
assortment of links in approximately 100 categories, including
many for various academic disciplines, with some emphasis on
environmental subject links.<P>

<a href="http://garnet.acns.fsu.edu/~msalo/">Cool Links
Pages</a> provides an eclectic list of approximately 300 links,
including some real gems.<P>

<IMG ALIGN=bottom SRC="rwb6line.gif">
<B>INTERNET RESOURCE SEARCHES:</B><P>

<A HREF="http://lycos.cs.cmu.edu/">Lycos</A> is one of the most
powerful World Wide Web search systems. It currently has
cataloged approximately 3,000,000 Web documents.<P>

Search the World Wide Web for pages which contain any word, or
words, you are interested in, by using the fill-in form on the:
<a href="http://webcrawler.cs.washington.edu/WebCrawler/
WebQuery.html">WebQuery search page</a><P>

```
<a href="http://alpha.acast.nova.edu/findtopic.html">"Finding
Topics on the Internet"</a> provides links to search programs
for Gopher, World Wide Web, Telnet, discussion groups, and
Usenet Newsgroups.<P>

<a href="http://alpha.acast.nova.edu/cgi-bin/news.pl">Usenet
News Finder</a> allows you to search a list of Usenet
Newsgroups for groups whose name or description contains any
word you've specified.<P>

<a href="http://alpha.acast.nova.edu/cgi-bin/lists">Discussion
Groups Search</a> allows you to search a list of nearly 6,000
discussion groups (mailing lists), for groups whose name or
description contains any word you've specified.<P>

<a href="http://web.nexor.co.uk/archie.html">List of WWW Archie
Services</a> is a compilation of links to various Archie sites
which can search the Internet for files at FTP sites.<P>

<IMG ALIGN=bottom SRC="rwb6line.gif"><BR>
<B>UNUSUAL AND USEFUL:</B><P>
```

WebCrawler has calculated which Web sites are linked to most
often by other sites, and offers them in a list of active links
through its: `<a href="http://webcrawler.cs.washington.edu/`
`WebCrawler/Top25.html"WebCrawler Top 25 List</a><P>`

`<A HREF="http://www.fagg.uni-lj.si/SHASE/">Virtual Shareware`
`Library</A>` offers searches of, and direct links to,
approximately 60,000 free and shareware computer programs
available on the Internet.`<P>`

KC Computing sponsors a large `<A HREF="http://www.automatrix.`
`com/conferences/index.html">database of Internet conferences,`
`expositions, courses, tutorials, and other gatherings</A>.<P>`

The `<A  HREF="http://cougarxp.princeton.edu:2112/bpd/`
`webweather.html">WebWeather</A>` site provides local weather
reports and forcasts for locations throughout the United
States`<P>`.

```
<IMG ALIGN=bottom SRC="rwb6line.gif"><BR><A
HREF="orr.html"><B>Back to the Oak Ridge Research
homepage</B></A><BR>
```

```
<IMG ALIGN=bottom SRC="rwb6line.gif"><P>
</BODY>
</HTML>
```

With the aid of some of programs mentioned in Chapter 10, writing these HTML documents is not as daunting a task as it may seem at first glance.

What's Happening Now on the World Wide Web

Certainly business is taking place on the World Wide Web, in a big way, and much of this book will deal with how businesses are using the Web. For now, however, let's just take a step back and look at the incredible diversity in ways the Web is being used for business, education, communication, and entertainment by looking at a few examples.

Web pages are available on the Internet in tens of thousands of styles and subjects, with almost as many reasons for posting them on the Web. There really is no good place to start to sample them, so we'll just start randomly at SportsLine (see Figure 2.2). This page provides daily sports news, scores, statistics, and analysis. It also features contests, sports merchandise, and talks with sports personalities.

The large TV networks such as NBC and CBS have a variety of Web pages relating to specific shows, and to departments such as news and sports. Figure 2.3 shows the CBS homepage. Each of the boxes shown in the large graphic image can be clicked on to get pages with information about the subject listed.

It's not just the big networks that have Web pages; some individual shows do as well. An interesting example is the Red Green Show Web page (see Figure 2.4). The Red Green Show depicts the activities at "Possum Lodge" in the Canadian wilderness. Its humor is some combination of off-beat, sophomoric, wacky, and dry.

Many entertainers have Web sites designed and maintained by their fans. The Grateful Dead have several of these fan sites. Figure 2.5 shows the top page of a group of pages offered by the publication *People Magazine*.

The sciences are very well covered on the Web, with pages for scientists and for the general public as well. The National Museum of Natural

Figure 2.2 SportsLine USA's Web page.

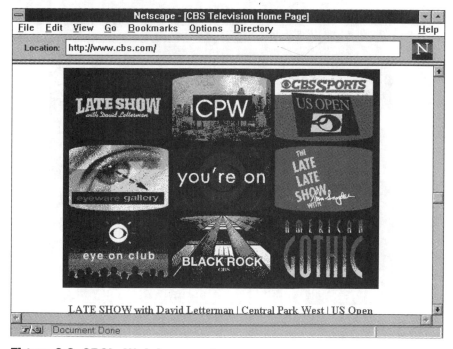

Figure 2.3 CBS's Web homepage.

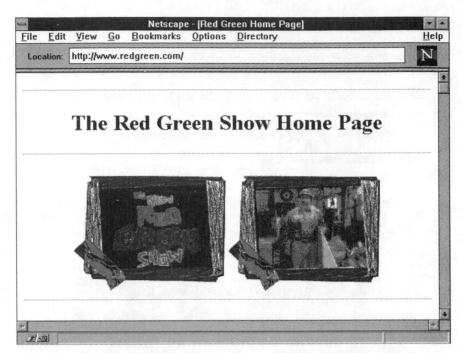

Figure 2.4 The Red Green Show's Web page showing yet another use for duct tape.

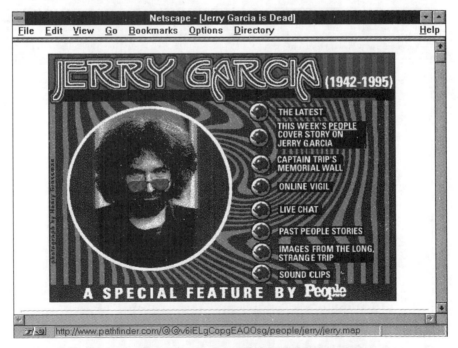

Figure 2.5 *People Magazine*'s Greatful Dead top page.

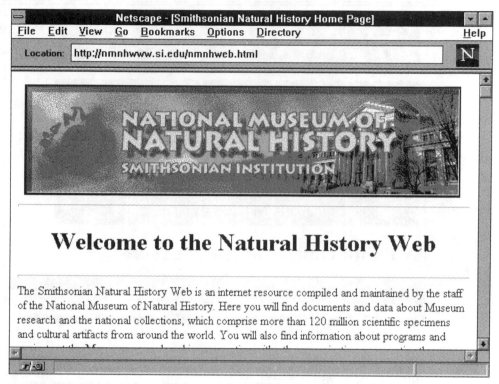

Figure 2.6 Homepage of the National Museum of Natural History.

History, for example, describes the nature of its exhibits and programs in its Web pages (see Figure 2.6).

The Hubble Space Telescope Web site is a good example of a site offering information to working astronomers and other scientists, and to the general public as well. Figure 2.7 shows one of the pages oriented to the lay public, with pictures of some of the more unusual findings of the Hubble telescope. Each small picture is a link to a large, high-resolution, color version of that image.

The Web is also excellent for reporting fast-changing information and news. Major news events such as earthquakes, storms, and deaths of public figures often lead to the creation of a Web site, which may appear within an hour or two of the original event. Figure 2.8 shows an hourly updated satellite image of the Atlantic Ocean made available during the stormy 1995 season.

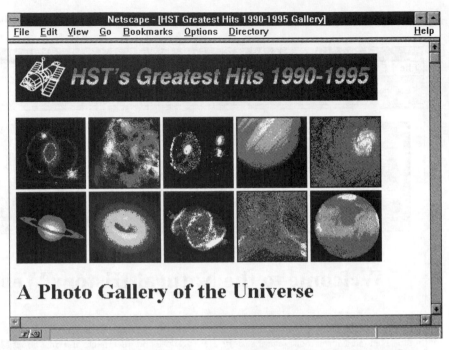

Figure 2.7 One of the Hubble space telescope's Web pages for the general public.

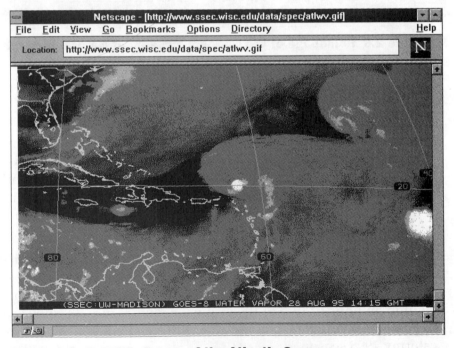

Figure 2.8 Satellite image of the Atlantic Ocean.

These sites give only a glimpse of the diversity of Web sites. There are thousands of sites in each of these subject areas:

- Commercial, Shareware, and Freeware software
- Business, marketing, commerce
- Finance, stock market, corporate information
- University level education
- K–12 education
- Online books
- Online magazines
- Government sites and information
- Legal information
- Health and medical information
- Daily and categorized news
- Travel/booking/ticketing information and purchase
- Reference books
- Scientific sites from astronomy through zoology
- History
- Museums and libraries
- Philosophy
- Religion
- Languages

As we said, it's hard to tell where to start telling what's on the Web, and hard to tell where to end. Here are two other sites: Vatican City, where an effort is being made to offer images of 150,000 original documents dating from as early as the second century A.D. on the Internet, and the Securities and Exchange Commission in the United States which maintains free Internet access to its library of corporate records.

From Here...

The best way to get a feel for the World Wide Web is to get online and start surfing. The next two chapters discuss getting access to the Internet (Chapter 3), and obtaining and using browsers (Chapter 4). These should provide you with the information you'll need to get on the Web and start experiencing it yourself.

Internet Access Types and Providers

How to Get Access to the Internet

Gaining access to the Internet is getting easier and easier. The cost is going down, while the number of choices is rising. Your connection to the Internet can be as simple as opening an account on a commercial service like CompuServe or America Online, or as complex as dedicating a portion of one of your company's computers to becoming an Internet node with a full-time presence on the Internet. Many businesses fear that connecting to the Internet is too expensive. Because of the range of Internet access types available, this is absolutely not the case.

Connecting to the Internet is not difficult. In the last four years, many companies called Internet Service Providers (ISP) have begun to offer dial-up SLIP/PPP and other Internet connection services. For a fee, these service providers will give you access to the Internet.

Get Access Now

You can spend a lot of time researching the best ways to get access to the Internet, but the most important thing is to get access now if you do not already have it. You don't have to make any long-term commitments with an access provider—if you don't like the service or your needs change, you can cancel your service at any time. Get online now and start learning.

You will need an account in order to use the Internet—be it on your corporate system, or through a commercial dial-up service. Business people in large corporations and high-tech industries may find that their companies are already on the Internet through their engineering or research departments, so you may already have access and not know it. Contact your network system administrator or MIS department for help in getting an account.

Whether you access the Internet from your company's network or from your own stand-alone personal computer, you will need some equipment. For stand-alone PC use (often called *dial-up* use) you will need a computer, a modem, a telephone line, and some type of communications or browser software. For LAN use you will need a personal computer, a LAN connection, and some kind of communications or browser software. (See Chapter 4 for information on browser software.)

This chapter cannot cover every Internet service provider—there are just too many, and the number of providers is growing rapidly. It will, however, show where lists of these providers can be found, supply a short list of current providers, and provide information for deciding on the type of service that could be useful to your business.

Throughout the rest of this chapter, you will find advice on deciding how to connect with the Internet. To do this, you'll be guided through the following steps:

1. Define which Internet services are available and the types of connections they require.
2. Choose which Internet services you need and which types of connections you'll need.
3. Choose a service provider and get an Internet account.

Access to Internet Tools

There are four basic tools to look for when selecting an access provider: e-mail, World Wide Web, Telnet, and FTP.

E-mail

E-mail is a basic service that you will usually get no matter how you hook up to the Internet. E-mail lets you exchange text messages with anyone else who has an Internet account. You have many choices, most of them fairly inexpensive and very easy to sign up for. Commercial services like CompuServe, Prodigy, and America Online may meet your needs. Look for a provider that supplies MIME-compliant e-mail. (Chapter 12 explains more about the business use of e-mail.)

World Wide Web

The World Wide Web is the fastest growing segment of the Internet for business use. You will want to be sure that your Internet account includes SLIP/PPP access (or SLIP emulation), or if it is a shell account, that you have access to the Lynx browser for surfing the Web. Many of the commercial services including CompuServe, AOL, and Prodigy now include Web access. (Chapter 4 explains the use of Web browsers.)

Telnet

With Telnet, you can connect to an enormous number of remote computers on the Internet and interact with programs on those computers. You can use a SLIP/PPP connection, or you can use a shell account for telnetting.

FTP

The Internet File Transfer Protocol (FTP) enables you to send and receive software and other files such as spreadsheet files, word processing files, graphics, etc. to and from other computers on the Internet.

Primary Types of Internet Access

If you are just starting to explore the Internet, you will probably only need a dial-up account available via normal phone lines. As you plan to put your business online, however, you may want to consider faster service and/or full-time service.

Each type of access has its own cost and its own equipment requirements, and gives you different Internet services. The goals you have for using the Internet will shape which one (or more) of the primary service types you select. Here are some options to consider.

Full-Time Connections

Full-time connections to the Internet can be made via regular phone lines, ISDN lines, 56K, or T1 lines. While these full-time connections may be made to a consumer-level Internet access provider, they are usually made to a high-speed network access point, and steps are taken to register a domain name, and make the business's computer a full-time node on the Internet. With a full-time, dedicated connection, your computer can become an Internet node, that is, a "permanent" part of the Internet.

Dedicated leased lines are used by large institutions and corporations and offer complete access to all Internet facilities. Table 3.1 compares the connection methods.

The up-front costs of a high-speed dedicated line are considerably more than for any other connection. It normally requires fairly sophisticated minicomputers, and a router costing $7,000 to $10,000. Also needed are the costly installation and maintenance of the dedicated leased line. The charges for a leased line may range from $70 per month for an ISDN line to $2,000–$4,000 per month or more for a T3. Installations often require considerable personnel time; in addition, in some locations, these higher-capacity lines are very expensive to install, or are not even available.

Many businesses have their company name as a node name, like *oak-ridge.com*. You can do this by becoming a true node, either through a full dedicated line connection, or through certain full-time SLIP/PPP connections and registering your domain name. In addition, though, many dial-up service providers are allowing companies to have domain names through the use of mailboxes or aliasing. This means that a

Table 3.1 Internet connections and phone line types.

Connection	Type of Line Required	Speed	Uses
Dial-up	Regular voice line	0–28.8KB	Individual or small business
Node	Leased line	56KB	Dedicated data link
Node	ISDN	128KB	Dedicated data link
Node	T1	1.54MB	Dedicated data link for heavy user
Node	T3	45MB	Major network or corporate

provider furnishes a service, allowing you to look as if you are *oak-ridge.com* without actually being a node.

An organization wanting to start a new Internet node contacts the Inter-Networking Information Center (InterNIC) for a domain name. InterNIC assigns and keeps track of all domain names in the United States. These names are currently assigned on a first-come, first-served basis, although there are further limitations on names that are associated with trademarks. The domain name is then registered for use by one organization. Currently, new registrations are charged a $100 registration fee per name for commercial and net designations; this fee is waived for government, military, and educational institutions.

To Node or Not to Node, That Is the Question

A node is a computer that forms a full-time part of the Internet, with a registered domain name such as *oak-ridge.com*, *ipc.org*, *wiley.com*, or *binford.net*.

While there are pseudo-nodes available through ISPs or Web service providers, these aliases are generally the property of the provider, not the business involved. It is far wiser to go ahead and register your own official domain name. You may have to use some creativity in registering if your preferred domain name is already taken. If someone already has *coke.com*, how about *fizz.com* or *notpepsi.com*? Some companies are even trademarking their domain name.

Dial-Up Connections

Dial-up connections are far less expensive than full-time connections. They are excellent for exploring and using the Internet in many ways. The main down side is that you will need to lease space at a Web service provider's site to offer your business Web pages. Even so, this is usually a less expensive package, and it reduces the amount of Internet expertise your company must have before putting your Web pages on the Internet. The dial-up connection to an Internet service provider is usually made over regular phone lines or ISDN lines.

Regular Phone Lines

With the currently available 28,800 baud modems, regular phone lines are now able to handle normal Internet activities very well. Pages download quickly, and even audio is possible. Depending on the size and quantity of files handled, phone line connections are suitable for many small-to-medium-sized businesses.

Integrated Services Digital Network (ISDN)

This is a *digital* service using the same twisted-pair phone lines used by normal phone service. ISDN lines can handle four (or more) times as much data as normal phone lines. They also can be used by several computers at one time. Within the last year, availability of ISDN lines has gone up dramatically, and cost has come down. Medium-sized businesses make extensive use of ISDN, and even some very small businesses are finding ISDN worth the extra expense. ISDN services range from $50 a month to $200, and the hardware needed represents an investment of $2,500–$4,000.

Types of Access Provider Accounts

Four of the most common types of dial-up accounts are:

- SLIP or PPP
- Shell accounts
- Commercial service providers
- Freenets

SLIP/CSLIP/PPP Accounts

If you want to use a graphical browser to explore the World Wide Web—to have immediate access to the color graphics, sounds, and movies—it is best to get either a SLIP, a CSLIP, or a PPP account. SLIP (Serial Line Internet Protocol), Compressed SLIP, and PPP (Point-to-Point Protocol) provide the opportunity to run Internet client software such as Gopher, FTP, and Telnet clients on your own computer. With this type of account, your personal computer is communicating directly with the Internet. The access provider usually does little more than transfer the information between your computer and the Internet. The account can also be used with e-mail programs.

The cost of these accounts is usually a bit more than for shell accounts, but prices continue to drop. A pricing schedule might look like this: a basic account with 40 hours of use for $20–$35 a month, with extra hours priced at $1–$2 each. Many providers have plans for heavier usage that are priced at $35–$45 a month for 90–120 hours, with additional charges for additional time. In some areas, full-time SLIP/PPP can be obtained for $99–$120 a month.

Commercial Service Providers

Internet access in some form is now available through commercial providers such as America Online, the MicroSoft Network, and CompuServe. The major online services are offering a subset of Internet tools—e-mail and WWW are available on all of them, with some limited access to the other Internet tools (FTP, Telnet, Gopher). The mix of services offered is one of the main ways these providers compete, and so is likely to change in the future. In this category, pricing plans vary but are typically around $9.95 a month for 10 hours, with additional charges by the hour. Some plans include extra charges for premium or special services.

Freenets

For personal Internet access, many community organizations have created Freenets, and some computer user groups are also beginning to make the Internet available to their members. Many organizations provide Internet access for individual use—for example, academic institutions provide accounts for current students, community members, or alumni. Businesses should, however, consider the acceptable use limitations of these services before deciding to use them for commercial purposes (see Chapter 6).

Shell Accounts

Shell accounts are designed to let you use a remote computer much as if you were sitting at a terminal directly wired to that computer. With a shell account that is connected to the Internet, you can run Internet client programs on the access provider's computer. You can then interact with these programs using almost any standard communications program on your personal computer. This type of Internet connection can provide e-mail, FTP, Telnet, Gopher, and the World Wide Web (though the pages are displayed without graphics).

The hourly usage rates usually range from $1 to $3 depending upon the service, and $15 to $30 per month for the account and a set number of hours. Most services have moderate usage plans such as 20/20, where you pay $20 a month for the first 20 hours, and then $1 or less per additional hour.

The programs available on these accounts are text-based. Graphics and sound files can be downloaded and displayed or played later, but these are generally not available for online, immediate use. This, however, makes the shell account the best choice if you are currently limited to computer equipment without graphics capabilities, or to slow-speed modems or noisy phone connections.

Deciding What Internet Services and Connections You Need

For business use, you will first want to consider the types of resources that your business intends to utilize and the services that your business will be providing on the Internet. Next, it is important to research access providers in order to decide which provider can best meet your business needs. What do you want and need to do? Do you want to use the World Wide Web? Use e-mail, read Usenet, Telnet, find files using FTP, create a virtual storefront? Does your business want its own node, or would a pseudo-node provided by someone else work just as well?

You do not have to know how all of these connections and hardware work to get started. Chapters 4 and 5 and will help you in making these decisions, too.

Issues to Consider When Choosing the Type and Level of Service

The checklist below may prove helpful in making decisions about your Internet services.

What type of uses of the Internet are you interested in?

❏   E-mail
❏   World Wide Web
❏   SLIP/PPP—GUI Web interface

❑ Lynx—text Web browser
❑ Telnet
❑ FTP
❑ Usenet newsgroups
❑ Multiple users at your business site
❑ Node

If you are only interested in e-mail, any type of account will probably be sufficient, but most businesses will want to consider a SLIP/PPP account to take full advantage of the Web.

What kind of computer system do you currently have or will you be using?

❑ DOS
❑ Windows 3.X
❑ Windows 95
❑ Macintosh
❑ OS/2
❑ Workstation
❑ UNIX
❑ Minicomputer
❑ Mainframe
❑ Other

Will your main computer system support the connection you wish to install? If you checked DOS, Windows, OS/2, or Macintosh, you can support all shell accounts and most SLIP/PPP connections including SLIP/PPP, but not full T1 connectivity. OS/2 Warp and Windows 95 offer integrated TCP/IP stacks, making connectivity easier. Workstations and UNIX boxes can easily support SLIP/PPP, as well as some leased-line connectivity.

For full-time connections: Will you be using a LAN?

❑ Yes
❑ No

If you are not using a LAN, you will lose some of the advantages of a full-time dedicated line, such as multiple user accounts at your business.

For dial-up connections: What speed modem do you have or will you be purchasing?

❑ 2,400 baud or slower

❑ 9,600 baud

❑ 14,400 or 28,800 baud

It is best not to consider working with a SLIP/PPP account with less than a 9,600 baud modem, though 14,400 or 28,800 would be better. With a 2,400 or slower modem, you will be able to support a shell account but it will be frustratingly slow for uploading and downloading information. Even 28,800 baud modems can be purchased for $170. If you have a slower modem, upgrade—it's the best money you'll ever spend.

How would you rate the importance of reliability and availability?

❑ Low

❑ Medium

❑ High

❑ Very high

If reliability is important, you should choose a provider with experience, a T1 connection, and multiple lines. Noisy lines or breakdowns can cause a loss of productivity; users who depend on their e-mail for conducting business, telecommuting, or while traveling will want to make sure that the service is always available, and does not have a lot of down time.

How fast is the service provider's system?

Some systems are faster than others, so you may want to use some of the services on a trial basis to see if they have substantial delays in responding to you or transferring pages while surfing or in delivering e-mail. Be sure to ask service providers what speed modems they use.

Are there long distance charges?

In urban areas there are many services available through local calls, whereas smaller cities and rural areas must depend on long distance for their service. Try to find a service provider that will give you a local number to call when you want to connect. Otherwise, you'll be paying a long distance charge in addition to the service provider's hourly rate.

Price: The Bottom Line

Once you have put together a service plan, you will, of course, want to price the various providers' plans and services. There are many differences among them, so you may wish to take bids as well.

Internet and Web Service Providers

Web service providers make it possible for you to present your Web pages on the World Wide Web. Some service providers may provide consulting, Web page design and authoring, statistical analysis of visitors to your pages, gathering of data from your Web pages input forms, and other services. Fees for these services vary widely, so always price and compare.

Some Internet *access* providers offer these Web services, while other companies specialize in offering only Web services.

The best documents and resources concerning Internet providers are on the Internet itself. This presents the new user with a chicken-or-egg problem for selecting the right provider. A good approach to handling this is to select one of the providers listed in this chapter, with the understanding that it may be a temporary account to be used while you learn about the Internet.

Here are some sources of information available on the Internet:

- Yahoo! has a listing of Internet presence providers at: *http://www.yahoo. com/Business_and_Economy/Companies/Internet_Presence_Providers/*.

- Open Market has a guide to Web service providers, categorized by the number of sites that they host: *http://www.directory.net/dir/ servers1.html, http://www.directory.net/dir/servers2.html*, and *http:// www.directory. net/dir/servers3.html*.

- To find ISDN services, take a look at Dan Kegel's list of ISDN providers: *http://alumni.caltech.edu/~dank/isdn/isp.html*.

- POCIA maintains a directory of providers in the United States, Canada, and other countries, and hotlinks to numerous other listings: *http://www.isp.net/pocia/index.html*.

- Colossus provides THE LIST, perhaps the most comprehensive list of Internet service providers: *http://thelist.com/*.

Here are some national and international Internet service providers:

Databank, Incorporated

1473 Highway 40
Lawrence, KS 66044
Voice: 1.913.842.6699
Fax: 1.913.842.8518
info@databank.com
http://www.databank.com

Institute for Global Communications

18 DeBoom Street
San Francisco, CA 94107
Voice: 1.415.442.0220
Fax: 1.415.546.1794
support@igc.apc.org
http://www.igc.apc.org

JVNCnet

Global Enterprise Services
3 Independence Way
Princeton, NJ 08540
Voice: 1.800.358.4437
Fax: 1.609.897.7310
market@jvnc.net
http://www.jvnc.net

Netcom On-Line Communication Services

3031 Tisch Way
San Jose, CA 95128
Voice: 1.408.983.5950; 1.800.353.6600
Fax: 1.408.241.9145
info@netcom.com
http://www.netcom.com

PSINet

510 Huntmar Park Drive
Reston, VA 22070
Voice: 1.800.827.7482
Fax: 1.800.329.7741
info@psi.com
http://www.psi.com

UUNET Technologies

3060 Williams Drive
Fairfax, VA 22031-4648
Voice: 1.703.206.5600
Fax: 1.703.206.5601
info@uu.net
http://www.uu.net

Channel One Internet Services

Sonetis Corporation
280-55 Metcalfe Street
Ottawa, Ontario
Canada K2P 6L5
Voice: 1.613.236.8601
Fax: 1.613.236.8764
getwired@sonetis.com
http://www.sonetis.com

Demon Internet Limited

Gateway House
322 Regents Park Road
Finchley
London N3 2QQ England
Voice: (44) 181-371-1000

Fax: (44) 181-371-1150

internet@demon.net

http://www.demon.net

Where from Here

With this information, and the information in the next chapter, you should be ready to go online and get a firsthand view of the Internet's World Wide Web.

CHAPTER 4

Web Browser Basics

Graphical Web browsers make navigating the Internet very easy, quick, and productive. The ability to receive colorful, formatted pages that can have pictures, sounds, and movies also makes surfing the Web more enjoyable, and the pages more memorable. Most of this chapter, therefore, will cover the installation and use of graphical browsers. If, however, you don't have access to a SLIP or PPP account, or don't have access to a computer system with a graphical display, the use of a text-based browser can offer you access to the Web. The use of Lynx will be explained in the last section of this chapter.

The GUI browsers can be found in the major platform flavors such as Windows, Macintosh, or X-Windows.

Most of the GUI browsers work as interfaces for several protocols in addition to the World Wide Web's HTTP, indicated by URLs that start with these prefixes:

- *gopher://*
- *ftp://*
- *telnet://*
- *news:*

Browsers are currently being developed and improved very rapidly. It is worthwhile to have a look at newly released versions as they appear.

Installing and Using Graphical Web Browsers

There are dozens of different Web browsers (with various versions of each available), and thousands of Internet access providers. You will need to consult the documentation that comes with your software and contact your access provider for some browser configuration details. But, installing Web browsers and connecting to Internet access providers is a lot easier if you know the basic, common steps needed. That is what this section will cover.

The First Steps

To get connected, you need to get software, install it, and configure it. The good news is that you only need to do this once. Connecting to and navigating the Internet thereafter will be quick and easy. If you are new to computing or to use of modems, see Appendix A, "Hardware and Software Considerations for the Newcomer."

Obtaining Software

Besides the browser itself, if your computer uses the Windows 3.1 operating system, you will also need a Winsock software. Winsock is an application that runs at the same time the browser does, and provides an interface between the browser and the Internet. It also provides a means to dial the phone and make initial contact with the Internet access provider. Windows 95, Windows NT, and OS/2 Warp come equipped with software to handle the Winsock functions; therefore, you will not need to install Winsock.

An additional piece of software called ws32.exe is also needed if you are running Windows 3.1 on a 16-bit machine and the browser you select is a 32-bit browser. (The browser's documentation will tell you if you need this.)

Browsers are now readily available in local retail stores and mail order outlets. Many of them come packaged with Winsock and ws32.exe, and with "helper" programs (explained later in this chapter). Information on locating and obtaining each browser mentioned in this chapter is listed along with the browser's review.

The Netscape browser is used in the first example in this chapter. In addition to retail stores and mail order suppliers, Netscape can be obtained by phone directly from Netscape Communications, Mountain View, California. Call (415) 528-2555 between 7:00 A.M. and 5:00 P.M. PST. One version, Netscape Navigator—Personal Edition, is specifically designed to help Internet newcomers get started online, while version 2.0 Gold integrates HTML editing functions and some Java technology.

For more information about Netscape, and to download updated versions of the software, visit Netscape's Web site at *http://www.netscape.com/*.

While the Winsock software is included with some browser software packages, it is also available on the Internet. The Trumpet Winsock program by Peter Tattam is shareware. The Winsock software can be downloaded with FTP (see Appendix D for instructions on how to use FTP). The files are located at *ftp://ftp.ncsa.uiuc.edu/Web/Mosaic/Windows/sockets/* or at *ftp://ftp.utas.edu.au/pc/trumpet* or at *ftp.ncsa.uiuc.edu/* in the */Web/Mosaic/Windows/sockets* subdirectory as file *winsock.zip*.

Installations

Installation of Winsock and browser programs proceeds in a manner very similar to other software installations: The "install" or "startup" program is run, a new subdirectory is made, files are transferred to it, and changes are made to the computer's configuration files. During the installation there are the usual dialog screens asking questions, and often offering default answers (which are usually best taken).

Winsock will definitely need to be configured. As you read through the Winsock documentation, develop a list of questions for your Internet access provider. There are a number of configuration parameters that can't be guessed—they are unique to your access provider and your account. Some of the questions you will likely need to ask:

- IP address—This is your online address. It many be permanently assigned, or dynamically assigned. If it is dynamically assigned you may need to change this number in Winsock each time after you sign on. The IP address is made up of four groups of numbers separated by periods, for example, 192.74.137.5.
- Name server—This is another group of four numbers needed for correct routing of information from your computer. It is unlikely to change very often.
- Connection protocol—Is your account a SLIP, CSLIP, or PPP?

- MTU, TCP RWIN, and TCP MSS—Ask your access provider for recommendations on these settings; otherwise go with the default settings.
- Your account's name (ID) and password—If you arranged the opening of your account by phone, you will need to know your assigned password. For extra security, change this password regularly.
- What phone number should your modem dial?

You will need to answer some questions yourself. For example, Winsock will need to know which port your modem is installed in, and what baud rate it is.

While browsers have many features that can be configured, most browsers can be used right away without initial configuring. Later, after you are used to how the browser works, you can start experimenting with variations in the configuration of the browser's various features.

Making the Connection

When starting an online session, the Winsock is run first. It will provide either a way for you to enter the Internet access provider's phone number each time, or some method for you to create a script that will do the dialing for you each time. (Some Winsocks come with prewritten scripts for some of the larger Internet access providers.)

If you don't have a script, after the number is dialed you will be prompted to enter your account's name, and then your password. Check

---

Ending a Session

When you are finished with an online session, you should switch to the Winsock program and execute the "bye" or "hangup" or similar command to disconnect the phone line. Just closing both the browser and the Winsock is not enough with many installations—you will still be connected to the access provider. Check your documentation, and for your first few sessions, after you close the applications, pick up a phone on the same line and listen to be sure the dial tone has returned.

your Winsock documentation to see if you need to do anything at this point to change the Winsock to a "SLIP Enabled" mode. Once this connection is established, click on the browser icon. When the browser is loaded, it is ready to use.

Browser Operation

Browsers offer many features and choices, but you can successfully start using them by learning how to do just a few things. Later you can learn additional features and techniques and become a "power user." The features and techniques shown here on the Netscape browser are also available on most other Web browsers.

Navigation

The GUI browsers are, for the most part, configured to bring up a homepage upon launching—and it is no accident that the homepage in question is often the homepage of the company or organization that created the browser. Netscape brings up the Netscape Communications ("Mozilla") homepage, while NCSA Mosaic brings up the NCSA page, and so on. You can change the configuration to load a different homepage—for example, your business page—or not to load any page at all. Figure 4.1 shows the Netscape browser with no Web page displayed.

To start navigating the Web, you need to give the browser a URL. To do this, click on the OPEN button. A dialog box will appear. Type in the URL and then press Enter.

URL Sources

URLs for Web sites are listed throughout this book. Particularly good URLs for starting an online session are listed in Chapters 15, 16, and 17.

After the URL is entered, the browser will start sending a request for information to the site that holds the Web page referred to in the URL. The Web page will start to appear. The page may finish loading in a few seconds, or if it has many or large graphics, it may take several minutes.

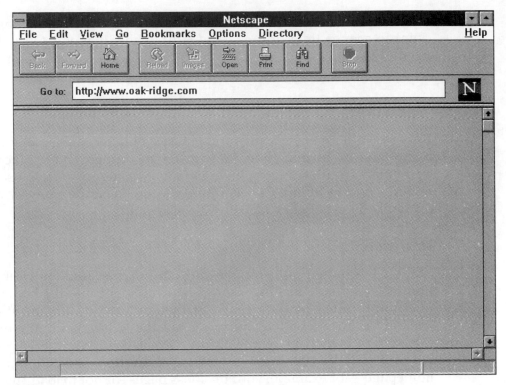

Figure 4.1 The Netscape browser with no Web page displayed.

When the page is loaded you can use the Page Up and Page Down keys or the scroll bars and mouse to move up and down on the page.

Links to other documents are highlighted on a Web page in some distinctive way (depending on the browser). Linked words or phrases may be a different color, or underlined, or have a box around them. Pictures that are links usually have a thin-lined box around them, in the same color used for linked text (Figure 4.2).

When you move the cursor on the screen over one of these highlighted areas, the status line on the browser will display the URL of that link. If the mouse button is clicked while over that area, the browser will retrieve that new page and display it. One can wander from page to page and from Web site to Web site this way.

It is easy to go back to an earlier page, since the browser keeps track of where you have been. To go back one page at a time in Netscape, click

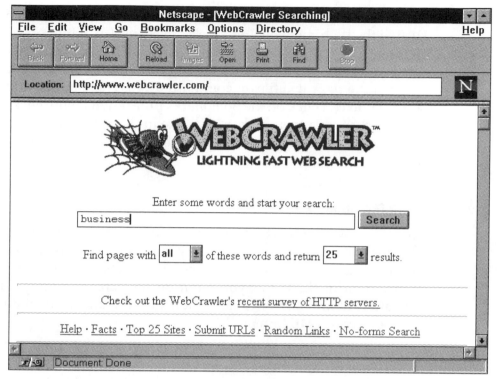

Figure 4.2 The Netscape browser with a Web page loaded.

on the BACK button. To go back several pages, click on the GO menu, and then click on the page you are interested in going back to.

You can also go forward again along the same path you traveled before, by clicking on the FORWARD button.

If you come across a large Web page and you are looking for specific information, you can click on the FIND button and do a text search of the document you are viewing.

If, however, you are waiting for a large document to be downloaded from the Web, and you can tell from the top of the page that you are not interested in it, you can click on the STOP button, or ESC. Sometimes, due to network problems, or problems within your computer, a page will be displayed in an obviously incorrect way. To check if the page can be used, you can click on RELOAD, and the same page will be requested and downloaded again.

Bookmarks are a very valuable navigation feature. When you are surfing the Web, and you find a particularly useful or interesting site, you can save its URL. To do this in Netscape, open the Bookmarks pull-down menu and select the "Add Bookmark" item. This records the URL and the name of the page in a file on your hard drive. Then, in any future online session you can click on the Bookmarks pull-down menu, click on "View Bookmarks," and then click on that site in the list of added bookmarks. (This sure is easier than writing down the name and URL of every site of interest.)

Page Management

There are several browser features that allow you to refer back to a page without going online. A page can be printed out. In Netscape this is done by opening the File pull-down menu and clicking on "Print." Most browsers print the file as you see it on the screen—with pictures and formatted text. Some offer an option to view and print the file in its unprocessed HTML format.

You can also save the page on your hard drive as a file. In Netscape this is done by clicking on "Save As..." in the File pull-down menu. The file is saved in its HTML text format. To view this file again later, choose the "Open File..." item in the File pull-down menu. The file is then loaded from the disk drive and displayed in formatted form. This can be done whether Netscape is connected to an Internet access provider or not. While all browsers display such files with formatted text, many do not retain the pictures that were originally displayed with the page.

If you wish to save only a portion of a page, the Copy command in Netscape's Edit pull-down menu can be used. Highlight the portion of the page that is desired in the usual Windows manner and click on Copy (in Edit menu). Now you can switch to another application such as a text editor or word processor, paste the copied material into it, and then save it to disk or print it.

If you want to save an image with Netscape, place the mouse cursor over the graphic and click the *right* mouse button to get a menu for saving and displaying the graphic.

E-mail and Newsgroups

Most browsers will allow you to send e-mail as you surf on-the-fly, using a fairly rudimentary mail utility. Some will let you send a Web page as you browse in either text format or HTML.

Some browsers are beginning to include an integrated full-function e-mail package. Version 2.0 and 2.0 Gold of Netscape includes such an integrated e-mail function in which you can embed Web links. It contains functions for listing, viewing and sorting messages, the creation and reading of e-mail off-line, and the creation and use of mail folders to organize messages.

Of particular interest to business users, in addition to the POP3 and SMTP mail protocols, this version supports the Secure MIME protocol, allowing for the encryption of messages, and for digital signatures.

Set up this e-mail feature clicking the Preferences pull-down menu, and then clicking on the Mail tab. To get up and running you will need information about your Internet service provider, and mail server addresses. Continue through the e-mail preferences to set up your personal information, such as e-mail address, company name, and so on.

Helper Applications

Web browsers generally can display GIF and JPG picture files, the types used on almost all Web pages. To play movies or sounds on your computer, or display formatted files other than HTML files (such as Adobe Acrobat files), the appropriate hardware and software must be installed on the computer, and your Web browser must be configured to be aware of the presence of the software.

Netscape has a dialog window in which the three-letter file name extensions are associated with a particular piece of software. For MPEG movie files, for example, the extension *.mpg* would be linked to an MPEG movie player program. Then, whenever an MPEG movie link is selected, the movie file will be downloaded, the MPEG movies player will automatically open up, and the movie will be played.

Netmanage's Chameleon uses a different approach, employing the associations that have been set up in Window's File Manager program to determine which piece of software to automatically open up and use.

For sounds, your computer must have a sound card or other sound generation hardware. Various types of sound files (with their unique file name extensions) are then linked to the appropriate program to play them.

Some of the programs you will want to link as helper programs may already be on your computer as part of the operating system package. Other helper programs may be packaged with the browser software you selected. If there is anything else you need, it is probably available on the Internet.

Graphical User Interface Browsers

While Web browsers all share some basic features and abilities such as those discussed in the previous sections of this chapter, there are many differences. Browsers vary in ease of use, speed, extra features and abilities, ease of installation, cost, and compatibility with current Internet standards. We have already looked at Netscape; here is a brief review of several other popular browsers.

Each of the browsers mentioned here will show the same WebCrawler page for comparison. This page is also shown in Figure 4.2 using the Netscape browser.

NCSA Mosaic

Mosaic, the free GUI Web browser created by NCSA at the University of Illinois, has inspired other browser programs based on the original Mosaic programming and concepts. NCSA Mosaic comes in three flavors—one for the PC (Windows), one for the Macintosh, and one for UNIX systems. New updated versions are developed quite regularly.

The "original" Mosaic for Windows, NCSA Mosaic version 2.0, is a 32-bit application and requires the Win32S extensions to run or a true 32-bit winsock such as found in Windows 95. This is a classic Windows application including a menu bar with pull-down menus, and mouse navigation bars. The menu bar has menus for working with files, editing, options, navigating, annotating documents, and a set of pre-installed bookmarks (starting points). An option to go into Presentation mode puts the loaded page on the whole screen, replacing all borders and bars.

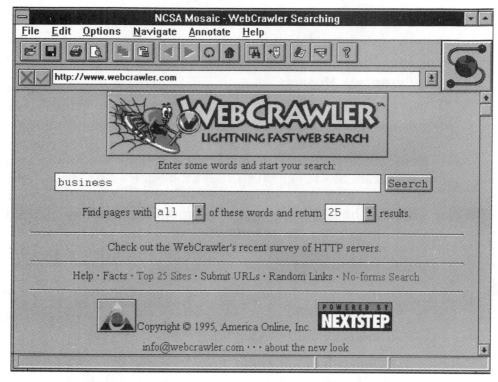

Figure 4.3 NCSA Mosaic

This browser has most of the tools you'll need, including the ability to send e-mail on the fly, a newsreader, and numerous customizations, and it handles hotlists (bookmarks) well. It puts graphics placeholders on the screen while it downloads the graphics, but you can still click and go before it finishes a download. One thing it does lack is a manual. Figure 4.3 shows NCSA Mosaic with the WebCrawler search page loaded.

The software can be obtained via the Net: *http://www.ncsa.uiuc.edu/ SDG/Software/Mosaic/NCSAMosaicHome.html* or *ftp://ftp.ncsa.uiuc.edu/ Mosaic/Windows*.

It can also be obtained directly from NCSA:

NCSA Documentation Orders

152 Computing Applications Building

605 Springfield Avenue

Champaign, IL 61820-5518

1.217.244.4130

orders@ncsa.uiuc.edu

Quarterdeck Mosaic

This is a classic Mosaic for Windows style browser with a couple of nice enhancements. The menu bar covers file management, editing, the viewing of documents in source or as rendered, navigation, hotlist management, tools (such as FTP, e-mail, and Telnet), window placement and configuration, and help. It also has a toolbar for navigation, hotlist access, and file saving. The management of your documents, recently visited sites, and hotlists is enhanced by an optional window which can drop down, which has file tabs for Hotlists, Link Tree, Global History, and Local History. Figure 4.4 shows the Quarterdeck Mosaic browser with WebCrawler loaded.

The browser comes bundled with an e-mail program that includes a Usenet newsreader.

To contact Quarterdeck:

Quarterdeck Corporation

150 Pico Boulevard

Santa Monica, CA 90405

Product information:

Phone: 1.310.392.9851

Fax: 1.310.314.4217

e-mail: info@qdeck.com

Cello

Cello version 1.01 was developed at the Cornell University Law School. This interface is very plain, without many of the bells and whistles found in Netscape and Mosaic. A new version, 2.0, is in the works and promises many improvements. On the simple button bar, there are just four options—stop, up, the name of the page, and home. Figure 4.5 shows the WebCrawler page loaded into Cello.

One advantage of Cello, aside from being free, is its ease of setup—with a configured Winsock, just unzip it and go. It supports FTP, Gopher,

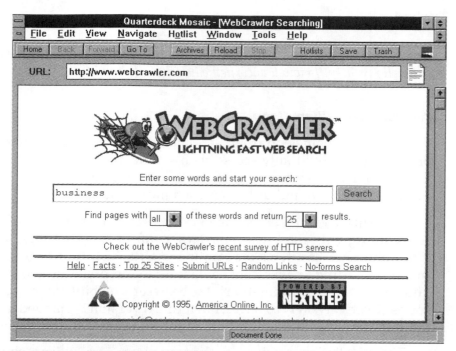

Figure 4.4 Quarterdeck's Mosaic

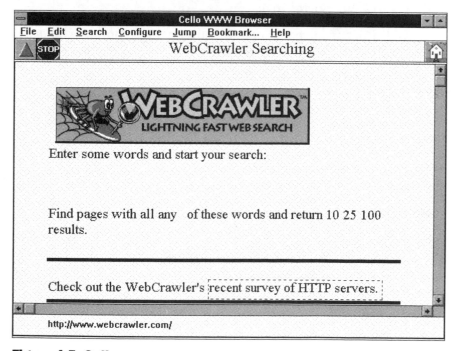

Figure 4.5 Cello

news, and e-mail send. You can find Cello at *ftp://ftp.law.cornell.edu/pub/ LII/Cello* or *http://www.law.cornell.edu/cello/cellotop.html.*

NetManage's Chameleon

The Internet Chameleon from NetManage is a commercial suite of tools and utilities individually accessible from the main window: WebSurfer, Gopher, NEWTNews, e-mail, Telnet, Archie, FTP, Finger, and Whois. Each of these tools and utilities is used individually.

WebSurfer is the NetManage WWW browser. Its menus offer items for working with files, loading pages, configuration settings, and help. The ribbon bar has items for printing, a URL history, a hotlist of book-marks, reloading images, tool navigating to the previous and next page, and home. A current limitation is the browser's inability to use data-input forms effectively on Web pages, but the next version is planned to provide this.

The installation is quite easy, signing up for a provider is simple, and the browser can be configured to use CSLIP, SLIP, or PPP. Figure 4.6 shows the WebSurfer in action.

Get more information about purchasing from *http://www.netmanage. com* or directly from the company:

> NetManage
>
> 10725 North De Anza Boulevard
>
> Cupertino, CA 95014
>
> 1.408.973.7171
>
> sales@netmanage.com

Hot Java

Sun Microsystems has created the Java programming language which uses a new HTML tag <APP> to provide for downloadable applications (aplets) which could range from 3D animations, sound files and games, to active spread sheets.

Their browser is called Hot Java. When Hot Java reads an <APP> tag it downloads and executes the program. At the Hot Java homepage you will find Duke, the Hot Java mascot who pops into their page from time

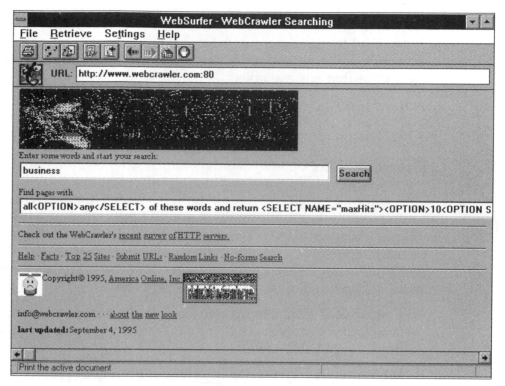

Figure 4.6 Chameleon's WebSurfer.

to time doing cartwheels accompanied by music. For business users, Web pages can be designed to provide real-time aplets with stock quotes, banking transactions, to animate products, and more. Currently it is ported to Microsoft Windows NT and Windows 95, SPARC Solaris, and Sun Solaris. It is available from: *http://java.sun.com.*

Note:

Netscape 2.0 and 2.0 Gold incorporate some Java functionality.

Sun Microsystems, Inc.

2550 Garcia Ave.

Mountain View, CA 94043-1100

Other GUI Browsers

It is helpful to experiment with several browsers, to find ones that meet your personal needs and style. Here are a few more browsers from among the dozens that are available.

VOL 1.0   VOL 1.0 was created by Video On Line, and is available in 15 languages. It can be downloaded for free from *http://www.vol.it/VOLB/ browser.html*.

Embarque   Developed by SandyBeach, Seattle, Washington, Embarque is a collection of freeware and shareware programs, including, among others, the Netscape Navigator browser and Trumpet Winsock. Embarque installs the client programs and configures them to work with The Internet Adapter (TIA). (TIA is a program designed to be run on an Internet access provider's shell account to simulate a SLIP/PPP connection.) When any of the applications are launched, Trumpet Winsock is also launched, and dials up the access provider.

Embarque is available for free from *ftp://marketplace.com*, at the Web site *http://marketplace.com*, or by phone from SoftAware, in Los Angeles, California—(310) 314-1466.

VRML Browsers   Virtual Reality Modeling Language (VRML) browsers are growing in number, and represent a rapidly changing market. VRML provides for virtual environments with varying levels of detail, manipulable objects, and all sorts of 3D rendering. Some browser examples:

- Paper Software—WebFX is an add-on for Mosaic and Netscape, and as a stand-alone called WebFX Explorer: *htttp://www.paperinc.com*.
- Silicon Graphics—WebSpace is a stand-alone product: *http://www. sgi.com/Products/WebFORCE/WebSpace*.
- InterVista Software—World-View, for Windows 95 and Macintosh: *http://www.hyperion.com/intervista/worldview.html*.
- NCSA—VRweb from the Mosaic people: *http://www.ncsa.uiuc.edu*.

Lynx—A Text-based Browser

Lynx is a Web browser that runs on your Internet access provider's computer. You view and interact with Lynx on your personal computer by using standard communications software and a connection to your

Internet access provider via a modem and phone lines to a "shell" type account. (See Chapter 3 for information about shell accounts.) When using Lynx with most Internet access providers, the communications software should be set to "VT100" terminal emulation.

Basic Lynx Commands and Navigation Methods

After dialing your Internet access provider's number, giving your ID and password in response to the prompts, and following any other procedures required by your access provider to get to the main system prompt, you will be ready to start Lynx. Just type **lynx** and press the Enter key. The Lynx program should then start. If it doesn't, check with your system administrators to see if Lynx is available.

Lynx usually opens by displaying a page chosen by the Internet access provider; therefore, your opening Lynx screen will likely look different from the following example:

```
                          Overview of the Web

                WWW ICON GENERAL OVERVIEW OF THE WEB

There is no "top" to the World-Wide Web. You can look at it from many
points of view. Here are some places to start.

Virtual Library by Subject
        The Virtual Library organizes information by subject matter.

List of servers
        All registered HTTP servers by country

by Service Type
        The Web includes data accessible by many other protocols. The
        lists by access protocol may help if you know what kind of
        service you are looking for

If you find a useful starting point for you personally, you can
configure your WWW browser to start there by default.

See also: About the W3 project.

Commands: Use arrow keys to move, '?' for help, 'q' to quit, '-' to go back
Arrow keys: Up and Down to move. Right to follow a link; Left to go back.
H)elp O)ptions P)rint G)o M)ain screen Q)uit /=search [delete]=history list
```

In the examples in this book, the words or phrases shown in bold are links to other Web pages. The one link that is bold and underlined is the currently selected link. If the Enter key (or the right arrow) is pressed, the page that is referred to by the currently selected link will be requested and displayed by the browser.

If You Can't See These Differences

Depending on your particular communications software, the differences between plain text, linked text, and selected links may be displayed as differences in color, boldfacing, underlining, reverse video, italics, and brightness. If you don't see differences in plain, linked, and selected text, experiment with the display preferences/configuration of your communications software. In particular, if your communication software allows text to be displayed in high and low intensity, select low intensity for standard text, to allow Lynx to use high intensity for marking the anchors (linked text).

To select one of the highlighted links, use the up and down arrow keys, which will cause the selection to jump up or down one link on the page for each arrow key press. If there is more than one link per line of text, the down arrow will cause the highlighted link to jump from left to right across the screen, and then down to the next line with links on it.

As mentioned, the right arrow key press will initiate the retrieval and display of the page referred to by the currently selected link. The left arrow key will return you to the previous page that you viewed.

At any time, you can go back to the homepage you started from—just press the **m** key, and answer the prompt about whether you really want to go back.

Most requested pages are displayed in just a few seconds. If one is taking too long, you can stop the process by pressing the **z** key or holding the **Ctrl** key while pressing the **g** key. The transfer process will be stopped, and you can resume using the browser.

If the Web page is more than one screen long, use the plus sign (+) to move down the page, and the minus sign (-) to move up the page.

To exit from Lynx, type an uppercase **Q** (**shift-Q**).

Navigation Tools

In addition to the links provided on the homepage used by your Internet access provider, your providers may also offer an additional set of links to serve as starting points for surfing the Web. To view these links, press the **i** key.

At any time while viewing a Web page, you can get more information about the current page and the page whose link is currently selected. To do this, use the arrow keys to move to the link you are interested in. Then press the equals key (=). In the homepage example shown above, the selected link is "Virtual Library by Subject." If the equals key is pressed, the following report will be displayed:

```
        Information about the current document

        YOU HAVE REACHED THE INFORMATION PAGE


  File that you are currently viewing

     Linkname: Overview of the Web
          URL: http://info.cern.ch/default.html
     Owner(s): None
         size: 20 lines
         mode: normal


  Link that you currently have selected

     Linkname: Virtual Library by Subject
     Filename: http://info.cern.ch/hypertext/DataSources/bySubject/Overview.
          html
```

This process allows you to see what the linked page's URL is. If the site is of particular importance or interest, you can write the URL down—allowing you keep a record of good sites for yourself and others.

These URLs can be used later, any time you are in Lynx. Just press the **g** key and an input line will be displayed near the bottom of the screen. Type in the URL, press Enter, and the page will be retrieved and displayed.

To return to the page you were viewing before the equals sign was pressed, just press the left arrow one time.

Bookmarks

Another good way of storing the name and URL of Web pages is to use Lynx's Bookmarks features. To add a page to your Bookmarks list, use the arrow keys to move to the link for the page you want to be able to return to, then press the **a** key. Bookmarks are stored in a file at your Internet access provider's site, so they will be available for future online sessions.

To view and use the Bookmarks list press the **v** key. The bookmarks that you have accumulated will be displayed as a list with selectable links. The list can be used like any other Web page—you can use the up and down arrow keys to move around in the list, the right arrow to display a selected item, and the left arrow to go back to the page you were viewing when you pressed the **v** key.

Options Configuration

A number of Lynx's features can be custom configured for use within an online session, or configured and saved for future sessions. To display the Options menu, press the **o** key.

```
Options Menu

E)ditor                                   : NONE
D)ISPLAY variable                         : NONE
B)ookmark file                            : lynx_bookmarks.html
F)TP sort criteria                        : By Filename
P)ersonal mail address                    : NONE
S)earching type                           : CASE INSENSITIVE
C)haracter set                            : ISO Latin 1
V)I keys                                  : ON
e(M)acs keys                              : ON
K)eypad as arrows or Numbered links       : Numbers act as arrows
U)ser mode                                : Novice
```

Several of these options are particularly worth considering:

- Bookmark file—This is the file where Lynx stores your Bookmark list. If you know the name of this file, you can use an editor on your Internet access provider's computer to delete lines of Bookmarks you no longer want. You can also have several Bookmark files and use this configuration menu to switch between them.

- Personal mail address—If you enter your e-mail address here, it will make it easier to mail Web pages to yourself via e-mail.

- Numbered links—As has been mentioned earlier, the up and down arrow keys are used to move around on a screen. This can get to be time consuming when there are many links on one screen (some pages have as many as 50 per screen). Lynx offers an alternative: It can be configured to automatically number all the links on a Web page. Then, to activate a link you just type in the link's number and press Enter.

To make the change to numbered links, first press the **o** key for the Options menu. Now press the **k** key. If you press the spacebar, the prompt will toggle back and forth between two options; stop at "Numbers act as arrows" and then press Enter.

If you just want to test the changes you've made during this online session, press the **r** key. If you want to save the changes for future online sessions, first press the **>** key (note: this is not the right arrow key used for moving the cursor, but is the key that prints the > symbol).

History List

Lynx automatically keeps track of documents you have viewed during your current session. You can view this list of documents by pressing the Backspace key. The list is displayed as a Web page with highlighted links that can be used to return to the pages listed. To go back to the page you were at when you pressed the Backspace key, press the left arrow key.

Some Pages May Be Missing

If you move from page to page and then backtrack and branch off from one of the earlier visited pages, those pages below the page where you branched may not be displayed in the history list.

Searches

Lynx offers two types of searches:

- Searches within the Web page you are currently viewing
- Searches of a database

Searching Documents   To search a document that you are currently viewing, move to the top of the document. Then, press the / (forward, right-leaning slash) key. A prompt and input line will be displayed. Type in the word, part of word, or phrase that you are looking for, and press Enter. Lynx will move down in the document and stop at the first occurrence of the text you are looking for, displaying it on the top line of the screen. Press the **n** key to view each subsequent occurrence on the page.

Case Sensitivity

Lynx is usually configured for case-insensitive searches. If you want case-sensitive searches, open the Options menu (**o**) and change this option.

Searching Databases   Some documents on the Web have been prepared as databases. These may be dictionaries, price lists, financial information, and so on. When you activate the link for one of these databases you will receive an opening page explaining what the database is. Near the bottom of the screen you will see the statement: "This is a searchable index. Use 's' to search." (If you used the forward slash as described above, you would only be searching the Welcome page, not the actual database.)

Press the **s** key; a prompt and input line will be displayed. Type in the word(s) you expect will be associated with the data you are interested in, and then press Enter. Lynx will then request the information, display the

---

Deleting Text

On any Lynx input line you can delete words one character at a time with the Backspace key, or all at once with the **Ctrl-u** combination.

---

results (which may include highlighted page links), and be ready for another search when **s** is pressed again.

Retrieving Documents

Lynx provides several ways to download files. These download methods are grouped in two categories:

- The "Print" command for retrieving documents you are currently viewing
- The "Download" command for retrieving documents referred to by a highlighted link

Print Command

If, while viewing a page or other document, you decide you would like a copy of it on your personal computer, you can use the Print command. Start by pressing the **p** key. Lynx will present several options on a screen similar to this one:

```
               Lynx Printing Options

                   PRINTING OPTIONS

   There are 20 lines, or approximately 1 page, to print.
   You have the following print choices
   please select one:

   [1]Save to a local file

   [2]Mail the file to yourself

   [3]Print to the screen

   [4]Use vt100 print sequence to print from your local terminal
```

To choose one of these options, move the highlight with the up and down arrow keys to your choice, and start the process by pressing the right arrow key. (If at this point you decide not to proceed, the left arrow will take you back to the previous screen.)

These methods under the Print command are only for ASCII text files that you can view on your computer screen. The Download command must be used for binary files such as programs and graphics files.

Saving to a Local File   This option saves the file on your access provider's computer. If you want to have the file on your own personal computer, you will need to subsequently download the file from your access provider's computer (see Appendix C).

After selecting this item, Lynx will show you the file's current name. You can accept the current name by pressing Enter, or erase the old name and type in a new one before pressing Enter.

Mailing the File to Yourself   The file you were viewing can be e-mailed to yourself, or to anyone else with an Internet accessible e-mail account. When you select this item, Lynx displays an input box. Type in the address and press Enter, and the process is complete.

Printing to the Screen   If your communications software has a logging feature (ability to capture to a file everything that is displayed on the screen) then the Print to the Screen option can be convenient. To use it, follow these steps:

1. Highlight the Print to the Screen option.
2. Press the right arrow key.
3. Turn on you communication software's logging feature.
4. Press the Enter key.

Lynx will now scroll the text on the screen without stopping between pages.

5. Turn off your communication programs logging feature.
6. Press Enter.

Printing Without Downloading

If your communications software fully emulates a VT100 terminal and you have a printer connected to your personal computer, you may be able to print the document without first downloading it.

To print out the document you are viewing, highlight this option and press the right arrow; the printer should now start printing.

Download Command

The Download command can be used for viewable text files as an alternative to the Print command, but its real value is in being able to download nonviewable binary files. (Binary files include computer programs, graphics files, program-specific data files such as word processor, spreadsheet, or CAD files, and thousands of other types.)

To download a file, move the highlight on a Web page to the item you would like to download. Do not press Enter or the right arrow as is normally done. Press the d key and a menu similar to this one will be displayed (some sites offer different or more downloading protocol options):

```
                    Lynx Download Options

                       DOWNLOAD OPTIONS


   You have the following download choices
   please select one:

   Save to disk


   Use Zmodem to download to the local terminal
```

The default file name will be shown near the bottom of the screen. It can be erased and changed before selecting one of the download options.

Save to Disk Option   This option allows you to save the file on your access provider's computer. To use the file on your own personal computer, you will need to download it from there (see Appendix C if you are unfamiliar with this process).

Download to Local Terminal Option   This option allows you to download the file directly to your personal computer.

Check to see what download protocol options are offered on the Download Options screen. In this example only Z-Modem is offered, but other sites may have Y-Modem, X-Modem, or others. Decide which protocol you want to use and set your communications software to use that protocol. (Techniques for doing that vary from program to program—check your documentation.)

Now highlight the protocol option you have chosen and press Enter. If your communications software can auto-detect a download, the download will proceed. Many programs, however, need to be given a command to receive the file (check your documentation). When the download is complete, press the left arrow key to return to the Web page you were previously viewing. For more information on downloading, see Appendix C.

Navigating Services Outside of the World Wide Web

Lynx can be used with several Internet systems in addition to the World Wide Web. It can be used to interact with Gopher sites, FTP sites, and Usenet news. As with the GUI browsers, this means that by learning how to use just this one browser program, one gains access to at least four different Internet systems.

Gopher via Lynx

Some of the links you will find on the Web are links to Gopher sites. If you select one of these, Lynx will retrieve the Gopher menu, and display it as a list of highlighted links that can be navigated with the usual Lynx commands—you can move up and down the list with the usual up and down arrows, select a Gopher menu by positioning the highlight and pressing the right arrow key, and so on. Also, if you have a Gopher URL (for example, *gopher://gopher.std.com*), you can enter it just as you would a Web URL (press the **g** key, type in the URL, press Enter). See Chapter 14 for an explanation of the Gopher, and of Veronica, a Gopher search system.

FTP via Lynx

Some links on the Web are links to FTP sites that store files available to the public. If you select one of these links, Lynx will display the top public directory on the remote computer. Subdirectory names and file names will be displayed as highlighted links. These links can be selected, allowing you to move up and down in the directory tree. When a file is located, you can view it if it is a readable text file, or download it using the usual Lynx download methods. Also, if you have an FTP URL (for example, *ftp://ftp.std.com/pub/orr/*), you can enter it just as you would a Web URL (press the **g** key, type in the URL, press Enter). See Appendix D for an explanation of FTP.

Usenet via Lynx

Lynx can be used to read Usenet group postings, and to reply to them. To do this, press **g**. In the input line that Lynx displays, type **news:** and the name of the group you are interested in reading. For example, if the group's name is alt.business.misc, then **news:alt.business.misc** would be typed on the input line. When this has been entered, Lynx will display a list of postings to the group. You can use the arrows in the usual manner to move within the list and to select items to read.

Lynx also provides a header with highlightable items that allow you to respond to the group, to the individual who wrote the posting, and to other groups that received the posting. See Chapter 13 for an explanation of Usenet news.

Displaying Unprocessed HTML Files

Lynx, as other Web browsers, displays an HTML file as a formatted file with highlighted links. The actual HTML file is a plain text file with the HTML commands added at appropriate locations throughout the document. To see this unprocessed HTML file with Lynx, press the backslash (\). Lynx will display the HTML file itself. Because it is not processed by Lynx, there will be no active highlighted links, but other features of Lynx, such as the ability to download the file, are still available.

Refresh the Screen

If Lynx displays a page that appears to be damaged in some way, you can command Lynx to request another copy of the page and to display this new copy instead. This is done by holding down the Ctrl key and pressing the **r** key.

Lynx Commands Quick Reference

Frequently Used Program Commands

Arrow Keys

Up	Move highlight to previous link.
Down	Move highlight to next link.
Left	Request previously viewed document.
Right (or Enter key)	Request highlighted link's document.

+ (or Spacebar)	Move to next screen.
– (or b)	Move to previous screen.
z (or Ctrl-g)	Cancel a request or file transfer while it is taking place.
h (or ?)	Displays a list of help files.
q	Leave the Lynx program (asks whether you really mean to leave).
Q (Shift-Q)	Leaves Lynx (no questions asked).

In searches, manual retrieval of documents, comments to the document owner, or any other time there is an input line:

Backspace	Erases one character at a time.
Ctrl-u	Erases all characters on the line.

Navigation Aids

g	Displays an input line for retrieval of a specific document by entering its URL.
i	Displays starting documents (varies from site to site).
m	Returns to the homepage displayed when Lynx was first started.
=	Displays information on current file and highlighted link.
Backspace key	Displays list of documents you have viewed.

Document Retrieval

d	Download the currently highlighted link's document. Select from:
	—to your current directory on Internet access provider's system
	—to your personal computer
p	To download the currently displayed document, select from:
	—print to screen (does not pause when screen is full)
	—save to local file (sends file to your directory at provider's site)
	—mail file (to yourself or others)

—print document on your own printer (if using VT100 emulation)

Bookmarks

a	Add highlighted link to Bookmarks list.
v	View the Bookmarks list.
R (Shift-r)	Erase the currently highlighted bookmark (doesn't work at some sites).

Searches

/	Search for a word or phrase within the currently viewed document.
n	Search for next occurrence of same word or phrase.
s	Search for a word or phrase within a database.

Other Useful Commands

c	Send a comment (e-mail message) to the owner of the file being viewed.
\	Display currently viewed file as an unprocessed/unrendered HTML file.
o	Display Options screen to reconfigure how Lynx performs some tasks.
Ctrl-W	Reprint the screen using the previously requested file.
Ctrl-R	Request current file again and reprint screen.

Getting Started

Now is the time to get on the Internet—you've seen brief overviews of the Internet and the World Wide Web, you've read about access methods and providers, and now you've covered the basics of Web browsers. This is the background knowledge needed to get on the Internet. Other Internet tools, and techniques for doing business online, will be discussed in the next sections of this book. These will all be easier to understand if you get online now and start to explore the Internet.

PART II

Business on the Internet

CHAPTER 5

Why Businesses Are Using the Internet

Businesses are the fastest growing segment of the Internet for many reasons: You can gather information, communicate, and actually transact business on the Internet. Some businesses are creating a corporate presence on the Internet, sometimes using a virtual storefront. Corporations are using e-mail for communication; Web sites for marketing, PR, and selling; Gopher for providing information; and FTP for file and data transfers. (Information on practical techniques for doing business on the Internet and the Web will be explained in Chapters 8 and 9.)

There are both visible and invisible business users of the Internet. Many businesses use the Internet for transacting business, but their work is largely not seen by the average Internet user. The largest invisible users of the Internet tend to be financial and medical institutions and insurance corporations, industries with very high data traffic rates on the network. Most of these large companies have established "fire-walls" to separate their own local data traffic from the rest of the Internet.

The most visible businesses on the Internet have a multifaceted corporate presence. They are visible in product announcements, on lists, on Usenet newsgroups, on Gophers, FTP, and more importantly, on the World Wide Web. Many have established virtual storefronts.

Reasons for Using the Internet

Businesses use the Internet for almost as many reasons as there are businesses. The Internet is used by businesses for:

- Communication (internal and external)
- Corporate logistics
- Leveling the playing field
- Globalization
- Gaining and maintaining competitive advantage
- Cost containment
- Collaboration and development
- Information retrieval and utilization
- Marketing, PR, and sales
- Transmission of data
- Creating a corporate presence

Let's have a closer look at some of these reasons.

Communication (Internal and External)

Maintaining good corporate communication is critical to businesses, and e-mail is a low-cost method for maintaining local, regional, national, and international communication. Messages can be exchanged in minutes, as opposed to days or even months using regular mail. E-mail is a shared information utility and is one of the most important productivity packages going. Often, the first and most frequent business use of Internet connectivity involves internal and external communications. The Internet lets a business stay in touch with branches and work teams at many locations, and permits high-speed access to vendors and customers. This can even create a virtual community in which people who might normally never meet or even communicate find themselves in conversation about substantive matters. E-mail is also popular because it can be sent to groups of people as easily as to one person, whereas phone calls tend to be in series.

Corporate culture is being affected by e-mail—for example, some people become more communicative because they prefer sending e-mail to talking on the phone. (See Chapter 6 for more information on computer-mediated communication and corporate culture.) E-mail can be a richer and more complete source of information than the telephone as well.

Businesses use the Internet to keep departments, work groups, and individuals in close contact. Just think—an end to busy signals and playing phone tag with your colleagues by using e-mail. Listserver software (discussed in Chapter 13) allows work groups to communicate in an open manner similar to virtual meetings, and can serve as an *ad hoc* tool for Total Quality Management (TQM) or process reengineering projects. This can help team members keep in touch and involved even while they are traveling. Listservs can also assist group members in obtaining the most up-to-date versions of collaborative work, and provide current versions and comments to all members simultaneously.

Many companies are using internal Web sites (intranets) to maintain good communication with branches and distant offices. Web documents provide a way to add and link related information from divisions such as marketing, accounting, sales, and planning—for example, to create an integrated set of documents.

It is not uncommon today for telephone conferences to occur, but not without considerable investment of time and effort in scheduling, planning, and discussion about who should and should not be included. Use of e-mailing lists can greatly facilitate such group conferencing, since the members can participate at various times and from various locations. Electronic mail messages can be read and posted at convenient times and places.

Improving communication with colleagues, government agencies, the academic community, researchers, and even competitors can help improve an industry in general. The culture of the Internet is such that genuine exchanges on industrywide questions and improvement are increasingly common.

E-mail is the primary way that people on the Internet communicate with each other. Many people use the Internet daily because they prefer communicating by e-mail, rather than over the phone or by postal mail. Businesses can make use of this increasing public enthusiasm for e-mail by interacting with customers via e-mail. Because some people prefer using e-mail, you are more likely to receive a quick but thoughtful reply if you send your message by e-mail.

Customers are increasingly finding that they can obtain up-to-date information readily through e-mail, company-sponsored discussion lists, auto-responders, and the other tools used by businesses: the Web, Gophers, and FTP sites.

Corporate Logistics

When communicating via e-mail, listservs, and electronic conferences, not all participants have to be in the same place at the same time to conduct business. Actual "real-time" communication is also possible, however, through the use of Talk, MOOs, and Internet Relay Chat (IRC). Online, real-time meetings are possible among individuals worldwide—whether they are in Siberia, Singapore, or Saskatchewan.

The increasing use of videoconferencing techniques such as CUSeeMe and Virtual Places, or telephone-like software such as I-Phone, is making virtual meetings easier. Distance and time barriers are lessened by using the Internet for communication.

Logistical concerns that can dominate production planning can be eased by better contact through the Internet. The Internet is the "anywhere, anytime" network, so exchanges with markets in Europe and Asia (across time zones) can be facilitated by the use of e-mail and conferencing.

It is increasingly common for companies to support telecommuting employees (even tailors are complaining because business people do not need as many suits anymore), and some corporations have employees in such far-flung places that they never come in to work. Work teams can be formed online, allowing these telecommuters to become part of a team. This can also be accomplished when employees are out of town or temporarily off-site.

In some cases, businesses have created a virtual company composed of individuals who work at a distance from one another. They may meet face-to-face only occasionally. I collaborate with colleagues regularly, forming temporary partnerships as the need arises, in some cases with people I have never seen.

Globalization and Leveling the Playing Field

Using the Internet, many organizations are able to bring a global edge to a provincial business. With the Internet, you are much less aware of national boundaries and distance. Individuals from Taiwan converse easily with others in Toronto, Moscow, and Okemos, Michigan. This opportunity for rapid communication can increase a business's visibility from local to global overnight.

Because access to the Internet has gotten cheaper, even tiny "cottage industries" can compete in the larger marketplace. Isolated businesses can compete at a much higher level. There are books being sold from Nova Scotia, mutual funds being managed from a ranch in Utah, and a software company that flourishes in the foothills of Appalachia.

For many companies, the use of the Internet creates a more level playing field. Very small businesses can create an image on the network that allows them to compete with large businesses. It makes the pursuit of customers, vendors, and resources possible worldwide—allowing competition in a world market. This is particularly true when using the World Wide Web—a well-designed Web site can overcome the difference between having an office in Trump Towers in New York, and one in Mason, Michigan.

Businesses that use the Web and, to a lesser degree, the other parts of the Internet, will need to think about the use of the global Internet, and their ability to do product fulfillment on a global scale.

Gaining and Maintaining Competitive Advantage

Increasingly, businesses are taking a look at their own organizations, structures, and processes in an effort to become more competitive. The Internet is a wonderful tool for engaging in these activities. Many companies are using e-mail and group conferencing to engage in business process reengineering projects. Maintaining good communication and the exchange of data and documents is critical in undertaking the reengineering of business processes.

In addition, many companies use the Internet in the search for "best practices." As businesses try to become more competitive, many want to find existing practices that can help them improve their activities. In some cases, businesses are using the communications abilities of the Internet to engage in a Total Quality Management plan. Additionally, some companies use the Internet to maintain corporate process control across all company locations (even on different continents).

What are other businesses doing? What kinds of information are available? The Internet mailing lists and the Usenet newsgroups are terrific sources for keeping track of industry and government standards and trends; in addition, various government databases also maintain online regulatory and standards information. Using the Web for such research is increasingly common.

Companies can gain a competitive advantage by having access to state-of-the art information on products, materials, and new ideas, and an increased ability to evaluate the status quo in a given industry. Many corporations use the Internet to engage in "techno watch"—keeping a finger on the pulse of emerging and new technologies, and the market response to those technologies, by gathering anecdotal information as well as data on financial performance and the stock market.

Many People Prefer E-mail

You will find that many people prefer being contacted via e-mail. It can be a more informal or private exchange, or simply more convenient. In addition, some users appreciate that you are Internet-literate and have chosen to use that kind of approach. I often find that my contacts are much more responsive to an e-mail message than to a telephone, voice-mail, or postal-mail message.

The public information and discussion groups available on the Internet provide insight and feedback that is hard to get in any other manner. Here, workers at all levels of industry, researchers, and the public exchange information on marketing, research, technological developments, internal processes such as accounting and personnel, and external activities such as purchasing and public relations. These discussion groups are useful both for the information presented in them and for the pointers they provide to important sites, contacts, and databases. Having the most up-to-date information about your markets and the state-of-the-art in your industry allows you to keep or increase your competitive edge.

In addition, many businesses are using their Web sites to make available corporate information such as is typically found in annual reports, including information regarding financial performance and more.

In some cases, the Internet is a tool for solving problems by accessing information, documents, and experts. Many companies cannot afford in-house experts on every process or activity, and use the Internet to locate and network with experts, through the mailing lists, newsgroups, or e-mail.

Cost Containment

Many business are using the Internet to contain long-distance telephone and mailing costs. Recent studies have shown that businesses can save thousands of dollars using e-mail, in lieu of some long-distance phone calls and postal deliveries. And these e-mail messages can increasingly contain data files (such as spreadsheets or CAD files), pictures, graphics, sound and movie files, and software.

With first-class letters costing 32¢ each, a mailing of 1,000 pieces to customers would cost $320 for postage alone, whereas the same information sent by e-mail would cost $2 to $3—and the messages would arrive in seconds as opposed to days or (weeks). Overnight mail (which typically costs $8–$12 for each delivery) can't compete with e-mail for speed or cost.

Long-distance telephone charges, particularly international long-distance charges, are greatly reduced by use of e-mail. In addition, fax gateways allow further savings on those long-distance charges by transferring the data via the Internet. Web sites allow customers to access catalogs, brochures, and technical information quickly, and that information can be updated swiftly and easily, without incurring reprinting costs.

In addition, the e-mail, data exchange, and conferencing abilities of the Internet are reducing the need for travel. This saves time, effort, and money.

Collaboration and Development

It is increasingly common for companies to form partnerships and collaborative development efforts—even IBM and Apple have done so. The development teams and project participants often use the Internet to keep in touch over long distances, and to exchange data, programs, and working papers. The Internet also allows several small businesses to band together much more easily for product development.

Formerly, companies tended to maintain separate projects, or to create a new division or production unit to handle a specific problem. Now, many companies are temporarily pooling resources to put out a new product or service, and are using the Internet to do this through e-mail, group conferencing, and exchange of spreadsheets, documents, drawings, pictures, and sound files. Web sites often are used in support of such projects. Such collaborations allow those in marketing, research, engineering, and accounting to keep track of and provide input on a project through every step of its development. This ongoing discussion helps to keep projects on track by ensuring that the needs of sales, marketing, accounting, and so on, are included as integral parts of a plan. Groups working in this way also tend to develop enthusiasm and a creative atmosphere.

Additionally, these work teams and partnerships typically allow for faster interactions and product development turnaround time, bringing products to market more rapidly.

The Internet has given rise to *virtual corporations* and *virtual partnerships*, which take telecommuting to another level. Such businesses may have no physical home office, and the employees probably don't come into work in the same place or time. Virtual corporations or partnerships can be formed for the purpose of single projects, or as permanent, incorporated units.

Information Retrieval and Utilization

The coin of the realm for the Internet is information. If the key to success in real estate is location, location, location, the key to success in business on the Net is *content, content, content*. Rich in resources, the Internet provides software, communications connections worldwide, and files of text, data, graphs, and images (from this world and from out of this world via the orbiting Hubble telescope). The Internet provides access to databases, books, manuals, training information, experts in various fields, even sound and video clips.

And much of that information is free. In the movie *The Graduate*, the young man played by Dustin Hoffman is told that the secret to his future success is "plastics." Today, the secret to success is "information." With roughly 6 million machines connected to the Internet, with databases, the World Wide Web, Usenet, Gopher servers, FTP archives, and conferences, the amount of information available is staggering.

Scientific and research data is available in large quantities. There are electronic newsletters, searchable databases, online experts—in some cases causing information overload. Some have compared using the Internet to drinking from a fire hose.

Some businesses find that the Internet is useful in helping employees learn new tasks and processes. There are many simulations, manuals, training aids, and tools available for software running on a variety of platforms. Also available online are large quantities of instructional materials regarding the use of the Internet itself.

Marketing and Sales

As businesses use the Internet more, and Internet users become more accustomed to marketing activities, Internet marketing is becoming much more popular. Marketing on the Internet involves both research and active outflow of information—marketing through information.

Marketing and sales on the Internet, both business-to-business and direct to the consumer, have been revolutionized by the World Wide Web. Business on the Web allows for:

- Full-color catalogs that are easily and frequently updated
- Online graphics, sound, and textual information
- On-screen ordering, customer feedback, and surveys
- Online technical support
- Worldwide distribution of announcements and PR information

As an example, Figure 5.1 shows Faucet Outlet's huge catalog of hardware.

Best of all, having a Web presence nullifies most of the netiquette issues that surround in-your-face advertising. Because customers come to the page and request information, there is less need to worry about stepping on Internet culture.

Marketing research is common on the Internet; attitudes are tested, conversations actively pursued, and opinions solicited from many

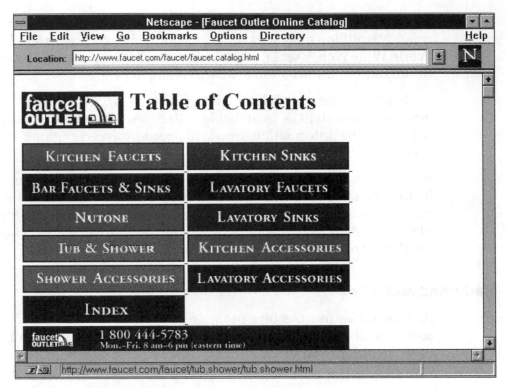

Figure 5.1 The Faucet Outlet online catalog.

groups. (For example, NBC regularly polls viewers through polls using its e-mail address, nightly@nbc.com.) Marketing plans are increasingly counting on Internet access for success.

One of the prime business uses of the Internet is in the area of customer support. Customers can reach a company on their own schedules—day or night—and obtain information from conferences, FTP, e-mail, Gopher, and especially, from the World Wide Web. The customer support information only has to be transferred to an archive once, and yet it may be accessed by thousands of customers and potential customers—a very labor-efficient and cost-effective way of distributing information. In addition, a business with a presence on the Internet is perceived as modern, advanced, and sophisticated.

Customer and product support and technical assistance by way of the Internet is time-efficient. Many companies provide e-mail assistance, including both individual and automated replies to e-mail questions and requests for information. Technical sheets, specifications, and support are offered through Web sites, e-mail, Gophers, and FTP. Relationships with vendors and outlets are maintained via the Internet.

Unsolicited Advertising

In a word—*don't*. Never send unsolicited e-mail advertisements to people on the Internet. This is just about the surest way to damage your reputation. There are plenty of stories about recipients of unsolicited advertising who have boycotted a company and even contributed to having the company thrown off the Net.

In a business atmosphere promoting the concept of "getting closer to the customer," the Internet is becoming increasingly important. In these days of a highly competitive global marketplace, the company that can reach and continue to satisfy customers will have an advantage—and the Internet can help in maintaining positive relationships with customers.

The Internet is also a fast and efficient way of networking with vendors and suppliers. With its global reach, the Internet can assist businesses in locating new suppliers and keeping in better touch with them—for example, to aid in zero, or just-in-time, inventory planning. A business might locate and coordinate with suppliers in Ecuador, Egypt, and Estonia; and the Internet system in some countries is often more stable than telephone service.

Maintaining up-to-date postings and a Web site of your company's product information and prices also allows your vendors to have continuous access to the information that is needed in order to promote and sell your products. Small suppliers find that they can compete with larger companies by being easily available via the Internet.

Internet-assisted sales, where customers are sought and served online through Web sites, Gophers, and a variety of virtual storefronts, are also popular. Customers are thus sought before the sale and supported after the sale.

In an increasing number of cases, companies are doing actual product sales transactions on the Internet, particularly through the Web. In addition, if the product is amenable to electronic delivery, as with software and information, it is actually delivered via the Internet. Some companies are arranging product delivery and services through the Internet, where companies can create and support actual distribution channels.

Transmission of Data

Many companies have been using the Internet for the transmission of data. The major financial and medical institutions in the world use the Internet extensively for exchanging information and files. Publishers are using the Internet to receive manuscripts, and to transmit files for printing over the Internet. Books are written and edited collaboratively using the Internet.

The Internet protocols and MIME-compliant e-mail allow for the exchange of both ASCII and binary information. Binary information includes executable programs (software), program data files (word processing files, spreadsheets, databases, etc.), graphics (pictures, maps, digitized images, CAD/CAM files, etc.), and sound files. The network's backbone can send the equivalent of a 20-volume encyclopedia in just seconds. (Secure MIME is discussed in Chapter 7.)

Research and scientific organizations and educational institutions, the original inhabitants of the Internet, are using the Internet to transmit large quantities of data as well, but corporate users now transfer the largest portion of data over the Net.

Corporate Presence on the Internet

By creating a corporate presence on the Internet, businesses can participate in all the benefits of online marketing, publicity, and sales. They can use such tools as the Web, Gopher, FTP, Telnet, e-mail, and Usenet to build and support a virtual storefront, create catalogs that can be browsed online, announce products, take orders, and get customer feedback. Chapter 8 focuses entirely on techniques and tools for creating this corporate presence on the Internet. Figure 5.2 shows the homepage of Ameritech, a large telecommuications conglomerate.

Figure 5.2 The Ameritech homepage.

Growth of the Commercial Domain

It is said that the Internet as a whole is growing at the rate of 10 percent per month, and that the largest and fastest growing segment of the Internet is business. According to statistics gathered by InterNic, Network Wizards (*http://www.nw.com*), and others, commercial addresses now make up more than 80 percent of network registrations—and this does not include companies that are registered under some research- or education-related functions. The graph in Figure 5.3 shows the distribution of network registrations. These are counts of network registration only, not of individual users. Substantial growth in the commercial domain is expected to continue, particularly as the World Wide Web grows.

The World Wide Web is now the fastest growing segment of the Internet, surpassing Gopher traffic since mid-1994. The rise in WWW

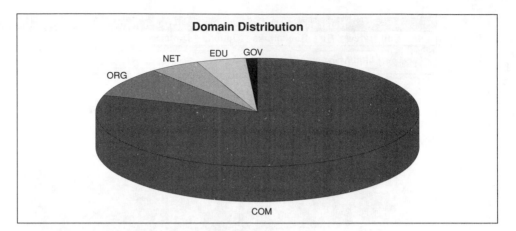

Figure 5.3 Network domain distribution.

traffic has three components: the increase in the number of WWW servers, and also the use of the HTTP protocol, plus the use of the Web browsers to access Gopher, Telnet, and FTP sites. This growth is almost cyclical—the more servers in use means more access, larger numbers of businesses on the Web, and more information. And at the same time, the easier-to-use browsers means that more people will be able to make use of the Web, too, and become potential customers. The growth of Web servers can be seen in Figure 5.4.

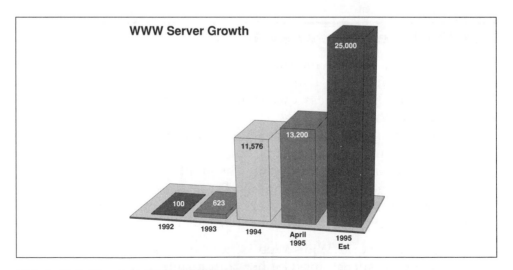

Figure 5.4 The growth in WWW servers.

The "power users" of the Internet still include some of the major computer corporations, health care organizations, pharmaceutical companies, banks and financial services, and high-technology manufacturers, but traffic patterns are becoming more diverse. Based on figures from the Internet Letter (Levin), InterNic, and Net Wizards, the 10 companies accounting for some of the heaviest traffic on the Internet according to the number of externally reachable hosts are:

- Ameritech
- Bell Communications
- Cisco Systems
- Dell Computer
- LSI Logic Corporation
- Motorola Manufacturing
- Performance Systems International (PSI)
- Portal Communications
- Sterling Software
- Xerox Corporation

Major financial institutions such as J. P. Morgan, Lehman Brothers, Paine Webber, and the Federal Reserve Board are all using the Internet for data transmission and research. According to the statistics from InterNic, Net Wizards, and others, they are retrieving 10 times as much data as they are sending out. This suggests that they are using the Internet in support of their financial research. Medical institutions such as Massachusetts General, Health and Welfare Canada, and Rush Presbyterian also have a 10:1 ratio, and are major Internet users.

Some useful resources for looking at network traffic, network demographics, and statistics can be found at the Merit Network (*http://nic.merit.edu*), NetGenesis (*http://www.netgen.com*), and Network Wizards (*http://www.nw.com*). The Internet Business Center maintains excellent links to these resources at *http://tig.com/IBC/stats/html/*, and Mike Walsh offers a variety of statistics on his page at *http://www.webcom.com/~walsh*.

There are other indicators of the growth of the business sector on the Internet. To illustrate, there are a growing number of paper-based and electronic publications about the Internet— *Internet World, The Internet*

Business Journal, Internet Week, The Internet Business Advantage, WebWeek, The Internet Letter, NetGuide Magazine, The Internet Business Report, Websight, Interactive Week, Bits and Bytes Online, E-D-U-P-A-G-E, and more. Some of these new publications are specifically about doing business on the Internet.

Increasingly, URLs are seen on television, and in newspaper and magazine ads. URLs can be spotted on business cards, letterheads, mouse pads, and coffee mugs. They even show up on billboards, airport displays, and motorcycle license plate holders.

Examples of How Companies Are Using the Internet

The Internet is not just used by large corporations! Many individuals, nonprofits, and small businesses use the Internet thorough the access service providers mentioned in Chapter 3. The ways in which businesses use the Internet are as varied as the businesses themselves. Some just use it for communication or the transfer of data. Others do market research and go so far as to create a virtual storefront.

Following are some current business residents of the Internet with a brief description of how they are using the Internet. These include a variety of online business models:

- Free services with expanded services for subscribers
- Online shopping and selling
- Online advertising and marketing with offline purchase or consumption
- Marketing through information.

The Ford Worldwide Connection at *http://www.ford.com/home.html* is where the Ford Motor Company is offering an electronic showroom, access to financial information, historical information, and a customer link to survey customers and promote its line of cars. "Have you driven a Ford lately..." on the Internet? But you cannot purchase the cars online—yet! The Ford homepage can be seen in Figure 5.5.

Tadpole Computers keeps its offices in Cambridge (England), Austin (Texas), San Jose (California), Dallas, New York, and Paris (France) in constant communication using the Internet.

Figure 5.5 The Ford Worldwide Connection.

Many publishers are using the Internet to market and sell their products. **John Wiley & Sons**, for example, uses the Internet to communicate with its authors, to stay current with the computer industry, and to market products through its Web site: *http://www.wiley.com.*

Numerous publications and radio and TV stations are seeking feedback via the Internet, including e-mail and Web sites. *The Houston Chronicle, The Village Voice, The New York Times, The Economist,* and the *National Broadcasting Company* (NBC) regularly query readers/viewers for interests and comments.

Schneider National of Green Bay, Wisconsin, one of the nation's largest trucking firms, uses the Internet to manage logistics and scheduling, and even to alert drivers of adverse road and weather conditions. *Newsweek* (1994) says that Schneider may be an information system masquerading as a trucking line. By keeping its equipment and drivers busy, Schneider doubled its revenue from 1989 to 1993.

Even the **IRS** is using the Internet for data exchange and customer service (*http://ustreas.gov*), and is accepting electronic submission of returns, though not via the Internet—yet.

Greenville Tool and Die makes automotive sheet metal stamping dies in Michigan. The dies are used by some of the large automobile companies. As with many manufacturing companies, its manufacturing and stocking processes have become heavily computerized. It uses the Internet to keep its computerized design and manufacturing (CAD/CAM) software up-to-date and running smoothly. Because of tight time lines for production, it must keep its software up and running at all times. It serves as a beta test site for software from a variety of sources. (Beta software is software that is almost ready for release, but needs a bit more testing.)

Greenville Tool and Die formerly used the telephone for technical support and postal mail for software patches and updates. Now it uses the Internet for both. In addition, it uses the Internet to locate high-tech information, and to download public domain software. It also uses the Internet for internal and external (global) connectivity.

McCrerey Farm in rural Pennsylvania sells handicrafts, dolls, natural fibers, and crafts supplies through an online catalog using the Gopher at *gopher://ivory.lm.com:70/11/Shopping%20Plaza%3A%2Businesses%20and%20Services/McCrerey%20Farm%3A%20handcrafts%20%26%20natural%20products*. The opening Gopher screen reads like this:

```
Gopher Menu

About McCrerey Farm
    Dolls and Santas
    Handcrafted Traditionals and Gifts
    Kits
    Natural Fibers & Crafter's Supplies
    Order Form
    Ordering Information
    The Legend of the McCrerey Angels
```

When you choose "About McCrerey Farm," you find a letter to potential customers, outlining products and services; the emphasis is on local natural products and crafts that are environmentally friendly. McCrerey Farms also includes educational materials regarding the care and use of the items for sale, and also offers some local legends about angels.

McCrerey Farm provides a postal address and phone number for orders, in addition to its online e-mail ordering address: kristen@telerama. pgh.pa.us.

The Internet's Online Career Center is a nonprofit employer association originally formed by a group of 40 U.S. corporations, and designed to help job seekers and employers to match job-related interests and skills. Job seekers may post their resumes and use the service for free, while the companies listing jobs have to pay a small fee for file maintenance (send mail to occ@occ.com). Currently there are more than 8,000 jobs listed. The opening screen of the homepage can be seen in Figure 5.6.

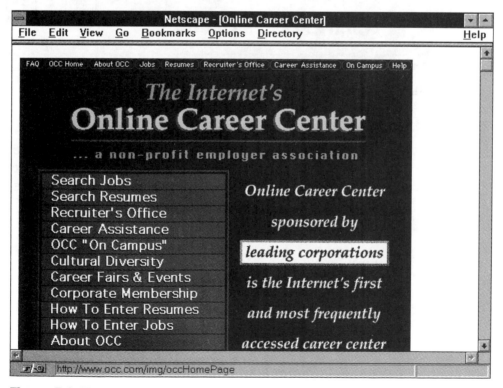

Figure 5.6 The Online Career Center homepage.

Figure 5.7 The True North homepage.

NSTN's **True North** site features True North Services, Tupilak the Cyberspace Searcher, and listings under Commerce, the Cybrary, and Entertainment. Figure 5.7 shows the opening page at *http://www.nstn.ca*. True North's CyberMall™ features vendors in a variety of categories:

- Bookstores
- Child Safety
- Computer Services
- Computer Networking
- Consumer Services
- Disability Services
- Distance Education
- Engineering and Environment

- Health Care
- Hobbies
- Real Estate
- Telecommunications
- Training
- Travel Services

Roswell's Bookstore was a traditional bookstore in Halifax, Nova Scotia before it went on the Internet to sell books. Now it is a traditional bookstore with a storefront on the world (*http://www.isisnet.com/roswell*). You can browse the "shelves," search by author, title, or ISBN, and look at its recent news releases. Roswell's provides access through both WWW and Gopher, and also maintains an e-mail mailing list for specials and sales. Ordering is accomplished through prearranged accounts so that orders can be placed via e-mail without concern for exchanging banking or credit card information online.

The Schlumberger Corporation is a company that provides oil field services and high-technology measurement devices to customers world-wide. This is a corporation with service locations ranging from Oklahoma to Japan and Siberia, and includes drilling platforms and a fleet of ships. All of its products and services are related to petroleum.

As a highly distributed conglomerate with more than 2,000 locations, it has a need for very high-quality, rapid communication. It uses the Internet for e-mail, and for data transfer via FTP. The Internet is an important tool for information sharing, minimizing the vast time zone and location differences. Schlumberger even maintains Gophers and Web pages with pictures of employees so that they can communicate effectively, and verify identities.

It also uses the Internet to disseminate information to customers, with sophisticated security measures to protect proprietary information. It is engaged in collaborative projects with academics and other corporations, and trades information via e-mail, Gopher, and FTP. In addition, it is able to share software on the Internet. The homepage (*http://www.slb.com/*) can be seen in Figure 5.8.

Lombard Institutional Brokerage offers online trading, stock market, and investing information. The LIST (Lombard Internet Securities Trad-

Figure 5.8 The Schlumberger homepage.

ing) service provides a rich variety of information to users, enabling them to make decisions and choices about investments.

This San Francisco firm is a traditional discount brokerage that extended its business on the Internet using one of the most common Internet business models: a two-tiered model, with a range of free services available to anyone, and then for subscribers, a much richer set of tools, services, and in-depth information.

Charts and graphs of historical information on all securities are provided, as well as information on all publicly traded companies. Some of the information is updated in real time. Subscribers can obtain more extensive information. Using a secure server, transactions are encrypted. Lombard's Web site also provides portfolio management services, and buy, sell, cancel, and change orders are accepted online. Research and analytical tools such as Dow Vision and Holt's Stock Market Reports are

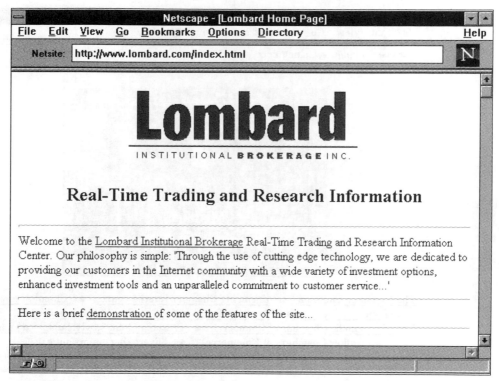

Figure 5.9 The Lombard homepage.

also available. Figure 5.9 shows the Lombard Web page at *http://www. lombard.com*.

Many cities, chambers of commerce, and other local organizations are putting businesses and business information online. Two interesting examples are the city of Indianapolis and a very small rural town—Calvert, Texas.

In support of more than 3,400 local businesses, the Indianapolis Chamber of Commerce has created a Web site called the **Indianapolis Chamber of Electronic Commerce**. It provides information about the chamber, the city, news and events, members, links to members' business pages, and links to other chambers. In addition, in order to promote electronic commerce, free e-mail accounts are offered for local businesses. Figure 5.10 shows the page, *http://www.bit-wise.com/icec*.

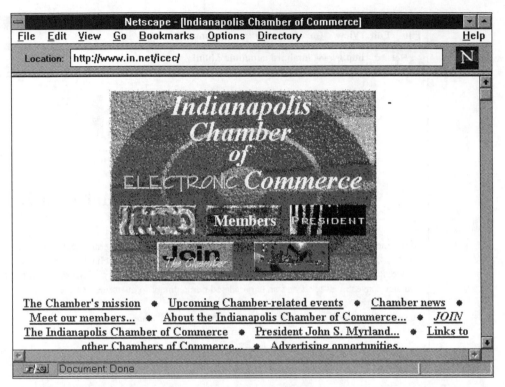

Figure 5.10 The Indianapolis Chamber of Electronic Commerce Web page.

But large urban centers are not the only ones going on the Internet to promote and support business. The **Calvert, Texas** Web page (*http://www.rtis.com/reg/calvert/*) has tourist information, information on the city and community, contacting local businesses, historical material, local events, and contact information.

This is a very small, rural town, presenting its businesses to the larger world. Local businesses listed on the homepage include physicians, banks, dry goods stores, cotton gins, antique dealers, CPAs, welders, car dealers, gas stations, restaurants, plumbers, bed-and-breakfasts, artisans, civic institutions, and more. The Web site is used to stimulate the tourist trade, and to give local businesses visibility beyond the city limits. Many of the businesses have gotten access to e-mail to support the Web page and customer interaction. Figure 5.11 shows the main street of Calvert.

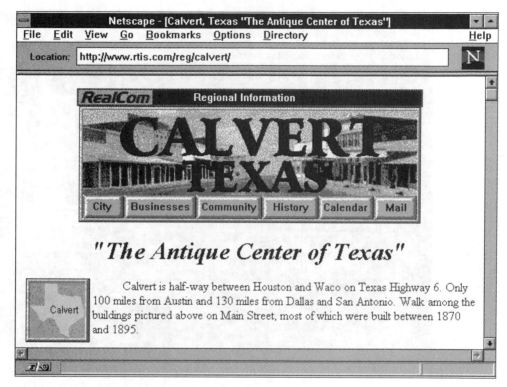

Figure 5.11 The Calvert, Texas Web page.

City.Net at *http://www.city.net* demonstrates how other cities, regions, and states are providing businesses with visibility on the Net, and a vehicle for transacting business.

A very large entertainment company is using the Net to stimulate business on and off the Net. **LucasArts** has a Web site designed to provide information on its movies and games, plus entertainment news, special offers, and even how to apply for jobs with the company. This business model is one of providing information, customer support, actual software, and the enticement to use its offline products.

Game demos, screen shots, technical support for their games, and downloadable software patches are available. The Company Store provides access to a variety of Star Wars collectibles, and an online magazine is offered called *The Adventurer*.

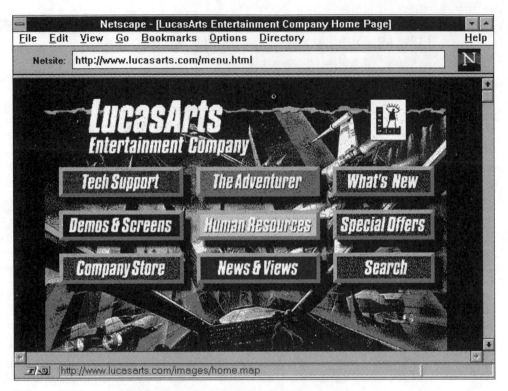

Figure 5.12 LucasArts Entertainment page.

Their site for LucasArts Entertainment (*http://www.lucasarts.com/menu.html*) is shown in Figure 5.12.

The Smart Food Co-Op in Cambridge, Massachusetts, has gone on the Internet to provide local customers online ordering, offering significant savings for shoppers plus the convenience of delivery.

An example of a virtual business, the Smart Food Co-Op has no physical grocery store, only a virtual store. It has been online since 1990, but only recently has the co-op offered a Web page (*http://thinkpix.com/sfc/*) for ordering and customer interaction. The page supplies information in addition to groceries: Clicking on the broccoli, for example, will not only give you price information, but nutrition data and recipes. You can even choose from among ripe, near ripe, and green bananas.

Customer profiles are created that include preferences such as "no okra," or "milk in paper cartons not plastic." The groceries are delivered

Figure 5.13 The Smart Food Co-Op homepage.

to the customer via vans, using a computer program that maps out the most efficient routes.

Customers include MIT students, new mothers, the elderly, and people too busy to shop. The co-op is considering expansion into other large markets. Figure 5.13 shows the homepage.

DealerNet is a group of over 25 automobile dealers who have joined forces to provide potential car buyers with information, choices, brochures, full-motion video, and inventory searches. They have created virtual showrooms for each dealer, manufacturer, and auto-related company.

The site is service oriented—it does not allow the consumer to purchase online (gee, and I was hoping to click on a new Taurus and get it delivered). The focus is on education, data, and availability, helping users

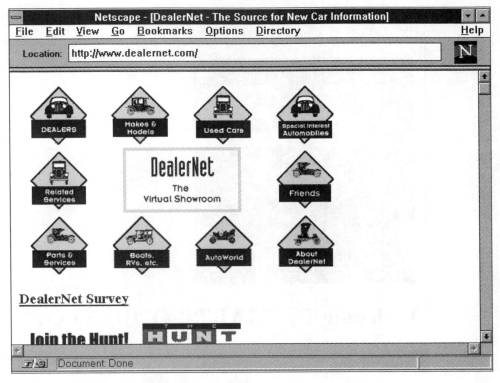

Figure 5.14 The DealerNet homepage.

make more informed choices about their car purchases. It also has communication links with each dealer.

This business model represents pure advertising and marketing, with no online selling. Figure 5.14 shows the Web site for DealerNet (*http://www.dealernet.com/*).

Lufthansa Airlines maintains a scheduler at its Tourism Info Internet site, which includes special flights, prices, and travel packages. The service is available in English (*http://www.tkz.fh-rpl.de/tii/tii-e.html*) and German (*http://www.tkz.fh-rpl.de/tii/tii.html*). **Southwest Airlines** has a much bolder presence at *http://www.iflyswa.com*, where they offer lots of information on schedules, policies, travel information, and more. They plan to begin actual ticketing soon through their site as well.

Ticketmaster is a very large ticket distribution company that lists information on over 10,000 live events through its WWW site at

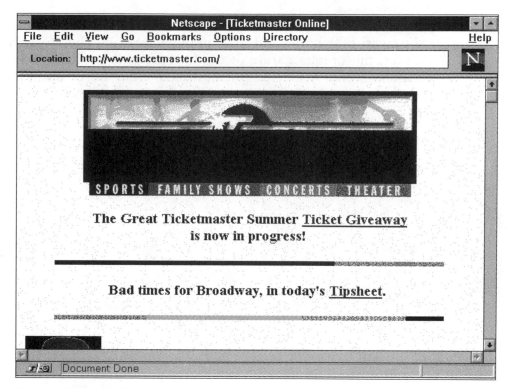

Figure 5.15 The Ticketmaster Online homepage.

http://www.ticketmaster.com. Its site is extensive (over 12,000 HTML pages) and includes information on schedules, artists, and venues across the United States, listing sports events, concerts, theaters, and other entertainment venues. The homepage can be seen in Figure 5.15.

Allergy Clean Environments (*http://www.w2.com/allergy22.html*) sells everything from air cleaners to vacuum cleaner bags on its Web site. In addition, it offers a broad variety of information about allergy products and books.

Moving On from Here

As you can see, all kinds of businesses are using the Internet in a variety of ways, and the development of the Internet system and its software will bring thousands of additional ways to use the Internet. But to maintain a good business image and access to the Internet, all businesses will need to be aware of the rules and customs of the Internet. Therefore, in the next chapter, the unique nature of the Internet will be discussed. Then, in Chapters 8 and 9, specific practical techniques for creating a business presence on the Internet will be explained in detail.

CHAPTER 6

Acceptable Uses and Customs of the Internet

To operate on the Internet successfully, businesses need to be aware not only of the written rules of the Internet, but of the customs and culture of the Internet. Just as the Internet has great power to magnify the reach of your business, it has power to damage your business if you jump in unprepared, and unaware of your surroundings.

Acceptable Use of the Internet

There are several controls on the nature of advertising on the Internet: formally written *acceptable use policies*, the informal concept of "giving back to the Internet," and legal concerns.

Acceptable Use Policies

Acceptable Use Policies (AUP) are a written set of rules governing your use of, and access to, your Internet service provider or network. Most Internet service providers and networks have AUPs. Even some "AUP-free" sites (a misnomer from the past) have written AUPs. Sometimes the AUPs are part of the overall agreement for services that you sign.

One policy that is nearly universally present in AUPs is a prohibition against sending unsolicited messages or advertising. Even within a commercial environment, it is not acceptable to send unsolicited advertising. ANS CO+RE, for example, a provider of commercial network links, has in its AUP the statement: "Advertising may not be broadcast or otherwise sent on an intrusive basis to any user of the ANS CO+RE network or any directly or indirectly attached network."

Sending unsolicited e-mail or posting inappropriate ads to newsgroups or mailing lists will, legal issues aside, result in swift, large-scale, angry responses from those on the Net. Those who have violated this custom have found negative messages about their company posted on discussion group sites read by millions worldwide, and have received so many negative responses that their Internet service providers have cut off their business accounts.

When you are selecting an Internet service provider or network, ask about their AUP and service agreement. Look for ones that are business-friendly and provide guarantees of data, log file, and message privacy.

Giving Back to the Internet

As you can see, even on the most commercially oriented networks, unsolicited advertising, or junk e-mail, is prohibited. This leaves one primary mode of advertising: attracting potential customers to connect to your virtual storefront or other online presence (Gopher or Web site, BBS, etc.). A business can attract people to its advertisements by providing free information, databases, software, or other goods and services along with the information about its business and products. (Chapters 8 and 9 explain techniques for doing this.)

Legal Issues

State and federal legislatures and regulatory agencies are also involved in determining what is acceptable use of the Internet. They have been dealing with issues of freedom of speech, legalities surrounding online transactions, issues related to government rights to "wiretap" encrypted messages, copyright and trademark protection on the Internet, and dozens of other issues. While a legal structure is needed to support activities on the Internet, Internet citizens need to keep track of legislative activities in this area—many legislators have never seen the Internet and therefore have incomplete or inaccurate impressions of it.

While the Internet was originally built and populated by adults, the increasingly easy and inexpensive access to the Internet in the last few years has brought many children online. These children are often not properly supervised by adults while online. Businesses should, therefore, give some consideration to the material they present both for legal concerns and for the protection of the children. While parents can use site blocking software (such as Surfwatch and Net Nanny), the legal issues surrounding a business's responsibilities in these matters are very much up in the air, so caution is advised.

Ways to Get Into (and Stay Out of) Trouble

As with any group or community, the Internet has some common practices, customs, conventions, and expectations. On the Internet these are often referred to as "netiquette" (net etiquette). Being aware of netiquette will help make you look less like a "newbie" and also help you get more and better responses to your requests for help. It is also valuable to be aware of what is considered inappropriate behavior.

Unsolicited E-mail

Never, under any circumstances, send unsolicited e-mail to a list of Internet users. The Internet cannot be used as an alternative method of sending card decks, flyers, and other advertisements. If, however, you receive a request for information about your products or company, you can respond with a "canned" e-mail advertisement. (Tips on how to get requests for your advertisements are presented in Chapters 8 and 9.)

Hacking

Hacking has a variety of meanings relative to the Internet. To some, hacking is a positive activity that involves the use of software and networks in new, creative ways, or a virtuoso demonstration of technical genius (even if what was accomplished is of limited practical value). Most people, however, refer to the negative aspects of using these technical skills: gaining unauthorized entry into private computer systems, damaging computer files, software, or communications systems, or causing disruption of other network activities. Obviously, this is unacceptable activity, and will probably result in your Internet access provider dropping your account. In some situations, at state and federal levels, hacking is a crime.

Passwords and some of the strange, convoluted login methods are measures taken by system administrators to protect their systems from hackers. System administrators can also protect files from changes, and directories can be protected from having new files put in them by unauthorized individuals. Firewall software and hardware provide much stronger protection than is provided by the systems built into most computer operating systems (see Chapter 7). Because of these various safeguards, hacking is usually not a big problem for most sites on the Internet.

Those new to the Internet are often amazed at how many networks and computer systems *are* open to the Internet public. Unless you've played "let's try 250 passwords" to get into a system, or you see warnings that you have reached a private system not open to the public, the system is probably intended to be open to the public and you are welcome.

Overloading

Commercial sites on the Internet are usually pleased to have many visits from many people, and seek to expand as needed. However, many sites that offer information and Internet tools as a free public service have some other primary reason for being there—as campus academic and administrative computers, as research computers, or as government agency computers. This means that many computer systems offer the public resources as their secondary function. During normal business hours these systems may be used heavily and begin to respond to their primary tasks more slowly. Despite this, most sites do not shut off the Internet community even during peak hours—but they do request that people voluntarily limit the number and length of connections during these peak hours. So far this voluntary system has worked quite well, so few system administrators have had to "pull the plug" on the Internet community.

This doesn't mean avoiding these services entirely during your business day, but just doing a little planning if you have a computer-intensive or long job for the remote computer. For instance, if you are on the East Coast of the United States, you could use the services of some West Coast sites before 11 A.M. Eastern time, so you would be finished before West Coast users got to work at 8 A.M. Pacific time. After 11:00 A.M., the workday is over in Europe, so it is a good time to connect to European sites. If your demands on the remote system are light, it is fine to connect any time, but if it is a time-consuming job, give scheduling some thought—the computers will respond faster for both them and you.

Opinions and Flaming

With over 30,000 discussion groups on the Internet, just about every topic imaginable (or absolutely unimaginable) is discussed. These discussions sometimes provide more heat than light. Something about the nature of network communications seems to lead some people to lose perspective and respond in overly harsh ways (someone could do a good psychological study here). These incendiary reactions are called "flames" or "flaming" on the Internet. Some who have strong opinions but have retained perspective and a sense of humor will write "set flame on," then proceed to have their say, followed by the words "set flame off," just to let you know that they feel strongly about the subject, but are still open to reason. It is good for the newcomer to be aware of flaming so as not to take it too seriously—and end up responding in anger.

In addition to the normal social reasons for not flaming, there are two Internet-related reasons to limit flaming. First, your communications on discussion lists are available worldwide—whichever group, individual, or institution you are flaming is probably reading the flame. Second, most discussion groups archive (keep) their past messages so that newcomers to the discussion can see what has been going on; therefore, others may still be reading your ill-advised words worldwide, three years down the road.

When sitting alone at your computer, writing to a discussion group may give the impression of anonymity, but it may be one of the most public things you ever do.

Passwords

A password can protect your account with an Internet access provider. The password is important to protect the privacy of your account, and if you pay for your account by credit card or a checking account automatic withdrawal, it will protect you from someone running up large connect time charges or using extra-cost services available at your access provider's site. In addition, with access to your account, someone could post messages and send e-mail in your name in a manner that could damage your reputation, or he or she could destroy or change information that you have stored. Generally this has not been a large problem, but you can do two things to help secure your account: First, store reminders of your password in a location separate from your account's user ID, and second, change your password frequently so that if someone does get it (e.g., through some sort of hacking), he or she will have a limited time to use it.

Password Cautions

To protect yourself from hackers, select passwords that are not real words, and are not anything someone who knows a little about you could guess, such as your street name, occupation, or dog's name. Strings of unrelated words and numbers or misspelled words (e.g., "pencil7dog" or "bwerddog") are quite secure and easy to remember.

Computer-Mediated Communication (CMC)

The history of the Internet, the types of people who use it, the text-based nature of much of the communication, and the unique storage, search, and retrieval systems available on the Internet have led to the development of customs and characteristics unique to the Internet.

The Great Equalizer

Because a person's gender, education, age, ethnic origins, appearance, handicaps, wealth, and social situation are not readily apparent in discussions and many e-mail exchanges, the Internet has become something of a leveler. It provides access to the world of information and ideas that ignores the social restrictions often put on each of these categories.

Corporate CMC

This equalizing effect carries over to some extent to communications within a corporation. People at all levels, from CEO to mailroom clerk, seem freer to join in discussions about the business. Participating in e-mail discussion groups within a company can improve the sense of participation and openness within that company—like a giant corporate water cooler for all sites and divisions of a company.

Smiley Faces and Other Communicons: The New Internet Punctuation

Because it is difficult for the text-based messages on the Internet to express things like humor, sarcasm, surprise, anger, or bewilderment, a variety of symbols (*communicons*—communication icons) have evolved and come into popular use. One of the first of these communicons was the "smiley face," which was a combination of a full colon and a right parenthesis :) (just tip your head to the left to view). Other communicons were developed so that the reader would better understand the intent and context of the message, and the message would therefore be less likely to be taken in the wrong way (see Table 6.1).

Another shorthand way of communicating on the Internet is through a set of commonly understood abbreviations such as those in Table 6.2.

Table 6.1 Communicons.

Smiley	Meaning
:)	basic smiley—an expression of good will
:-)	another basic smiley
;>	mischievous smile
:]	goofy smile
;)	wink
8-)	smile with glasses
:-l	blank look
:-o	surprise
:-O	shock
:(	frown
:-<	sad face

Table 6.2 Commonly Used Abbreviations

Abbreviation	Meaning
<g>	grin
AKA	Also Known As
BTW	By The Way
IMHO	In My Humble Opinion
IMNSHO	In My Not So Humble Opinion
IMO	In My Opinion
LD&R	Laughing, Ducking & Running
LOL	Laughing Out Loud
OTOH	On The Other Hand
SYSOP	SYStem OPerator
TIA	Thanks In Advance

Since fonts, italics, and other ways of highlighting are generally not available in discussion groups and e-mail, several common methods of showing emphasis have evolved:

`_pseudo-underlining_`	Using an underline character at the beginning and at the end of a phrase to be emphasized
`*asterisks for emphasis*`	Using stars at the beginning and end of the emphasized phrase
`ALL CAPITAL LETTERS`	Using all capital letters for emphasis of words and *short* phrases—overuse of all capital letters annoys some people and will often elicit responses such as *quit shouting!*

Another aid to communications used in discussion groups are parenthetical phrases that are intended to give some perspective to the text of the message:

`(as I rise to the soap box...)`

Here the author of the message makes his opinions known.

```
(stepping to the side of the soapbox I wait to see who will
join me)
```

Or someone might write:

```
(hiding in my bunker, I throw out this idea),
```

and then present a controversial statement.

With the rise of HTML, some people use HTML-like tags to indicate humor or emotion:

```
<sarcasm>
I find DOS so easy to use.
</sarcasm>
```

These are all useful for warming up the relatively cool medium of the Internet.

Some Other CMC Concerns in Transition

E-mail privacy and log file privacy are trends heading in opposite directions. While a great deal of effort is going into providing more secure e-mail, there is a proliferation of programs and companies designed to harvest the demographics and personal data from log files on the Internet.

E-mail and Privacy

Standard post office mail (known to the Internet community as "snail mail") has privacy protections established in law. There are a few laws relating to the confidentiality of private e-mail, but generally the level of privacy is determined by the trustworthiness of the computer system administrators.

Ordinarily, e-mail communications are read only by their intended recipients, but system administrators do, in most cases, have access to private e-mail on their systems. On a day-to-day basis, the sheer volume of e-mail traffic provides some privacy, but matters of a highly sensitive nature should not be transferred on the Internet without encryption or other protection. (See Chapter 7 for information on e-mail protection.)

Log Files and Privacy

Many sites on the Internet keep log files of who used their systems and what documents were accessed. Log files store system logins and system activities automatically, tracking who entered the site and what files and programs they accessed. In the case of Web sites, traffic and activity logging is almost universal. These log files are primarily used for statistical purposes, to aid in planning which computer systems resources are to be dedicated to Internet communication, and to help figure out what is happening in case of network problems. They do, however, create some issues of privacy. Librarians, by contrast, have a tradition and, in some states, laws that prohibit anyone from getting a record of what books another individual has checked out. Some Internet sites provide privacy protections, but this is far from the norm. In day-to-day activity on the Internet this is a relatively minor issue—just something to be aware of.

From Here. . .

Chapter 7, "Security, Authentication, and Online Transactions," discusses specific dangers of doing business online, along with current and forthcoming solutions to these potential problems.

Security, Authentication, and Online Transactions

Overview

To do business on the Internet, it is important to understand the issues that surround site security, data integrity, authentication, and the broad implications of secure transactions. Beyond all of these discussions about security is still the need for businesses and individuals to check out the claims and representations of online businesses in the same way as they would offline—what kind of company lies behind the homepage?

In order to make purchasing from Web pages more attractive, there are several groups working on various kinds of secure transactions systems. To sell products directly on the Internet, some form of secure end-to-end transaction is needed. There are several models for this, including analogies to cash and checks, credit cards, the exchange of tokens, prearranged payments, encrypted payments, and on-the-fly secure transactions.

Tangible money serves several functions. Its most important function is as a medium of exchange: We can use money to buy services and goods. Money also acts as a standard of value—if an item costs $10.11 at one store and $11.00 at another, we can distinguish between the two because we trust what the unit of $1 means. Money also sometimes has intrinsic, stored value—independent worth.

Notational money (stored electronically and transferred via electronic means) is the current focus of most secure transactions on the Internet.

Some security measures are embedded in the Internet systems, including Secure HyperText Transfer Protocol (SHTTP) and Secure Sockets Layer (SSL). Secure servers can use these to create an on-the-fly secure environment for the duration of the online transaction. For example, this type of online secure transaction is used by CDnow. CDnow sells many kinds of music CDs online. They have a page that describes the purchasing process, shown in Figure 7.1.

Encryption

The encryption of material for use in electronic commerce is becoming much more common. The process works this way: First you encrypt a message or file with encryption software, using a unique "key" or algo-

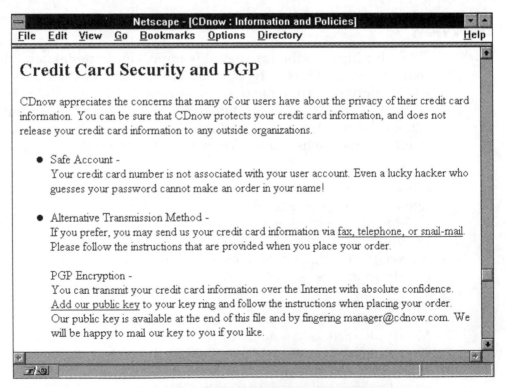

Figure 7.1 The CDnow page discussing secure transactions.

rithm (similar to a password—this is your secret decoder ring). The encrypted, unreadable message is then sent via the Internet to someone else, who, using decryption software compatible with your software, and the message's key, reprocesses the file back into its original, readable form. Encryption methods, called strong encryption, are now available that would take 100 years of computer time to break for someone who doesn't have the key.

A single key that encrypts and decrypts is called a one-key algorithm. A system that needs two keys typically uses a public key to encrypt the message, and a private key to decrypt the message. This means that anyone can use your public key to encrypt a message to you, but only you can decrypt it with your private key. A good example of a two-key system is the program Pretty Good Privacy.

Pretty Good Privacy (PGP)

Pretty Good Privacy (PGP) is a secure encryption system developed by Phil Zimmerman. Currently, it can be downloaded from the Internet. To begin using PGP, obtain version 2.6.1 of the software from the directory *ftp://net-dist.mit.edu/pub/PGP*. It is legal to distribute PGP in the United States and Canada but not elsewhere.

You use the software to generate your pair of public and private keys. You make the public key available to others through e-mail, FTP, a web site, and so on, so that others can encrypt information for you. You then use your private key to decrypt these messages.

Business to Business

Business-to-business transactions usually involve purchase orders, invoices, and delayed billing. These are easily handled with encrypted communications. Consumer or retail transactions, on the other hand, usually involve immediate financial transactions. Secure transactions methods for retail are discussed later in this chapter.

Site Security

Many companies are concerned with protecting their internal networks and computers from access via the Internet in order to avoid breaches in security. The protocols of the Internet such as Telnet, FTP, and e-mail are open systems, meant to be used easily. Several approaches can be taken to protect your systems and files from viewing and alteration.

Firewalls

Many companies place firewalls around their networks and computers to restrict access and services. A firewall is a secure path for incoming and outgoing traffic between an internal network or computer and the Internet. This serves to restrict traffic to authorized users. Most firewalls restrict any kind of protocol except e-mail, passing along only those packets that meet certain criteria. In some cases this is just a software filtering function on e-mail, but it can be more sophisticated—using separate hardware with only outward connectivity.

Firewalls are normally a combination of software and hardware, typically involving a computer, a router, and security software. The firewall is the link and gatekeeper between the internal network and the Internet. Firewalls that work very well are difficult to create, and require consistent monitoring for effectiveness. None are foolproof, but some are getting fairly close.

Another system that some companies are using now is what we call the "castle and the moat" system. A company places its internal network inside the castle and pulls up the drawbridge. The public server is then outside the moat, unconnected to the internal system, and allows for outside access. The down side of this is that since there is no connection between the two systems, information has to be duplicated and managed separately.

Passwords

Some security precautions are fairly simple; such is the case for password management. Here are just a few very quick ways that you can safeguard your system:

- Change your password frequently.
- Don't use the same password for all of your accounts.
- Don't put your password on a Post-it note on your computer or monitor.

- Mix upper- and lowercase characters in your password (if your system is case sensitive).

- Do not use ordinary words as passwords—combine words and numbers in unusual ways, or use odd spellings.

- Do not use as passwords names, other words, or numbers associated with you such as hobbies, your spouse's name, your ham radio call sign, or your birthday.

A password such as *C-2Steve* is better than just *steve*, and *C-2s_V* is even better, but be sure that you can remember it as well. Many companies are using security algorithms to generate good passwords, so passwords may be assigned to you.

Secure E-mail

A new secure extension to MIME called Secure Multipurpose Internet Mail Extensions (S/MIME) is under development. This will provide security for messages and other files sent between S/MIME-compatible mail programs. Several leading software companies are supporting the S/MIME specification developed by RSA Data Security, including Microsoft, Lotus, Banyan, VeriSign, ConnectSoft, QUALCOMM, Frontier Technologies, Network Computing Devices, FTP Software, Wollongong, SecureWare, RSA Data Security, and IBM. This means that e-mail with sensitive documents contained or attached as files can be securely transmitted over the Internet and cannot be "opened" (read) in transit. (S/MIME is included in Netscape 2.0.) S/MIME is based on the popular Internet MIME standard (RFC 1521). More information on S/MIME can be obtained at RSA's Web site, at *http://www.rsa.com*.

Computer Emergency Response Team (CERT)

The Computer Emergency Response Team is the official Internet body that deals with Internet attacks and viruses of all kinds. It was formed in 1988 in response to the Internet "worm" that attacked the Net.

CERT provides around-the-clock technical assistance for help in responding to security incidents. The volunteer group also offers information, discussion lists, documents, and training sessions, and posts advisories to the Usenet group *comp.security.announce* and through a variety of mailing lists. Some of CERT's documentation can be accessed through the Carnegie Mellon Software Engineering Institute: *http://www. sei.cmu.edu/FrontDoor.html.*

CERT

E-mail: cert@cert.org

Telephone hotline/24 hours: 1.412.268.7090

Fax number: 1.412.268.6989

What are some of the signs of a break-in? There are some things to look for in your log files that might indicate that someone has tried to break into your system. Your system log files can keep track of e-mail, WWW, Telnet, and FTP access to your system, and a look at them may alert you to a possible break-in. Look for:

- Repeated attempts to connect to ports that your site does not use
- Large numbers of attempts to use the *Finger* program to look at your site
- Large numbers of attempts to log in that are unsuccessful
- Repeated login attempts from a single address or group of similar addresses

If there is some evidence of break-in attempts, a contact to CERT would be in order.

Data Security and Integrity

Keeping your data safe from both casual and determined intruders is increasingly important. In addition to firewalls, there are other systems available to secure your data.

Kerberos (named for the dog in Greek mythology who guards Hades) is an authentication system that enables people and systems to identify each other for permission to use files and systems. It also helps to prevent the unauthorized modification of files.

You can find more information about Kerberos on the Usenet newsgroup *comp.protocols.kerberos* and from the Web site *http://www.cs.cmu. edu:8001/afs/andrew.cmu.edu/usr/db74/www/kerberos.html.*

Increasingly, companies are looking at ways to transform accessible data into objects. Data files are relatively easy to change, while data that have been transformed into an object are much more difficult to change. One example of this method is called Portable Document Format from Acrobat. Acrobat takes documents of all kinds and makes them into a single unit (a single unitized document), as opposed to lots of units (letters). While this objectification does not utterly prevent tampering, it makes it very much more difficult.

Authentication

On the Internet, security issues include authentication, because, in general, you cannot see or hear the people that you are doing business with. Authentication of identity is essential to business transactions, particularly those involving signed documents and contracts. Are they who they say they are—really?

This concern comes into play in many phases of business dealings. Suppose you get an e-mail offer of employment. Important questions are, who sent this (really); is this an authentic, valid document, electronically signed by an authorized individual; and is the document you receive an exact copy of the document that was sent?

Issues of authentication are increasingly important as more business moves online, and the need for online contracts and interchanges increases. There are a variety of ways to accomplish verification, including the use of PGP, secure envelopes, and packet "stamping" schemes.

Secure Packaging

One approach to both security and authentication uses secure bundling or packaging. A secure package or digital virtual envelope is created for the information (in some cases the information is first encrypted). After the files are placed in the secure envelope or container, it is sealed—like using the old wax seals of the Middle Ages. Netscape, for examples, has developed Secure Courier—a kind of secure "envelope" that contains sensitive data. This envelope can be transmitted using MIME mail, through a Web server, Telnet, or FTP.

Secure Transactions

In retail business on the Internet, secure transactions are increasingly important. Customers need to feel that their sensitive data is protected, and that credit card and customer information is secure. There are a variety of methods for making the Internet more secure for business transactions.

Secure Transaction Models

There are several popular models being used or developed for increasing the security of transactions on the Internet. These include:

- Prearranged account or billing—This involves shopping online, but arranging for ordering offline. The consumer makes offline arrangements (by phone, mail, fax, etc.) for payments though a credit card or by establishing a line of credit. Orders are then made via input forms on a Web page or through e-mail, or even through telephone or fax. These solutions are often called account billing systems, where each customer registers with each vendor. This requirement of a separate arrangement with each vendor tends to stifle impulse purchases. In some cases, virtual malls allow for the creation of one payment account that can be used with any of the merchants in the mall.

- Virtual bucks or tokens—this system involves the purchase of tokens, coupons, or virtual bucks, to be used with a variety of vendors who accept this kind of payment. This is more flexible than a prearranged account, but there is still the matter of security of the codes transmitted across the Internet, and the limited number of vendors using these systems.

- Encrypted Web page entry—In this case encryption is offered on-the-fly through the use of secure HTTP or through Secure Sockets Layer (discussed in the following section) so that you can transmit credit card or other data directly to each vendor.

- Cyber credit cards—The credit card model allows a customer to purchase from any participating vendor. Often, the credit card information is encrypted and transmitted through some secure channel.

- Electronic checks—These are another model that involves the use of a third party—an online bank.

Secure Software and Hardware

There are several security solutions that combine secure browsers such as Netscape and servers such as Netsite Secure to create a secure connection in which the two can communicate with each other in their own language without others being able to eavesdrop. This usually involves some level of on-the-fly encryption of information between the client and the server. In addition to providing for security, it enhances the privacy of the transaction. Look for the number of secure servers and clients to increase sharply.

The Netsite server provides an example of the secure server method. Figure 7.2 shows the Netsite server in the "shopping" mode—the key at

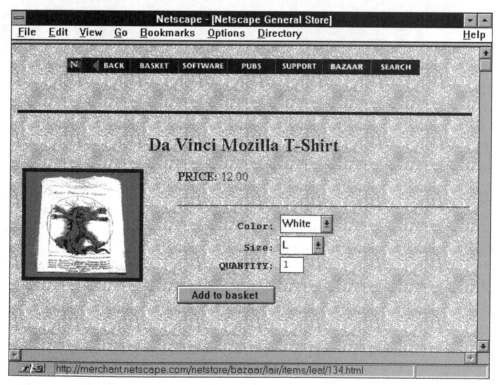

Figure 7.2 The Netscape shopping page.

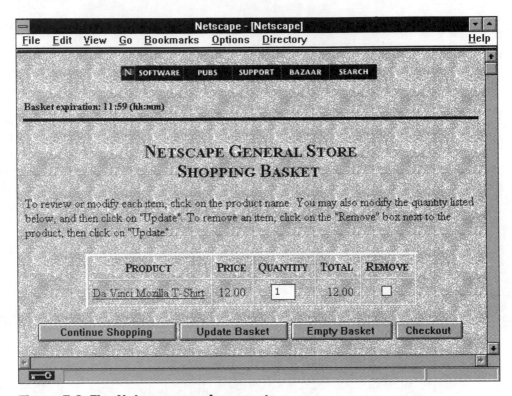

Figure 7.3 The Netscape purchase page.

the bottom left of the screen is "broken," meaning that it is not a secure connection, and the bar at the top is gray.

Figure 7.3 shows the server in secure mode; the key is turned and the bar would be green if this figure was in color, meaning that a secure connection is in effect, allowing the connection to move from shopping mode to purchasing mode.

Secure HTTP and Secure Sockets Layer (SSL)

Developed by Enterprise Integration Technologies, NCSA, Terisa Systems, and RSA, secure HTTP (S/HTTP) is a protocol available for a variety of commercial browsers that allows customers who are using the Web to order online to transmit credit card or other private financial information in a secure environment. This can include all manner of forms online, including purchases, applications for jobs and loans, and so on, and typically takes the form of momentary, on-the-fly encryption.

More information can be found on the CommerceNet page at *http://www.commerce.net/information/standards/drafts/shttp.txt*.

Secure Sockets Layer is an Internet security protocol that provides privacy. The protocol allows client/server applications to communicate in a way that prevents eavesdropping. Under SSL, servers are always authenticated, while clients may be authenticated optionally. The SSL protocol is designed to provide privacy between two communicating applications (a client and a server), keeping the channel secure end to end.

More information can be obtained from: *http://www.mcom.com/newsref/std/SSL.html*.

Digital Money (or Its Equivalent)

In addition to prearranged purchases and the use of traditional credit cards, business on the Internet makes use of digital cash.

Cash in the nonvirtual world offline has some characteristics that make it very useful.

- It is *anonymous*. No one keeps a record of what was bought or who bought it.
- It is *reputable*. The value of the "bill" is not in question—it is backed up by a banking and currency system that is trustworthy.
- It is *hard to forge*. Currency in the offline world is engraved in particular ways, printed on special paper, and difficult to counterfeit.
- It is *divisible*. A variety of units of the money are available ($1, $5, $10, etc.). You are not stuck paying $20 for a piece of bubble gum.
- It has *atomicity*. A transaction either happened or it did not—the money changed hands or not.

These are the same characteristics needed by digital cash, and a number of systems have sprung up that emulate these characteristics.

Approaches to E-money

There are several online analogies to cash, checks, and credit and debit cards. The following are some of the most developed.

CyberCash

CyberCash relies on special software and an intermediary for its workings. The company is creating relationships with banks (Wells Fargo for instance), and is attempting to create a link between the Internet and the more secure banking networks. CyberCash's server can communicate with both systems.

For more information, see *http://www.cybercash.com*.

First Virtual

First Virtual calls itself the first virtual bank on the Internet. Its credit card transactions are processed through First USA Bank, and its direct deposit transactions are processed by Northern Trust. Its confidential financial records are managed by the Bank Card Processing division of EDS. Currently, First Virtual is used only for those purchases involving information—not hard goods.

First Virtual's system does not require encryption, nor any special software—it makes use of e-mail. First Virtual is a credit card broker operating between consumer and vendor. It has adapted the offline credit card system to the online environment. To begin, the customer creates an account by giving First Virtual a credit card number via telephone or fax, and the customer is given a First Virtual ID, which can be a number or phrase of the buyer's choosing. To use the account, the buyer places an order with a vendor using this ID; the vendor contacts First Virtual to verify that the buyer has an account, and then sends the product (the information) to First Virtual. The buyer can then look at the product before closing the purchase. The buyer's account is then debited to finish the transaction.

More information on First Virtual can be obtained from its Web site: *http://www.fv.com*.

NetCash

NetCash has been created by Software Agents, and focuses on micropayments. In concept, NetCash wants to make it easy for someone to pay 10 cents for a bit of online information—the online equivalent to handing a newsstand vendor a dime for a paper. The controls on its use do not guarantee anonymity or heavy protection against forgery or fraud. Because the company only deals in small change—transactions under $100 per coupon—these issues are less important.

NetCash is entirely e-mail based. It involves buyers, sellers, and a bank that converts the coupons into real money. To begin, a buyer creates an account with NetCash, purchasing coupons from the bank using standard forms of money—credit cards or money orders. The NetBank keeps track of the use of the coupons, invalidating coupons as they are used. The buyer sends coupons to vendors, who then present them to the NetBank for conversion into money. More information is available from *http://www.teleport.com/~netcash/*.

NetCheque

NetCheque is an electronic payment system analogous to standard checks which was developed for the Internet by the Information Sciences Institute of the University of Southern California.

Users who register through prearrangement with NetCheque accounting servers are able to write electronic checks to other users. The checks may be sent through e-mail or through other network protocols. As with a conventional paper check, when it is deposited, the check authorizes the transfer of funds from the buyer to the seller. The signature on the check is authenticated using Kerberos. NetCheques can also be used for micropayments (payments of a few cents or less). More information can be obtained through the Web page at *http://nii-server.isi.edu/info/ NetCheque/*.

DigiCash

Created by David Chaum, DigiCash is an encrypted cash system relying on public key encryption and what Chaum calls a *blind digital signature*. It is this characteristic that makes DigiCash so different from other digital money schemes. The blind signature guarantees the anonymity of the user. DigiCash is anonymous, and provides for a direct transaction. It requires special software. More information can be obtained at the DigiCash site: *http://www.digicash.com*.

NetBill

NetBill is a system that allows micropayments on the Internet—small transaction charges can be made for accessing information and services.

Created by researchers at Carnegie Mellon, it offers a method for making money "a little at a time," and is useful for a Web site with a high volume of hits to ensure income from the site.

The transaction flow works this way: The buyer arranges a NetBill account, the information goods are transferred from the seller to the buyer, the buyer's NetBill account is debited, the seller's account is credited. This is all done within a secure environment, including access controls, user certificates, certified delivery, and a certain degree of anonymity. More information can be obtained at the NetBill Web page: *http://www.ini.cum.edu/netbill/*.

iKP

Credit card–based systems for electronic transactions such as iKP are growing in popularity on the Internet. iKP (i-Key-Protocol) is a suite of electronic payment protocols based on public-key cryptography that can be implemented at a hardware or software level. The protocols also can be applied to electronic checks and debit cards. More information can be obtained from *http://www.zurich.ibm.com/Technology/Security/extern/ecommerce/*.

Legal Issues for the Online Business

There are a variety of legal issues concerning intellectual property of importance for online business. These include:

- Copyrights
- Trademarks
- Advertising practices

Copyrights

Material that you find online is most likely to be copyrighted, although there are some exceptions for material in the public domain and certain government documents. For the most part, this means that all text, image, and sound files and homepages are copyrighted, and as such, cannot be used in certain ways, particularly for profit, without the permission of the owner/creator.

This covers Usenet and discussion list postings, homepages, FTP files, and other online material. Since 1978, in the United States, any original material that you create is copyrighted immediately upon creation, and cannot be used without permission, except as defined by fair use—in attributed excerpts, quotes, and reviews.

Trademarks

A trademark is some distinguishable word, symbol, design, or phrase that identifies the source of goods or services. Many companies are now trademarking their domain name: **bigcompany.com**®. This protects them from its use by someone else. The use of the ® is restricted to trademarks that are fully registered with the Patent and Trademark Office.

Advertising

There is a large body of law related to advertising of products and services, and its laws, policies, and rules apply for the most part to your business online. This is especially important for businesses advertising products for sale on Web pages, or actually selling directly from a Web page.

Resources

Here are a number of online resources for finding more information about security, secure transactions, authentication, legal matters, and related issues.

The Internet Engineering Task Force (IETF)

The IETF currently has a number of projects underway that relate to security issues. These relatively long-term projects are aimed at examining and creating several standards that will effect cyberbusiness. The Security Working Group has some draft standards underway, including:

- Authorization and Access Control
- Authenticated Firewall Traversal
- Commercial Internet Protocol Security Option
- Common Authentication Technology
- Internet Security Protocol

- Network Access Server Requirements
- Privacy Enhanced Mail

The developments in these areas can be tracked on the homepage of the IETF at *http://www.ietf.cnri.reston.va.us*. The goal of much of this work is to make secure transactions and authentication as easy as just clicking your mouse.

The Security for Businesses on the Internet Site

A useful site for getting more information about security is maintained at *http://www.catalog.com/mrm/security.html*. Called the Security for Businesses on the Internet page, it has an organized set of links to resources covering practical examples and tools for securing your business on the Internet, as well as information on encryption and authentication.

The Internet Banking Page

The Internet Banking Page (*http://www.cts.com/~wallst/w_banks.html*) has links to financial information and institutions, and is one of the largest sites of its kind. Links include banks in the United Kingdom, the United States, Russia, Japan, Austria, and other countries. Other links include the Federal Reserve Board, EuroNet Electronic Banker, FutureBank Online, and Jobs in Commercial and Investment Banking pages. You'll also find information on electronic payment mechanisms and methods.

The GNN Personal Finance Center

The GNN Personal Finance Center maintains a number of interesting pages. A page called e-Money Focus—Network Money Sites on the Internet can be found at *http://gnn.com/meta/finance/feat/links.html*. It has lots of information on electronic monetary systems, plus links to information on encryption and other forms of secure electronic commerce. The Network Money page is part of this same site, and focuses on the future of banking and commerce on the Internet (*http://gnn.com/meta/finance/feat/emoney.home.html*). GNN is now part of America Online (AOL).

TradeWave Galaxy (Formerly EINet)

TradeWave Galaxy has a very useful set of links to many kinds of documents and resources related to electronic commerce at *http://galaxy.tradewave.com/*. This page includes the budget of the United States government, various guides, information on Network economics, game theory, the SEC, electronic commerce, and more.

The Advertising Law Internet Site

The Advertising Law Internet site at *http://www.webcom.com/~lewrose/ home.html* contains information on advertising, marketing, and related law. The site is maintained by Lewis Rose, an advertising and marketing law partner with the law firm of Arent Fox Kintner Plotkin & Kahn. This site also contains a wealth of information on United States advertising law and FTC information.

Usenet Newsgroups and Discussion Lists

Some Usenet newsgroups that discuss online security and related topics are:

alt.security
alt.security.index
alt.security.keydist
alt.security.pgp
comp.security.announce
compt.security.misc
comp.risks
sci.crypt
talk.politics.crypto

Discussion lists related to electronic commerce include:

com-priv@psi.com
internet-marketing@popco.com

A Final Word or Two about Privacy

It is important to remember that Internet protocols and e-mail afford little if any real privacy. Because of the sheer volume, Internet traffic in general offers a degree of privacy, but nothing is guaranteed.

Currently, unsecured e-mail is somewhat private, but just how private depends upon a system administrator's behavior and ethics. Messages can be trapped if someone wants to work at it. The legalities are particularly muddy about this when an employer is involved in providing the Internet access. While the privacy of postal mail is clear under law, the privacy of e-mail is not. On a practical day-to-day basis, this has not been a large problem, but if you are involved in sending sensitive data, you should consider using encryption of some kind.

Many Internet sites keep a running log of those people who access the system and what files they used—this is particularly true of Web sites. This means that your activities are often logged while visiting Web, FTP, or Gopher sites. Someone can, therefore, track your activities on the Net to some degree.

For Web sites, this can even include information about your login site and even your user name. From a business and marketing standpoint this is very useful data—you may want to know who is visiting your site, which pages they hit, how frequently they visited, which domains they are from (*.edu*, *.com*, etc.), what time of day they hit the page, how many people visited after a big promotional campaign, and so on. From a personal privacy point of view, however, this is something to keep in mind as you surf the Net.

Where from Here...

The security issues, customs, possibilities, and limitations of the Internet covered so far in this book provide a good background for exploring the techniques used to create a business presence on the Internet and the Web presented in Chapters 8 and 9.

PART III

Creating a Business
Presence on the Internet

CHAPTER 8

Techniques for Creating a Business Presence on the Internet

Using the Internet as an entrepreneurial tool is an audience participation sport—two-way communication is the valued and expected norm. Here is an appropriate Internet business motto to follow:

Think Dialog, Not Monolog. Think *Information*, Not Hype.

Acceptable use policies and current practices have made the model of top-down delivery foreign to the Internet. The Internet encourages interaction, and encourages consumers to be providers as well. The "look and feel" of the Internet is normally friendly and casual, and despite having perhaps 50 million users, there is a sense of community. On the Internet, straightforward content-rich exchanges are valued. Marketing on the Internet must also be creative, interesting, and constantly changing, because you must make your information stand out.

The virtual community of the Internet has strong opinions about how the Internet should be used. To develop and maintain a positive image and customer acceptance, businesses need to be aware of the norms and customs of the Internet (as discussed in Chapter 6). It is very helpful to use and experiment with the tools of the Internet—the World Wide Web, e-mail, FTP, Gopher, discussion lists, and so on—and get a sense of what is customary before starting to do business online. While a positive image of a company can spread networkwide quickly, so can a negative impression. Since the broadcasting of advertising is restricted on virtually all networks, the only way a marketing plan will work is if the Internet community has a good impression of, and wants to come to, your company.

The denizens of the network are vocal, and will very quickly respond negatively to hype. The Internet is not a traditional mass market—businesses market one on one, group by group, or to temporary groupings and virtual communities. Also, because of its global reach, the Internet is breaking down the distinctions between some of the traditional market segments such as urban and rural, local and global.

This virtual community is very content-oriented, and does not respond well to the slogans and soundbytes of the almost content-free advertising found on TV. Traditional "in-your-face" advertising is not successful on the Internet, and in fact, such activities garner considerable bad press. On the Internet, despite the fact that there are millions of users, it *is* a small world when it comes to bad news.

"Giving back to the Internet" is an important concept for networkers. The Internet custom is that you can market your services and products if you return something of genuine value. A similar concept is "value added" services, again pointing to the idea of an obligation to provide something to the network. These kinds of contributions are needed in order to maintain good will, cooperation, and attention to your online presence. The Internet is a place where valuable information and assistance are routinely given freely. This freely given information accounts for the large amount of the information available on the Internet.

Although using the Internet to promote services and products can be challenging, it is well worth the effort.

Marketing vs. Advertising

Advertising as practiced for the most part these days has an "in-your-face" attitude. You are bombarded with flashing images and loud sounds and music, all designed to get your attention and sell the product. Almost none of this kind of advertising is content-rich. It is this noisy, intrusive, content-free nature of advertising that makes it unwelcome on the Internet.

As viewed on the Internet, advertising is intrusive, whereas marketing can be active and discourse-based, and can provide valuable information and services as part of its efforts to sell products and services. Businesses must be seen to be giving something back to the Net. Businesses for the most part have to make a paradigm shift from something highly intrusive and image-oriented to something highly content-oriented.

The key to living comfortably with network neighbors is to observe the simple rule that solicited information is good, but unsolicited is not. In doing business on the Internet, the unsolicited information you offer must be subtle and unobtrusive. Information that is requested, either through e-mail or because the individual accesses your business Web site, Gopher, or FTP site, is then *solicited* and may be more detailed and promotional.

The coin of the realm on the Internet is information. Overt hucksterism is met with flaming e-mail and virtual raspberries: You will receive irritated, pointed, negative messages demanding that you stop what you are doing. Don't even think about mass unsolicited e-mailings to the Internet. Acceptable-use policies maintained by providers and networks prohibits this in general terms, and inhabitants of the network will not tolerate it. On the other hand, if you provide something of genuine value, you will be met with collegiality.

What is needed, then, is for a business to create opportunities for interaction and the exchange of information: to create a business presence and, possibly, an information service on the Internet. This can require some ongoing labor—maintaining information, sites, a list or a database.

Models for Creating a Business Presence on the Internet

There are numerous ways to create a business presence on the Internet, and the choice among them depends upon your business goals, your marketing plan for the Internet, and the level of market penetration you wish to achieve. Taking advantage of the size and speed of the network, commercial ventures are finding a place for themselves where they can reach customers, promote their products, and provide information to others. There are four common models for creating a business presence on the Internet. You may want to start with one of these approaches, and then expand to another as you become accustomed to working on the Internet and have more resources to do so.

Billboard

The Billboard model involves the posting of "come-on" information for others to read and take action on. The object is to place a small bit of your information in view, without coming on too strong. Usually this kind of notice is for telling others where more complete information is available. People usually put notices in the following places:

- plan.txt, .plan, or .project files
- Signature (.sig) blocks
- E-mail headers or footers
- Greeting cards

The plan.txt, .plan, and .profile files are stored at your Internet access provider's site and are available to others on the Internet when requested using a program called *finger*. The .sig files and e-mail headers and footers are methods for adding information about your business to e-mail messages sent to discussion groups, Usenet groups, and individuals (see Chapter 12). Greeting cards are quick timely announcements sent out based on a date or an event.

Yellow Pages

The Yellow Pages approach involves providing a directory or guide to information similar to the telephone yellow pages. Essentially, you create a menu, with each item on the menu pointing toward other sources and providing small bits of information. At the top of the menu you could advertise your company's name, and one or more of the menu items could contain advertisements and information about your products. By providing directory information and a useful service, you are definitely "giving back to the Net," something that your potential Internet customers will appreciate and that will bring them back to your site in the future.

You might use this approach on:

- Modest-sized Web sites
- Gopher servers
- BBSs

Brochure

The Brochure approach features the provision of dense content through data sheets, brochures, and informational items. For instance, you might offer a stock market "ticker tape" or worldwide weather information to anyone who wants it. The emphasis here is on the information itself, with only a small amount of promotional material. Some of the vehicles for brochures include:

- Web sites
- E-mail—especially, automated reply
- FTP archives
- Gopher servers
- Usenet news

Virtual Storefront

The Virtual Storefront is a full information service designed to include the marketing of your services and products, and in some cases, to allow online purchasing, customer support, and more. It combines some of the activities from all of the other models, but in a more coordinated approach. A Virtual Storefront:

- Is usually created on a Web site (occasionally on a Gopher or Telnet BBS), either by setting up your own server or by using "rented space" from an Internet provider
- Can just use Web pages, or can include links to support information on Gophers, FTP sites, Usenet news, and e-mail auto-responders

Choosing a Business Model

Each of these approaches is best suited to certain kinds of business ventures. In general, the Billboard approach works best for those just starting to use the Internet for business. It is a relatively low-cost strategy (in time, effort, and money) that can place your business information in view. This is a low-key approach, suitable for those with businesses that are traditionally outside of the Internet. It does not involve offering actual products or services over the network.

The Yellow Pages approach is a middle ground of involvement. It will require a heavier investment of time and money, but will create a higher profile for the business. This approach is good for those with some Internet experience, for products or services that are ready for Internet promotion, and for those with stable Internet access. The Brochure approach is similar, but with the added requirement that you maintain a good-sized inventory of useful information pieces, product information, and so on.

The Virtual Storefront should be approached cautiously by the Internet newcomer. It requires a fairly heavy investment of time and effort. A storefront can be fairly costly if you maintain your own dedicated line and site, but it can also be maintained on a rental basis with a full-service Internet provider. This is a sophisticated approach and will call for a more substantial investment in planning as well.

A Web site as a storefront can range from the fairly modest, inexpensive set of pages offered through your ISP's Web server as part of your account, up through million-dollar installations using your own equipment. Because it is such a powerful tool, the next chapter is entirely devoted to a discussion of the Web as a business tool.

Overall, it is best to take a low-key approach initially, since mistakes are broadcast to millions of users almost instantly—it is better to start slow and build from there. Chapter 18, "Putting Together a Complete Internet Business and Marketing Plan," will assist you in making some of these decisions.

Creating an Information Service: Methods for Building Content, Content, Content

Creating a business presence on the Internet can take many forms, from small tickler announcements as part of your e-mail signature file to the creation of a full-blown Web-based information service. Many regular business marketing and sales activities can be adapted to Internet methods.

A quick example: It is popular these days for businesses to provide information to potential customers who have circled a number on a "Bingo Card" tipped into magazines. The potential customer circles the numbers on the card, mails it off, and some six to seven weeks later, receives the information through the mail. Using a Web site, that very same customer will receive the information by way of the page, or through e-mail, in seconds—while his or her interest is still high. A Web site can even offer immediate, on-site sales.

What other kinds of traditional marketing strategies can be approximated on the Internet? Here are a few examples:

- Product announcements
- Product flyers or introductory information
- Product specification and data sheets
- Pricing information
- Catalogs
- Events and demos
- Free samples
- Company contacts
- Customer support
- Promotional notices of special sales
- Documentation and manuals
- Multimedia productions
- Marketing or customer surveys and needs assessments
- Product performance data
- Service evaluations
- Reviews and product commentary
- Customer service information and functions
- Job placement or recruitment notices
- Dialog with customers, suppliers, and others

Some Internet Resources and Tools for Creating a Business Presence

Creating your own business presence on the Internet is a multifaceted undertaking. It can involve almost every Internet tool, but can also be based on a more modest approach, depending upon your goals, resources, and marketing plan.

World Wide Web (WWW)

The World Wide Web is the premier Internet tool for doing business. Based on hypertext linkages, the Web allows you to browse information on the Net, following up on items of interest, and make use of multimedia. It is like a combination of TV, radio, and print media. Because of its major role in online business, the Web is discussed at greater length in Chapter 2 and especially, as a tool for business, in Chapter 9.

E-mail

E-mail is perhaps the most important *support* tool for communicating on the Internet to market services and products, or to get your business some publicity. In addition to being the ubiquitous communication tool of the Internet, it provides quick and easy ways to work with people and information. Some businesses and customers do not have access to full Internet services, so e-mail may be the only way of reaching them electronically.

Advertising Your E-mail Address and Your URL

Always put your e-mail address and your homepage URL on all electronic and nonelectronic communications; put it on your business card, stationery, catalog, ads, and all your e-mail messages.

In addition to traditional individual e-mail, most mail programs allow you to set up an automated reply "mailbot" which will send out a standard information reply of your making to any request for information. Replies are automatically generated by the mail program, which grabs the sender's e-mail address and mails out a reply with a message you have stored for this purpose. Reply mailboxes need little human attention once they are set up.

The addresses for automated reply mailbots often look something like this: *info@oak-ridge.com*, or *info-request@whippet.com*. These mailbox addresses might appear in a .sig file (discussed in the next section) such as this one:

```
[[[[[[[[[[[[[[[[[[[[[[[[[[==+==]]]]]]]]]]]]]]]]]]]]]]]]]]]
[  Claire Fincher                 Purebred Whippets   ]
[  Contact me for more information about Whippets      ]
[  1-555-555-555              info@whippets.com        ]
[[[[[[[[[[[[[[[[[[[[[[[[[[==+==]]]]]]]]]]]]]]]]]]]]]]]]]]]
```

Mailbots also can be configured to store the address of the sender so you can follow up on the lead. Most mailers (mail software) can create distribution mailing lists through the use of address book files with named groups of addresses or group aliases. You can then create listserv-like e-mail "exploders" in order to set up your own discussion list, either for inside personnel working on a project together, or for interested others. It is increasingly common to see notices like the one following that provide pointers to e-mail addresses, and that can be included in both electronic customer information and paper-based materials:

```
++++++++++++++++++++++++++++++++++++++++++++++++++++++++
      Customer Relations Representatives
      If you have a questions, e-mail us!
            --------
John Jones all products              jones@steel.com
Mary Smith all queep products        smith@steel.com
Bob James all poketa products        james@steel.com
++++++++++++++++++++++++++++++++++++++++++++++++++++++++
```

MIME (Multipurpose Internet Mail Extensions), which is now part of many mailer programs (such as Eudora, Pegasus, and Pine), allows you to e-mail even binary data such as image, word processing, or spreadsheet files. MIME is very common, and as Secure MIME (a method for sending secure messages) becomes more available, you can expect that the business uses of e-mail will expand.

Signature Blocks or .sig Files

Signature blocks, also called .sig ("dot sig") files, are very short attachments or preformatted text at the end of e-mail messages and Usenet postings designed to identify you. They should be limited to five or six lines at most, or you will risk getting flamed—also, some mailers will truncate these files if they are attachments. At least include your name, Web URL, and e-mail address, but you can also include an institutional or business affiliation, a "snail-mail" address, and/or a telephone number. Business users often include a small "ad," composed of a line or two of information on their product or services, such as "contact mary-jones@starcomp.com for information on CAD peripherals." Some .sigs even have a small embedded corporate logo.

Here are two examples of .sig files containing business information:

```
Vern Matthews      vmatthews@genes.cows.com              (__)
Hybrid Genetic Engineering Corporation                   (oo)
Research Park                                 /-------\/
E. Lansing, Michigan                         /  |      ||
http://www.cows.com                         *  ||----||
Contact me about do-it-yourself kits.          ^^      ^^


+=-=-=-=-=-=-=-=-=-=-=-=-=-=-=-=-=-=-=-=-=-=-=-=-=-=-=-=+


Harrison Wilson   TECHNOLOGY COMMUNICATIONS
HWP@saturn.tec-com.com
Voice:555-555-5555    Cell:555-555-5555     FAX:555-555-5555
Are you looking for Communication Business Consulting?
We can provide a wide range of services.
info@jupiter.tec-com.com
                     http://www.tec-com.com
+=-=-=-=-=-=-=-=-=-=-=-=-=-=-=-=-=-=-=-=-=-=-=-=-=-=-=-=+
```

Before constructing your own .sig, look at examples from discussion lists and from Usenet postings for ideas and to get a sense of the discussion list and group norms.

Each mailer program will support different methods for inserting signatures automatically at the end of e-mail and Usenet messages—check your mail program's documentation for details.

Using Discussion Lists

Discussion lists are popular for the distribution of information and the discussion of issues related to businesses. The lists are a method for maintaining discussions and group conferencing, by distributing each incoming message to all members automatically.

The number of existing lists is in excess of 10,000, and like everything else on the Internet, is growing. Some lists have been started to discuss a subject or product of interest, such as business in Russia, polymers, or WordPerfect. Many companies have started discussion lists focusing on their industries as a way to invite exchanges on important issues, government regulations, technologies, techniques, and so on. Some have even started lists focusing on a particular product.

Usually, individuals join lists of interest, both personal and professional, as a way of keeping up to date, taking the pulse of the industry, gauging public opinion, or just exchanging ideas. The best uses of lists for marketing are for marketing research and for making product announcements (on appropriate lists that permit such announcements). Use caution in posting to new lists—you are safer if you read the group's messages for a while before sending an announcement out. An announcement like this would generally be well tolerated on a list with some kind of MIS focus:

```
***************** NEW BOOK ANNOUNCEMENT *****************
*************** From Churchill Publishers ***************
******* MANAGEMENT INFORMATION AND THE INTERNET: *******
******************** TOWARDS 2001 **********************

                        edited by
        David Simmons, HAL-N-DAVE Computer Corporation

Table of Contents and Order Form are attached below.

More information, including Preface, can be obtained via
    anonymous FTP from 2001.hal-n-dave.com in the directory
            simmons/books as 2001.txt or 2001.pdf
                  http://www.hal-n-dave.com
```

Usually an announcement like this will be 20–40 lines or so, and might, as in this case, include the table of contents, and—here is the angle—a handy e-mail order form. In addition to posting a single announcement to a few appropriate mailing lists, it is common for publishers to put a free chapter or section on their Web or FTP site. Product specifications, could also be made available at an FTP site.

> ### Read the FAQ!
>
> Be sure to check the FAQ (file of frequently asked questions) for any list or newsgroup before making a commercial posting. If commercial postings are prohibited, don't post such announcements.

Active participation on appropriate lists can give your business good Internet visibility if you spend the time to make useful contributions to the list with thoughtful postings. Remember to use a .sig with each message, mentioning your business, URL, and e-mail address.

It is important to sample many lists before deciding on a few on which to be an active participant. After you sign up for a list, all messages sent from the list will start arriving—30 or more a day for a high-volume list, a few messages a month for a low-volume list. Remember, many lists prohibit advertising, but will tolerate the short signature. Information on subscribing to lists is found in Chapter 13.

Don't SPAM

As you use the discussion lists and newsgroups, do not be tempted to send out the equivalent of bulk mail. Sending out messages that are unrelated to the list or group is not tolerated. This practice is called spamming, and spamming is bad business.

Usenet Newsgroups

Usenet newsgroups are sometimes confused with the Internet itself, since they are distributed to so many sites. These newsgroups are just one application running on the Internet. Usenet is a distributed messaging interchange focused on topics. The groups number in the thousands, and range from the practical to the esoteric. They are used in similar ways to discussion lists. The Usenet system provides public postings of individual messages. Instead of being sent out via e-mail, these messages are read and responded to with special newsreader software. See Chapter 13 for a discussion of how to read and post to Usenet.

The newsgroups are very active venues for the exchange of ideas and information. The newsgroups are very fluid, with some groups having hundreds of postings a day.

On Usenet, you will find numerous brief product announcements, press releases, and many signatures with business information. Under the *alt.* and *biz.* categories you will find commercial groups. Some companies such as Zeos and O'Reilly have created their own newsgroups. Each newsgroup has its own charter, so be sure to check for commercial or business restrictions by reading the FAQ or charter. Here is a sampling of the business-related groups available for exploration:

- alt.business.import-export
- alt.business.misc
- alt.business.multi-level
- biz.americast
- biz.americast.samples
- biz.books.technical
- biz.clarinet...
- biz.comp...
- biz.comp.telebit
- biz.comp.telebit.netblazer
- biz.config
- biz.control
- biz.dec
- biz.dec.ip
- biz.dec.workstations
- biz.digex...
- biz.jobs...
- biz.jobs.offered
- biz.misc
- biz.next...
- biz.oreilly...
- biz.oreilly.announce
- biz.pagesat
- biz.pagesat...
- biz.sco...
- biz.stolen
- biz.tadpole...
- biz.test
- biz.univel...
- biz.zeos
- biz.zeos...
- misc.business.facilitators
- misc.business.records-mgmt
- misc.entrepreneurs
- misc.entrepreneurs.moderated

Some newsgroups are moderated, while others are not. Moderated groups are monitored by a group administrator, who will, in some cases, screen posts for excessive flaming and appropriateness of content. Unmoderated groups are those where every message is posted as is—no changes.

Usenet is popular for postings of business networking opportunities, including opportunities to form business partnerships. For example, the posting shown in Figure 8.1 shows a message seeking business partners in American saying:

> We want to resell in Russia low-cost computer parts and systems like 486/P2 motherboards, SIMM 4M & 8M, sound cards, sVGA cards, hard drives & streamers, sVGA monitors, high speed modems, 386 and 486 notebooks, CDROMs, software under Unix, OS/2 and MS Windows95, MS Windows NT and so on. Used equipment will be good too.

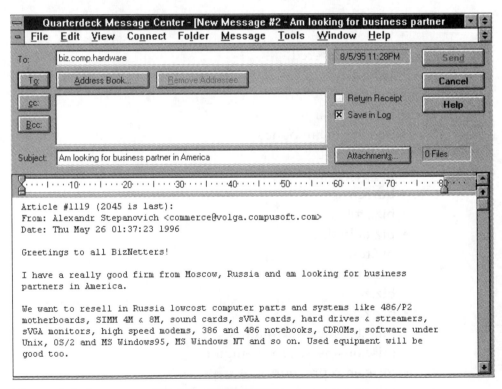

Figure 8.1 A news posting from Moscow.

It is common to see price lists, brochures, product announcements, and all kinds of business-related information posted to *.biz* groups that allow them:

```
Newsgroups: biz.comp.hardware,biz.comp.software
From: csquare@lobby.computersquare.com
Subject: Pricing on BNE products
Reply-To: gstone@office.computersquare.com
Date: Sat Sep 17 06:17:44 1996

NOTICE

Computer Square is pleased to announce significant price
reductions on BNE products currently in our warehouse. We are
offering a 25% automatic markdown for all individuals who
mention this ad in their price query. Tell them you saw it on
biz. Call our toll free order line at 555-555-5555, or e-mail
your query to info@office.computersquare.com to get further
ordering information or send it directly to me. George.
```

Gopher

Gopher is a system with menus of documents, images, software, other materials, and other menus and resources. This system allows for searching, viewing, downloading, and e-mailing of files. Now much less popular than the Web, it is used to support business functions for users who do not have WWW access.

Gopherspace—that is, the global collection of files available to Gopher servers—can be searched using a utility called Veronica, either by file name or by menu entry. (Gopher and Veronica are discussed more fully in Chapter 14.) Having a Gopher will increase your business online visibility by providing a path through which people can find you.

You can set up your own Gopher menus on your own site, or rent space on the Gopher of an Internet access provider, much in the same way that you might use their WWW server. Pointers to your information are set up, allowing users throughout the world to access the items you have made available. The information can include product information, brochures, surveys, up-to-date price lists, catalogs, images, even binary files of software. Many sites provide sample products, services such as access

Figure 8.2 The Kaleidospace homepage.

to Usenet or the Clarinet news service, access to other Gophers, and full text of important documents.

Many businesses create a full-function online presence by have a WWW site, a gopher, an FTP site and support for all of it via e-mail. As an example, Kaleidospace is a site focusing on the needs of independent artists, providing a very rich business environment that includes:

- A Web site: *http://kspace.com*
- A Gopher: *gopher://gopher.kspace.com*
- An FTP site: *ftp://ftp.kspace.com*
- E-mail support: *editor@kspace.com*

Figure 8.2 shows the Kaleidospace homepage. Contrast that with the opening Gopher screen:

```
Root gopher server: gopher.kspace.com
1.   About_Kaleidospace (2k).
2.   articles/
3.   Artist_Info.txt (15k).
4.   Artist_List.txt (15k).
5.   artist_rooms/
6.   helper_pgms/
7.   Kspace_logo.gif (5k) <Picture>
8.   more_gophers/
9.   newsletters/
10.  Web_Develop.txt (10k).
```

Choosing the first item brings up the "About Kaleidospace" document:

```
*******************************************************
        Welcome to the Kaleidospace FTP/Gopher Archive!
                   Last Modified 7/05/95
*******************************************************
Kaleidospace Independent Internet Artists promotes, distributes
and places work by independent artists, musicians, performers,
writers, animators, filmmakers, and software developers. In
addition to the independents we run an Artist-in-Residence
(A-i-R) program (see the Spotlight Section) giving high-profile
artists an Internet presence. Kaleidospace also builds Internet
"presences" for other groups including american recordings, A&M
Records, and the J. Paul Getty Center for Education in the Arts.

This site is functions as a complement to our World Wide Web
site, Kaleidospace (http://kspace.com). Please send questions,
comments, and bug reports to editors@kspace.com.


*******************************************************
To access visual art, audio and video by Kspace artists, go
into the "artist_rooms" directory.
*******************************************************


As of July 1, 1995


A global list of all Kspace artists is available in the
Artist_List.txt file. All of these are available on the Kspace
web site; a subset are available via ftp/gopher.
```

```
As of June 1995

Check the Artist_Info.txt for how to become an artist on
Kaleidospace, and Web_Develop.txt for consulting on web design,
space rental, bandwidth rental, netpublicity and regular
publicity.

PAN Users:

Note that the Delphi FTP client requires you to enclose
case-sensitive directory and file names in (") characters.
-------------------------------------------------------
```

Kaleidospace's FTP site offers a somewhat narrower set of information, and includes a very long "banner" of announcements and information:

```
ftp open ftp.kspace.com
Connected to ftp.kspace.com.
220 Peter's Macintosh FTP daemon v2.4.0 (Unregistered) awaits
your command.
Name (ftp.kspace.com:oakridge): ftp
331 Guest log in, send Email address (user@host) as password.
Password:
230-********************************************************
Welcome to the Kaleidospace FTP/Gopher Archive!
                Last Modified 12/16/94
**********************************************************
Kaleidospace promotes, distributes and places work by
independent artists, musicians, performers, writers,
animators, filmmakers, and software developers. In addition
to the independents we run an Artist-in-Residence (A-i-R)
program giving high-profile artists an Internet presence.
Kaleidospace also builds Internet "presences." Current
projects include:
* american recordings (http://american.recordings.com)
* The J. Paul Getty Center for Education in the Arts (Spring 1995)
* The A&M Woodstock '94 site: http://woodstock94.com/album

This site is currently being developed as a complement to
our World Wide Web site, Kaleidospace (http://kspace.com).
Please send questions, comments, and bug reports to
editors@kspace.com
```

```
As of 12/16/94
* Over Christmas we'll be upgrading our Internet connection.
If you have trouble accessing Kaleidospace, try the following
addresses during Dec 20-30:
ftp: ftp.home.kspace.com
gopher: gopher.home.kspace.com
web: http://www.kspace.com
After the connection is complete the old addresses will
work again.

As of 11/94
* Thomas Dolby audio and video clips are available in the
Spotlight, as part of his tenure as a Kaleidospace
Artist-in-Residence. You can join his mailing list/
```

This continues with a longer set of notices about special events, and ends with:

```
Here at the ftp/gopher site, you can download the following files:
---------------------------------------------------------
GENERAL INFO
*Frequently asked questions, utility programs,
helper programs for Mosaic and other World Wide Web-related
information.

ROOMS
   *Artist/Organization Portfolios - Information on our artists,
    for those of you who don't have access to the World Wide Web.

ARTICLES
   *Kaleidospace in newspapers and magazines.

BROCHURES
   *Artist and Internet consulting brochures. How to get your
   work onto Kaleidospace, and how to create your own web site.

RATES
   *Artist and company rates for promoting and distributing
   your own work through Kaleidospace, and design and construction
   of word wide web sites.

ORDER FORMS
   *Phone (800-771-7223), fax (310-396-5489), or email
   (editors@kspace.com) to order material from our artists.
```

```
GOPHER SITES
    *Other sites for gopher users.

PAN Users:
Note that the Delphi FTP client requires you to enclose
case-sensitive directory and file names in (") characters.
---------------------------------------------------------


230 Anonymous login to 1 volumes.  Access restrictions apply.
"/space/kspace".
Ftp
```

A directory listing of the site reveals the files available for downloading:

```
ftp dir
200 PORT command successful.
150 ASCII transfer started.
-------r--          332      1679      2011 Jul 16 03:29 About_Kaleidospace
drwxrwxrwx               folder         14 Mar 12 10:59 articles
-------r--          336     14749     15085 Jul  7 00:13 Artist_Info.txt
-------r--          332     14547     14879 Jul 11 11:03 Artist_List.txt
drwxrwxrwx               folder         11 Jul 16 01:52 artist_rooms
drwxrwxrwx               folder          5 Mar 12 10:59 helper_pgms
-------r--            0      5094      5094 Mar 26 13:42 Kspace_logo.gif
drwxrwxrwx               folder          1 Apr 26 02:25 more_gophers
drwxrwxrwx               folder         14 Apr 26 02:28 newsletters
-------r--            0      9718      9718 Aug  2 12:06 Web_Develop.txt
226 Transfer complete.
692 bytes received in 0.085 seconds (7.9 Kbytes/s)
ftp bye
221 Nice chatting with you.
```

Gopher sites are searchable with Veronica, FTP sites are searchable with Archie, and the Web is searchable with search engines such as Lycos, Excite, WebCrawler, and Tupilak. This use of multiple delivery systems is valuable for making sure that your business is visible on the Internet.

Greeting Cards

Greeting cards are not used very frequently, and are just a variation on an e-mail message. Some companies are using them as mailings to current customers. They should not be sent out to individuals who do not already have a relationship with your business, but depending upon the content, they can be mentioned in a .sig file. Greeting cards usually look something like this:

```
     Grandstaff, Fincher and Harrison, Esq.
              Attorneys-At-Law
   Wishing You a Happy and Prosperous New Year

        You are cordially invited
   to a Holiday reception at our Chicago offices
        December 31st from 6 to 8 P.M.

           R.S.V.P. rsvp@lawlook.com

  We will be upgrading our LawLook System in January
    Request information from upgrade@lawlook.com
```

Using FTP to Support a Business Presence

Many businesses are using an anonymous FTP site to provide information, product descriptions, price list updates, news releases, catalogs, demos, text files, and executable software files and demos for customer use. These archives are publicly accessible using the anonymous FTP protocol described in Appendix C.

Users can FTP to your business archive site, look around a little, and download files (both ASCII and binary). Many businesses (like Kaleidospace) put a "banner" at the top of their listing to welcome you and give a bit of information about the archive. The following is at the Dell Computer site:

```
ftp open ftp.dell.com
Connected to dell1.us.dell.com.
220 dell1.dell.com FTP server (Version wu-2.3(7) Wed Mar 22
13:50:58 CST 1995) ready.
Name (ftp.dell.com:oakridge): ftp
331 Guest login ok, send your complete e-mail address as
password.
Password:

230-*************************************************************
230-==
230-==   Welcome to the Dell Computer Archive
230-==                       AND
230-==   Anonymous FTP Computing Server
```

```
230-==
230-*********************************************************
230-**
230-**All transfers are logged with host name and email address
230-**
230-*********************************************************
230-*************IN CASE OF PROBLEMS********************
230-**
230-** File Content: send EMAIL to dellbbs@dell.com
230-**
230-** Server Problems: hostmaster@dell.com
230-**
230-** Mosaic Problems: webmaster@dell.com
230-**
230-*********************************************************
230-Please be advised that use constitutes consent to monitoring
230-(Elec Comm Priv Act, 18 USC 2701-2711)
230-
230-Please read the file README
230-it was last modified on Tue Dec 13 18:28:59 1994 - 235 days ago
230 Guest login ok, access restrictions apply.
ftp dir
200 PORT command successful.
150 Opening ASCII mode data connection for /bin/ls.
total 32
-rw-r--r--    1 root    wheel       757 Sep 20  1994 .message
-rw-r--r--    1 root    wheel      1838 Dec 14  1994 README
drwxr-xr-x    4 root    wheel       512 May 11 22:49 asia
drwx--x--x    2 root    wheel       512 Apr 14  1994 bin
drwxrwxr-x   19 root    dellbbs    1024 Aug  4 15:19 dellbbs
dr-xr-xr-x    4 ftp     daemon     1024 Oct 10  1994 donate
drwx--x--x    2 root    wheel       512 May 16  1994 etc
drwxr-xr-x    4 root    wheel       512 May 11 22:49 europe
drwx-----x   10 root    wheel       512 Jul 25 17:09 hidden
drwxr-xr-x    2 root    daemon     1024 Mar  3 21:46 notes
drwxr-xr-x    2 root    wheel       512 May  3  1994 pcca
drwxr-xr-x    2 root    daemon      512 Mar  3 21:40 support2.0.1
drwxr-xr-x    2 root    daemon      512 Mar  3 21:42 support2.1
drwxr-xr-x    2 root    daemon      512 Mar  3 21:43 support2.2
drwxr-xr-x    2 root    daemon      512 Mar  3 21:45 support2.2.1
226 Transfer complete.
862 bytes received in 0.15 seconds (5.7 Kbytes/s)
ftp bye
221 Goodbye.
```

Following the opening banner, this offers you information about the server, and about whom to contact in case of problems. You can then ask for a directory listing of the files and subdirectories. (For more information on how to decipher this directory listing, see Appendix C on FTP.) Getting the README file is always a good idea, since as you can see, the subdirectory names may be a little cryptic.

Dell also maintains a Web site: *http://www.dell.com*.

Newsletters and 'Zines

Electronic newsletters are used by businesses to provide information of many kinds to current and potential customers. The ease of selling or distributing for free via the Web, e-mail, and Gopher makes these powerful sales vehicles. Like traditional paper-based newsletters, electronic newsletters usually target a particular audience, and contain a mix of articles about the business itself and other articles and information to keep the reader's attention. Successful Internet newsletters have a high percentage of information, articles, and features, relative to advertising (high signal-to-noise ratio). Most newsletters are distributed upon request through e-mail, listservs, Web sites, or Gophers. Many are archived at FTP sites. Some newsletters are redistributed on Usenet or network information mailing lists.

Electronic 'zines are creative, small, often experimental magazines. A few companies have created 'zines in order to grab attention, particularly in industries that are on the creative cutting edge and want to be a bit avant-garde. Some businesses underwrite a newsletter or 'zine produced by others and thus get a free blurb in each issue, something like:

```
Newsbytes is sponsored by TechnoWoofer Inc.
TechnoWoofer is a major producer of speech recognition hardware.
1/555-555-5555. info@bark.woofer.com    http://www.woofer.com
```

Newsletters also provide a vehicle for doing some marketing research about your customers—ask them to fill out a form in order to be placed on the mailing list.

Plan.txt, .plan, and .profile Files

Many sites connected to the Internet allow other users on the Internet to obtain a small file of information about you by using a utility called "finger." If you finger someone's account, almost immediately you will receive back some information about that individual or business. Often this information will tell you the account owner's name ("real name"), login name, whether the account has mail waiting, and the time of last login. For example,

```
finger dave@zeus.hal-n-dave.com
```

would look for a user named Dave at the machine named *zeus* at HAL-N-DAVE Corporation.

Many business people create a file to be sent in response to a finger, along with the basic information; this is called a *plan.txt* file, or *.plan* (said "dot plan") or *.profile*, depending upon the software. Job hunters have been known to put their whole resume in their plan file; others include price lists or corporate information. A sample .plan file might look like this (where the first three lines are automatically provided by finger):

```
-User--Real Name--------------------------------
drew   Drew Allen Arkins  Last Login Fri 6-May
10:01 AM from netnet.com

Plan:
       ***DAA and Associates Internet Training Services***

We specialize in services to small and medium sized businesses
who want to provide employee training on the use of the
Internet. We offer both on- and off-site training with small
classes, or on an individualized basis.

DAA and Associates is a group of 9 trainers with combined
expertise in all facets of the Internet. The DAA team can help
you.

*On Site Training: $500.00 per day, plus travel and expenses
for three trainers

*At our headquarters in San Francisco, $300.00 per day

Call 555/555-5555 for more information or e-mail me at
dave@zeus.hal-n-dave.com
FAX 555/555-5555     homepage: http://www.hal-n-dave.com
```

This kind of plan file provides information about the business, a little price information, and more about how to contact them:

```
        THE DYNAMIC COMPUTER EQUIPMENT CORPORATION^
                    17554 IH - 35 ACCESS^
                  SPRING, OKLAHOMA 12345^
Voice: (555) 555-5555  (days, nights or weekends)^
                    FAX:   (555) 555-5555^
  http://sooner.dcec.com      terry@sooner.dcec.com^
---------------------------------------------------------

* NOTE: Some prices are dependent upon foreign suppliers, or on
market prices so E-mail for a custom quote. Ask about any items
that you don't see listed *

%%% SPECIALS FOR JUNE %%%   June    %%% SPECIALS FOR JUNE %%%
486-90hz CPU Heat Sink Fans                   Only $ 18!
8Mb VESA Local Bus 24-bit SVGA Video Card     Only $195!
Sound Galaxi BXII (100% Blaster Compatible)   Only $ 65!
Pongate 3390A FASTEST 1.6 GIG DRIVE           ONLY $600!
Eastern Digital 940Mb IDE Hard Drive,3yr warranty ONLY $475!
```

Some finger files are designed to be news updates on products, people, and so on.

Animated finger files can often be constructed on UNIX machines. Because plan files are requested (via finger) they may contain fairly specific information and promotionally oriented material. Most individuals mention that the plan file is available via finger in their signature, in newsletters, or in other documents that they distribute. Check with your user services contact person to discuss the use of a plan file. Some providers offer an information file similar to a plan file but that provides only the information that you wish to share.

Real-Time Conferencing

IRC—Internet Relay Chat, allows for real-time interactive text-based "conversations" where all parties are online together. This means that your business can directly interact with customers and potential customers, or provide an online expert to answer questions while using the opportunity to let people know about your business in a very low-key manner.

In addition to IRC, there are a rapidly growing number of conferencing and real-time interactive software packages emerging. I-Phone resembles an Internet telephone—users can talk across the Net. Currently I-Phone is half duplex meaning that users must talk one at a time, as opposed to full-duplex which allows the users to interact as they would on a telephone, but a new full-duplex version is in the works.

Other new technologies include CU-SeeMe, which is an interactive video and text system, Real-Time Audio which provides audio streaming for sound in real-time, and Virtual Places which emulates video conferencing. Global Stage offers Global Chat, an interactive chat system built over IRC.

All of these technologies are making Internet conferencing more realistic and affordable.

Wide Area Information Servers (WAIS)

WAIS is a distributed text-based tool that will let you search through Internet archives for articles containing groups of words. The system is based on the Z39.50 standard. Businesses are running WAIS servers with information on products and services. The information is indexed, using software called waisindex, which allows others to use your indexing to locate information. WAIS is a fairly uncommon network tool, and one that is not easily used.

Time, Effort, and Money

These methods for creating a business presence on the Net vary in their relative need for human and capital investment. The creation of .sig and .plan files requires little initial investment, only a couple of hours of planning and design, and almost no ongoing maintenance. Once you have created the .sig file, just attach it to all your e-mail and you are up and running. A .plan file, once created in your account, is available to anyone who seeks it, and requires no further effort. Both kinds of files should be reviewed for periodic revisions, but they are definitely low-cost/low-maintenance options.

Using discussion lists and Usenet newsgroups for *participation* will take some time and effort. You must read your e-mail frequently and take the time to respond in ways that benefit your business. Time and effort go into thoughtful participation and the placement of announcements. Depending on the level of participation, this could mean between 1 and 15 hours of effort a week.

To "own" or moderate a list or a newsgroup is a much more substantial commitment, usually requiring 20 hours a week or more depending upon the size and activity level of the list or group. To moderate a list or group also requires learning the software and locating a site for the list or group. Your local systems manager can help you set up a list on your site, or you can purchase services from an Internet access provider.

Making high-quality information available through the Web, Gopher, Telnet, FTP, WWW, and so on, requires a substantial investment in the planning, monitoring, and creation of materials. The materials must be kept current. If you provide feedback options—and you should—there is the need for a commitment to timely response, or you will defeat your purpose. After up-front development, these options typically require 2–6 hours a week in information maintenance if response is low to moderate, and another 3–20 hours of e-mail and request processing depending on traffic to your site. Of course, these numbers could skyrocket if your efforts are attractive to customers! Not a bad problem to have.

Making use of an Internet access provider, to set up your information on existing servers such as WWW, Gopher, and FTP varies tremendously in costs even for similar services. Some sites provide modest access to all of these resources for little more than disk storage fees ($15 a month), while others charge a hundred times that amount, and have development and one-time charges. Like anything else, the more you want to do with these tools, generally, the more it will cost. Information about costs, both initial and ongoing, is best sought as part of your research for choosing service providers.

Setting up your own node and running your own server for a Web, Gopher, or FTP site is a big undertaking. The initial costs of equipment, configuration, and training are considerable, and these servers require monitoring and maintenance. Considerable technical know-how is also needed; thus a company planning for this large an investment generally hires a consultant to work with it in its planning and implementation.

Chapters 9 and 18 can assist you in creating your marketing plan using these tools.

Under Construction for Business Use

There are some Internet tools that have yet to be fully utilized for businesses because they are relatively new and/or take considerable bandwidth (network resources) to use. Creatively used, one of these might prove to be the perfect vehicle for your business:

- Mbone Radio, from Carl Malmud, uses direct links to the Internet to broadcast real-time digital audio and video. Businesses can "broadcast" information with an advertising slant, provide added value by doing interviews, and so on.

- MUDS, Multi-User Dialog/Dimension/Dungeons, are text-based virtual environments allowing several individuals to interact in real time. Currently, these are often used for games. TinyMUD is used for social gatherings. These and other virtual environments will provide almost endless opportunities for businesses to create an entire community, store, or setting for customers to browse.

- MOO, MUD Object Oriented, is a MUD based on an object-oriented language, and offers a richer experience than MUD.

- MUSE, Multi-User Simulation Environment, is a facility that combines elements of Internet Relay Chat and role-playing games. Users create their own virtual reality, or can participate in existing scenarios. Currently this is being used for K–12 education, but it has possibilities for use by businesses.

- Virtual reality will offer almost endless opportunities on the Internet for customer interaction and enjoyment (a separate programming language called VRML, or Virtual Reality Modeling Language, has been developed for this purpose). Businesses can let customers try out a product, visit a virtual store, or play an adventure game. All kinds of virtual reality software is becoming available which can create virtual environments for conferencing, merchandising, and creating "what-if" designs. It is possible to create "walkthrough" models, as well as objects (merchandise) which can be manipulated.

- Sometimes called the new "killer ap," the Java programming language, and the browser called Hot Java, allows for the creation of two-and three-dimensional movable objects through downloadable programs called aplets. Netscape has licensed some of this technology, and is available in their version 2.0 and 2.0 Gold. Businesses can create objects and applications which can be used on-the-fly by their Web page users.

Where from Here?

As you can see, using the Internet to create a business presence can take many forms, from simple e-mail signatures to virtual storefronts. (If you are new to the Internet, refer to the appendixes to understand how to use some of the other tools of the Internet.) Right now, go on to Chapter 9 to learn how to use the most popular of the Internet tools for business—the World Wide Web.

Using the Web for Doing Business Online

Overview

The World Wide Web is the fast growing, most popular place for business on the Internet right now. It is *the* place to be for doing business. In the preceding chapter, ways in which most of the Internet tools could be used for business were discussed. Now let's explore the potential of the WWW as a business tool. Like the other Internet tools, the Web can be used for numerous business functions.

From Content to Content Again: From Newspapers to the Net

For hundreds of years, newspapers have been a rich source of information. Primarily textual in nature, they offered dense information in an easy-to-use form.

When radio came along, the communication became less information-rich, more entertainment driven; and television brought yet another lowering of the level of content.

With the Net and the Web, the opportunity exists to return to an information-rich environment, but now enhanced by the multimedia features of the Web.

Business Uses of the Web

To use the Web effectively, you must become part of the Web through the creation of a Web site. This can be accomplished in a number of ways, and these are explained Chapter 10.

To use the Web, you become part of the Internet by creating your own place on the Net—a Web site. This site will consist of a homepage, and any number of other pages linked to it. Each page will have a unique address called a URL (Uniform Resource Locator) in a form such as *http://www.oak-ridge.com/orr.html*. Because all of your business's pages will be linked, usually only the URL of the homepage will need to be publicized. In some cases, it may be useful to publicize additional pages if they have a different audience.

The Web can be used for many business functions, and in many cases the Web is more effective and easier to use than the other Internet tools discussed in Chapter 8:

- Communication
- Information management and distribution
- Customer service and technical assistance
- Public and community relations
- Cost containment
- Research
- Recruitment
- Marketing and sales

Communication

The Web is a multimedia communication powerhouse. You can use text, images, and sound to communicate with the user, and the user can interact through data-entry forms and e-mail. This communication can be internal and external to your enterprise. Many companies are using the Web to create a suite of documents and exhibits in support of other business functions; they use the forms and pages to communicate with employees, solve problems, coordinate projects, and create online manuals.

Some companies use the page to communicate with far-flung offices and employees, as well as with customers for customer support and technical feedback. The newsletter is a very popular means of using the Web internally, and externally, and it is one of the most popular communications activities in support of marketing.

Information Management and Distribution

Some companies use the Web for information management and distribution—again, sometimes internally, between employees, workgroups, and offices, and sometimes externally, for exchanges with product users and potential customers. This is sometimes called the Intranet.

Finding that Web documents are easily updated, many companies use the opportunity to create dynamic catalogs of information: price lists, specifications, and other information can be updated as frequently as is useful.

Because of the powerful linking capabilities of the Web, information from other sites can be made available on your local pages for your own business use, or for the use of your customers.

Customer Service and Technical Assistance

One of the most successful uses for the Web in business is in the area of customer support and technical assistance.

Customer feedback can be obtain online through data-entry forms and through the "mailto" field. Many companies are providing technical support to customers that includes online information, software, and interaction with technical staff, plus, in some cases, assistance in solving problems by way of a database of frequent "fixes."

These pages can provide:

- Announcements of special sales
- Company product descriptions
- Documentation
- Newsletters
- Pictures and drawings of products
- Price sheets
- Product problem alerts
- Software patches

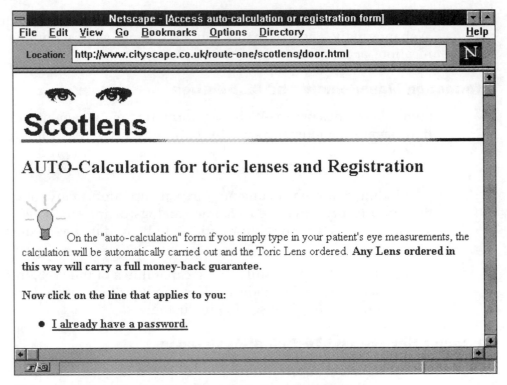

Figure 9.1 The Scotlens page on toric lens calculation.

- Specification sheets
- Technical notes
- Upgrade information

Two companies that provide various kinds of customer support and technical assistance from their pages are Scotlens (see Figure 9.1) and Apple Computers (Figure 9.2).

Scotlens (*http://www.cityscape.co.uk/route-one/scotlens/*) is an independent contact lens laboratory based in Scotland, dealing directly with practitioners. Scotlens features a unique service to its customers that allows automatic calculation of toric lenses online on the Internet.

The Apple page provides access to technical bulletins, certain appropriate Usenet newsgroups, a release notes archive, information on updates, a technical information library, product information, and other customer support information.

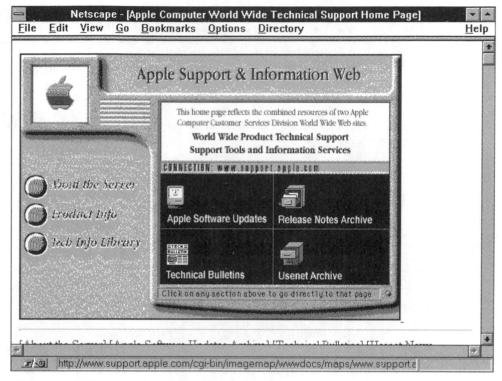

Figure 9.2 The Apple technical support page.

Public and Community Relations

For some small and start-up companies, a Web site may be the only public face of the company. The Web can help a small business compete on the larger, global playing field. The Web then becomes the company's headquarters on the Internet. The image presented needs to be professional, functional, and eye-pleasing. If your pages look good and work well, your business looks good as well.

There are numerous public relations activities that are possible on the Internet and the Web. One can appropriately distribute news releases, sponsor events, make publications available, or support nonprofit groups.

Many companies use their Web pages as a place to make information such as the corporate annual report or news releases available online. Figure 9.3 shows one of the AT&T pages of press releases.

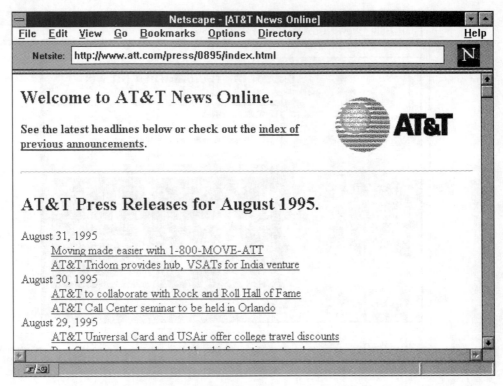

Figure 9.3 The AT&T News Online page.

Another way that businesses are using the Web for increased visibility is by providing sponsorship on their page for conferences, public information, or nonprofit organizations. This is a little like sponsoring a public television show—you can support useful and important activities, and gain visibility for your efforts. Some companies sponsor a set of Web pages for large industry events or conferences.

NSTN, through its True North Web site, provides a wide variety of community information on its Cybrary pages (Figure 9.4). This includes access to other sites, as well as resources maintained by NSTN.

Cost Containment

Although e-mail is one of the premier tools for cost containment using the Internet, the Web can provide cost savings to businesses in a variety of areas—it has a *very* good cost per user ratio. In marketing and adver-

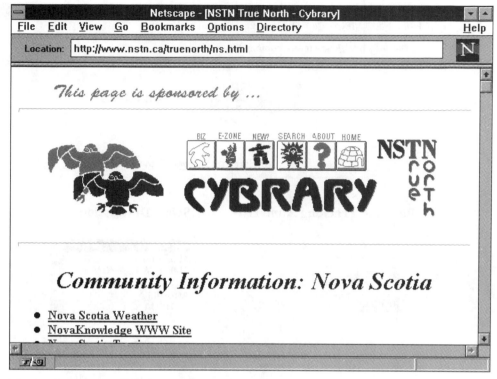

Figure 9.4 The NSTN Community Information Cybrary page.

tising, it allows you to reach a large number of potential customers rather inexpensively. Also, the Web allows a company to keep its information and price sheets fresh, without reprinting expensive four-color brochures. The Web can replace some printed materials, or at least provide support for printed materials.

In addition, the Web provides opportunities for business-to-business transactions, which can result in greater efficiency. FedEx, for example, provides a page on which you can track the delivery of your packages easily, cutting down on long phone calls searching for lost packages. Figure 9.5 shows the FedEx tracking page.

Research

The Web can be used to locate existing databases and other collections of information, and as a place to carry out marketing and customer research.

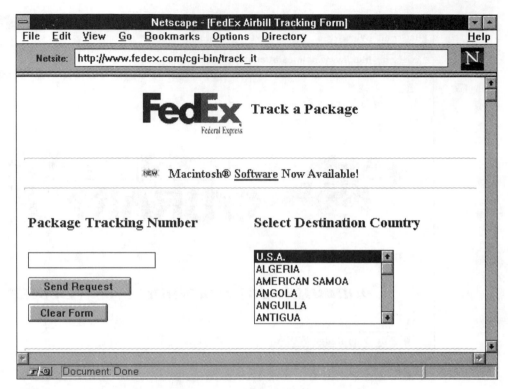

Figure 9.5 The FedEx package tracking page.

The amount of information currently available on the Web is amazing—business people can get everything from travel information, reservations and advisories, and weather, to stock market quotations, up-to-date news reports, and information on thousands of other topics. Information is one of the strengths of the Internet, and the GUI Web browsers make hunting it down and retrieving it much easier. The browsers can handle not only Web searches, but also Gopher, Telnet, and FTP. Chapters 11, 15, 16, and 17 demonstrate the wealth of information available, and discuss how to manage "drinking from the fire hose" of information. The Web can become a source of information that gives your business a competitive edge.

Businesses are using the Web to carry out many types of customer surveys, product interest and reaction surveys, some experimental focus group activities, preference polls, and other marketing research functions. In order to attract people to their Web site and induce them to fill out a survey form, businesses often offer something of value such as contests with prizes, give-aways, and newsletters. While these survey methods are not based on statistically sound random sampling techniques, they nonetheless can provide useful feedback from potential customers who have reached your page.

In addition, a good Web site can track the number of visitors, and the number of times your pages have been accessed or "hit." This logging of page activity can include the domain type of the visitors, such as *.com* or *.org*, the frequency and length of their visits, and which pages were hit the most often. On Web pages, we can get better information on site visitors than we can from traditional advertisements. For example, we can track how long they spent on a page, and the order in which they accessed the pages. With newspapers and TV, it is difficult to discover: Who saw your ad? Did they read it? How long did they spend looking at it? You don't know, but with Web pages, you can find out.

Recruitment

Many businesses are using Web pages to recruit employees, consultants, and contractors. Your Web pages have a long reach, and can provide in-depth information about your business to potential employees. You can even provide information on the community, schools, realtor contacts, and other aspects of local life of interest to a potential employee considering a move to your area.

Dell Computers, for example, uses a Web page for recruitment, offering information about the company, its future, employment opportunities, and information about the local Austin, Texas community (Figure 9.6).

Marketing and Sales

Last but not least, the Web is being used extensively for marketing and selling. This is becoming the most popular business use of the Web—for advertising, visibility, brand name recognition, public relations, press releases, corporate sponsorship, and direct sales.

On your business Web site, you can create short flyers, teasers, and full product descriptions, and you can provide pricing and purchase information, as well as online order forms.

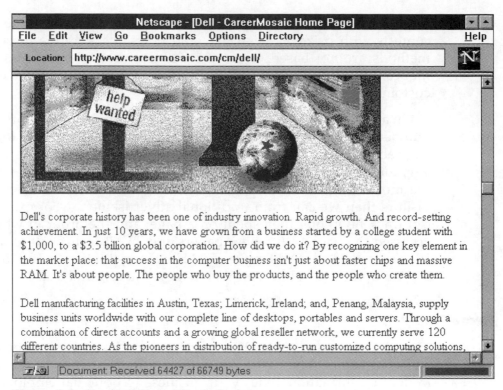

Figure 9.6 The Dell Help Wanted page.

A critical task in Web marketing is to get people on the Internet to visit your homepage. You have to make your page visible on the Web and the Internet through:

- Site registration with the Web search engines, listings, and catalogs
- Participation in discussion lists and Usenet newsgroups and the use of informative .sig files
- Online announcements and news releases
- FAQs
- Use of Gopher and FTP to support the pages
- Cross-linking of pages

Site Registration

Keeping your Web site visible on the Internet and in your print media is important for attracting new visitors—building foot traffic.

Registering your page with the search engines, listings, and catalogs may be the single most productive action you can take to ensure that your Web site is visible on the Internet. There are a large number of these, but among the most important are:

- Search engines:

    Lycos: *http://www.lycos.com*

    Webcrawler: *http://www.webcrawler.com*

    McKinley: *http://www.mckinley.com*

    Excite: *http://www.excite.com*

    InfoSeek: *http://www.infoseek.com*

    Open Text: *http://www.opentext.com*

    Tupilak: *http://moose.nstn.ca/cgi-bin/cgifind.pl*

- Listings and catalogs:

    Yahoo: *http://www.yahoo.com*

    Commercial Sites (OpenMarket): *http://www.directory.net/*

    TradeWave Galaxy: *http://galaxy.tradewave.com/galaxy.html*

    BizWeb: *http://www.bizweb.com*

Don't think of this as a one-time activity either. New sites emerge almost every day, and it is important to register with them as they are created. In some cases you can register Gopher and FTP URLs as well.

Once you get Web users to visit your site, it is important to get them to come back—by demonstrating that it is an active, useful, changing site that is worth repeated visits. People will return out of curiosity, because of item turnover, in order to use some indispensable tool or resource, or to get information on some unique event or resource. Good pages often are those that provide interactivity, engaging the potential customer in surveys, contests, and so on. The best pages are those that engage their visitors.

Integration of the Web Site as a Channel

Ultimately, to be successful, Web-based marketing must be an integrated part of a business and marketing plan that encompasses the Web, the larger Internet, and non-Internet strategies. Companies did not stop advertising in newspapers when radio came along, nor did they abandon radio when TV came on the scene. In the same way, Web marketing is not a replacement—it is another channel.

For successful online marketing, use discussion lists, Usenet newsgroups, e-mail, and other Internet resources to support your Web page, in conjunction with your existing traditional advertising and marketing efforts. Encourage cross-fertilization between your Web site marketing efforts and your marketing and advertising in traditional marketing media.

Be sure to put your URL and e-mail address in all your print-media advertisements—magazines, newspapers, newsletters, flyers, brochures, and so on.

URLs and E-mail on Your Business Card

Putting your homepage URL and your e-mail address on all of your office stationery and on your business cards can stimulate interest and conversation. If the recipients are Web-wise, they will appreciate it; if they are not, they just might ask about it, opening the door for dialog.

Television advertising is just starting to show URLs and e-mail addresses. If you use them in your TV ads, be sure they are displayed long enough for the viewer to write them down correctly.

URLs are showing up in an increasing number of places. Creative ways of presenting your site's URL are useful in focusing attention on your site, and letting people know your business is on the Internet. Here are a few recent URL sightings:

- The Southwest Airlines URL (*http://www.iflyswa.com*) can be spotted on outdoor billboards underneath a picture of one of their planes.
- The URLs for the support and fan pages of many TV shows are shown at the ends of shows. For example, on the Red Green Show, *http://www.redgreen.com* flashes on the screen. The site has quotes from the show, background information, and merchandise for sale.
- The Harley-Davidson Motorcycles URL (*http://www.hd-stamford.com/hd.html*) has been spotted on the back of a Harley.

Figure 9.7 The Ford Worldwide Connection homepage.

The Web Site and Corporate Identity

Businesses spend a great deal of time and money in creating and maintaining their corporate identity. Companies seek to have consistent images, styles and messages in their advertising and on company materials. Figure 9.7 shows Ford Motor Company's Worldwide Connection page. You can easily see the "look and feel" of Ford in the logo and layout.

Integrate the public image, logos, graphics, colors, and other unique aspects of your company into your Web pages whenever possible. This can magnify your other advertising efforts, rather than splintering from them.

To promote the online part of your corporate identity, consider putting your URL and e-mail address on most promotional materials and corporate literature:

- All stationery
- Binders
- Brochures
- Bulk mailing items
- Business cards
- Diskettes
- Fax cover sheets
- Flyers
- Folders
- Letterhead
- Magazine bingo cards
- Mouse pads
- Mugs
- Newsletters
- Notebooks
- Pens
- Post-it notes
- Press packets
- Press releases
- Report covers
- And more…

Direct Sales

More and more businesses are using the Web as a vehicle for direct sales to consumers. Direct sales are possible because Web pages can be programmed to accept data entry. Sales can take place either through your own site, or by placing your products in a cybermall or virtual storefront.

Online ordering is becoming increasingly common and secure. Chapter 7, which deals with security, outlines some of the models for online purchasing through prearranged accounts, credit cards, secure online forms, and more.

An example of online order capabilities is the BookStacks online bookstore at *http://www.books.com*, shown in Figure 9.8. Here you can browse, talk to authors in forums, look at reviews, and place an order online.

Adding Value—Giving Back to the Internet Community

Placing your business on the Web creates an opportunity to be a good Net citizen by participating in the tradition on the Internet called "giving back to the Net." (Chapter 6 discusses this as well.) In planning a business Web site, consider ways in which to add value. The tradition of giving back, or the gift economy, is very strong, and any business using the Web is well advised to pay attention to it. And, of course, providing interesting

```
┌─────────────────────────────────────────────────────────────────────────┐
│ ─          Netscape - [Book Stacks - Order Form]                ▼ ▲       │
├─────────────────────────────────────────────────────────────────────────┤
│  File   Edit   View   Go   Bookmarks   Options   Directory        Help    │
├─────────────────────────────────────────────────────────────────────────┤
│  Location:│ http://melville.books.com/scripts/order.exe?sid˜oLGsxe0uefR8W2R │  N  │
├─────────────────────────────────────────────────────────────────────────┤
│                                                                           │
│  Current Order List:              Shipped Via:                            │
│                                                                           │
│  Qty  Title                       Author      Binding    Price   Amount   │
│                                                                           │
│  1    TO KILL A MOCKINGBIRD       LEE, HARPE   Trade      23.00   23.00    │
│                                                                           │
│  Alter Current Order List                             Sub Total:  23.00   │
│                                                       Sales Tax:    .00    │
│  Apply Bookmarks                                      Shipping:     .00    │
│                                                  Order Total:$    23.00    │
│  Credit Card Information:              Example Information:                │
│  Card Holder's Name: │            │    Jane Doe                           │
│           Card No: │            │      1234567890123456                   │
│         Exp Date: │Jan  ▼│ │1995 ▼│                                       │
│  ☐ I prefer to call in my credit card number via telephone.              │
│     NOTE: This option only works with TOUCH TONE phones.                  │
│     Card Holder's Name and Exp. Date must be filled in on this form.     │
│                      │   Place Your Order   │                             │
└─────────────────────────────────────────────────────────────────────────┘
```

Figure 9.8 The BookStacks online order form.

and useful information also attracts many more people to your Web site than would normally visit.

The type of services, products, and information used to add value to a Web site should fit the business providing the site. Some companies offer only a collection of links to related sites. This is useful, but unless it's a particularly good collection, it is not really in the spirit of "giving back." Some businesses maintain directories of businesses and resources, some offer free copies of their software, and others offer news feeds. Major sites should consider providing some of the following:

- Internet services such as servers to provide Veronica and Archie searches

- Mirroring of major services and archives (offering duplicate content of overloaded sites such as software archives)

- Major collections of resources and archives, particularly in digitizing existing or archival material from paper (or audio) into digital collections; access to unusual or rare information
- Access to free software
- Space and services for groups and individuals that would otherwise not be able to have a presence on the Internet

As an interesting new example of "giving back" to the Internet, America Online (*http://www.aol.com*) is providing support for the Internet search system WebCrawler as a service to the Internet, and is also providing FTP mirror sites for a group of the most popular FTP sites in the world, as shown in Figure 9.9.

See Chapter 6 for additional discussion on "Acceptable Use and Customs of the Internet."

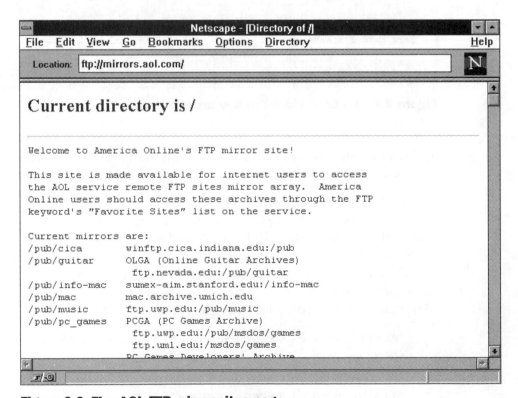

Figure 9.9 The AOL FTP mirror sites page.

Keys to a Successful Business Web Site

Successful business Web sites have some characteristics in common:

- *There are no Invisible Webs.* It is difficult sometimes to find Web pages in the haystack of the Internet. To keep the site from being invisible, register it with all of the online search engines such Lycos, WebCrawler, Tupilak, McKinley, and InfoSeek, and with the catalog listings such as Galaxy, Yahoo, the Commercial Sites Index, etc. In addition, the registrations are kept up to date with new categories and new sites.

- *There are no Dead Webs.* Some Web pages have a "ghost town" feel about them because it seems as if no one has been tending them in a while. On good sites, the content is always fresh—new pages are added and old pages are updated and given face-lifts.

- *Successful pages are information-rich.* A successful site offers good content, content, content, more than a visitor can absorb in one visit.

- *The pages have clear navigation.* Users can move around and through the site easily. The navigational elements (icons, arrows, etc.) are consistent. Moving around on the pages and among the pages feels intuitive—you can see where you are going, and can return to previous pages easily.

- *The pages do not funnel the user out too quickly.* Some pages have links out every time you turn around. You have spent considerable effort to bring users to your pages; don't send them away with too many links out to other sites.

- *The site has true value added.* Services, content, products, or other resources are in evidence. A successful site is not just a place to market and sell; users can get real information and services for free.

- *The site maintainers are responsive.* Queries are answered quickly, and they troubleshoot problem links. Users don't get the dreaded "404, URL not found" messages that mean that links are "dead" because the document the user is hunting for is not available (or, the links are incorrect!).

- *The site has organizational and/or institutional support.* A successful site is not set up by guys "out back" where no one else in the organization knows anything about it. The site has budget and personnel support—it is not dependent on handouts.

- *The site is capable of gathering information.* Information about users is routinely gathered through contests, newsletters, or surveys, so that the maintainers know who has been visiting, and their preferences and reactions.
- *The Web site is a marketing channel integrated with other channels.* The Web and the Internet are integrated with print media, TV, and radio.
- *The Web site is supported through other Internet tools.* A good Web site has related Gopher and FTP sites, and is supported by e-mail.
- *The site has good design.*

    There are text and small image alternatives for large images.

    Interactivity with people is available.

    The site is sensible vs. "hot"—graphics, design and colors are in synch with the corporate image.

    The site has relatively consistent imagery and content from page to page—providing a sense of visiting one site, not just a collection of pages.

    The URL is not a "funny-looking" URL with lots of mixed cases and tildes.

From Here...

Chapter 10 will guide you through the process of creating the actual Web documents that make up your business Web site.

PART IV

Preparing World Wide Web Pages

Preparing World Wide Web Pages

Web sites can vary from simple one-page, text-only displays, to elaborate and large collections of pages with extensive graphics, input forms, linked databases, sound, animations, movies, interactive 3D renderings, and much more. Whether you decide to produce the pages yourself, have them done in-house by your own company, or hire a consulting firm, you should at least understand the basics of what an HTML file is, and how all of the features just mentioned are added to a site. This chapter will give you an overview of the basic building blocks of a Web site. If you decide to pursue do-it-yourself site building, make use of the online and offline materials mentioned in each section.

Elements of Web Page Production

While the basic building blocks of a Web site are the HTML documents, the support files related to graphics, sound, and databases also require planning and preparation. Here are some elements to consider when designing your site.

HTML

First, take a look at Figure 10.1. This is how a particular HTML document (orr.html) is displayed on the World Wide Web when viewed with a Netscape browser.

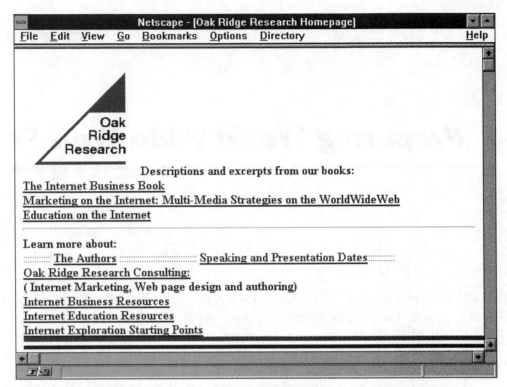

Figure 10.1 The Netscape browser displaying the HTML file orr.html.

Here is the same file (orr.html) as it is displayed by any ordinary text viewer or editor, with the HTML markings showing (HTML files are plain text files—there are no hidden symbols, commands, or control characters):

```
<HTML>
<HEAD>
<!-- HTML document prepared by Oak Ridge Research
oakridge@world.std.com -->
<!-- Revised August 17, 1995 -->
<title>Oak Ridge Research Homepage</title>
</HEAD>
<BODY>
<IMG ALIGN=bottom ALT="OAK RIDGE RESEARCH" SRC="r-w-b-sm.gif">
<B>Descriptions and excerpts from our books:</B><BR>
<A HREF="ibb.html"><B>The Internet Business Book</B></A><BR>
```

```
<A HREF="topmoip1.html"><B>Marketing on the Internet:
Multi-Media Strategies on the WorldWideWeb</B></A><BR>
<A HREF="topeoip1.html"><B>Education on the Internet</B></A><BR>
<HR>
<U><B>Learn more about:</B></U><BR>
::::::::::::
<A HREF="topautp1.html"><B>The Authors</B></A>
::::::::::::::::::::::::::::::::
<A HREF="ftp://ftp.std.com/pub/je/topspkp1.html"><B>Speaking
and Presentation Dates</B></A>:::::::::::<BR>
<A HREF="topconp1.html"><B>Oak Ridge Research
Consulting:</B></A><BR>
<B>( Internet Marketing, Web page design and authoring)</B><BR>
<A HREF="topibrp1.html"><B>Internet Business
Resources</B></A><BR>
<A HREF="topierp1.html"><B>Internet Education
Resources</B></A><BR>
<A HREF="topispp1.html"><B>Internet Exploration Starting
Points</B></A>
<IMG ALIGN=bottom SRC="rwb-line.gif"><BR>
<I>Send comments and inquiries to:</I>
<B>oakridge@world.std.com</B><BR><P>
<A HREF="c-rights.html"><PRE>Copyright 1995 Oak Ridge
Research</PRE></A><P>
</BODY>
</HTML>
```

This HTML document becomes more comprehensible when taken one component at a time.

HTML Document Structure

It is best to adhere to the HTML standards for structure in order to ensure that your page will display properly with current Web browsers, and future ones as well.

Each HTML document starts with <HTML> and ends with </HTML>.

Within the document surrounded by the <HTML> and </HTML> tags there are usually two sections, the HEAD, which is enclosed by the <HEAD> and </HEAD> tags, and the BODY, which is enclosed by the <BODY> and </BODY> tags.

Tags

Groups of characters enclosed by the arrowlike brackets <> are called tags in HTML documents. Tags are usually, but not always, used in pairs: one before the text that some action is to be taken on, and one at the end of that text. For example, to direct the browser to display the word "Texas" in bold letters, the start bolding tag <B> and the end bolding tag </B> would be used in this manner:

```
<B>Texas</B>
```

The HEAD contains various lines and tags telling the reader of the HTML text document who owns the document, when it was updated, and what its title is.

Some of this information is enclosed within HTML tags that tell the browser not to display the line on the browser's display. In the HTML document shown above, for example, the following line is viewable in the HTML document, but is not displayed when it is presented on a browser:

```
<!-- Revised August 17, 1995 -->
```

One element in the head is the TITLE. The browser doesn't show this element on the Web page, but rather, displays it in a status line or box somewhere on the browser screen. With Netscape, for example, this line of HTML:

```
<title>Oak Ridge Research Homepage</title>
```

is displayed at the top of the screen (see Figure 10.1).

The BODY contains the text of the Web page along with formatting information, URLs of links, and information about what and where images are to be displayed.

Upper- and Lowercase Are OK with HTML

HTML tags are not case sensitive. <BODY> and <body> will be interpreted by browsers in the same way.

HTML documents being prepared in Windows 3.1 or other environments that allow only a three-letter file name extension should be saved to disk with a file name extension of **.htm**. When the file is placed on the Internet, it is best to rename it with the four-letter **.html** (e.g., orr.htm becomes orr.html).

Linking to Other Pages

Of course, much of the power of Web pages comes from their ability to link other pages, sites, and Internet systems together. Though the systems, pages, and files may vary, there is a standard way to make these links. In the HTML example document shown, this line is listed:

```
<A HREF="topibrp1.html"><B>Internet Business Resources</B></A><BR>
```

On the browser screen this is displayed as a bold-lettered link (**Internet Business Resources**) to another page.

The HTML tags for making a link are <A HREF=""> and </A>.

Between these two tags the text that is to be marked as a link is inserted—in this case, "Internet Business Resources":

```
<A HREF="">Internet Business Resources</A>
```

The name of the file being linked to is then inserted between the quotation marks:

```
<A HREF="topibrp1.html">Internet Business Resources</A>
```

To make the words stand out even more, the tags for bold letters can be added:

```
<A HREF="topibrp1.html"><B>Internet Business Resources</B></A>
```

In this example, the tag <BR> is added, forcing the browser to display the next text it finds on a new line:

```
<A HREF="topibrp1.html"><B>Internet Business Resources</B></A><BR>
```

If the page being linked to is at another location, the address of that location, the subdirectory path to the file, and the file name will be included between the quotation marks. For example:

```
<A HREF="ftp://ftp.std.com/pub/je/topspkp1.html"><B>Speaking
and Presentation Dates</B></A>
```

Inline Graphics

Graphics can be displayed by using the inline image tag (just one, not a pair in this case):

```
<IMG ALIGN=bottom ALT="" SRC="">
```

To link an image file, insert the file name between the quotation marks after SRC. In this example, the company logo with the file name r-w-b-sm.gif is to be displayed:

```
<IMG ALIGN=bottom ALT="" SRC="r-w-b-sm.gif">
```

Because many people may be visiting your Web page using Lynx or another text-based browser, it is good practice to include some words that can substitute for the graphics image. In this case, OAK RIDGE RE-SEARCH is the alternative that Lynx will substitute for the image it can't display:

```
<IMG ALIGN=bottom ALT="OAK RIDGE RESEARCH" SRC="r-w-b-sm.gif">
```

External Graphics and Other Applications

Just as you can create links to other Web pages, you can create links to pictures. In this example, the link is to an image of the book's cover:

```
<A HREF="cover.gif"><B>Internet Business Book Cover</B></A>
```

You can also make links from inline pictures (images that are displayed automatically when the browser loads the page) to other images. This is useful for linking a small, quick-loading version of an image to a larger image that would slow down the initial transfer of your page if it were inline. For example, a small image of a book cover could be linked to an easier-to-read larger image:

```
<A HREF="large.gif"><IMG ALT="(FRONT COVER)" ALIGN=middle
SRC="small.gif"></A>
```

Input Forms

Input form pages provide a chance to interact with customers while their interest is still high and you have their attention. Input forms allow you to get response to your pages, individual products, and your business. They also can be used to survey public opinion on matters related to your industry or as a user interface with a database (see Figure 10.2).

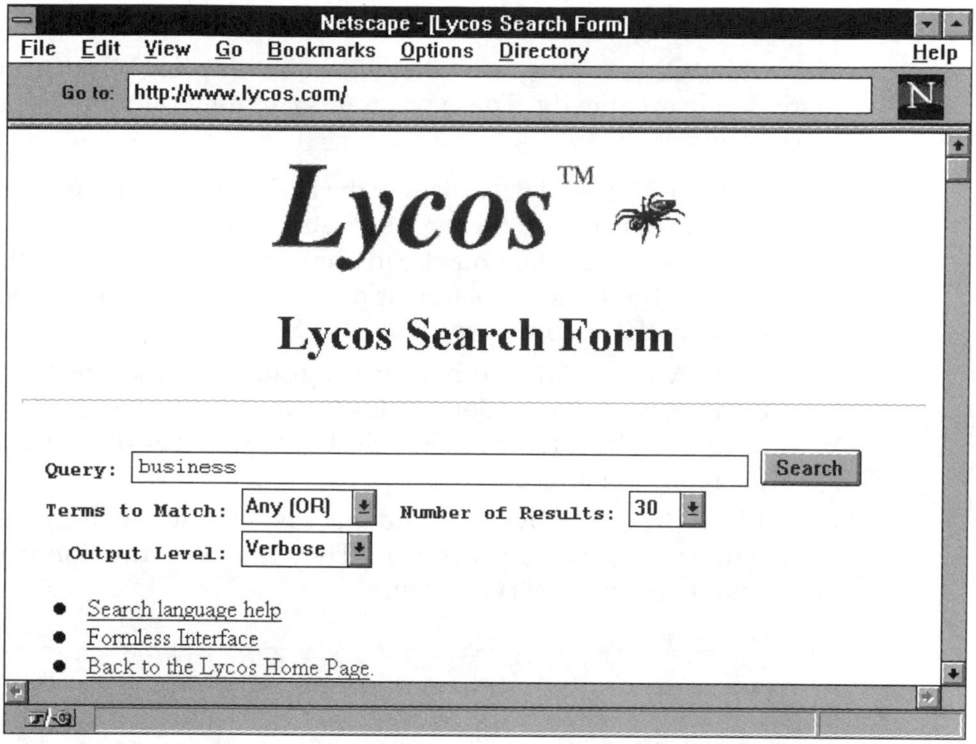

Figure 10.2 Lycos—one of the many uses for input form pages.

While receiving direct orders from customers is an immediately valuable use of input forms, forms are also available for allowing visitors to your site to request information packs, catalogs, and so on; their requests help you to build a database of individuals or businesses interested in your products or services.

One or more forms can be incorporated within an HTML document. The basic HTML tag for doing this is:

```
<FORM METHOD= ACTION="">
```

In addition to text input lines, an input form can contain checkboxes, action buttons, sets of checkboxes that only allow one to be checked at any one time, and password protection.

A tutorial on creating forms is available from *http://www.ncsa.uiuc. edu/SDG/Software/Mosaic/Docs/fill-out-forms/overview.html*.

HTML Production Tools

The availability of programs that aid in writing HTML documents has increased dramatically. These programs can generally be categorized in three groups:

- HTML editors—These display the HTML file, and offer features that make it easy to add the tags, links, and formatting. They usually use a Web browser that you already have installed on your computer to display the HTML document during the development of the page the way the Web will see it.

- WYSIWYG HTML authoring programs—These are becoming increasingly popular. Some allow you to move images and text by drag-and-drop techniques, select font size, set up tables, and perform other manipulations.

- Word processor overlays and macros—These are designed to work with specific word processors. They range in function from HTML editors to WYSIWYG systems.

WYSIWYG

WYSIWYG stands for "What You See Is What You Get." When used in connection with browsers, it means that you work on the screen with a page that it is formatted and displayed just as it will be on a Web browser. The WYSIWYG HTML editor then converts the page shown on the screen to an HTML document. Most of the HTML coding goes on unseen by the user of the program.

Here are a few examples of currently available software:

- HTML Assistant—A Windows-based HTML editor/authoring tool with features for speeding up the production of HTML documents. It uses the Web browser installed on your personal computer to display the documents as they would appear to others on the Web. It is available online from *ftp://ftp.cs.dal.ca/htmlasst/htmlasst.zip*.

- HTML Writer for Windows—Available from *ftp://ftp.byu.edu/tmp/ htmlwrit.zip*.

- HoTMetaL—A WYSIWYG editor for creating and modifying HTML files. SoftQuad's HoTMetaL HTML editor—Available from *ftp://ftp.*

ncsa.uiuc.edu/Web/html/hotmetal/ or *ftp://doc.ic.ac.uk/pub/packages/WWW/ncsa/contrib/SoftQuad/hotmetal/*, in versions for Microsoft Windows 3.1 (386 or higher, 6MB RAM) and Sun/SPARC Motif (Solaris 1/4.1.x and Solaris 2.3 or later; needs X11).

- Claris 4.0—A commercially available product for MAC users with an HTML translator that allows you to create the page as it would be seen on the Web; Claris then automatically translates it into HTML script.

Resources for HTML Authoring

There are many books and online resources for learning to write HTML, and for keeping up with the standards. Here a few excellent starting points:

- *The HTML Source Book* by Ian S. Graham, published by John Wiley & Sons
- Netscape maintains a variety of information useful for HTML authoring. Check under "Assistance" on Netscape's home page at *http://home.mcom.com/home/welcome.html*
- The WWW Developer's Virtual Library (*http://WWW.Stars.com/*), a major source of information about developing Web sites, has links to over 1,000 sites with information about developing Web pages and sites.

Graphics and Movies

Good graphics make pages much more memorable, and they can display products in an attractive and accurate manner. Hardware and software for making and modifying graphics is now abundantly available and quite affordable, even for small businesses.

Producing Digital Pictures and Graphics

Digital pictures and images can be created many ways, but the most common methods are by scanning hard copy images, grabbing video pictures, using CAD and drawing programs, and capturing from a computer screen.

Image File Types

The image file formats that Web browsers can display varies from one browser to another, but there is nearly universal ability to display GIF and JPEG image file formats. (These files types are marked with the three-letter file name extensions .gif and .jpg.) Therefore, to ensure successful display of image files created in other formats, convert them to GIF or JPEG files.

Scanning Pictures   If you have a photograph or piece of artwork that you would like to display on a Web page, a scanner can be used to create a digital computer file of the image.

Size of the picture or artwork, the resolution of the scanner, and how accurately the color is recorded all affect the image file size dramatically. Generally, it is best to scan images at the highest resolution, with the most colors available to you, but expect that the digital image will need to be reduced in size and number of colors by post-processing the file. (See "Processing Image Files" later in this section.)

There are two common types of scanners: hand-held and flat-bed.

The hand-held units are pulled across the picture, and record the image in strips (often about 4 inches wide). These strips of image can be reassembled in the computer to re-create the larger image. Hand-held scanners usually cost $100 or more, depending on their resolution and the number of different shades of color they can detect.

Flat-bed scanners usually are made to accommodate pictures, pages, or artwork up to the size of a sheet of typing paper. They scan this size in one pass. These scanners often have higher resolution and color capabilities than hand-held units. They go for $1,500 and up.

If you only need a few images scanned in, consider having the images professionally scanned. Scanning services are increasingly available at copy centers and other graphics businesses.

Another approach to scanning is to send negatives or slides to one of the increasing number of photo finishers that will provide you with digital files of the images on CD-ROM or floppy disk. These are usually high-quality scans, and are convenient if your materials are already on film.

If black-and-white images are acceptable and your artwork is on paper, you can also fax the image to a computer that has a Fax/modem board. Most Fax board software allows you to convert the file to one of the standard image types. (If the file is not GIF or JPEG, it can be converted.)

Video Frame Grabbing Video images can be captured directly from a camera or from a video recording and converted to digital image files. This requires some extra hardware, such as a plug-in computer board or an external box.

While captured video images have a resolution much lower than most scanned images, they do have some advantages and uses:

- Pictures can be taken at regular intervals and assembled into a digital movie—either as a full-motion movie, or as a time-lapse movie.
- Businesses can also offer frequently updated pictures on their Web page using a frame grabber—showing their business in action in some way, or by just capturing pictures of an interesting location, to attract visitors for repeat visits.

Computer-Generated Images Some of the most stunning graphics on the Web were created in drawing programs. The range of tools available for creating images, even in low-end drawing programs, allows businesses to quickly create in-house Web graphics.

In addition to creating completely original artwork, drawing programs are excellent for modifying files made by any of the other techniques mentioned. They can add labels, pointers, or highlights, combine pictures, and perform dozens of other types of modifications.

Screen Capturing Capture programs allow you to make an image file of whatever you can get on your computer screen, which you can then display on your Web page. For instance, you can make a digital image of a portion of a spreadsheet, or an image of some software your business has developed, or an image from any other program that doesn't have the ability to save a graphics file.

Capture programs are usually launched on the computer first; then the program to be pictured is loaded, leaving the capture program to run in the background until some predesignated key combination is pressed.

Processing Image Files

Graphics viewing and processing programs allow you to take an image file created by any of the means mentioned, and change its size, number of colors, and color balance. They can also add special effects.

Image Size Modification   Image size needs to be controlled for two principle reasons:

- The image should be sized correctly for good Web page appearance.
- The image should load quickly enough to not annoy visitors to your site.

Most people using GUI browsers have screens with a width of 640 pixels (dots) and a height of 480 pixels. Part of that screen is used up by scroll bars, status lines, buttons, and pull-down menus. This leaves, at most, 600×400 pixels for a picture that won't run off the sides or bottom of the screen. However, full-screen pictures can require very large, slow-to-download files. A 600×400 pixel picture, for example, requires a file 24 times as large as a 100×100 pixel picture. Keep image files as small as is artistically acceptable.

Another way to keep image file size down is to use the minimum number of colors possible. Most people using GUI browsers have displays using 16 colors or 256 colors. Using larger numbers of colors dramatically increases file size, and few on the Web will see the difference.

The image size and number of colors can be adjusted by a graphics processing program, and balance can then be achieve between loss of image quality and image file size. When designing pages, view them in as many browsers and on as many platforms as possible—you will find many variations in how your HTML document and inline pictures are displayed.

Cropping

Image file size can also be reduced by using a graphics processing program to trim off unneeded portions of the image. Is there too much foreground? Background? Border? Crop!

Color and Special Effects Processing Many graphics programs available now are designed to work with photographs as well as artwork. They have all of the standard abilities of a traditional darkroom: They can adjust color balance, contrast, brightness, saturation, and sharpness.

In addition, special effects such as embossing, warping, texturizing, and posterizing are available to make more eye-catching images.

Movies

Movies are not yet in widespread use on the Web, but their use is increasing, and they do attract attention to Web pages that have them.

A movie file is assembled from a series of still pictures by programs designed for this purpose. The images can be any series of graphics files that show incremental changes (the video capture system is an excellent source for these). While the standards are still in flux, the MPEG type of movie file (file extension .mpg) is a good choice because it is widely supported.

One challenge in working with movies is keeping the file size down. A 5-second movie with an image size of only 260×120 pixels can easily add up to a 100K file.

Sound

Sound files can be recorded on most multimedia-equipped computers, and on many others with sound cards. Most multimedia computers and sound cards come with at least some software for editing these sound files. The software allows you to combine files, cut out parts, and change the audio sampling rate (to reduce file size).

Audio files can be offered from links on your Web pages. The type of sound file you offer is indicated by the file name extension. Commonly used audio file types on the Web are .au, .wav, and .snd.

Visitors to your site must have some sort of audio hardware installed on their system, and their browsers must be configured to be aware of this hardware, if they are to be able to hear your sound clips. As multimedia-equipped computers become more common, more visitors on the Web will be able to listen; but even with a limited installed base, sound links attract attention to your pages.

Databases

"Database" can mean many things on the Internet; it can be any collection of searchable information—searchable by people or computers. Databases are a good way to provide product information and customer support, and they can be used to draw visitors back to your site for repeat visits.

Links to Existing Databases

The easiest approach to providing databases from your Web pages is to find existing databases on the Internet that are appropriate to your business, and offer links to them. If you have a good, focused set of links, individuals interested in this type of information are likely to add your site to their browser's bookmark file—providing repeat visits to your site.

Offering Your Own Database

Offering your own database certainly requires more effort, but a well-planned and well-maintained database will encourage other sites throughout the Web to add links to your site. Additionally, a strong database will demonstrate your company's expertise and provide good public relations. There are several approaches to offering the data.

Web Page Databases   The easiest kind of database to offer is a text file of information that is converted to a basic HTML file. This basic file can then be searched using the word search system available in most browsers.

At the top of the page, visitors should be given a summary of the database contents, and be directions to use the word search feature of their browser.

If the database is over 100K, it should be divided up into several pages in some logical way, with links provided on a contents page. If the database sections are too large, download times will be long, and searching will be slow and frustrating to your visitors—just the opposite of the intended effect.

Link-Based Databases   A link-based database is more user-friendly, but will require a bit more effort by your business. This method can provide a high-quality, attractive, and easy-to-use database.

For this kind of database, you will need to divide the data into logical groups and subgroups. These are then linked in a hierarchical manner to a top page. Because searches within documents are done very rapidly by browsers, and because people tend to search more often within one topic area which can be localized in one document, this approach can provide a very efficient database.

For very rapidly changing data, small text-based files can be linked to any of the database pages. The data can then be quickly updated by deleting an old text file and replacing it with a new one of the same name.

The appearance and utility of the database can be improved by providing small graphics that aid in navigating. For example, a small icon might be used throughout the database to take the user to the top of the current topic, and another to link to the top of the database; these can be distributed throughout the database with little affect on downloading or browser response time.

Server-Based Databases The server-based database model is good for large databases, and ones which require frequent major changes in the data. To operate a server-based database, you need to make arrangements with your Web service provider concerning installation, storage, and maintenance of the database.

In addition, a Web page must be written to interact with the visitor to your site. The HTML file will contain a forms section with the <FORMS> tag and the <ISINDEX> tag. Depending on the nature of the database, the visitor to your site may see your welcoming messages, an explanation of the database, blank data entry lines to type in terms to search for, buttons to click on to, select categories or types of searches, and a button to click on to initiate the search.

Presenting Completed Pages on the World Wide Web

When your business's pages are completed, they and the supporting files need to be transferred to a Web services provider that has a computer connected to the Internet running Web server software. Because of the great variety in services and charges, it is best to get information about several Web services providers before selecting one. (See Chapter 3 for information about online Web services information.)

In choosing a service provider for your Web site, there are a number of things to consider beyond basic price:

- If you need a secure server, does the service provider have one? Which one?
- How will you collect orders and other information entered by customers and visitors to your page?
- What data will be collected about the visits to your Web site? In what way and when will it be made available to you?
- What steps will be taken to protect your data from others?
- What, if any, are the setup fees?
- What fees are there for changing or adding pages?
- What is the service provider's history of system down time?

After your pages are installed, test all pages and all links online. When things are working well, be sure to visit the Web sites such as Lycos, WebCrawler, SubmitIt, and Yahoo to register, register, register.

CHAPTER 11

Meta-Sites and Searching for Information on the Web

All Internet tools sites and resources are not created equal. There are some sites that are much more likely to provide complex, dense, useful information than others. This chapter is designed to describe some of these sites to aid you in locating high-quality information germane to your business. (For more on searching Gopher and FTP sites, see the discussion of Veronica and Archie in Chapter 14.)

Thomas Ho's Favorite Electronic Commerce Sites

This is one of those business sites worth regular visits to track new developments. The URL is *http://www.engr.iupui.edu/~ho/interests/commmenu.html.*

This very useful site, maintained by Thomas Ho, provides access to a huge collection of information about electronic commerce, advertising, marketing, economics, Internet and Web service providers, intellectual property, and more. It is unique in that it focuses exclusively on electronic commerce, and is organized into thematic headings covering the background and development of electronic commerce. Ho's top-level subject headings include:

Background
    General articles
    Economic development

An industry is born in cyberspace
    Service providers
    Technology providers
    Library providers

Electronic commerce examples
    Company lists
    Electronic "storefronts"
    Industry groups
    Corporate presence
    Individual outlets
    Electronic publishers
    Financial & professional services
    Emerging services
    Co-operative efforts and consortia
    Directories and clearinghouses ("yellow pages")
    Sponsorable sites

Innovative solutions to common problems
    Innovative solutions to ordering
    Innovative solutions to gaining visibility
    Blacklists

Information resources
    Reading list
    Journals, newsletters, & books for information-based
    industry
    Conferences & training for information-based industry
    User groups for information-based industry
    Research groups for information-based industry
    People
    Teaching resources
    Repositories
    Internet mailing lists
    Calls for papers and stories
    News
    Jumpstations

```
Related areas
    Government services
    Consumer protection
    Community networking
    Related technology
        World Wide Web research
        Z39.50
        Agent technology
        Network and Computer Security
        World Wide Web security
        Payment mechanisms
        Electronic data interchange
        Commercial WWW browsers
        IETF
    Regulation, law, and policy
    Miscellaneous
```

Yahoo!—A Guide to WWW

Reach Yahoo! at *http://www.yahoo.com.*

An example of a small start-up that has become a major player on the Internet is Yahoo!. Started by two graduate students, Yahoo! has now become one of the premier sites on the Internet. Yahoo! is a very large catalog of hierarchical, categorical listings that cover a huge range of topics, all linked to WWW sites. Information and links are arranged under these main headings:

```
Arts
Business and Economy
Computers and Internet
Education
Entertainment
Government
Health
News
Recreation
Reference
Regional
Science
Social Science
Society and Culture
```

A search feature allows for keyword searching, and a menu system lets you navigate the hierarchies. In addition, you can add your own WWW entries to the hotlist.

The homepage has links to pages for Headlines, What's New, What's Popular, What's Cool, feedback, a place to add your URL to the database, and a chance to have a look at a Random Link—click on it and it picks a link from the Yahoo! database—you never know what you'll find. The business hierarchy is very complete.

WWW Virtual Library

This virtual library maintains a distributed subject catalog, even attempting an experimental Library of Congress classification. In addition to a very large subject tree, it has links to the Top Ten most popular fields, information on Internet and Web statistics, and an index. Use the following URL: *http://www.w3.org/hypertext/DataSources/bySubject/Overview.html.*

The Virtual Library subject menu (shown below) covers a lot of ground, from engineering and the sciences to commercial services, education, and more, and each subject links to further menus, lists, documents, and images. This is a very active site where information is constantly updated.

```
Aboriginal Studies
Aeronautics and Aeronautical Engineering
African Studies
Agriculture
Animal health, well-being, and rights
Anthropology
Applied Linguistics
Archaeology
Architecture
Art
Asian Studies
Astronomy and Astrophysics
Autos
Aviation
Beer & Brewing
Bio Sciences
Biotechnology
```

Broadcasters
Cartography
Chemistry
Climate research
Cognitive Science
Collecting
Commercial Services
Communications
Community Networks
Computing
Conferences
Cross-Connection Control/Backflow Prevention
Cryptography, PGP, and Your Privacy
Crystallography
Culture
Dance
Demography & Population Studies
Design
Developmental Biology
Drosophila (fruit fly)
Earth Science
Education
Electronic Journals
Encyclopaedia
Energy
Engineering
Environment
Epidemiology
Finance
Fish
Forestry
Fortune-telling
Furniture & Interior Design
Games
Geography
Geophysics
German Subject Catalogue
History
Home pages
Human Computer Interaction
Human Factors
Humanities

International Affairs
Italian General Subject Tree
Journalism
Landscape Architecture
Languages
Latin American Studies
Law
Libraries
Linguistics
Literature
Mathematics
Medicine
Medieval Studies
Men's Issues
Meteorology
Middle East Studies
Movies
Museums
Music
Mycology (Fungi)
Non-Profit Organisations
Oceanography
Paranormal Phenomena
Pharmacy (Medicine)
Philosophy
Physics
Physiology and Biophysics
Political Science
Politics and Economics
Prospectus
Publishers
Recipes
Recreation
Reference
Religion
Remote Sensing
Roadkill
Russian and East European Studies
Secular Issues
Social Sciences
Sociology
Spirituality

```
Sport
Standards and Standardization Bodies
Statistics
Sumeria
Technology Transfer
Telecommunications
Tibetan Studies
Transportation
Treasure
U.S. Federal Government Agencies
US Government Information Sources
Unidentified Flying Objects (UFOs)
United Nations and other international organisations
Vision Science
Whale Watching Web
Wine
World-Wide Web Development
Yeasts
Zoos

Other virtual libraries
```

Open Market's Commercial Sites Index

This index is another good example of how some major resources for Internet users have evolved from small projects into large useful sites. It started life at the MIT Laboratory for Computer Science as an informal listing, but very quickly became one of the best listings of commercial services on the Web. Open Market now maintains the list as a free public service for the Internet community.

Open Market also facilitates commerce on the Internet through assisting in the development of storefronts and other services involving store creation, account management, buyer authentication, and secure payment processing. They are deeply involved in creating methods for secure transactions, most notably through the Secure Sockets Layer (SSL) technology.

The index is searchable through keyword searching, or users can browse via categories.

TradeWave Galaxy (Formerly EINet)

You can reach TradeWave Galaxy at *http://galaxy.tradewave.com/*, or go directly to information on business and commerce at: *http://galaxy.trade wave.com/galaxy/Business-and-Commerce.html*.

TradeWave is an example of a multifaceted company that provides software for the Web and electronic commerce, and a variety of commercial Web services. They support electronic commerce through their software, services, and through TradeWave Galaxy, a subject guide to Internet resources.

TradeWave Galaxy provides a guide to the Web through a page that organizes information into broad subject areas. The directory includes access to both public and commercial information:

```
Arts and Humanities -- architecture, language, literature,
performing and visual arts, philosophy and religion

Business and Commerce -- business administration, business
policy and strategy, financial information, human resources,
legal and regulatory issues, commodity and consumer prices,
dictionaries and glossaries, foreign statistics and trends,
reading sources, libraries, newspapers and periodicals,
statistical trends, consortia and research centers, consumer
products and services, electronic commerce, commodities and
financial futures, investment sources, management,
communications, MIS, marketing and sales, advertising

Community -- community service, consumer issues, culture,
education, gender issues, health, liberties, lifestyle,
networking, communication, politics, religion, the environment,
the family, the workplace, states, urban life, veteran's
affairs, world communities

Engineering and Technology -- agriculture, biomedical,
electrical, mechanical, civil and construction engineering,
computer technology, human factors, manufacturing, processing,
transportation

Government -- Government Agencies, Regulations, Military,
Politics, Public Affairs
```

```
Law-- Administrative, Commercial, Constitutional, Criminal,
Environmental, Intellectual Property, Legal Profession,
Military, Research, Societal, Tax

Leisure and Recreation -- Amateur Radio, Games, Humor, Reading,
Recipes, Speleology, Sports, Travel

Medicine -- Community Medicine, Exercise and nutrition,
Medicine, Human Biology, Medical Applications specialties
Technologies and practice, Nursing

Reference and Interdisciplinary Information -- Census Data,
Conference Announcements, Dictionaries and directories, Grants,
Internet and Networking, Library Information and Catalogs,
Publications

Science -- Astronomy, Biology, Chemistry, Geosciences,
Mathematics, Physics

Social Sciences -- Anthropology, Economics, Education,
Geography, History, Languages, Library and Information Science,
Psychology, Sociology
```

Interesting Business Sites on the Internet

This is not just a series of listings; rather, each section lists selected sites with comments about them. The URL for this site is *http://www.rpi.edu/ ~okeefe/business.html*.

This resource is called, very plainly, "Interesting Business Sites on the Internet." Maintained by Bob O'Keefe at Rensselaer Polytechnic Institute, it organizes information regarding commercial use of the Net into the categories. Each category features a selected number of products, companies, and services. Some recent entries have been:

```
Pick of the Month -- something new and interesting each month

Successes -- a focus on successful Web-based businesses.
Previous entries are archived in their Hall of Fame

Large "Name" Companies -- Bank of America, Cellular One, Digital,
IBM, Novell, Pizza Hut, Coca-Cola, Goodyear, Molsens, TDK
```

```
Small Companies -- Arctic Adventures, Future Fantasy Bookstore,
Nine Lives Women's Clothing Consignment, The Virginia Diner,
Cars-at-Cost, The Icelandic Astrology Forum, The Peanut Roaster

Financial Services -- Chicago Mercantile Exchange, Dun &
Bradstreet, QuoteCom, Wells Fargo, The American Stock Exchange,
First Virtual

Advertising and Marketing -- Internet Business Connection,
Multimedia Ink Designs, HomeBuyers' Fair

Legal Services -- Venable

Publishing -- Wired Magazine, InfoWeek, PC Week, PC Magazine,
The Wall Street Journal

Consulting Services -- PreCom, Toyo Engineering, CareerMosaic

Event Information -- Helsinki '94, Woodstock '94, World Cup

Travel -- Canadian Airlines, Embassy Suites, Norfolk Airport

Public Corporations -- Ministry of Posts and
Telecommunications, Slovakia, European Economic Community

Virtual Catalogs -- Catalog Mart, Discount Tire Direct, Earth
Stewards, Phantom Bookshop, Staples - The Office Superstore

Virtual Malls -- CyberSales Internet Mercantile, Internet Green
Marketplace, The London Mall, MegaMall, World Mall.
```

Washington and Lee University Netlink

Washington and Lee University sponsors Netlink, which is a very large site organized by subject, kind of resource (Telnet, Gopher, WWW, WAIS), or geographic location or domain. This is a very broad site with numerous options—it is often a good starting place for hunting down subject-related material. It is a well-maintained site, and frequently updated: *http://honor.uc.wlu.edu:1020/*. The menus cover:

```
Non-classified
General Reference
-----------------
```

Agriculture
Animal Culture, Veterinary Science
Anthropology, Archeology
Architecture
Biology, Genetics
Botany
Careers, Jobs, Employment
Chemistry
Commerce, Business, Accounting
Computers
Directories of People/Institutions
Earthquakes
Economics
Education
Education - Primary/Secondary (K-12) Schooling
Engineering (Civil, Electrical)
Environment, Health/Safety
Film, Television, Radio
Fine Arts
Forestry
Games, Sports, Recreation
Geography
Geology, Paleontology
Grants, Funding
History
International Law
Journalism
Language & Literature
Law
Law--Primary Materials (legislative, executive, judicial)
Library and Information Science
Library Catalogs
Library Catalogs (Major U.S. and Canada Libraries)
Mathematics
Medicine
Military Science
Music
Naval Science, Navigation
Oceanography
Pharmacology
Philosophy
Physics

```
Plants, Gardening
Politics
Psychology, Mental Health
Religion
Retail Trade
Science
Social Science
Social Science Statistics, Census
Space Science, Astronomy
The Internet
Weather, Meteorology
Z39.50 Information Retrieval Clients
Zoology
----------------------------
Bibliographic Indexes
```

December's Guides

The Internet and Computer-Mediated Communication is a resource maintained by John December. Located at *http://www.rpi.edu/Internet/Guides/decemj/icmc/top.html*, this set of pages organizes information concerning the Internet and computer-mediated communication, including information on applications, resources, the social implications of the Internet and Web, technologies, culture, discussion forums, and bibliographies. It is highly organized and always up-to-date. The pages cover:

```
1. ABOUT this information
      + Notes
      + Formats
2. INTERNET
      + Introduction
      + Collections
      + Training
      + Navigating
      + Searching
      + Directories
      + Services
3. APPLICATIONS
      + Commerce
      + Communication
      + Education
```

```
        + Entertainment
        + Government
        + Information
        + Multiple
        + Scholarship
    4. TECHNOLOGY
        + Computing
        + Developing
        + Human Interaction
        + Multimedia
        + Virtual
        + Networks
        + Telecommunications
    5. CULTURE
        + Art
        + Community
        + Language
        + People
        + Society
    6. FORUMS
        + Academic resources in communication and related fields
        + Meetings and Activities
        + Discussion
        + Periodicals
        + Usenet
    7. ORGANIZATIONS
        + Academic
        + Research
        + Commercial
        + Internet
        + Network
        + Non-profit
        + Standards
    8. BIBLIOGRAPHY
        + Online
        + Special
        + Books
```

Yanoff's Special Internet Connections

Scott Yanoff has created a guide called Special Internet Connections that is organized by subject and covers sites, tools, and resources. It is updated twice a month, so it is especially useful for new information. It is located at *http://www.uwm.edu/Mirror/inet.services.html*. Top level headings for the guide are:

```
Agriculture
Art
Astronomy
Aviation
Biology
Botany
Business/Economics/Financial
Chemistry
College Prep
Computers
Consumer/Commercial Information/Resources
Education/Teaching/Learning
Employment
Food/Recipes/Cooking
FTP
Games/Fun/Chat
Geophysical/Geographical/Geological
Gopher
Government/Politics
History
Internet
Law
Literature/Books/Languages
Math
Medical/Health
Movies
Museums/Laboratories/Exhibits/National Parks
Music/Sounds
News/Electronic Journals/Magazines
Paranormal/Occult/Spiritual/Astrology
Physics
Religion
Software
Space
Sports And Recreation
Television
Theatre/Drama
Travel
```

```
User Lookup Services/Whois Services
Weather/Atmospheric/Oceanic
WWW/HTML/Mosaic
```

And Just a Few Other Resources

For those wanting to do business on the Internet, there are numerous other resources that can be useful for gaining information, doing research, or locating other sites and references. Here are just a few more:

- Discussion and News Group Searching—Nova University makes a very complete searchable index of discussion groups available at *http://alpha.acast.nova.edu/cgi-bin/lists* for lists, and *http://alpha.acast. nova.edu/cgi-bin/news.pl* for newsgroups.

- The MetaIndex at *http://www.ncsa.uiuc.edu/SDG/Software/Mosaic/ MetaIndex.html* is an excellent starting point for surfing the Web in general.

- Inter-Link—The Inter-Link Internet Access page contains one of the largest collections on the Web. To visit, go to *http://alpha.acast.nova. edu/start.html*.

- Internet Conferences Page—Automatrix makes a WWW page listing of Internet-related conferences available at *http://www.automatrix. com/conferences*.

- Spider's Web—An offbeat site on the Web, the Spider's Web connects to more than 1,000 sites. The links can be accessed through a page that sorts them into categories, or a menu bar across the top. This site has one of the best sets of links to WWW resources. The WWW page points you to various Web FAQs, HTML writing resources, and more. The URL is *http://gagme.wwa.com/~boba/spider. html*.

- BizNet is an umbrella for a variety of cyber-marketing opportunities, including a shopping center, yellow pages virtual vending, a grocery store, and more: *http://128.173.241.138/*.

- BizWeb maintains a very large listing of commercial products. Each month it has a "what's new" section with featured companies and products. Listings are organized in a similar way to the Usenet hierarchies. You can see the site at: *http://www.bizweb.com/*.

Searching the Web

Searching on the Web is unlike searching the other Internet "food groups," because there is no one single tool to use. Instead, there are some very useful search tools, but if you really want to be thorough, you will need to use more than one of these. They each have strengths, so you will need to choose your tools to suit your particular purpose.

Back in the Internet dark ages (a couple of years ago), the Web was very small and we relied on Gopher and Veronica, FTP and Archie to help us locate information. Now, there are a number of search tools for the Web, but no one of them will find everything.

Options

As you begin your searches, it is good to be aware that the search entry form may offer you a variety of options for style of search (Boolean to include AND and OR), the number of "hits" it will return, the size of the database to search (small or large catalog), and the type of search (Web only or to include Gopher, for example) that you wish to undertake.

Some search pages such as Galaxy and Yahoo! will use a simple string (plain words and phrases), but will also let you search a variety of Internet tools such as FTP, Gopher, or WWW. Some will let you describe how in-depth and wide-ranging you want the search to be—you can tell them to use files, directories, and/or addresses. Other engines such as Lycos offer fewer options on the search page, but return more information on each item. Some searchers return just URLs (WebCrawler and Tupilak), others return listings ranked by relevance (Tupilak), and a few will give you in-depth descriptions of the items (like Lycos and InfoSeek).

InfoSeek, a fee-based engine, is perhaps the most comprehensive, adding certain news and magazine databases to your search. Several search engines, including Open Text, Lycos, and JumpStation, search only their own database of entries.

There are a few meta-pages such as CUSI and All-in-One that will let you access several different engines from one page.

Lycos

http://www.lycos.com.

This search system was developed by the Lycos Project at Carnegie-Mellon University. The Lycos database contains a large collection of WWW pages, plus some Gopher and FTP archives. Structurally, Lycos provides alternative access to subsets of its data, using a variety of databases.

Lycos, the largest of the search databases, provides a wealth of information about each item, and using the small Lycos search catalog will result in a quicker search. You can use the search form to choose your terms, maximum number of hits, and minimum score for relevance to make your search more effective. In addition, you can decide if you want the full output or a truncated (terse) output. Figure 11.1 shows the Lycos search form.

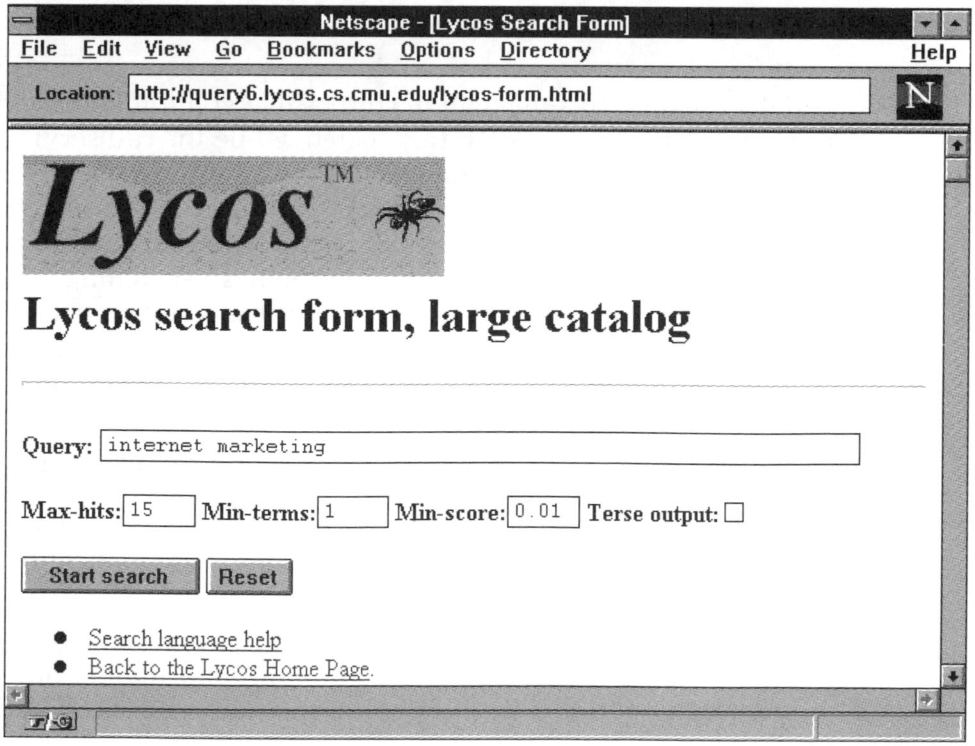

Figure 11.1 The Lycos search page.

In choosing the words that you will use in your search, these are a few important considerations:

- Searches are case insensitive—"marketing" is the same as "Marketing."
- The word or text string must be at least three characters long, and must start with a letter, not a number.
- Words cannot contain a hyphen.
- A hyphen in front of a term means that you *don't* want hits that include that term in your search—"market -food" when you want "market" but not "food."
- A period at the end of a search word means that you want the search to be exact—"market." when you want "market" but not "marketing."

InfoSeek

http://www.infoseek.com.

InfoSeek is a commercial search engine, but you can use a subset of its database for free—this will of course give you limited search results. You can get 100 hits for each free search, while the full service search is much more complete. The InfoSeek search screen begins with a data entry box for your search string as shown in Figure 11.2. The search page lets you restrict the document to certain dates and to choose from among sets of document types. InfoSeek allows for Boolean searching (+ means the words are sought together, - means that you want to exclude terms). When you use those operators, be sure that you don't leave a space between the operator and the keywords. (Be sure to read the online help files provided onsite for additional information.)

InfoSeek has a number of specialized subject-specific collections:

- MDX Health Digest—Both current contents and summaries of articles from more than 200 health and medicine publications broadly related to medicine and health.
- Hoover's Company Profiles—A database based on Hoover's Handbook of American Business, containing information on more than 800 major U.S. public companies, and key private companies
- Wire—A database containing current articles from the *Business Wire*, the *PR Newswire, Reuters Business Report*, and *Newsbytes*

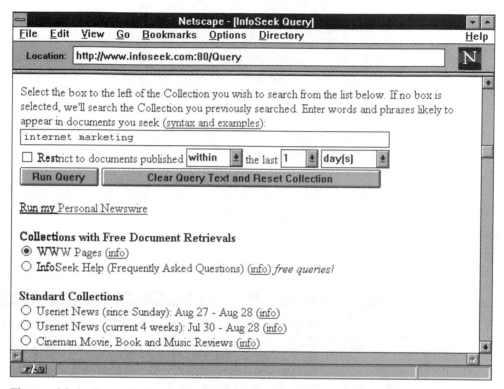

Figure 11.2 The InfoSeek search form.

- Computer Periodicals—Articles from three computer-related journals: *Computerworld*, *InfoWorld*, and *Newsbytes*
- Computer Select—Both full-text articles and abstracts of articles from business and computer business publications

WebCrawler

http://www.webcrawler.com.

WebCrawler, like some other search tools, works by going out on the Web and sniffing out new URLs for its database. It then builds an index of these URLs that can be searched through the Query page. The database is indexed by content, which means that the contents of documents, not just the page titles and URLs, are indexed. Also, like other search engines, it allows individuals to enter their page into the database.

Like many search engines, WebCrawler does not search on terms that it finds too commonly in documents. For example, while Lycos finds a different number of documents with a search for "business internet" than for "business," WebCrawler finds the same number for both searches because it throws out the word "Internet" (since it is so common in Web documents) and just looks for "business" in both cases.

WebCrawler ignores case, and it truncates words before checking its index. For example "business" and "Businesses" are the same in a WebCrawler search.

The WebCrawler data entry form (Figure 11.3) has a space for the search string, and you can indicate how many results to return and whether you want to include hits for either of your terms or for all of them.

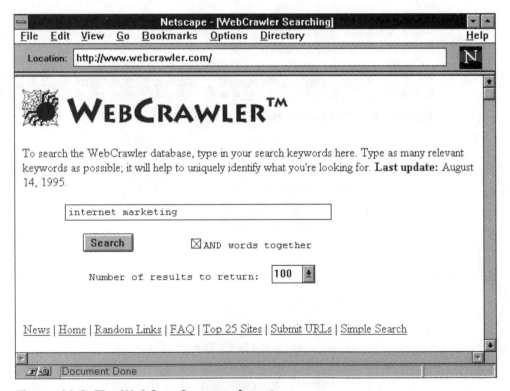

Figure 11.3 The WebCrawler search page.

McKinley

http://www.mckinley.com.

The McKinley Internet Directory takes a different approach to searching by providing evaluative information on sites through its rating system. This allows a better focused search, but currently the database is smaller than that of some other search engines.

The McKinley search page (Figure 11.4) assumes that you want to begin with full text searching. You can do a regular search, or a search that approximates and expands your words by concept. In addition, you can narrow your search using filters based on McKinley's rating scheme and by category—restrict it or use all categories.

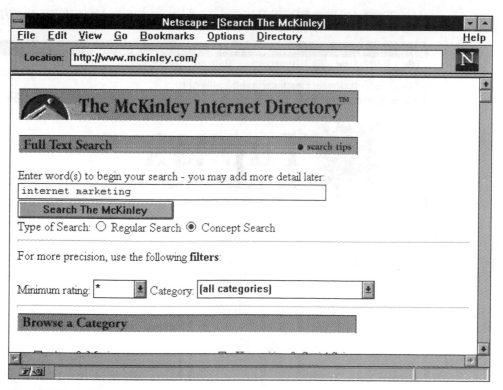

Figure 11.4 The McKinley search homepage.

Tupilak

http://moose.nstn.ca/cgi-bin/cgifind.pl.

Tupilak: The "Lost Soul" Searcher has been created at NSTN. The name comes from Inuit stories about the shamans who were seeking the mystical helper called the Tupilak in order to gain power. This database is updated automatically by a URL miner developed by NSTN, which "mines" the Internet for new URLs and adds them to the database. Individuals can add their URLs to the database as well.

The Tupilak search page shown in Figure 11.5 is a very simple data entry form for your search string.

Meta-Searchers

There are a few places where you can carry out searches on multiple databases from a single page. The All-in-One search page at *http://www.*

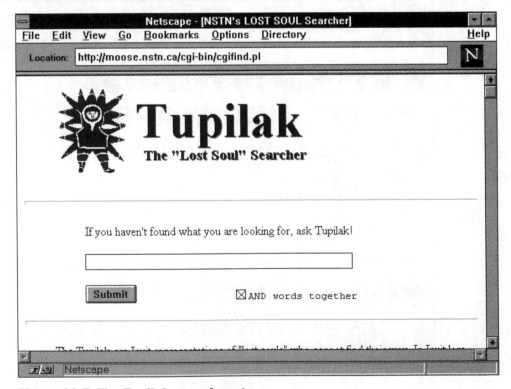

Figure 11.5 The Tupilak search page.

albany.net/~wcross/all1srch.html is one that will let you search numerous sites from its page:

- CityScape Global On-line Directory
- CUI World Wide Web Catalog
- DA-CLOD Project Distributedly Administered Categorical List Of Documents
- EINet Galaxy
- Global Network Academy Meta-Library
- Harvest Broker WAIS-based search of WWW Home Pages
- InfoSeek
- IWeb URL Review Database
- JumpStation
- Lycos
- Mesch Multi-WAIS Engine for Searching Commercial Hosts
- NetSearch
- NIKOS
- NorthStar Search WWW document headers
- Open Text Web Index
- RBSE's URL Database Search WWW document full text
- SavvySearch Simultaneous Search
- Spry Internet Wizard
- Tribal Voice Internet Trailblazer Search
- Wandex net.Genesis Wanderer Index
- WebCrawler Search WWW document content
- WWW Worm
- Yahoo!

SavvySearch at *http://www.cs.colostate.edu/~dreiling/smartform.html* is another place that will allow you to search more than one site. SavvySearch acts as a form of intelligence agent that contacts multiple Internet search engines. It will gather information from several sources, and then return the results as URL hotlinks. It lets you search by sources of information—you can choose up to three of the following:

- Academic
- Commercial
- Entertainment
- Images
- News
- People
- Reference
- Software
- Technical reports
- WWW resources

Search Strategies

In using the various search tools of the Internet, it is important to have a plan in mind. The Internet is a bit daunting to search, and nowhere is that more true than in using the search engines and tools of the World Wide Web. Here are some tips on searching:

- *Define your search.* What particular question are you trying to answer, what site are you trying to find, what resources are you trying to locate? Clearly defining your search will help you make decisions about the appropriate tools. For example, if you are simply looking for a URL, your best bet is WebCrawler, since is will quickly return a listing of URLs when you do a query. If you are looking for information on a company, you might begin with WebCrawler, but you will soon want to try both Lycos and Yahoo! as well in order to locate more information.

- *Think about the variants for your search.* If you are looking for information on advertising, you may find something under the related terms *ads, adverts, advertise, public relations,* and *marketing* as well.

- *If your search returns hundreds (or thousands!!) of hits, you should narrow your terms.* Look over your results and try to be more specific.

- *Once you have started to gather your information, analyze and use the results from your search to clarify and revise your terms.*

- *Narrow your search by using the AND feature present in many search engines.* For example, if you want to look for small businesses, search for "small" *and* "business." If the result meets your needs, you probably don't need to go on—if not, you might try "small businesses," "small office," "entrepreneurs," or "SOHO," for example (SOHO is short for small office home office).

- *Remember that it works well to try the same search at several sites.* Try "small business" at several sites like Lycos, InfoSeek, and Tupilak and see what you get.

Strengths of the Search Engines

Each search engine has some strengths, in its database, its organization, its speed, or the way it displays the results.

- WebCrawler—A big database, works quickly, very good for finding a specific URL, ranked results, easy to use
- Lycos—Huge database, weighted scoring for documents, several databases to increase speed, rich information about the document
- Yahoo!—Large database broken down by category; relatively fast to use
- Tupilak—Easy searching, smaller database for speed
- InfoSeek—Large database, good descriptions, customizable searches, specialized databases
- McKinley—Sites that are described and rated, allows complex searches

Hunting the Wild URL?

The first stop would be WebCrawler, Tupilak, or InfoSeek. Hunting for in-depth information? Go to Lycos with a side trip to Yahoo!

Search Results Comparison

To compare these search engines, let's look at the results they returned on a search for the terms "internet" and "marketing." Figures 11.6 through 11.10 compare the results of the searches.

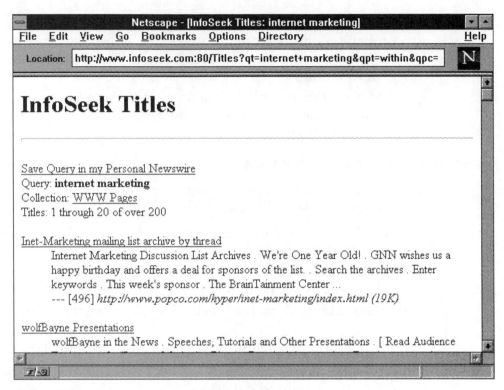

Figure 11.6 The search results from InfoSeek.

InfoSeek returned over 200 entries related to Internet marketing. In this case, the first entry is the Internet-marketing discussion list archives. InfoSeek gives you the option of saving the search to your personal area.

The McKinley search returned more than 60 records, which are rated by the service for utility. The first entry here with a four-star score is the Hajjan/Kaufman New Media Lab. The search results are presented with a narrative description, a rating, and a hotlink to the site. You can refocus your search to narrow it by adding additional keywords. You are also given an opportunity to go to McKinley's unrated Magellan database.

Tupilak returned a scored list of over 50 entries, the first of which is John December's Internet and Computer-Mediated Communication. The listing gives just the title of the resource.

The WebCrawler search found 3,082 URLs, ranked by relevance. The first entry is the Internet-marketing mailing list archives.

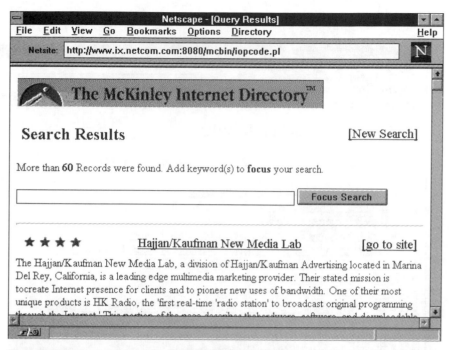

Figure 11.7 The search results from McKinley.

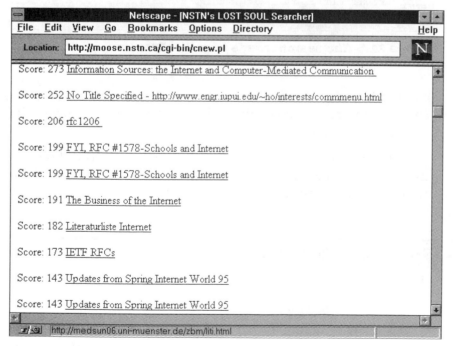

Figure 11.8 The search results from Tupilak.

Figure 11.9 The search results from WebCrawler.

The Lycos search found 94,228 documents matching one or the other search term, and 24,089 with both search terms. It returned 100 of those with the highest relevance scores.

The number of items returned ranges from around 60 to more than 24,000; and some are just URLs, while others include full-blown descriptions with relevance and quality ratings.

Sites, Sites, and More Sites

There are many other sites to try out when searching:

- AliWeb: *http://www.cs.indiana.edu/aliweb/form.html*
- CUI W3 Catalog: *http://cuiwww.unige.ch/cgi-bin/w3catalog*
- Find-It: *http://www.cam.org/~psarena/find-it.html*

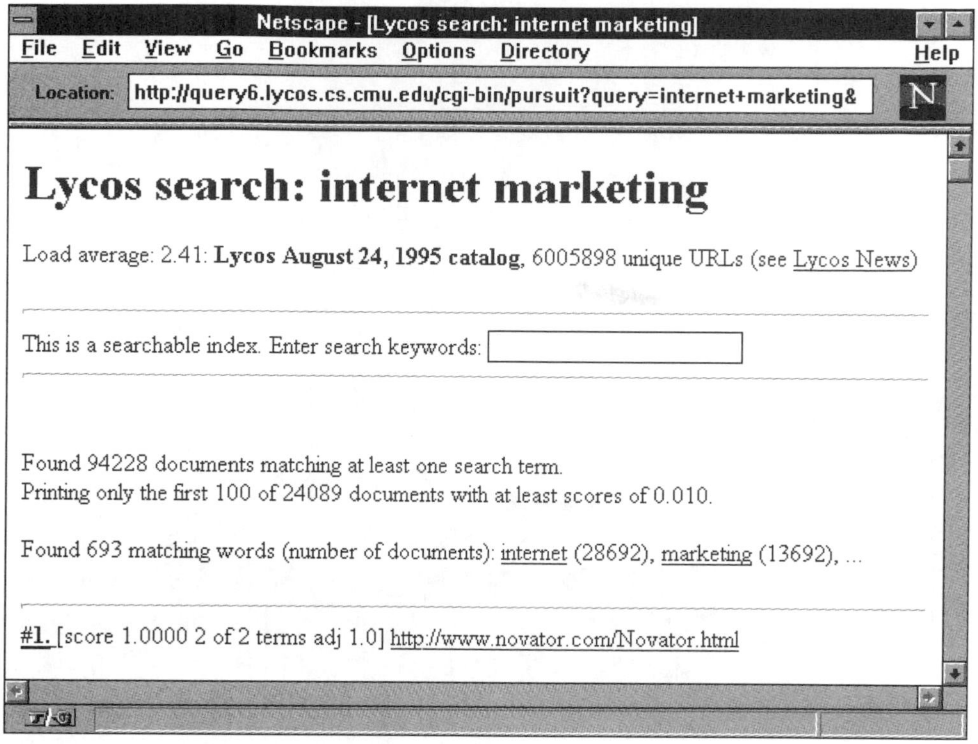

Figure 11.10 The search results from Lycos.

- CUSI: *http://pubweb.nexor.co.uk/public/cusi/doc/list.html*
- Internet Exploration Page: *http://www.amhahl.com/internet/meta-index. html*
- JumpStation II: *http://js.stir.ac.uk/jsbin/jsii*
- Open Text: *http://www.opentext.com*
- WWW Worm: *http://www.cs.colorado.edu/home/mcbryan/WWWW.html*

And from Here...

Part V describes some of the most popular Internet tools for doing business, including e-mail. For more information on Internet searching, have a look at Chapter 14, which covers Veronica (for searching Gopher) and Archie (for finding files on the Internet).

The Other Internet Tools

CHAPTER 12

Electronic Mail

Electronic mail (e-mail) is the most popular of the Internet tools. It is also the easiest to use, and the most frequently used by businesses. It is the key Internet resource for most people, and may be the first reason for a business to get connected to the Internet. E-mail is used for:

- Sending single or multiple messages to individuals
- Sending single or multiple messages to several individuals, or to groups of associated users
- Sending text files
- Sending binary items (such as a spreadsheet data files or graphics)
- Distributing electronic newsletters, flyers, and magazines
- Broadcasting notices or updates to a group of individuals
- Supporting business functions

I typically receive 150–200 e-mail messages a day. They include messages from various discussion lists that I have joined, related to professional and personal interests. They also include communications with colleagues and companies that I am working with on a variety of projects. Other messages come from an electronic news clipping service, my former graduate students, and friends and relatives around the world.

Overview

In the electronic maze of the Internet, e-mail is perhaps the simplest tool for the business user to access and utilize in corporate communication. In addition, it is available on the greatest variety and number of computing systems and Internet access providers. E-mail, like its counterpart, postal mail (often called "snail mail" on the Internet), can be used to send all manner of letters and documents.

An important thing to remember about e-mail is that of the 50 million or so people with Internet access, by far the vast majority of them have e-mail access. (Only 25 or so million have other Internet tools such as the World Wide Web, FTP, and Telnet.) E-mail therefore becomes very important for doing business on the Internet.

It can be used to exchange not only messages, but almost any material that can be stored electronically on a computer. It makes the distribution of material to individuals or groups easy, and allows for impromptu, *ad hoc* group conferencing and working groups, making it a powerful tool for business and corporate users. It is also a popular format for customer feedback and technical support.

There are numerous other advantages to e-mail communication:

- *E-mail is fast.* Messages are often delivered in minutes, as opposed to the weeks or months that "snail mail" can take in some parts of the world. You can exchange numerous messages in the time it would take to send one piece of mail via the post office or even via one of the express document delivery services. In fact, during times of low message traffic, delivery takes just a few seconds. If, by chance, the recipient of the message happens to be online at the time that your message is received, a response may be back in minutes.

- *E-mail is inexpensive.* Messages can often be sent for less than the cost of a first-class stamp, and with most Internet providers, the cost is the same whether a message is going across the street or to the far side of the world. With many Internet access providers, after you pay a monthly fee, all e-mail messages are free.

- *E-mail is convenient.* E-mail can be read and sent at work, home, or anywhere, and at any time that a computer can be hooked up to a phone line. Business travelers find this particularly useful, since it eliminates most concerns about time zone differences, and reduces the dependence on the home office for sending and receiving messages.

- Many VBPs (Very Busy Persons) will respond more readily to e-mail than to some other forms of communication because it is more convenient.

You should be aware of some further characteristics of e-mail:

- *E-mail is not a fully secure medium.* Unlike postal mail, your messages can be read by others either intentionally or unintentionally, such as system administrators or individuals with access authority. The confidentiality of the postal and telephone systems is established in law, but that of e-mail is still in flux. While this is not a big problem on the Internet, you can't assume confidentiality, so exercise caution in sending certain financial, personnel, or proprietary information. Encryption for security and authentication (proving identity) is a hot topic on the Internet, and you can expect new protocols and algorithms to be available in the near future which will make e-mail more secure and useful. Currently, Pretty Good Privacy (PGP) is useful for providing authentication and encryption through public/private keys for verification. (Chapter 7 explores issues surrounding security and authentication.)

- *E-mail is a form of asynchronous communication.* Information does not flow in both directions at once as it does in a telephone conversation. As with postal mail, a "conversation" is made up of a series of messages and replies. This asynchronous method makes communication across time zones much easier. Unlike postal mail, however, e-mail combines advantages of synchronous and asynchronous systems: Like letters, e-mail messages can be composed, sent, and read at any convenient time and at many locations; and, as on the telephone, messages travel quickly (sometimes they are delivered within seconds).

- *The formality of e-mail varies according to your purpose.* Most messages are very informal, but some emulate "snail mail" by having a letterhead and using formal formats, styles, and language.

- *E-mail messages may be fugitive unless you make a point of downloading and saving them.* Some internal company systems, access providers, and mailer software will even delete messages if they are left in the electronic in- or out-box too long.

Understanding E-mail Addresses

To use e-mail, you need an account with an Internet access provider or with your company or organization, and a computer address. That is to say, an e-mailbox is needed—a "place" to send and receive e-mail. Addresses for e-mail are like postal addresses in some ways. For example, a postal address might look like this:

John Grandstaff
New York Stock Exchange
Wall Street
New York, NY 12345

Via the Internet, John Grandstaff's address might be something like this:

`jgrandstf@nyse.sec.com`

An Up-Close Look at Internet Addresses

The actual name of your correspondent has almost nothing directly to do with the automated network routing of the e-mail message—all of the routing information is embedded in the address itself. E-mail is called a *store and forward system* because it moves through the Internet by leaps and bounds, guided by the information in the header. Internet addresses typically have a form that looks like this:

m_smith@jupiter.cedar.com

- **m_smith** This is the individual's name as known to the local computer that collects and processes his or her e-mail. Some systems allow users to use full first and last names, others confine the user to cryptic names and/or numbers such as *msmit01*. In all cases, however, there are no spaces allowed, so the underline or dash character is often used instead of a space, for example: *digi_com* or *oak-ridge.com*.

- **@** The @ (at) sign is used to separate the individual user's name from the rest of the address.

- **jupiter** Like pets, ships, and big buildings, computers on the Internet have names. This is the name of the computer that collects m_smith's e-mail. In other words, m_smith is @ (at) jupiter.

- **.cedar** This represents the name of a group of computers (of which jupiter is one) that are connected together and operated by a group or organization. Often, computers in a cluster have related names, like saturn, mars, and pluto. (Or pluto, goofy, and mickey!)

- **.com** Within the United States, a three-letter designator usually identifies the type of Internet network. Table 12.1 shows Internet user types. In addresses outside of the United States, this three-letter domain name is usually replaced by a two-letter country designator. Some are easy to figure out, like .fr for France or .uk for United Kingdom, but some are more obscure, like .za for South Africa or .pn for Pitcairn Island.

Return to Sender, Address Unknown

Just as with a phone number, one wrong letter or number in the address could unintentionally send your e-mail to someone that shouldn't have received it, or it could result in a "bounced message" which is returned to your e-mail box.

Notice that the computer group name and the user type (or country code) are each preceded by a single period (usually said "dot"). Notice, too, that the address is given in lowercase letters. Most systems on the Internet are case insensitive for Internet traffic, but not all are. It is best to observe carefully the case of any addresses you receive from others (check the header of their messages to you), but generally, using lowercase letters will work with most sites. Table 12.1 contains a list of Internet network types or domains that are used in the United States.

Table 12.1 Internet network (domain) types.

Code	Network (Domain) Types
.com	Business and commercial users
.org	Organizations and nonprofit groups
.mil	Military and related groups
.gov	Nonmilitary government and related groups
.edu	Educational institutions
.net	Network service providers

There are numerous conventions for mail addressing to commercial, European, and Asian sites which may involve many other symbols and signs, leading Brendan Kehoe in *Zen and the Art of the Internet* to call this addressing "the symbolic cacophony." Some networks use exclamation marks (!), called "bangs," in their addresses. Information on the more unusual addressing schemes can be found in *!%@:: A Directory of Electronic Mail Address and Networks* (Frey and Adams, 1990).

E-mail travels well beyond the Internet backbone, to and from many associated nets and commercial services such as MCImail, America Online (AOL), CompuServe, Prodigy, the MicroSoft Network, SprintMail, and ATTmail. These commercial services have different addressing conventions (see Table 12.2).

E-mail on Commercial $ervices

Some commercial services charge their users for receiving mail (by item and/or by size), so be sure that the message will be useful and not too large.

Table 12.2 E-mail address conventions for commercial service providers.

Service	Address Example
America Online	Maryjones@aol.com
Applelink	Maryjones@applelink.apple.com
ATTmail	Maryjones@attmail.com
CompuServe	12345.678@compuserve.com (the comma used on CompuServe user IDs changes to a period when e-mail is sent from an Internet address)
Delphi	Maryjones@delphi.com
Genie	Maryjones@genie.geis.com
MCImail	Mary_Jones@mcimail.com
Prodigy	Maryjones@prodigy.com
Sprintmail	/PN=Mary.Jones/O=anycom/ADMD=telemail/ C=US/@sprint.com

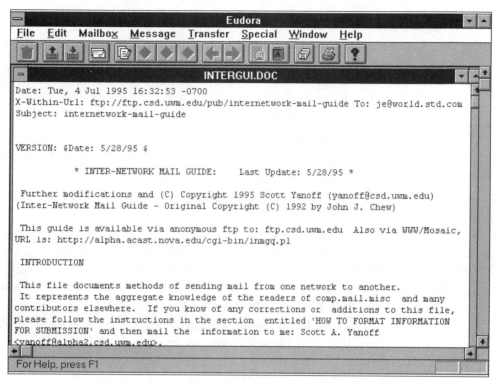

Figure 12.1 The InterNetwork Mail Guide.

More information on mail and gateways can be obtained from *The InterNetwork Mail Guide* (Figure 12.1) which can be browsed via WWW at *http://alpha.acast.nova.edu/cgi-bin/inmgq.pl*, or obtained through FTP at *ftp://ftp.csd.uwm.edu/pub/internetwork-mail-guide*. (Remember that a WWW browser can be used to obtain FTP files with this URL.)

Proliferation of E-mail Addresses

An individual or business can have numerous e-mail addresses. Many business people have one e-mail account for work, and another one from an ISP for personal use.

Locating E-mail Addresses

Locating an e-mail address can be simple: Just call the individual on the phone and ask. This is not, however, the usual method, nor is it always feasible. Sometimes, finding an e-mail address is tricky—there is no one listing of all Internet addresses. A variety of tools have been developed for locating a person, machine, or node:

- White pages directories (essentially, electronically stored telephone books) are maintained by several groups, most notably the Knowbot Information Service (KIS), which maintains experimental online electronic white pages designed to help you locate e-mail addresses. It can be found at *http://info.cnri.reston.va.us/kis.html*.

- A WWW interface for The Internet Tools Summary covering a large number of services can be found at the URL *http://www.rpi.edu/Internet/Guides/decemj/itools/internet-tools.html*. Specifically, information on searching for people is located at *http://www.rpi.edu/Internet/Guides/decemj/icmc/internet-searching-people.html*.

- At the Info Bank's WWW page (*http://www.clark.net/pub/global/find.html*) there are assembled a large number of links to services to help you locate addresses, including Knowbot, Whois, Netfind, and other sites.

- Using Gopher (explained in Chapter 14), you can search for phone books, and you will be presented with a menu of electronic phone books from cities, campuses, organizations, and businesses. (Currently, over 500 phone books are available to search.)

- Netfind is a utility designed to locate machine and node names at institutions, and can help you locate people at those sites. To use Netfind, point your browser to *gopher://ds.internic.net:4320/1netfind*.

- For more information on finding addresses, read the "Finding-Addresses" FAQ, which provides detailed information on this subject: *http://www.cis.ohio-state.edu/hypertext/faq/usenet/finding-addresses/faq.html*.

- Many Internet access providers and institutional systems allow for remote testing of an address, using a utility called *finger*. Finger will return information about the remote user and his or her login activity. Type **finger** *user@node* (for example, **finger jgrandstf@nyse.sec.com**).

Most sites have an e-mail postmaster or a staff member who maintains the e-mail functions for the company or institution. You can send e-mail to **postmaster@***address*, with a request for assistance in locating someone. (Replace *address* with the specific Net address, for example, **postmaster @nyse.sec.com**).

There is an address database of those who have posted messages to Usenet groups that can be queried using e-mail. Send an e-mail message addressed to **mail-server@rtfm.mit.edu**. There is no need for a subject field entry. In the body of the message put: **send usenet-addresses/***name* (replacing *name* with the actual name you wish to locate).

Commercial providers such as AOL and CompuServe will allow their own members to search a membership list. CompuServe, for example, will allow searches by last name, first name, state, and city.

How to Use E-mail

There are numerous mail programs for a full variety of computing platforms. Different software requires different techniques and processes. In the appendixes and chapters on Telnet, FTP, Gopher, and other Internet tools, this book gives you step-by-step directions. For e-mail, general principles and some examples will be discussed, but you will need to read your documentation for the specifics of your system.

The particular commands and techniques that you will use when sending and receiving e-mail will vary depending upon the services and software that you use. Learning basic e-mail commands and techniques, however, will greatly enhance your understanding of what your particular e-mail host can be expected to do.

There are four major methods for handling e-mail tasks:

- Shell accounts—Often UNIX, often using the Pine e-mail program
- SLIP/PPP accounts—Often using programs like Eudora and Pegasus
- Commercial services—Usually using proprietary interfaces
- Corporate services—Using the software supplied by your employer, ranging from custom interfaces to off-the-shelf applications

Increasingly, mail programs are being bundled or integrated with Web browser software as in the case of Netscape 2.0. The fastest growing segment is the SLIP/PPP method, explained below.

Sending and Receiving E-mail

For many people, access to e-mail is gained through company or institutional computing systems, sometimes through IBM or VAX/VMS environments, LANs, or UNIX systems. You may already have an Internet e-mail address and not know it—call your computer user assistance staff and ask! These people are often in the MIS department.

Getting online may mean learning to connect to a corporate system, to a LAN, or to your Internet Services Provider. Virtually any system that handles Internet mail will have some kind of mail program installed. If you are using a SLIP/PPP account with an ISP, you can use any number of mail programs on your local machine. Eudora and Pegasus are just two examples.

All mail programs have a set of commands or menus that allow you to send and receive mail, but they vary in their capabilities for composing, editing, and managing messages. Some require that you compose the message as a file outside the mail program, and some will not let you edit it before sending. Others, however, provide much more user-friendly features such as full-screen editing, named electronic file folders for storing and organizing received messages, spell-checking, and various sort and search utilities to help you to manage your messages.

E-mail software often contains provisions for functions equivalent to those used with paper-based mail. You can carbon copy (cc) or blind carbon copy (bcc) someone, forward mail, request a return receipt, and send a reply. The reply function will have a method for extracting the address of the sender and the subject line. This will help you to send a return message without having to type in the address or subject line. Use caution with this, since you may have received the message via a list or via another person, and the reply might then go to the wrong person. Each mailer treats the reply function differently; some mailers will reply to the sender, others will reply to the address identified in the *From:* field. Read the program documentation for the particular details of your mailer. The reply function will be particularly useful when managing discussion list

Table 12.3 E-mail commands.

Command	Meaning
compose/create	To create an e-message (usually starts the process of addressing, typing in the subject, composing the message, etc.)
reply	To reply to a message taking the address information from the received mail's header
file save or extract	To convert the message(s) into a separate ASCII file
delete	To erase a message
forward	To send a received message on to another user
open/view	To open a message for reading
queue/send	To send the message immediately or put it into a queue (or out-box) for batch sending
attach	To attach a file to the message (a text file, or a binary file like a spreadsheet, database, or word processor document)

messages. (See Chapter 13 for more information on the discussion lists.) Most mailers have commands like those shown in Table 12.3.

In addition, many mail programs will let you scan or sort existing messages by subject and sender, print messages, and place messages in a wastebasket folder until you exit the program (as opposed to getting rid of them instantly). Some systems will allow you to filter the messages as they arrive, automatically putting them into separate in-boxes or folders. Most mail systems also will alert you when you first log in that you have new mail waiting, and some will notify you with a beep when new mail has arrived.

The specific command structure and mailing procedures differ depending upon the particular mailer provided by your local system or access provider, but the following procedure is typical of many Windows-based mailers.

After launching your mail program (such as Eudora, shown in these figures), to create a new message, you will begin the process by clicking on the **Message** menu and choosing **New**, as shown in Figure 12.2. This menu provides options for creating a new message, replying, forwarding messages, and for attaching files.

When you have clicked on New Message, you will be presented with the New message pane as seen in Figure 12.3. Fill in the fields as follows:

1. **To**: Identify the recipient with the user's complete e-mail address.

2. **From**: Most mailers such as Eudora and Pegasus will automatically fill in this field with your own e-mail address. If not, enter your complete address.

3. **Subject**: Enter the subject of the message in this field.

4. **Cc**: Enter the full e-mail addresses of individuals to receive "carbon copies" of the message. Some people cc themselves as they do with postal mail. (Don't you find the reference to carbon paper interesting in an electronic environment?)

5. **Bcc**: Enter the full e-mail address of those individuals to receive a blind carbon copy of the message.

6. In the message pane you can then enter your message. Many mailers have word wrap and spell checking to make this easier.

7. You may then choose to **Queue** the message for sending later, **Send** the message at once, or simply file it to work on later by closing it or saving it.

The mail can be sent to individuals, such as *steve@west.com*, a program, such as *archie@sura.net*, or a mailing list, such as *internet-marketing@popco. com*.

Make the subject entries descriptive. A subject that says "Re: your mail" is not very helpful to a busy person with dozens of e-mail messages to sort through, but one that says "Marketing meeting on Friday canceled" is much more useful and likely to be read.

Using Your Browser to Send E-mail

While using a good mail program will be your usual method for managing your mail needs, it is possible to send mail on-the-fly while using a Web browser. In Netscape, for example, choose the **File** pull-down menu, and then **Mail Documents**. You will be presented with a form to send an HTML or text document that you are browsing, post it to a newsgroup, or just send a simple mail message. In other browsers, this function can often be found under the **Tools** menu.

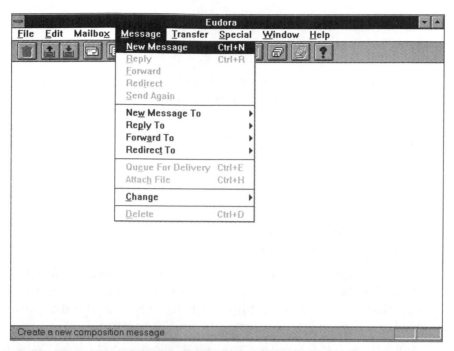

Figure 12.2 The Message pull-down menu in Eudora.

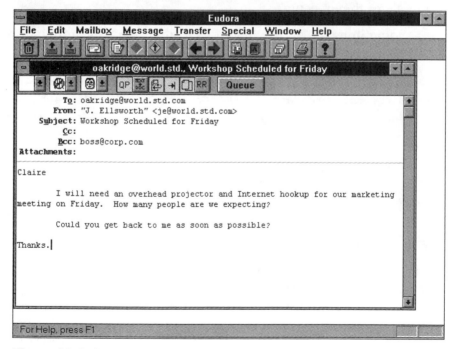

Figure 12.3 The New Message pane in Eudora.

Sig Files

It is common to include what is called a sig (or .sig—"dot sig") at the end of e-mail messages. This is a short identifier that may include your name, company name, phone and fax numbers, e-mail address, URL, and sometimes, a short quotation or thought. Most business users find that the sig file offers them a chance to have a small advertisement for their business. The e-mail program can be directed to automatically append this information at the end of your message.

It is a good idea to be cautious with sayings and quotations (especially humorous ones), since the Internet crosses so many cultural boundaries, and thus your sig may be misunderstood.

Many mail programs allow you to have several different sig files to append to the message. In Eudora, choose the **Window** menu, and choose **Signature** or **Alternate Signature** to create and edit these files; in Pegasus, choose **File**, **Preferences**, and **Signatures**.

Sig files of more than five lines are considered to be a breach of netiquette, since some users pay for their e-mail based on the size of the messages they receive.

Sometimes the sig file includes a small ASCII graphic, or a discrete advertisement, for example:

```
=-=-=-=-=-=-=-=-=-=-=-=-=-=-=-=-=-=-=-=-=-=-=-=-=-=-=-=-=-=-=-=-=-=-
Harrison Grandstaff     GHG Computing        g01@greyhound.ghg.com
Business Phone: 555-555-5555                 FAX: 555-555-5555
Are you looking for Internet Business Consulting?
                                        We Provide Solutions!!!
For more information, send a message to:
info@greyhound.ghg.com
=-=-=-=-=-=-=-=-=-=-=-=-=-=-=-=-=-=-=-=-=-=-=-=-=-=-=-=-=-=-=-=-=-=-
```

E-mail Management

Many mail programs allow you to create an address book—a vehicle for storing your frequently used addresses. With those long cryptic strings of numbers and characters, it can be a real time-saver. Address books can also facilitate group messaging. Eudora calls its address books Nicknames, and you can have a nickname for individuals and for groups of people as a distribution list. By using the Nickname of a group in the To: field, you can send one message to each person in the group.

Eudora and many other mail programs provide for the arrangement of your messages in "mailboxes" and "folders." A **Mailbox** pull-down menu is shown in Figure 12.4.

E-mail message management will differ by user, platform, and system. Depending upon the particular mail services you use, you may read mail online, or download it all at once for reading and management on a personal computer. Because of the volume of mail and files that is generated by becoming active on the Internet, information management is absolutely critical. Once the files are on your personal machine, it is best to organize the messages by category or subject thread, using subdirectories, floppy disks, zip disks, and so on. Text and file search programs are valuable in making the downloaded files useful.

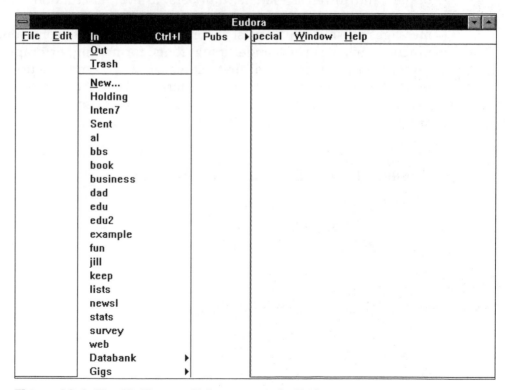

Figure 12.4 The Mailbox pull-down menu in Eudora.

One Very Small Caution

One very small caution—not all e-mail messages are authentic. They may have been sent by someone other than the named sender, or the text may have been changed. This does not happen very often, but a small grain of salt may assist you in sorting through odd messages. A new mail specification under development called Secure/Multipurpose Internet Mail Extensions (S/MIME) will enable secure e-mail. (See the discussion of security and authentication in Chapter 7.)

Creating Emphasis in E-mail

Generally, e-mail messages are sent in ASCII (7-bit format), which contains upper- and lowercase letters, numbers, a few punctuation marks, and some control codes. Because the Internet involves millions of computers, messages must use this lowest common denominator to communicate. In practice, this means no underlining, fonts, formatting, or graphics. This can be a little frustrating at first. However, with some practice, you can learn to accentuate words by using asterisks, dashes, or carets. For example, emphasis is usually expressed *this* way or as pseudo _underlining_. (See Chapter 6 for more information on *communicons*.)

Don't Type E-mail in All Capital Letters

Don't try to create emphasis or a sense of urgency in your e-mail message by typing it in ALL CAPITAL LETTERS. This is considered rude—it is the electronic equivalent of shouting.

Understanding Message Headers and E-mail That Goes Awry

When you receive Internet e-mail, you cannot fail to notice one of its most striking characteristics: its long, complex header that seems to go on and on, with many lines iterating and reiterating the sender, the receiver, some intermediary routing information, when it was sent and received, and message identifications.

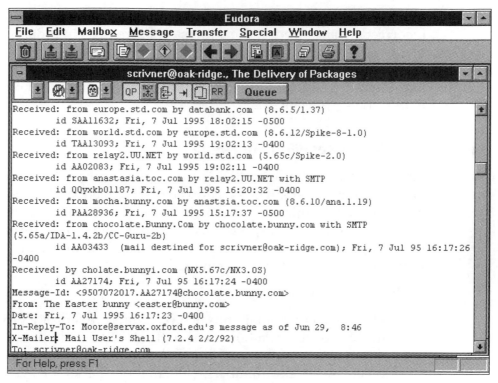

Figure 12.5 An example of an e-mail header.

Headers can take 40 lines or more, as you can see from Figure 12.5. Although they are complex and confusing at first, with practice, they become decipherable. Fortunately, you can ignore most of the information they contain, or set your mailer to conceal these—Eudora, for example, has a button called Blah, Blah, Blah (really!) that you can use to toggle between full and shortened headers. Unless you need to do some troubleshooting, just ignore headers. Most users need only to be concerned with the *Date:*, *From:*, and *Subject:* fields toward the bottom of the header.

From time to time, a piece of e-mail, like postal mail, is undeliverable. "Bounced mail" is e-mail that has been returned to the sender because of an incorrect address, an unknown host, an unknown user, faulty hardware or software, hardware or transmission lines that are malfunctioning ("down"), and so forth. It is here that the header becomes important in figuring out what happened. The first step in troubleshooting bounced mail is to check the exact spelling, case, and syntax of the address. The most frequent error made is typographical: Simply, the address was incorrectly transcribed. If the address appears to be in order, resend the message after a few hours, since the second most frequent problem is that the system linkages are temporarily down. Finally, the local sysadmin may be able to help, or a message to the postmaster at the remote site may help resolve problems.

How to Send Computer Files via E-mail

There are two common methods for sending computer files (or *binary files*) with regular e-mail messages: The first is called MIME, and the other is UUENCODE. This is especially important, since business users often need to send formatted spreadsheets, graphs, and word processing files to colleagues. In addition, you can send images, sounds, and animated files using UUENCODE (see below).

First, a couple of definitions:

- **ASCII**—When 7 binary bits of on/off data are sent as a group, there are 128 possible combinations. In the ASCII standard, each of these combinations is assigned a meaning: one of the uppercase letters, lowercase letters, numbers, punctuation marks, or symbols. The Internet uses this ASCII standard for transferring e-mail. ASCII files are often called "text" files.

- **Binary**—While ASCII files are, in fact, binary, in the sense that they are made of groupings of binary numbers (0s and 1s), when you see the term "binary" it usually refers to 8-bit files—that is, files where eight binary numbers are sent as a group. Eight binary numbers in a group allow for 256 possible combinations. Unlike ASCII, binary code has no standard assignment for what each of these 256 numbers means—the meaning has only to do with their use with specific software programs. The number 212, for example, might mean "draw a blue dot" in a graphics program or "start showing letters in bold" in a word processor file. Examples of binary files include spreadsheet and word processor files, graphics files (such as .PCX and .GIF), some database files, and software program files.

In Eudora, if you wish to attach a text or binary file to the message, pull-down the **Message** menu and **Attach a file**. On the toolbar of the message pane you may choose to attach the file in MIME, Bin-Hex, or

UUENCODED format. In Pegasus, press the **Attach** button, and fill in the resulting form.

MIME

This is not about Marcel Marceau. A special protocol called MIME (Multipurpose Internet Mail Extension, RFC 1341) can be used by some mail programs to distribute and receive binary files such as digitized pictures and executable programs if the MIME protocol is available on both the sending and receiving machines. Created in 1992 by the Internet Engineering Task Force (IETF), it is a set of information exchange standards for non-ASCII e-mail. Secure MIME is a new protocol you will be seeing more frequently as well; for example, it is available in Netscape 2.0.

Not all mailers support MIME. When a mailer that does not support it receives a MIME message, it will display all of the ASCII information, but only a notation about the items that cannot be processed. MIME-capable mailers allow word processing documents, spreadsheets, images, audio, and other binary data to be attached to an e-mail message. Multimedia mail also allows for information in alternative formats to be attached at the same time, so that it can be read by a variety of mailers. Check with your correspondents to determine if they can receive MIME attachments. It is in increasingly common usage, but users who are on an internal LAN may have trouble with MIME. (Further information on MIME is available from *http://ww.oac.uci.edu/indiv/ehood/MIME/MIME. html.*)

Using UUENCODE and UUDECODE to Mail 8-Bit Files

There are several programs available that will allow you to encode a binary file and send it through regular e-mail. These programs encode files, they do not compress them. In fact, encoded files are larger than the binary files you started with. (Some mail programs such as Eudora will do all this for you.)

The sender encodes the file, inserts it in an e-mail message, and sends it. The recipient retrieves the message as usual, and then typically extracts it or saves it to a file, then decodes the file.

While the Internet has devised several systems that allow transfer of binary files (such as FTP), the Internet e-mail system is based on ASCII.

You can, however, send binary files through e-mail if you first convert them from binary to ASCII. Then, the recipient of your message converts the files from ASCII back into binary. A popular method for doing this is to use UUENCODE and UUDECODE.

UUENCODE is a program that can convert binary (8-bit) files, such as word processor files, spreadsheets, computer programs, and graphics images, into ASCII (7-bit) files. UUDECODE is a program that can convert ASCII (7-bit) UUENCODEd files back into exact copies of the binary (8-bit) files that they came from.

Finding and Getting UUENCODE and UUDECODE

From the Internet, uuencode.com and uudecode.com are available by FTP from wuarchive.wustl.edu in the */mirrors/msdos/starter* subdirectory using your browser, or FTP at the command line (see Appendix C for information on using FTP). If you can't locate these programs at that site, do an Archie search for uuencode.com and uudecode.com. Also, since these programs are so popular, you can get them from commercial services such as CompuServe, and from many free local dial-up BBSs.

Using UUENCODE in the DOS Environment

Suppose you want to send a spreadsheet file to a business associate. While some spreadsheets, databases, and word processors will allow you to save the data in ASCII format, you would lose all the special formatting, formulas, fonts, boldfacing, and other styling elements. Assuming the file you want to send is named january.wks and is located in the *c:\expenses\ atlanta* subdirectory of your PC, taking the following steps will convert this binary file to a mailable ASCII file:

1. Change to the subdirectory where you have stored the UUENCODE program using the cd command. For example, if you've stored it in a directory called *convert* in your *utility* subdirectory, at the prompt, you would type in **cd c:\utility\convert**.

2. Now type **dir** at the prompt to confirm that the UUENCODE program is there.

3. To do the actual conversion, at the DOS prompt type **UUENCODE** followed by the full path and name of the file to be converted, followed by a space, followed by the full path of where you would

like the converted file to be stored, including your new name for that converted file. If you want the file stored in the *temp* subdirectory and you want to call it jan-exp.uu, then the full command line would look like this:

```
C:\utility\convert\uuencode > c:\expenses\atlanta\
january.wks c:\temp\jan-exp.uu
```

The original binary file itself is not moved or changed in any way by this procedure.

In a few seconds the DOS prompt will return, the conversion will be complete, and jan-exp.uu will be ready for uploading and e-mailing. You can take a look at this converted file if you want to, but if you use a word processor, be very careful not to alter the file in any way or to "save" it—just view the file and then close it without changes. What you will see when viewing the file is line after line of uniform length, containing letters, numbers, and characters, without spaces.

For details on how to upload this file to your Internet e-mail host computer, see Appendix E. For details on how to send an encoded or any other kind of ASCII file, see the information on sending files earlier in this chapter.

Using UUDECODE in the DOS Environment

Looking at UUENCODEd files and becoming aware of their characteristic appearance is helpful, since you may get files or messages that are encoded without your correspondent or file source mentioning this. When you view one of these files, if you are not familiar with the file's appearance, you may think that your mail program has gone berserk. If you have the UUDECODE program on your PC and you download an encoded message or file, follow these steps to convert it:

1. Change to the directory where the UUDECODE program is stored—for example; *cd c:\utility\convert.*

2. At the prompt, type **UUDECODE** followed by the name of the ASCII file containing the encoded binary file, followed by the path to the directory where you want the binary file stored. No name is needed for the binary file, since it will have the same name that the original binary file had when it was converted. The full command line, along with the prompt supplied by your computer, might look like this:

```
C:\utility\convert\uudecode > c:\download\from-bob.txt c:\database\
```

This would convert the file from-bob.txt from ASCII to a binary file that will be stored in the *database* subdirectory.

Don't worry about any message headers, .sig files, or other text in the message as long as it comes either before the word "begin" or after the word "end." If, however, some lines of text have gotten into the encoded material, they will need to be edited out. It is best to use a simple editor that does not do formatting, rather than a full word processor, since many word processors change margins or add characters, even when they are directed to "save as ASCII."

Windows UUENCODE/DECODE

There is a Windows version of UUENCODE/DECODE called UU Coder that has a user-friendly interface, created by Bruce Sabalaksey. The menus are very basic, with choices for **File** and **Configure** to start with. Choosing **File** presents you with just two choices: **encode** and **decode**. Choosing **encode** will prompt you for a file name; type it in and click on **OK**. The program will then suggest an output file name and path. Clicking on **OK** will initiate the encoding process.

Choosing **decode** from the **File** menu is the reverse process—choose the file to be decoded, and the program will automatically decode the file, using the embedded file name for the new file.

Special E-mail Applications

There area two special applications of e-mail that have proven to be particularly useful to business users: automated e-mail (mail servers, or mailbots), and e-mail for work groups.

Automated E-mail

Some e-mail addresses are not the addresses of an actual person; rather, they are addresses of what are called *servers*, or autoresponders. Servers are special computer addresses that use software for automated file distribution. For example, *almanac.@oes.orst.edu* is the address of a server maintained by the Oregon Extension Service. It maintains a large repository of files, among them Project Gutenberg's full-text books. Using your normal e-mail procedures, sending *almanac@oes.orst.edu* the message **send guten alice** would retrieve the full text of Alice in Wonderland.

Many businesses have autoresponders with addresses like **info@big.company.com** or **catalog@bc.com** which will automatically respond by sending out a file of information. Using an autoresponder means that your customers, or those interested in your products, can get information by reply mail. Check with your system operator or ISP about the availability of this kind of service on your system.

Using E-mail with Work Groups

Using e-mail, large groups can be reached as easily as one person, so work groups can communicate even when members are in different locations and time zones. Most mailers will let you create group address entries; for example, one group address entry called **marketing** might have the addresses of all of the people working in the marketing department, or all of the people working in marketing at all enterprise locations worldwide. (In Eudora, you can create group addresses under the **Window** menu under **Nicknames**.) You can also use a group address for an *ad hoc* short-term work team.

Using E-mail to Support Other Business Functions

E-mail forms an important support and enhancement for other Internet functions. The use of a combination of autoresponders and personal e-mail contacts is important for supporting customers and potential customers, particularly in support of your Web pages. To ensure that you can be reached via e-mail and interact with users, it is a good idea to include what is called a "mailto" link in your Web pages. (See Chapter 10 for more information on HTML and HTTP.) The mailto link allows page visitors to send e-mail to you while they are using your pages. On a page this might look something like this:

```
Send your comments to our customer service representative Steve
K. at stevek@oak-ridge.com.
```

By clicking on or choosing that link, a user can send e-mail to you or your business.

In An E-mail–Only World

Some users may have access to the Internet *only* through e-mail. The document called *E-mail as Your Only Tool*, by Bob Rankin, tells you how to access virtually all of the Internet tools using only e-mail. You can retrieve files from FTP sites, use Gopher, search with Archie, Veronica, or WAIS, obtain World Wide Web pages, and access Usenet newsgroups using just e-mail. The URL for this document is *ftp://rtfm.mit.edu/pub/usenet/news.answers/internet-services/access-via-email*.

Finding More Information...

What is the next step?

- Many of the items listed in Part VI, "Business and Professional Resources on the Internet," make use of these e-mail techniques.

- E-mail is particularly useful in creating a business presence on the Internet—Part III of this book will show you how to use e-mail in marketing, customer service, and other business applications.

- Chapter 6 can show you how e-mail can change corporate communications.

- Continue on to the next chapter to learn about one of the most popular uses of e-mail for getting up-to-date information on how to participate in discussions on thousands of topics.

CHAPTER 13

How to Use Discussion Lists

Early in the development of BITNET, e-mail–based discussion lists were originally created to provide the academic and research community with the ability to exchange ideas freely and quickly across long distances. These e-mail–based, subject-related exchange/distribution groups now number in excess of 10,000, and cover almost any subject you can imagine, including a wide variety of business subjects.

As with most Internet resources, the number of groups grows daily. These discussion lists have been compared to all kinds of things: meetings at the water cooler, discussions in employee lounges, presentations and conversations at conferences, and even talk radio. Each list has its own flavor, its mix of how frequently people post, how they post (formally, informally), how much flaming is tolerated, and other style issues. Reading the mail for a time is a good way to discover the customs and the "signal-to-noise ratio" of each list—that is to say, how many informative or interesting messages there are compared to the number of trivial or uninteresting messages.

Using the Internet Discussion Lists

The discussion lists can focus on virtually any topic: popular TV shows, scientific and academic research, current Internet practices, marketing, business practices, anything. They are useful for obtaining up-to-date

255

information, discussing current situations in organizations and industries, networking with colleagues, getting assistance, and more.

After you subscribe to (join) a list, the listserver software will begin e-mailing copies of all messages posted to the list directly to you. (We'll discuss exactly what a listserver is in the following section.) High-traffic lists can generate 30 or more messages a day, while low-traffic lists may generate one message every week or so. Subscribing to several high-volume lists could mean that you find 200 messages in your e-mailbox every morning! Try out a couple of lists before signing up for more, to be sure that the volume of e-mail does not overwhelm the time you have available to read and process it. Often, the best way to get started with the discussion lists is to subscribe to one or two lists and read them for a while before jumping in with both feet. This helps you get a sense of the issues being discussed, the style, and the level of formality of the group.

The lists are maintained, for the most part, by software programs that allow for automated message distribution, management, and retrieval. These programs are sometimes called mail exploders. Some of the most popular list management programs are LISTSERV from L-Soft (created by Eric Thomas), ListProcessor, a UNIX listserver by Anastasios Kotsikonas, Majordomo, and the Mailbase system in the United Kingdom. LISTSERV is the most powerful of these; created in 1986 for IBM mainframes on BITNET, LISTSERV is now ported to VM, VMS, UNIX, Windows NT, and Windows 95. If you are interested in starting your own list, ask your Internet service provider about using a listserver with your account.

Some lists are moderated, while others are not. Most lists allow open, unmoderated posting, with all messages automatically sent to members of the list without screening. Review by a moderator before posting allows for the screening of long, off-topic, or offensive postings. Some moderators have a *laissez-faire* attitude, or choose to direct the list by suggestion or persuasion, while others will even edit messages or combine related messages. Most moderators see themselves as maintaining list civility and keeping the list on track with its stated mission.

Open enrollment lists allow anyone to subscribe, usually letting the user sign up via an automated system with no human intervention. Closed lists, on the other hand, are often exclusively for members of particular organizations or groups with screened subscriptions. There are, for example, lists that are maintained to support ongoing corporate working groups, or for individuals in particular professions, or to serve as communication channels for specialized groups. These lists are typically private and may not be open for subscription without invitation.

Joining Lists

Signing up for, or subscribing to, lists requires an understanding of an important distinction between the *listserver* and the *list* itself. The listserver is the software that handles the tasks (administrivia) associated with list maintenance, including subscription processing, database management, and archiving. The list itself is the group of people who are currently subscribed.

The listserver software acts like an administrative secretary working for a group of, say, salespeople. The secretary handles administrative matters such as typing, filing, and making appointments. The *list* is the group of sales representatives themselves, who, assisted by the administrative secretary, communicate with each other by exchanging memos, messages, phone calls, and information.

Figure 13.1 first shows the traffic of the list, with messages going from one user out to all other members. Below that is the traffic between a single user and the listserver.

Often, messages sent to the listserver are read by computer, not human beings, so additional requests for help or additional information will be ignored or cause the request to be rejected. The software "knows" a limited number of commands that will carry out some basic instructions. To subscribe to a list, you send an e-mail request to the listserver, and if your request is accepted, you will be added to the list and begin receiving messages. Here is an example of a message sent to the administrative address for subscribing to a list:

```
To: listproc@mailer.fsu.edu
Subj: [leave this space blank]
Message:
subscribe market-l Meg Jones
```

This message to subscribe to the *market-l* (Marketing discussion) list is being sent to the address of the software that is managing the list, in this case *mailer.fsu.edu*. Meg's e-mail address does not need to be typed

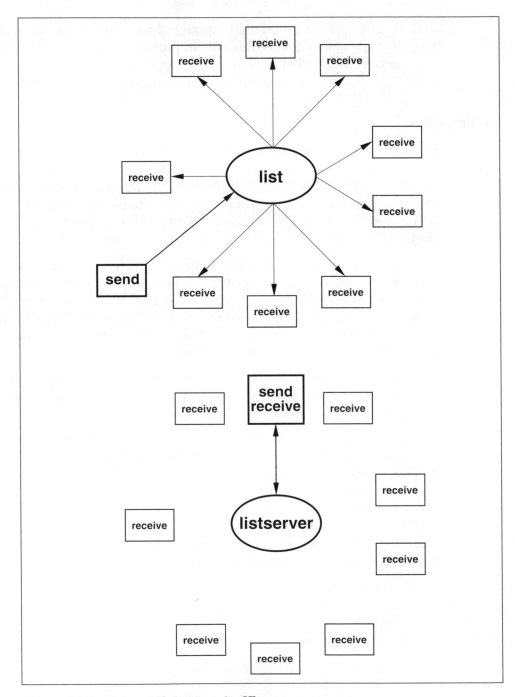

Figure 13.1 List and listserver traffic.

in, since the listserver grabs her e-mail address from her message header. Meg has instructed the listserver to place her on the *market-l* discussion list, and has given the name she wants to be known by on this list. In some cases, the correct syntax to reach a given listserver is to send the message to *listname-request* as with the list *com-priv,* which is concerned with the privatization and commercialization of the Internet: subscribe to *com-priv-request@psi.com.*

When you first subscribe to a list, you will probably receive two standard types of messages. One of these is from the listserver automatic software welcoming you or telling you that you have been added to the list. It often contains instructions for setting up your list options and for unsubscribing. The other message from "the system" shows system CPU use and the address that was extracted from your subscription request header. Always save both messages, as they contain the commands for leaving the list, suspending mail, and searching the archives, which you will need later. These commands differ considerably, depending upon the list moderator or owner. This is my subscription welcome from internet-marketing:

```
Internet Marketing Discussion list info

June 28, 1995

First Frequently Asked Question

Is there a FAQ for this list? This is more or less it.

The topic of marketing and Internet is a broad one and
controversial. This list was established to discuss
*appropriate* marketing of services, ideas, and items to and on
the Internet. At this writing, over 4,400 people and sites
involved in all aspects of marketing, sales, programming,
journalism, and other fields are actively participating in this
forum.

This list is a good source both for people who want to create
Internet sites, market products and goods in appropriate ways,
develop payment systems, or write about what's going on here.

Guidelines and Focus Of List
```

Topics

The topics of this list are limitless, but should be focused around:

How to reach consumers/end-users/purchasers
How to find out how many people are actually out there on the 'Net
How to advertise and market appropriately
Ordering and credit card purchasing, including how to get merchant status
Secure ordering systems (NetSite/SSL, SHTTP, etc.)
Digital cash and related systems (DigiCash, CyberCash, First Virtual Holdings, and other systems)
Trademarks and copyright

Posting Recommendations and Guideline

Be pithy.
Only a few posts per day per person.
New material is better than quoted material.
Posts with inappropriate material will be rejected out of hand. This includes attacks on other people and commercial appeals.
Don't quote entire posts. Please choose the necessary minimum to quote and reply to that.
Please keep signatures (.sig's) to 8 lines or fewer. Longer sigs will be shortened arbitrarily.
Make sure that any quoted material is properly cited (i.e., "Etaoin Shrdlu writes:" followed by the quoted material identified by some mark as quoted lines).

Moderated List

This list is moderated. That means that I review all posts before they get exploded to the list. There are options if you don't like that (see below).

I reject posts on very few grounds. Sometimes, it's because the post is far away from the guidelines above. Mostly, however, it's because the material is sufficiently unrelated to the list.

Getting On and Off the List

Subscribing

To join this list, send a message with any contents and subject (or none) to IM-SUB@POPCO.COM

Unsubscribing

Send a message with any contents or subject (or none) to IM-UNSUB@POPCO.COM

Posting

Posts to this list should be addressed to INTERNET-MARKETING@POPCO.COM

Mail Digests

By default, when you subscribe, you will get the digest. The digest is a daily compilation of posts. To get the list in single-mail-message format (also called NOACK format) send the message to the listproc address above SET INTERNET-MARKETING MAIL NOACK

To change back to the digest form, send SET INTERNET-MARKETING MAIL DIGEST

Sponsor Site

This list was maintained for several months through the generous gift of time, expertise, space, and processor time by EINet <<http://galaxy.einet.net> and Bruce Speyer.

The current site is run by Point of Presence Company, a high-end Web site developer. The moderator and administrator of the list, and president of POPCO is Glenn Fleishman <<glenn@popco.com>.

Other Information on This Topic

Newsgroups

For information in current newsgroups, check out alt.internet.services and alt.internet.media-coverage, and

```
comp.infosystems.www.* for info on internet providers or World
Wide Web issues. Also, look at biz.misc and alt.entrepreneurs.

WWW

Mail archives are at:
http://www.popco.com/hyper/internet-marketing/

Moderator

I've been on the Internet in various forms since 1986. I've
worked as a typesetter, designer, technical support person,
curriculum planner, instructor, and editor. Currently, I have
several lives. I'm the president of Point of Presence Company;
a columnist and contributing editor for Adobe Magazine; and a
freelance feature writer for InfoWorld and the Seattle Times.

Glenn Fleishman, Seattle, Washington
```

Posting a Message to All Members of a List

Now, you can send a message to all of the list members. Your message might look something like the following, depending upon the mailer that you use:

```
To: internet-marketing@popco.com

Subj: Trade Shows

We have been invited to exhibit at the Office Product trade
show in Cobo Hall (Detroit) in November. Has anyone else been
to this show before? If you have, please contact me --I need
some advice about clientele and set-up. Thanks

  <><><><><><><><><><><><><><>
Meg Jones <mjones@sumaron.com>
Marketing                                      555/555-555
Sumaron Industries                         FAX 555/555-555
  <><><><><<><><><><><><><><>
```

In posting to a list, use the reply feature of your e-mail software carefully if you are replying to a message from a list. If you intend the message for one person, do not use the reply feature, or your message will go out to all and sundry on the list. Almost every veteran list member can tell a story or two about a private message that was broadcast to a list—some of these are fairly innocuous, but a few have been embarrassing.

Listserver Commands and Protocols

Most listservers respond to a small group of common commands sent in messages to them such as Meg's request to subscribe. This group of commands depends upon which listserver is managing the list. There are several popular listserver software packages currently in use on the Internet. While they operate in a similar manner, there are some differences, based on both the software and the platform running the software.

Perhaps the most popular software is LISTSERV from L-Soft by Eric Thomas, which runs on a variety of platforms. If you subscribe to a list that is managed by LISTSERV and you send an e-mail message consisting of the word help to the site serving the list (listserv@vm1.nodak.edu, for example), you will get back a quick reference guide to the most common commands:

```
LISTSERV version 1.8b - most commonly used commands

Info       <topic|listname>       Order documentation
Lists      <Detail|Short|Global>  Get a description of all lists
SUBscribe  listname <full name>   Subscribe to a list
SIGNOFF    listname               Sign off from a list
SIGNOFF    * (NETWIDE             - from all lists on all servers
REView     listname <options>     Review a list
Query      listname               Query your subscription options
SET        listname  options      Update your subscription options
INDex      <filelist_name>        Order a list of LISTSERV files
GET        filename filetype      Order a file from LISTSERV
REGister   full_name|OFF          Tell LISTSERV about your name
```

LISTSERV uses more commands than are given by requesting help (AFD, FUI, PW, etc.). Send a message of INFO REFCARD for a comprehensive reference card, or just INFO for a list of available documentation files.

Another popular listserver is ListProcessor by Anastasios Kotsikonas. Again, when you put help in the message to ListProcessor (*listproc @mailer. fsu.edu*, for example), you will get a file of information:

```
                  ListProcessor 6.0

Here is a brief description of the set of requests recognized
by ListProcessor. Everything appearing in [ ] below is
optional; everything appearing in <<>> is mandatory; all
arguments are case insensitive. The vertical bar ("|") is used
as a logical OR operator between the arguments. Requests may be
abbreviated, but you must specify at least the first three
characters.

Keep in mind that when referring to a <<list>>, that list may
be of two kinds: local or remote, unless otherwise noted. When
referring to a local list, your request will be immediately
processed; when referring to a remote list (a list served by
another ListProcessor which this system knows about), your
request will be appropriately forwarded. Issue a 'lists'
request to get a listing of all local and known remote lists to
this ListProcessor.

Recognized requests are:

help [topic]
------------
Without arguments, you receive this file. Otherwise gets
specific information on the selected topic. Topics may also
refer to requests. To learn more about this system issue a
'help listproc' request. To get a listing of all available
topics, generate an error message by sending a bogus request
like 'help me'.
set <list> [<option> <arg[s]>]
------------------------------
Without the optional arguments, get a list of all current
settings for the specified list. Otherwise change the option to
a new value for that list. Issue a 'help set' request for more
information.

subscribe <list> <your name>
----------------------------
The only way to subscribe to a list.
```

```
unsubscribe <list>
signoff <list>
------------------
```
Two ways of removing yourself from the specified list.

```
recipients <list>
review <list>
-----------------
```
Get a listing of all non-concealed people subscribed to the
specified list.

```
information <list>
------------------
```
Get information about the specified list.

```
statistics <list> {[subscriber email address(es)] | [-all]}
-----------------------------------------------------------
```
Get a listing of non-concealed subscribers along with the
number of messages each one of them has sent to the specified
list. If the optional email addresses are given, then
statistics will be collected for these users only. For example:
        stat foo user1will generate statistics about these two
subscribers. "-all" lists statistics for all users that have
posted on the list (whether currently subscribed to not).

```
run <list> [<password> <cmd [args]>]
------------------------------------
```
Run the specified command with the optional arguments and
receive the output from stdout and/or stderr. To get a listing
of all available commands to run, omit the arguments, i.e.
issue a 'run <list>' request. You have to belong to the
specified list, and must have obtained the password from the
list's owner; the owner's address may be found in the
Errors-To: header line of each delivered message. <list> may be
local only.

```
lists
-----
```
Get a list of all local mailing lists that are served by this
server, as well as of all known remote lists.

```
index [archive | path-to-archive] [/password] [-all]
```

```
------------------------------------------------------
```
Get a list of files in the selected archive, or the master
archive if no archive was specified. If an archive is private,
you have to provide its password as well.

get <archive | path-to-archive> <file> [/password] [parts]
```
-----------------------------------------------------------
```
Get the requested file from the specified archive. Files are
usually split in parts locally, and in such a case you will
receive the file in multiple email messages -- an 'index'
request tells you how many parts the file has been split into,
and their sizes; if you need to obtain certain parts, specify
them as optional arguments. If an archive is private, you have
to provide its password as well.

view <archive | path-to-archive>] [/password] [parts]
```
-----------------------------------------------------
```
Same as "get" but in interactive mode just catenates the file
on the screen.

search <archive | path-to-archive>] [/password] [-all] <pattern>
```
----------------------------------------------------------------
```
Search all files of the specified archive (and all of its
subarchives if -all is specified) for lines that match the
pattern. The pattern can be an egrep(1)-style regular
expression with support for the following additional operators:
'~' (negation), '|' and '&' (logical OR and AND), '<' '>'
(group regular expressions). The pattern may be enclosed in
single or double quotes. Note: . matches any character
including new line.

fax <fax-number> <archive | path-to-archive> <file> [/password][parts]
```
----------------------------------------------------------------
```
Same as 'get', but it faxes you the files instead to the
specified number.

release
```
-------
```
Get information about the current release of this ListProcessor
system.

which
```
-----
```
Get a listing of local mailing lists to which you have subscribed.

The popular listserver called Majordomo, by Brent Chapman, offers information in a similar way. You can make a request for help from *majordomo@csn.org*, and get the following:

```
This is Brent Chapman's "Majordomo" mailing list manager,
version 1.93.

In the description below items contained in []'s are optional.
When providing the item, do not include the []'s around it.

It understands the following commands:

    subscribe <list> [<address>]
Subscribe yourself (or <address> if specified) to the named
<list>.

    unsubscribe <list> [<address>]
Unsubscribe yourself (or <address> if specified) from the named
<list>.

    get <list> <filename>
        Get a file related to <list>.

    index <list>
        Return an index of files you can "get" for <list>.

    which [<address>]
Find out which lists you (or <address> if specified) are on.

    who <list>
Find out who is on the named <list>.

    info <list>
Retrieve the general introductory information for the named
<list>.

    lists
Show the lists served by this Majordomo server.

    help
Retrieve this message.

    end
Stop processing commands (useful if your mailer adds a
signature).
```

```
Commands should be sent in the body of an email message to
"Majordomo@lists.csn.net".

Commands in the "Subject:" line NOT processed.
```

A system that is popular in the United Kingdom is the Mailbase system. You can receive a lengthy description of how to use the service by sending the command **send mailbase user-card** in an e-mail message to *mailbase@mailbase.ac.uk*. A comprehensive introduction to Mailbase can be obtained by sending the message **send mailbase user-guide** in a message to *mailbase@mailbase.ac.uk*.

There are other systems, but these are the most common. A guide to the most popular listserver commands is maintained by Jim Milles at *http://lawlib.slu.edu/home.htm*. It can be obtained via e-mail by sending a message containing only the line **get mailser cmd nettrain f=mail** to the listserver, *listserv@ubvm.cc.buffalo.edu*.

Database/Archive Searching

Some lists make previous postings available in a variety of forms for both list members and nonmembers. The index command can be used to obtain these listings of archived information. Some lists group the postings by subject and then distribute them in digest format, while others maintain postings in chronological order. Archives of long documents or documents not sent out to the list members are often available. Some lists have frequently asked questions (FAQ) documents available for new or potential members. In many cases, archives can be searched for items to be retrieved by using the following search structure, sent as the body of a message to the appropriate listserver:

```
To: listserv@ukanvm.cc.ukans.edu
Subj: [blank]
Message:

//
database search dd=rules
//rules dd *
search management in TQM-L
index
/*
```

This search will locate all messages that contain the word "management" in the archives of the Total Quality Management (TQM-L) list, located @ukanvm.cc.ukans.edu, and return a listing of the files containing "management" to you as an e-mail message. To carry out another search, replace "management" with any keyword, "TQM-L" with the list name, and "@ukanvm.cc.ukans.edu" with the address of the listserver. You can then request that the listserver get any files found in the search.

There are many other archiving systems; for example, the internet-marketing list archives are maintained at *http://www.popco.com/hyper/ internet-marketing*.

List and File Management

Some mailers aid the reader in keeping track of the subjects of the discussions by allowing for searching and/or sorting of the subject field. On most lists there are several topics being discussed simultaneously; for example, on one list there might be an ongoing discussion of advertising, acceptable use, and what AT&T and the telcos (telephone companies) are up to, all at once. Each of these subjects is called a *thread*. Some users prefer to follow the subject thread rather than read the messages chronologically as sent. Threads may be tracked, since they usually maintain identical wording in the subject line of each message.

Finding Appropriate Lists

Finding interesting lists can involve looking through several documents and listings, since, surprisingly, there is no master list. Some places to look:

- You can search for appropriate groups by having a look at a Web page at Inter-Links that provides a way of keyword searching— *http://alpha.acast.nova.edu/cgi-bin/lists*. Figure 13.2 shows a search for "marketing," locating 12 lists. Another source of lists is *http://www. tile.net/tile/listserv/index.html*, where you can search by topic as well.

- Useful lists can be found in various of the guides found in The Clearinghouse for Subject-Oriented Internet Resources at *http:// www.lib.umich.edu/chhome.html*.

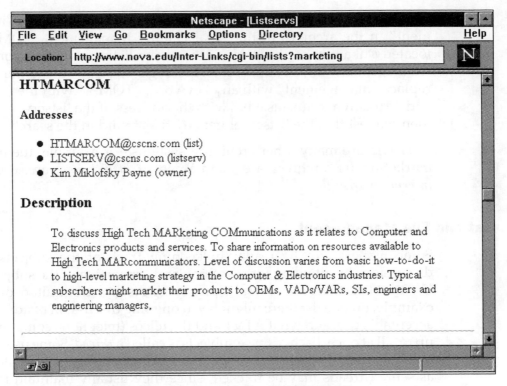

Figure 13.2 The results of a search for "marketing."

- Two documents available from listserv@vm1.nodak.edu are "How to Find an Interesting Mailing List," and "Some Lists of Lists." To get a copy of these, send an e-mail message to the listserver reading:
  - **get new-list wouters**
  - **get listof lists**
- An annotated list of lists can be fetched via FTP from the URL *ftp://ftp.cu.nih.gov:network/interest.groups* (note that the size of this file is currently almost 1 megabyte). It can also be obtained via e-mail: Send a message to mail-server@sri.com with the message **send interest-groups**.
- You can also go to *ftp://rtfm.mit.edu/pub/usenet/news.answers/mail/mailing-lists* and find the files *part1* through *part14*.
- The Internet Dog-Eared Pages can found at the URL *gopher://sunsite.unc.edu/11/ref.d*.

Here are some lists that are focused on discussions of business use of the Internet and marketing:

- *internet-marketing@popco.com*—The premier list for the discussion of all facets of marketing on the Internet. Subscribe to the address *im-sub@popco.com* with a message of **internet-marketing yourname**.

- *com-priv@psi.com*—This list discusses all facets of the commercialization and privatization of the Internet. Subscribe by sending the message **subscribe com-priv yourname** to the address *com-priv-request @psi.com*.

- *ritim-l@uriacc.uri.edu*—Sponsored by the Research Institute for Telecommunications and Information Marketing, ritim-l is a lively discussion list focusing on technology and marketing. Subscribe with a standard listserver subscription.

Usenet Newsgroups

Usenet is an odd phenomenon—descriptions of Usenet almost always include the story of the blind men discussing the elephant, because it is so large and diverse. Often no one has a full understanding of what Usenet is.

Usenet is a worldwide community of discussions called *newsgroups*. Each host on the network pays for its own transmission costs. No one "owns" Usenet—it is a self-regulating network of newsgroups. Some have said that Usenet is the CB on the Internet. It resembles the conferences found on BBS systems, both commercial and nonprofit. Usenet is a group of people posting public messages, often called articles, that are organized by subject category. They are tagged with a standardized set of labels for distribution from site to site.

Generally, Usenet does not allow commercial messages—though the discussion of products you have purchased and how you feel about them is okay as long as there is no financial gain. For most groups, no unsolicited advertising is permitted. Some *alt.* groups have a specific charter stating that commercial messages are fine, and the *biz.* domain encourages commercial discussions (you will see *biz.* at the beginning of the name of the group: *biz.computers*).

The Usenet messages are organized into thousands of topical news-groups (approaching 13,000 now). You read and post (contribute) at your local Usenet site. That site distributes the postings to other sites. The group names are always in lowercase, separated by periods (said "dot"): *comp.fonts*, *misc.forsale*, *rec.skiing*, *sci.archaeology*, or *alt.fan.monty-python*. The group topics are organized hierarchically, going from the general level to the more specific level:

```
rec
rec.sports
rec.sports.baseball
```

The first word in a Usenet name indicates the general topic of the list. Table 13.1 shows the Usenet naming scheme.

Outside of the regular Usenet hierarchies are some unregulated topics. Under unregulated hierarchies, groups can be formed without any regulation as to subject or commercial content and without a formal vote to approve the formation. Usenet has no "management." To start a group, you must poll the readers for permission (except in *alt.*, where you can start a group unimpeded). The groups organized under *biz.*, and under *.biz* under some other classifications (e.g., clari.biz), are quite useful for business or commercial discussions and actual product information. The other groups are good for asking and answering questions, participating in discussions of interests, and getting information on files, programs, and other resources. Table 13.2 shows a few of the unregulated Usenet topics.

Usenet users and sites require special software packages. The software for users, often called a newsreader, allows for thread tracking, and

Table 13.1 The regulated usenet newsgroup names.

Group Name	Topic
comp:	All computer-related topics
misc:	Things that do not fit elsewhere
news:	Happenings around the Internet and networks
rec:	Hobby and recreation
sci:	All the sciences
soc:	Social issues and culture
talk:	Debate-oriented

Table 13.2 The unregulated Usenet newsgroup names.

Group Name	Topic
alt:	Alternatives (highly unregulated, and your taste may be offended)
biz:	Business and commercial
clari:	ClariNet news (ClariNet does not refer to the woodwind instrument; it is the name of the news sponsor)
bit:	Newsgroup echoes
k12:	Education

kill files to sort out what you *don't* want to read. Popular newsreaders are *tin* and *nn* for shell accounts, and *WinVN, Free Agent,* and *News Xpress* for SLIP/PPP accounts running Windows, *Newswatcher* for the Macintosh. Many browsers, including Netscape and the various flavors of Mosaic, can be used to read news as well. In Netscape, for example, you would choose the **Directory** pull-down menu, and then select **Go** to Newsgroups.

To read the news, you have to find a news site. Your Internet access provider may be a news site, and may provide the needed reader software. Most SLIP/PPP accounts have a news server, usually called something like *news1.site.com.* You must locate an online source in order to gain access—there are "readers" available for your local PC, but they can only read the messages you have downloaded from a news site.

The best way to approach Usenet is to start reading some groups of interest. Many newsgroups have a frequently asked questions (FAQ) document full of useful information about the newsgroup and its operation.

Use the Usenet News Finder at *http://alpha.acast.nova.edu/cgi-bin/news.pl* to find useful newsgroups. Figure 13.3 shows a news finder search for business newsgroups.

Frequently Asked Questions Documents

Many mailing lists and Usenet groups have what are called frequently asked questions (FAQ) documents. A FAQ (rhymes with "tack") is struc-

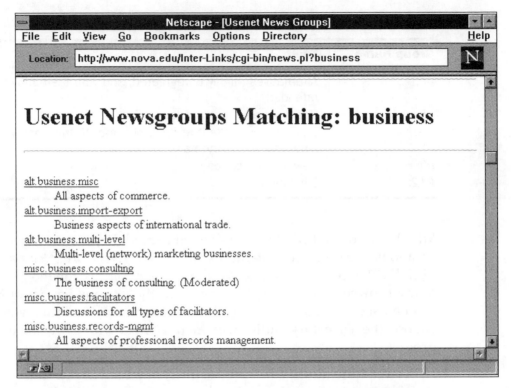

Figure 13.3 The results of a search for business-related Usenet newsgroups.

tured as a list of common questions that a newcomer might have about the group and the subject of the group.

These are the "start here" documents of the Internet. They help avoid discussing the same old subjects over and over. Often these documents have evolved over time.

One good location for getting FAQs is *http://www.cis.ohio-state.edu/ hypertext/faq/usenet/finding-groups/faq.html*.

A typical FAQ might have sections similar to the one shown in Figure 13.4 about the World Wide Web.

For some cases discussion lists and Usenet newsgroups, the FAQ document is posted at regular intervals, sometimes monthly or every two months (or when the moderator thinks the readers need a dose of getting

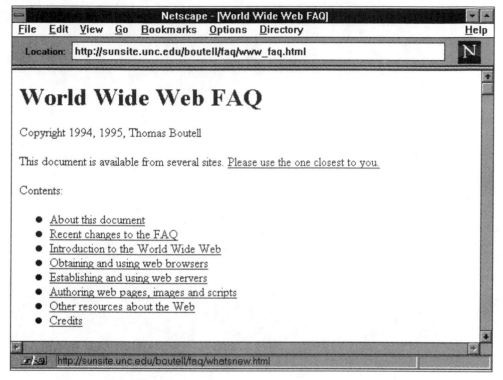

Figure 13.4 World Wide Web FAQ.

organized). Reading the FAQ is very important to understanding the ground rules for each group and list, particularly relating to its tolerance for advertising and marketing activity.

Where from Here...

Newsgroups and discussion lists are important factors in creating and maintaining an Internet business presence. To see how discussion lists and Usenet newsgroups can be used to help your business on the Internet, see Chapters 8 and 9.

CHAPTER 14

Text-Based Internet Search and Navigation Tools

The Internet has an enormous reservoir of information and resources on more than 7 million computer sites. Finding information at all of those sites can be difficult, but the search is made easier by a group of search tools that predate the World Wide Web, but that are still available and still very useful:

- Gopher
- Veronica
- Archie

All three are text based, and therefore they work well even with older, nongraphic personal computers. Most basic shell accounts with Internet access providers offer access to Gopher, Veronica, and Archie.

These search systems are even easier to use, however, with the aid of one of the many Web browsers that are able to navigate these services. To use these services, enter their URL in the appropriate input box just as you enter any normal Web URL. The ways each browser displays and interacts with these services varies from browser to browser, but most functions available in the nongraphic programs are available (and in a few cases, extra functions will be available).

In this chapter the text-based client programs that reside on Internet access providers' computers will be explained. Even if you plan to use a browser, read through these sections to find out what each service is about, and what functions are available.

Gopher

The Gopher system provides an easy-to-use, standardized user interface for finding and retrieving files of all kinds from all over the world. A basic feature of Gopher is that every Gopher session starts with a menu from which files, services, Internet tools, or other menus can be chosen. Some of the menu choices on this top menu lead to other menus, which lead to submenus, which can lead to more submenus, and so on. This huge linked system of menus providing links to services and files is often called *gopherspace*.

Gopher is based on what is called a "client/server" system. That is, client software running on many machines interacts with a smaller number of remote computers running the server software. If you are using a personal computer and a dial-up Internet access provider, you will just need your normal telecommunications software; the Gopher client software is installed on your Internet access provider's machine for all of its customers to use.

Why the name Gopher? Gopher was invented in the "Gopher State" (Minnesota) at the University of Minnesota, whose sports teams are called the "Golden Gophers"; and possibly, too, the name refers to a "gofer," an assistant that finds and delivers things and does all sorts of jobs.

If you are unsure whether your access provider offers Gopher service, you can do a quick check by typing **gopher** at your system's main command line prompt ($, %, >, etc.) and then pressing Enter. If you get a menu similar in style to the one shown in the next section of this book, then you probably have a working Gopher client. You can also go to Gopher sites by typing in the Gopher URL, which will look something like this: *gopher://gopher.std.com*.

A Plain Vanilla Gopher Session

Many Gopher sessions will be as simple as the following one in which Gopher is used to find and read a text file. To start a Gopher session, type

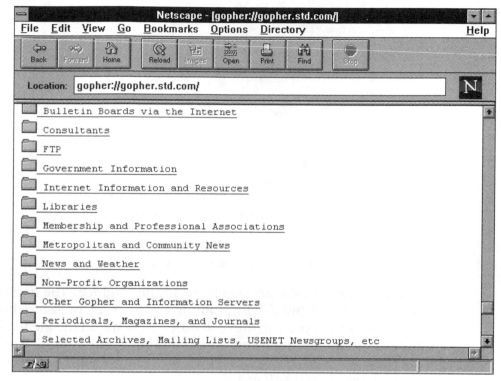

Figure 14.1 Netscape browser viewing a Gopher menu.

gopher at your access provider's main system prompt and press the Enter key. At the access provider World Software Tool & Die (world.std.com), the following screen is displayed. Your screen will probably show different menu choices depending on your access provider. (Figure 14.1 shows a Gopher menu as displayed by a graphical interface browser.)

```
             Internet Gopher Information Client v1.13
                  Root gopher server: gopher.std.com


       1.   Information About The World Public Access UNIX/
 -->   2.   The World's ClariNews AP OnLine & Reuters Newswire Index/
       3.   OBI The Online Book Initiative/
       4.   Internet and Usenet Phone Books/
       5.   Shops on The World/
       6.   Commercial Services via the Internet/
       7.   Book Sellers/
```

```
 8.  Bulletin Boards via the Internet/
 9.  Consultants/
10.  FTP/
11.  Government Information/
12.  Internet Information and Resources/
13.  Libraries/
14.  Membership and Professional Associations/
15.  News and Weather/
16.  Non-Profit Organizations/
17.  Other Gopher and Information Servers/
18.  Periodicals, Magazines, and Journals/
19.  Usenet Newsgroup and Mailing List Archives/
20.  University of Minnesota Gopher Server/
21.  software/


Press ? for Help, q to Quit, u to go up a menu          Page: 1/1
```

The arrow --> indicates which item is highlighted. The first time you see a menu, the arrow will be pointing to item 1. By pressing the up and down arrow keys you can move to different items on the menu. To select an item, press the Enter key. In our example, selecting 2. *The World's ClariNews AP OnLine & Reuters Newswire Index/*, would cause the following submenu to be displayed:

```
            Internet Gopher Information Client v1.13
        The World's ClariNews AP OnLine & Reuters Newswire Index


--> 1. Information About These AP OnLine and Reuters Newswire Indexes.
    2. Search ClariNews AP OnLine Newswire Index <?>
    3. Search Reuters newswire index <?>


Press ? for Help, q to Quit, u to go up a menu          Page: 1/1
```

To read the file *Information About These AP OnLine and Reuters Newswire Indexes*, press the Enter key and the file will be displayed on your screen:

```
The World provides full-text search and retrieval of Associated Press
OnLine and Reuters newswire feeds for the last seven calendar days.
These indexes are updated four times daily.
You will be prompted for words to search for. You can respond with one
```

```
or more words, any articles which contain these words will be listed for
viewing by headline. You can combine more than one search word with the
word "and" in order to limit matches to articles which contain both
words, or "or" for all articles that have either word. For example,
"bill and clinton" would only match articles which contain both the
words "bill" and "clinton" (note that searches ignore upper/lower case.)
If you do not specify "and" or "or" then "or" is assumed.
```

To leave Gopher after reading the file, just press the Enter key and then type in the letter **q**. You will be asked if you really want to leave Gopher with this prompt:

```
Really quit (y/n) ?
```

Since Yes is the default answer, you only need to press the Enter key, and your access provider's main prompt will be displayed again. For just finding and reading a simple short text file, that's all there is to it!

Gopher Sessions with Some Very Useful Bells and Whistles

Gopher can do a lot more than just finding and displaying a text file. It can connect to other sites and services and also find and download binary files of sound, graphics, and other data. This time we'll give Gopher a little more exercise and examine the screens more carefully.

As in the plain vanilla example, at your host system prompt type **gopher** and press the Enter key. Looking back at the first menu screen at world.std.com, you'll note that the first line tells which client software is running (since there are a lot of small differences in how Gopher clients operate, knowing which software is running can be helpful). The second line states: *Root gopher server: gopher.std.com*. This lets you know that this is the top menu (the menu from which all others can be reached) at this site. From wherever you are, in any menu, you can return to this top menu by pressing the **m** key.

Selecting Menu Items

As an alternative to using the up and down arrow keys to select a menu item, you can simply type the number of the menu item you want, and then press Enter.

The diagonal bar / at the right end of a menu item indicates that it leads to another menu rather than directly to a text file. In this example, all of the menu items lead to other menus.

Remembering Where You've Been with Bookmarks

With thousands of menus leading from one to another, it is very easy to get lost, or to find an excellent resource and then forget how to get back to it at a later date. To deal with this, Gopher has a system called "Bookmarks" which allows you to record important resources in a custom menu that you create. This is similar to the bookmarks systems provided by most GUI browsers.

In the following example, we will create several bookmarks, then show how to display a menu of bookmarks so that you can quickly jump to the menus you've marked. First we'll go to *OBI The Online Book Initiative/* menu by selecting item 3 from the root Gopher menu shown previously. The name of this new menu is *The Online Books*. To create a bookmark for *The Online Books*, type an uppercase **A** (**shift-a**)and the box shown near the bottom of the screen below will appear. To accept this as a bookmark entry with the name shown, press the Enter key.

```
           Internet Gopher Information Client v1.13
                        The Online Books

    -> 1.   Welcome to OBI.
       2.   A. Hofmann/
       3.   A.E.Housman/
       4.   ACN/
       5.   ATI/
       6.   Access/
       7.   Aesop/
       8.   Algernon.Charles.Swinburne/
       9.   Ambrose.Bierce/
      10.   Amoeba/
      11.   Anarchist/
      12.   Andrew.Marvell/
      13.   Anglo-Saxon/
      14.   Anonymous/
      15.   Ansax/
      16.   Antarctica/
      17.   ArtCom/
```

```
|-----------------------------------------------------------|
|Name for this bookmark? The Online Books                   |
|                                                           |
|                              [Cancel ^G] [Accept - Enter] |
|-----------------------------------------------------------|
```

```
Press ? for Help, q to Quit, u to go up a menu          Page: 1/6
```

Navigating Long Menus

In the lower right-hand corner of the Gopher screen shown above is the indication that this is page 1 of 6 pages (Page: 1/6). The other pages of menu choices can be reached by using the + and - keys to move up and down. (Unlike the World Wide Web, where one whole document is considered one page, no matter how many screens it fills, in Gopher, a page is whatever group of menu items fit on a screen at one time.)

By default, the program gives the new Bookmarks menu item the name of the current menu. You can, however, change the name to something that will help you better remember what was important to you about the menu. To do this, type **A** from any Gopher screen you want to bookmark—the Bookmark entry box will be displayed. Now, you can enter a new bookmark name by using the Backspace key to erase the existing name. Finish by typing in the new name, and then press Enter.

Alternate Name Erasing Method

Instead of using the Backspace key to delete a bookmark name one character at a time, you can erase the whole name at once by pressing the **u** key while holding down the **ctrl** key.

An example of a menu item that would be good for a Bookmarks menu is a frequently changing database such as one of the news search services shown in the plain vanilla example. No matter how far down the menu tree this item is, with it in the Bookmarks menu you will have direct access to it.

To view the Bookmark menu, press the **v** key and a menu similar to that shown below will be displayed. This custom menu can be used like any other ready-made Gopher menu that you find on the Internet.

```
              Internet Gopher Information Client v1.13
                            Bookmarks


    -> 1.  The Online Books
       2.  Census, Fed gophers, etc/
       3.  ClariNews AP OnLine & Reuters Newswire Index/
```

Any time you want to use this Bookmarks menu, just press the **v** key. To return to whatever menu you were using when you pressed the **v** key, press the **u** key (if you are several levels down in menus that started from one of your Bookmark items, you may need to press the **u** key several times to get back to the Bookmarks menu before pressing the **u** key again to escape from the Bookmarks menu).

To delete any item from the Bookmarks menu, just use the up and down arrow keys to move the --> pointer to the item to be deleted, then press the **d** key. Caution: There is no prompt asking if you really want to delete this item; it will immediately be deleted when the **d** key is pressed.

Capital **A** (**shift-a**) is used to make bookmarks for menu items that lead to other menus or to searches. The lowercase **a** is used for menu items that are files. You might, for instance, want to repeatedly come back to one file that is changed frequently—possibly a weather forecast or stock information file.

Going Directly to the Bookmarks Menu

To make your Bookmarks menu the top menu that shows up first when you start Gopher, start Gopher with the command **gopher -b**.

Searching Large Gopher Menus

When you encounter a Gopher menu as large as the one excerpted below (this is page 1 of 34 pages), it is often easier to do a search than to use the + and - keys and read all of the entries. To do a search, press the **/** key and a box will be displayed on the screen:

```
             Internet Gopher Information Client v1.13
                All the Gopher Servers in the World

     -> 1.   Search Gopherspace using Veronica/
        2.   ACADEME THIS WEEK (Chronicle of Higher Education)/
        3.   ACM SIGDA/
        4.   ACM SIGGRAPH/
        5.   ACTLab (UT Austin, RTF Dept)/
        6.   AMI -- A Friendly Public Interface/
        7.   AREA Science Park, Trieste, (IT)/
        8.   ARPA Computing Systems Technology Office (CSTO)/
        9.   AT&T Global Information Solutions (formerly NCR) Info Server/
        10.  Academic Position Network/
        11.  Academy of Sciences, Bratislava (Slovakia)/
        12.  Acadia University Gopher/
        13.  Action for Blind People/
        14.  Advantis Global Network Services, Applications &
             Outsourcing/
        15.  AgResearch Wallaceville, Upper Hutt, New Zealand/
        16.  Agricultural Genome Gopher/
        17.  Alabama Supercomputer Network/
```

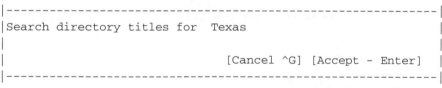

```
|-------------------------------------------------------------|
|Search directory titles for  Texas                           |
|                                                             |
|                            [Cancel ^G] [Accept - Enter]     |
|-------------------------------------------------------------|
                                             Page 1/34
```

Type in the word or phrase that you expect would be in Gopher menu items of interest to you. The search is case insensitive, so capitalization doesn't matter. Partial words are often best: For example, using "electron" as the search word would find menu items with "electron," "electronics," "electronically," and so on. After the search term is typed (in this case, **Texas**), press the Enter key and the pointer will move to the first menu item it finds that has your search word in it. To find the next menu item that contains the search term, press the **n** key.

Viewing and Downloading Gopher Text Files

Text files are often much larger than the few paragraphs shown in the plain vanilla example. Gopher therefore provides several methods for moving around within a document and several ways of downloading the document to your access provider's computer or directly to your personal computer. In the following example, the *GOES Data User's Guide* is selected to be read:

```
              Internet Gopher Information Client v1.13
              NOAA Geostationary Satellite Data Active Archive


    ->  1.   GOES Data User's Guide.
        2.   Information about the Browse Images.
        3.   GOES Browse Images/
        4.   Global Composite Geostationary Browse Images/
        5.   Information about the CRAS Forecast Images.
        6.   CRAS Forecast GOES Images/
        7.   Other NOAA Gopher Servers/
```

After a menu item is selected, Gopher displays enough of the file to fill the screen, then stops and, at the bottom of the screen, displays the word *More* and the percentage of the document that has been displayed so far. In this case 8% is displayed, so the full document is probably about 12 or 13 pages long:

```
    Geostationary Operational Environment Satellite (GOES)
                       Data User's Guide
                         (preliminary)


    I. INTRODUCTION


        The GOES system includes the satellite (with the GOES
    instrumentation and direct down-link data transmission
    capability), the NESDIS facility at Wallops Island, Virginia
    (that receives the direct transmission and generates the
    "stretched VISSR" transmission), and the ground systems at
    NESDIS and at the University of Wisconsin at Madison's (UW)
    Space Science and Engineering Center (SSEC).


    A. The GOES Satellites


        The original GOES instrument was the Visible and Infrared
    Spin Scan Radiometer (VISSR), which was an outgrowth of the
    spin scan radiometer flown aboard several of the Applications
```

```
Technology Satellite series of NASA research satellites. The
VISSR was first flown aboard SMS-1 and SMS-2 (Synchronous
Meteorological Satellite), also NASA satellites, that were
turned over to NOAA for operational use. GOES-1, GOES-2, and
GOES-3 were operational satellites that flew the original VISSR
instrument. GOES-4, GOES-5, GOES-6 and GOES-7 where flown with
a modified instrument package called the VISSR Atmospheric
Sounder (VAS). A set of infrared sensors were added to provide
an atmospheric sounder capability. Details of these instruments
are provided below.

    The data from these satellites have been archived at the
University of Wisconsin at Madison (UW) from 1978 to the
present. The holdings at the UW are currently about 120
terabytes. Data from the archive are available through the
National Oceanic and Atmospheric Administration (NOAA) National
Environmental Satellite Data Information Service (NESDIS)
facility at 301-763- 8111.
1. Visible and Infrared Spin Scan Radiometer (VISSR) Instrument

--More--(8%)
```

When a prompt such as **--More--(8%)** is shown, there are several options for moving around in the document: To see the next page, press the spacebar; to see the previous page, press the **b** key; to search for a word or phrase in the document, type the forward slash **/** followed by the word or phrase and then press the Enter key. This search may be case sensitive, so you may need to try the word in several forms, such as "house or House or HOUSE."

If you want to leave the document before getting to the end of it, press the **q** key.

If you want a copy of the document in your personal computer for searching or printing out or because it is too large to read at one time, there are several ways to get the file. One straightforward, but not too elegant, way is to turn on your communication software's "log" function, which saves to a file everything that is displayed to your screen. Once the log feature is turned on, press the spacebar repeatedly to quickly page through the document. All the screen text will be saved—including the prompts such as **--More--(8%)**. This method is fine for a short to medium-sized document that you just want for a quick look.

A good alternative for getting a full copy of the document is to mail the document to your e-mail account. To do this, at any time while viewing the document, press the **q** key and this prompt will be displayed:

```
Press <RETURN> to continue, <m> to mail, <s> to save, or <p> to print:
```

Now press the **m** key and press Enter. A box will appear in the center of the screen as shown below:

```
|                                                                    |
|Mail current document to:                                           |
|                                                                    |
|                              [Cancel ^G] [Accept - Enter]  |
|                                                                    |
```

Type in your full e-mail address (or that of anyone else you would like to send the file to) and press Enter. The words *Mailing File* will appear for a short time at the bottom of the screen. When the *Mailing File* words disappear, the mailing process is complete.

```
|                                                                    |
|Mail current document to:  oakridge@world.std.com          |
| [Cancel ^G] [Accept - Enter]                               |
|                                                                    |
|                                              Mailing File..|
```

An alternative to mailing is saving. With this method, the file you are viewing is saved to your home directory on your Internet access provider's computer. You can then use an editor on the access provider's computer to read the file or download it to your personal computer. (See Appendix C for details on downloading.)

To save a file, press the **q** key while viewing the file. A prompt at the bottom of the screen will be displayed. Now press the **s** key and hit Enter. A box will appear in the center of the screen with the current file's name. If you don't need to change that name, just press Enter—you will briefly see the message *Saving File...* at the bottom of your screen.

If you plan to download the file to a personal computer that does not allow long file names (such as an MS-DOS system, which is limited to eight characters plus a three-character extension), you can change the file's name before completing the save. Type **Ctrl-u** to erase the current name. Now type in the new name for the file and press Enter. The file will be saved to your home directory at your Internet access provider's site, under the new name.

Downloading Binary Gopher Files

The document files just described are ASCII files (also known as 7-bit or text files). Binary files (also know as 8-bit files) can be spreadsheets, formatted word processing files, desktop publishing documents, CAD files, sound files, picture and graphics files, software, and hundreds of other types of files. Binary files can't be downloaded to your personal computer by any of the techniques described so far. Gopher provides another technique for retrieving these binary files, which can also be used to get ASCII files.

In this example the picture file *2. Fluid Dynamics 2 (8-bit GIF image) <Picture>* will be downloaded directly from Gopher to your personal computer. Start by using the arrow keys to move the --> pointer to the item of interest.

```
          Internet Gopher Information Client 1.2VMS p10
                       Fluid Dynamics (list)


      1.   Fluid Dynamics 2 (24-bit RLE image) <Picture>
  >   2.   Fluid Dynamics 2 (8-bit GIF image) <Picture>
      3.   Fluid Dynamics 2 (text description).
```

Now type an uppercase **D** (**shift-d**). A box will be displayed in the center of the screen providing choices of downloading protocols. You must select the same protocol as you have your communications software in your personal computer set for. Type in the number of your protocol choice.

```
          Internet Gopher Information Client 1.2VMS p10


                       Fluid Dynamics (list)
      1.   Fluid Dynamics 2 (24-bit RLE image) <Picture>
  >   2.   Fluid Dynamics 2 (8-bit GIF image) <Picture>
      3.   Fluid Dynamics 2 (text description).
```

```
+       Fluid Dynamics 2 (8-bit GIF image)       +
|                                                 |
| 1. Zmodem                                       |
| 2. Ymodem                                       |
| 3. Xmodem-1K                                    |
| 4. Xmodem-CRC                                   |
| 5. Kermit                                       |
| 6. Text                                         |
|                                                 |
| Choose a download method:                       |
|                                                 |
| [Cancel ^G]   [Choose 1-6]                       |
|                                                 |
+-------------------------------------------------+
```

The screen will clear and prompt you to give your communications software the command to begin receiving a file. (The particular command varies greatly among communications programs, so you will need to check the software's documentation.) After the prompt, various lines of seemingly random characters will be printed on the screen, for example:

```
Start your download now...


è*_B00000000000000
```

Move quickly to get your software into receive mode, because after sending several of these lines, Gopher will stop trying to send the file.

After the file has been successfully sent, an additional report will be displayed on the same screen.

```
Download Complete. 109184 total bytes, 1186 bytes/sec
```

Press Enter and you will be back to the Gopher menu.

Searching a Gopher Database

A Gopher menu item that ends with a bracketed question mark <?> will perform a search of the indicated database. In the following example, a database of news articles is searched for particular words in the texts of the Reuters news articles. The search is started by first moving the pointer down to *3. Search Reuters newswire index <?>* and then pressing Enter.

```
Internet Gopher Information Client v1.13
The World's ClariNews AP OnLine & Reuters Newswire Index
```

```
    1. Information About These AP OnLine and Reuters Newswire
Indexes.
    2. Search ClariNews AP OnLine Newswire Index <?>
 >  3. Search Reuters newswire index <?>
```

In the search shown below, articles are sought that have somewhere in them either the word "stocks" or "bonds." OR is not the "exclusive or;" in other words, this search will provide:

All articles with the word stocks in them.

All articles with the word bonds in them.

All articles with both the words stocks and bonds.

```
+-----------------Search Reuters newswire index---------------+
|                                                             |
| Words to search for   stocks or bonds                       |
|                                                             |
|                        [Cancel ^G] [Accept - Enter]         |
|                                                             |
+-------------------------------------------------------------+
```

After typing in the search words, press Enter. The results will be presented as another Gopher menu from which you can select, read, mail, download, and so on. If you find the number of responses is too large, examine the list and decide how to redefine the search.

NOT can also be used to define a search. Defining the search as "cycle not bicycle" would result in finding menu items relating to, for example, business and stock cycles, without listing items relating to bicycle races. Searching for "bear not Chicago and bear not stock" would search for articles about the big mammals without also listing sports stories and articles about worried stock market analysts.

To leave Gopher, **q** can be used as mentioned previously, but to avoid the *Really quit (y/n) ?* question, type an uppercase **Q**, and you will be immediately returned to your access provider's system prompt.

Note:

AND, OR, and NOT may be entered in Gopher searches in lowercase or uppercase.

Table 14.1 Gopher commands.

Key	Command
Up arrow key (or **k** key)	Move the highlight/pointer up the menu.
Down arrow key (or **j** key)	Move the highlight down the menu.
Left arrow key	Go back up to the previous menu.
Right arrow key	Display currently highlighted item or menu.
Enter key	Display currently highlighted item or menu.
u	Go back to the previous menu.
m	Go back to the top (first) menu.
=	Display information about the current item.
> or **+** or **f** (also try spacebar and the Enter key)	Display the next page within a document.
< or **-** or **b**	Display the previous page within a document (some sites have no way to move back up in a document).
s	Save the current file to your directory on the Internet access provider's computer.
D (**Shift-d**)	Download the currently highlighted file directly to your PC.
/	Initiate a search.
n	Find the next menu item containing the search keyword.
?	Display list of available commands.
q	Leave the Gopher (prompts with *Really quit (y/n)?*).
Q (**Shift-q**) (or **ctrl-z**)	Same as q but does not display a prompt asking whether you really want to quit.

Summary of Commands and Symbols

Commands do vary from site to site, but the commands listed in Table 14.1 are a good starting point.

At the end of the line following each menu item, there is often some sort of symbol indicating what type of item that menu choice is. These vary a great deal from site to site, but are usually consistent within a site. Table 14.2 lists the most common symbols.

Table 14.2 Common Gopher symbols.

Symbol	Meaning
/	This item is another menu (subdirectory).
.	This item is a readable text file.
<?>	This item will initiate a full-text index search by prompting you to type in a word or phrase to look for.
<TEL>	Selecting this item will initiate a Telnet session with the named remote service.
<)	This symbol (representing a speaker) indicates an audio data file.
<PICTURE>	This is a graphics/image data file.

Using Gopher to Explore Other Gopher Sites

Each site on the Internet that installs the Gopher client software configures it to link, by default, to a particular Gopher server. When you start Gopher you can, however, "point" the Gopher to another site so you can start with a different root menu. Your Gopher client software will operate just as before, but you will have available a different set of menu choices reflecting the information available at this new site.

To point the Gopher, you need to know two things: the other Gopher's address and its port number. If the port number is not given with the information you have about the Gopher site, assume that it is the very common 70. The command for pointing the Gopher takes this form:

```
gopher server-name port-number
```

For example, the Gopher server at the University of Illinois's Department of Atmospheric Sciences has an address of wx.atmos.uiuc.edu. In most lists of Gopher servers, no port number is given for this site, so assume that it is 70. The command typed at your access provider's system prompt would be:

```
gopher wx.atmos.uiuc.edu 70
```

Veronica

Gopher allows searching for keywords within menus, but only within the menu that you are currently viewing. Veronica, however, maintains an index of thousands of Gopher menu items from many Gopher server sites, and can search them all at one time, thus the somewhat strained acronym Veronica—Very Easy Rodent Oriented Net-wide Index to Computerized Archives.

Veronica has server software installed at a few sites. The server software has features that allow it to collect an index of all Gopher menu items on all Gophers known to it.

At most Gopher sites, the top menu will have a menu choice such as *Gophers and other information servers,* or *Internet resources and services.* Try choosing this and you are likely to find a menu choice below it such as *Search titles in Gopherspace using veronica/.* (If you are unable to locate Veronica, point your Gopher client to one of the sites listed at the end of this section.) A typical Veronica menu lists some general background and instruction files, several places to do Veronica directory searches, and several sites for Veronica gopherspace searches. (Figure 14.2 shows a

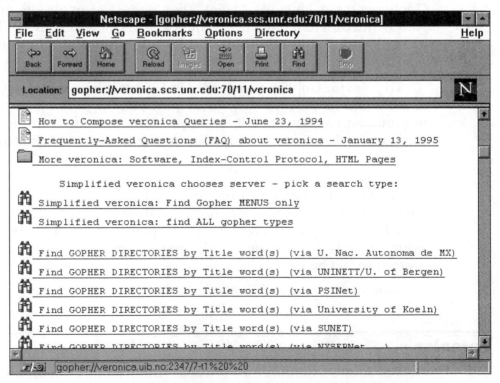

Figure 14.2 Using the Netscape browser for Veronica searches.

Veronica menu as displayed by the Netscape graphical user interface browser.) (Each of these sites usually maintain similar index files, so if you get the message *Too many connections* at one site, try another site.)

In this example, a gopherspace search will be performed (all Gopher menu items at all know locations), and in this example the (PSINet) server is chosen. Moving the pointer to *8. Search gopherspace at PSINet <?>* and pressing the Enter key causes a search word prompt box to be displayed on screen. In this case, all items with the word business in them will be searched. After the word business is typed in and the Enter key is pressed, the search is initiated.

Veronica Searches and Case

Veronica Searches are case insensitive—"Business," "business," and "BUSINESS" are all considered the same word.

```
                    Internet Gopher Information Client v2.0.12
                    Search titles in Gopherspace using veronica


        1.
        2.  FAQ:  Frequently-Asked Questions about veronica      (1993/08/23)
        3.  How to compose  veronica queries (NEW June 24) READ ME!!
        4.  Search Gopher Directory Titles at PSINet <?>
        5.  Search Gopher Directory Titles at SUNET <?>
        6.  Search Gopher Directory Titles at U. of Manitoba <?>
        7.  Search Gopher Directory Titles at University of Cologne <?>
    >   8.  Search gopherspace at PSINet <?>
        9.  Search gopherspace at SUNET <?>
        10. Search gopherspace at U. of Manitoba <?>
        11. Search gopherspace at University of Cologne <?>


    +------------------Search gopherspace at PSINet---------------+
    |                                                             |
    |Words to search for                                          |
    |                                                             |
    |business                                                     |
    |                                                             |
    |[Help: ^_]   [Cancel: ^G]                                    |
    +-------------------------------------------------------------+
```

In anywhere from a few seconds to a couple of minutes, the results of the Veronica search are displayed as a Gopher-style menu. This search yielded 13,008 items. By default, at this site only the first five pages (200 items in this case) are initially sent, but that number can be changed. If, for instance, you wanted 500 sent, you would type -m500 before the search word(s):

```
+-------------------Search gopherspace at PSINet---------------+
|                                                              |
|Words to search for                                           |
|                                                              |
|  -m500 business                                              |
|                                                              |
|[Help: ^_]   [Cancel: ^G]                                     |
+--------------------------------------------------------------+
```

Obviously, 13,008 items would be quite a list to browse through. Fortunately, Veronica can do complex searches, using AND, OR, NOT, and parentheses ( ). These are used as follows:

AND—The words before and after AND must both be in the menu item for that item to be listed.

OR—If either the word before OR or the word after appears in the menu item, the item will be added to the list. Also, if both words appear in the menu item, that item will be added to the list.

NOT—A menu item will be selected if the word preceding NOT appears in the menu item, but only if it doesn't also contain the word following NOT.

Parentheses—These are used to contain groups of words separated by AND, OR, and NOT. For example:

(sales and marketing) NOT wholesale.

(wood AND products) OR lumber

Veronica searches look for exact whole-word matches, so using "environment" as a search term would not find Gopher menu items with "environmental," "environmentalism," or "environments." To find menu items with all of these, the asterisk wild card character can be used. A search for "environment*" will find "environment," "environmental," "environmentalism," "environments," or any other variation that has additional characters at and after the position of the *.

There may be times, when you want some but not all of the variations on a word. In that case you can specify which variations you want by using parentheses to enclose word variations and OR. For example, to find all Gopher menu items that have the word "business," and either or both of the words "environment" and "environmental," use this search command:

```
business and (environment or environmental)
```

In the list of search results, some of the menu items may be truncated, so the words you search for may not be displayed in all of the menu items, but they can be assumed to be there.

Searching for Menus

Another approach to dealing with the very large lists that some searches produce is to do a search just for menus (directories). The resulting list will be much smaller, and will provide the added benefit of finding Gopher sites that customarily have the type of information you are interested in.

The following is a search for Gopher directory titles (menus), rather than a full Gopher search for all menu *items*. Item 4 is selected, Enter pressed, and the search is conducted in the same manner as a gopherspace search.

```
                 Internet Gopher Information Client v2.0.12
                  Search titles in Gopherspace using veronica


       1.
       2.   FAQ: Frequently-Asked Questions about veronica (1993/08/23)
       3.   How to compose  veronica queries (NEW June 24) READ ME!!
   >   4.   Search Gopher Directory Titles at PSINet <?>
       5.   Search Gopher Directory Titles at SUNET <?>
       6.   Search Gopher Directory Titles at U. of Manitoba <?>
       7.   Search Gopher Directory Titles at University of Cologne <?>
       8.   Search gopherspace at PSINet <?>
       9.   Search gopherspace at SUNET <?>
       10.  Search gopherspace at U. of Manitoba <?>
       11.  Search gopherspace at University of Cologne <?>
```

```
+-----------Search Gopher Directory Titles atPSINet-------------+
|                                                               |
| Words to search for  forest                                   |
|                                                               |
|                                                               |
| [Help: ^_]  [Cancel: ^G]                                      |
+---------------------------------------------------------------+
```

The items returned by the search are now *all* Gopher menus, rather
than the gopherspace search's mix of menus and files (note the forward
slash / after each menu item, indicating that it leads to another menu).
This search yields 130 menus. Each of these Gopher menus can now be
browsed and searched in the usual Gopher manner.

```
              Internet Gopher Information Client v2.0.12
              Search Gopher Directory Titles at PSINet: forest


  >   1.  FOREST PRODUCTS (ForP)/
      2.  FOREST RESOURCES (FR)/
      3.  Department of Forest Products/
      4.  Forest Products Course Info/
      5.  Forest Product Class Materials/
      6.  Forest Products Job Board/
      7.  Department of Forest Resources/
      8.  How To Reach Someone in the Dept of Forest Resources/
      9.  Schoolhouse of Forest Resources Courses/
      10. The Internet and Forest Resources/
      11. 01:Forest Resources:Regional, National, International/
      12. 17:Forest Management-General/
      13. 37:Non-Industrial Forest Products/
      14. Tropical Forest Conservation and Development Bibliography/
      15. Forest Resources/
      16. Nontimber Forest Products/
      17. Recreation in the Urban Forest/
      18. Wildlife in the Urban Forest/
      19. Planning the Urban Forest/
      20. Managing the Urban Forest/
      21. Forest.Conference/
      22. FWU...........Forest and Wood   /
      23. FWU...........Forest and Wood   /
      24. FOREST SERVICE FS  (36 entries)/
```

```
25. SOUTHERN FOREST EXP STATION  (2 entries)/
26. FOREST WILDLIFE FOUNDATION  (1 entries)/
27. FOREST SERVICE FS  (1 entries)/
28. FOREST SERVICE FS  (15 entries)/
29. FOREST SERVICE FS  (2 entries)/
30. WOOD WOOD SCIENCE AND FOREST PRODUCTS/


Press ? for Help, q to Quit, u to go up a menu        Page: 1/4
```

Limiting Your Search by Menu Item Type

Veronica allows even more control of the type of menu item that is returned with a search. Table 14.3 lists the types of Gopher menu items that you can selectively request. The instructions to Veronica to search for specific types of Gopher menu items are in the form of **-t** plus the file type code, followed by the search word or words. For example, if you wanted to just have binary file Gopher menu items returned from a search for "business," the search instructions would look like this:

```
+-----------------Search gopherspace atPSINet-----------------+
|                                                             |
| Words to search for  -t9 business                          |
|                                                             |
|                       [Cancel ^G] [Accept Ä Enter]         |
|                                                             |
+-------------------------------------------------------------+
```

Using **-t9** to search for binary files is especially useful if you are looking for any type of software, CAD files, spreadsheet data files, graphics, and so on.

Table 14.3 Gopher menu items.

File Type Code	Menu Item File Types
0	File
1	Directory
2	CSO (phonebook server)
7	Index search server
8	Telnet session
9	Binary file

You can specify more than one file type in a single search. For example, if you are interested in index searches of databases and Telnet sessions (such as with bulletin boards and information server sites), these can be returned in one search in this way:

```
+---------------Search gopherspace atPSINet------------------+
|                                                            |
| Words to search for   -t78 business                       |
|                                                            |
|                            [Cancel ^G]  [Accept - Enter]   |
|                                                            |
+------------------------------------------------------------+
```

Archie

Two of the problems with FTP are in knowing what files exist on the Internet and where they are located. Archie was created at McGill University in Montreal, Canada, to help solve these problems, and is now supported by Bunyip Information Systems.

Archie is a search system that scans a database containing the names and locations of files at most anonymous FTP sites in the world. The database is updated regularly to include new listings.

To use Archie, Telnet to an Archie server (see Table 14.5 for a list of Archie servers), and log in as archie. (See Appendix E for information on how to Telnet.) Your system may also have an Archie client; to determine this, type **archie** at your system prompt. If you have an Archie client, you will get some form of the *archie>* prompt or help screen.

It is possible, through use of command line switches (options), to specify the kind of search you wish, as well as whether you want the listing that Archie returns displayed on your screen only or displayed on your screen and put into a file for later searching and reference. In addition to finding files that may be of interest, Archie will identify subdirectories with the search word as well. When you find subdirectories that look interesting, you can use FTP to examine the files stored there. (See Appendix D for information on how to use FTP.)

Often, at the system prompt, you can obtain a listing of the command line options for Archie by typing in **archie** and pressing Enter; for example:

```
world% archie
Usage: archie [-acelorstvLV] [-m hits] [-N level] string
            -c : case sensitive substring search
            -e : exact string match (default)
            -r : regular expression search
            -s : case insensitive substring search
            -l : list one match per line
            -t : sort inverted by date
       -m hits : specifies maximum number of hits to return
(default 95)
    -o filename : specifies file to store results in
       -h host : specifies server host
            -L : list known servers and current default
      -N level : specifies query niceness level (0-35765)

world%
```

With the **-s** option, which makes the search case insensitive, "Next," "next," "NEXT," and "NeXT" are all the same, while with the **-c** option all of those searches are different. The default setting is case sensitive.

The **-t** option gives you the information sorted by date, which will allow you to locate the most recent versions of files and programs. Different sites have slightly different options, but most will contain options for case, the number of hits (matches) to return, a file storage option, sorting options, and the ability to choose which Archie server to access. Typing archie after you have logged in at one of the Archie sites will put you into interactive mode, with a prompt *archie>*. (Some sites will automatically place you in interactive mode with the *archie>* prompt.) Table 14.4 shows some useful commands that can be typed in at the *archie>* prompt. Table 14.5 is a brief list of some Archie sites and their locations.

Table 14.4 Archie commands.

Command	Meaning
help	To get information on Archie and currently available Archie commands
mailto	Lets you identify an e-mail address to which to send search results
list	Lists the sites covered by the archie database
set	Used to set up user setable parameters
prog	Searches the Archie database for a file
bye	Exits the program

Table 14.5 Archie servers worldwide.

Name	Country/State
archie.au	Australia
archie.univie.ac.at	Austria
archie.belnet.be	Belgium
archie.bunyip.com	Canada
archie.cs.mcgill.ca	Canada
archie.uqam.ca	Canada
archie.funet.fi	Finland
archie.univ-rennes1.fr	France
archie.th-darmstadt.de	Germany
archie.ac.il	Israel
archie.unipi.it	Italy
archie.wide.ad.jp	Japan
archie.kornet.nm.kr	Korea
archie.sogang.ac.kr	Korea
archie.nz	New Zealand
archie.uninett.no	Norway
archie.icm.edu.pl	Poland
archie.rediris.es	Spain
archie.luth.se	Sweden
archie.switch.ch	Switzerland
archie.ncu.edu.tw	Taiwan
archie.doc.ic.ac.uk	UK
archie.hensa.ac.uk	UK
archie.sura.net	USA (MD)
archie.unl.edu	USA (NE)
archie.internic.net	USA (NJ)
archie.rutgers.edu	USA (NJ)
archie.ans.net	USA (NY)

Following are the abbreviated results of a case-insensitive (**-s**) Archie search using the word "business," with the list arranged by date (**-t**). You can observe that some of the search results are directories, some are files, and some are software. The directory listings give you some starting places for further searching for similar files.

```
world% archie -s -t business

Host freebsd.cdrom.com
Location: /.1/cdrom/incoming
DIRECTORY drwxrwxrwx 512ÿ Jan 11 00:29 business

Host owl.nstn.ns.ca
Location: /pub
DIRECTORY drwxr-xr-x 512 Jan 4 14:17 internet- business-journal
Host sunsite.unc.edu
Location: /pub/academic/business/.cap
FILE -rw-r--r--        78- Jul-10 1993 internet-business-journal

Host calypso-2.oit.unc.edu
Location: /pub/academic/business/.cap
FILE -rw-r--r--        78 Jul 9 1993 internet-business-journal

Host sunsite.unc.edu
Location: /pub/academic
DIRECTORY drwxr-xr-x 512  Jul 1 199ÿ business


Host ftp.sunet.se
Location: /pub/mac/mirro umich/util/organization
FILE -r--r--r--   249933  Jan 15 1993
businessplanmaster.sit.hqx
```

Figure 14.3 shows the use of the Netscape browser for an Archie search.

> ## Archie Collection on the Web
>
> A Web-based collection of links to Archie sites is available at *http://web.nexor.co.uk/archie.html*.

Publicizing Your Business's FTP Resources

If you have an anonymous FTP site, or start one for your business in the future, the people who operate the Archie system encourage you to send

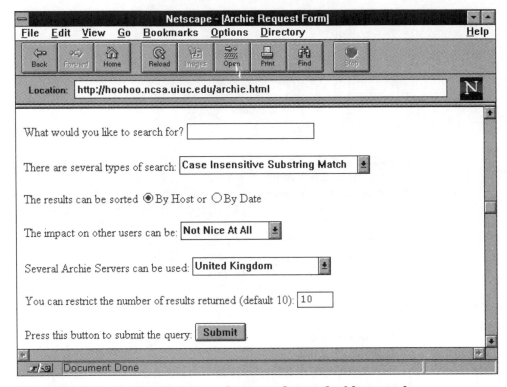

Figure 14.3 Using the Netscape browser for an Archie search.

them the details about your public files so that their server tracking software can be configured to update the information, making it easier for others to locate your information. To register with Archie, send electronic mail to **info-archie@bunyip.com**. Don't forget to link your FTP site on your Web page as well.

Where from Here...

Having just learned about Gopher and Veronica, and earlier, about the WWW search tools, continue on to Part VI to discover resources and starting points for doing business on the Internet.

PART VI

Business and Professional
Resources on the Internet

CHAPTER 15

Resources for Doing Business on the Internet: Business to Business and Beyond

Many people liken dealing with the amount of information available on the Internet to drinking from a fire hose. In the field of business, that fire hose is pouring out a torrent of information. Finding business-related information, databases, and World Wide Web, Gopher, Telnet, and FTP sites is an ongoing activity. New resources are coming online daily, and new online guides are being written. Addresses of resources change frequently, so you will want to use the search tools discussed in Chapters 11 and 14.

There are now numerous online businesses that can assist you in making your online business experience successful, including advertising agencies, venture capitalists, and others.

Following is an introduction to some of the most interesting and useful information resources for businesses, and some sources of assistance online.

Business to Business

There are a growing number of businesses operating on the Internet that are providing services to other businesses wanting to get online or to improve their online presence and activities.

307

Online Advertising Agencies

adfx(tm)—Virtual Advertising

URL: *http://www.shore.net/~adfx/top.html*

Virtual specializes in Net-appropriate nonintrusive ways to explore promotional opportunities. They offer consulting, design, and publication of information. As a part of their services, they have franchises for the FreeStyles Network virtual storefronts. They have a monthly Client Newsletter that helps clients keep up-to-date with electronic marketing.

Apollo Advertising

URL: *http://www.apollo.co.uk/*

Apollo is a free advertising service on the Web located in the United Kingdom. It integrates classified and business advertising in a single framework in which hotlinks are provided to most advertisers. The whole page is organized by continent and country, and you can search the entire database by keywords.

Dataquest Incorporated

URL: *http://www.dataquest.com/*

Dataquest Incorporated is a market research and consulting company focusing on high-technology and financial institutions. The company provides coverage of the semiconductor, computer systems and peripherals, communications, document management, software, and services sectors of the information technology industry. Dataquest is an international company of The Dun & Bradstreet Corporation.

Fine Marketing Communications

URL: *http://aragorn.solutionsrc.com:80/FINE*

Fine Marketing Communications is a traditional advertising agency offering services to businesses, attempting to merge "traditional methods with the information superhighway." Their technology-based marketing includes database marketing, internet marketing, multimedia, CD development, digital imaging, advertising, graphic design, and public relations. They offer services such as advertising strategies, media planning and purchasing, concept development, creative art and copywriting, and more.

Greenberg Seronick & Partners

URL: *http://www.tiac.net/users/gsandp/index.html*

Greenberg Seronick & Partners has an online portfolio to demonstrate the recent work of this Boston advertising agency. Their Web page contains an extensive categorized hotlist of business sites. The categories of the hotlist are advertising and marketing; business resources; research and statistics; academic resources; online services; TV, film, and music resources; interactive media; and Internet reference resources.

Hajjar/Kaufman New Media Lab

URL: *http://www.hkweb.com/*

This advertising agency provides a "radio station" to broadcast original programming exclusively through the Internet. They specialize in publishing, electronics, entertainment, and financial services. They use Sun Sparc hardware, operate a Netscape Netsite Commerce server, and will lease their CU-SeeMe reflector.

Lindsay, Stone & Briggs

URL: *http://www.lsb.com/*

This Madison, Wisconsin advertising agency presents a well-designed and sometimes humorous Web page focusing on the marketing concept of branding. Their Creative Gallery link leads you to examples of their work for Weyerhaeuser, Jewelers Workshop, Klarbrunn Mineral Water, and the Bach Dancing & Dynamite Society, among others.

The Online Ad Agency

URL: *http://advert.com/.*

The Online Ad Agency focuses on getting content to the customers via both traditional and new media, with a strong emphasis on brand name recognition. Their homepage provides access to menus emphasizing content, delivery, target audience, the opening of new channels, and clients, as well as to their portfolio. E-mail Larry Chase at *lchase@panix.com.*

Poppe Tyson Advertising

URL: *http://www.poppe.com:8400/cgi-bin/imagemap/pt2-poppe_home*

Poppe Tyson Advertising, a very traditional advertising agency, is a subsidiary of Bozell, Jacobs, Kenyon & Eckhardt, the world's fourth largest marketing communications company. Poppe Tyson has an online PR division, and database marketing capabilities, and they emphasize the mix of marketing strategies that include integrated online activities.

Sharrow Marketing: Sharrow Davies Townsend

URL: *http://www.dnai.com/~sharrow/enter.html*

Coming to you from San Francisco, California, Sharrow provides you with a mixture of marketing theory and examples of its own successful database marketing work. Sharrow specializes in strategic and marketing planning, marketing and strategic plan development assistance, market research and analysis, sales management, and sales support.

Werbal Advertising Agency

URL: *http://www.eunet.ch/werbal/*

Werbal Advertising Agency, based in Berne, Switzerland, provides consulting, programming, design, image-building, sales, promotion, and public relations services, and artwork. They use the Web not just as an advertising platform but as a two-way publishing and communication medium. The page is humorous and has hot links to example sites.

Werbel's homepage offers the visitor the chance to find out more about Werbal services, reasons to advertise in global networks (document in German), a price list of WWW advertising services (document in German), an online communications form for further information, a reference list, and overnight translation services for U.S. companies (English to German).

Winkler-McManus Advertising

URL: *http://www.winklermcmanus.com.*

Winkler-McManus is a traditional advertising agency branching out to the Internet. Their visually compelling homepage features the Virtual Agency, and offers links to their Portfolio, Staff Office, Philosophy, Late

Breaking News, and Boardroom. The Portfolio page has a large image of a portfolio and lists some of their clients.

Other Online Business Services: From Sites to Money

There are a few miscellaneous sites that have services and information of particular interest to those wanting to promote and carry out business on the Internet.

Open Market: The Companies Providing Web Space Page

Open Market provides a three-tiered guide to Web service providers, broken down by the number of sites that it hosts: *http://www.directory.net/dir/servers1.html*, *servers2.html*, and *servers3.html*.

NetPost

NetPost is a service that will, on an individualized basis, research, announce, list, and register WWW sites, e-mail catalogs, and companies and organizations that are using the Internet for business. Their specialty is World Wide Web site announcement and registration campaigns. This service is designed to make your business visible on the Internet. Reach them at *http://www.netpost.com*.

Advertising Law Site

The Advertising Law Internet Site offers access to a large body of advertising and marketing information. In addition, there is a "what's popular" page so visitors can see what everybody else has been using. The topics include:

- Fundamental Advertising Principles
- Articles about Advertising Law
- FTC Advertising Guidelines and Enforcement Policy Statements
- FTC Trade Regulation Rules
- FTC Consumer Brochures
- Testimony and Speeches
- About the Advertising Law Internet Site

The URL is *http://www.webcom.com/~lewrose/home.html*.

Where Is the Money? Venture Capital Firms and Other Funding Sources

InterSoft solutions maintains a page (*http://www.catalog.com/intersof/finance/vent_cap.html*) called Venture Capital on the Web, which currently lists 16 venture capitalists and 10 regional funding organizations.

For the United Kingdom, The InternetWeb company maintains a page connecting to numerous venture capital firms: *http://www.internetweb.co.uk/WEBPAGES/VENTURE/venll.htm*.

Ottawa Online Ventures at *http://ottawa.microworks.ca* is a resource of venture capital in Canada.

The MCI Small Business Center has a page for business financing: *http://www.mci.com/SmallBiz/fina.html*. The Small Business Center site is also a good source for general business information (*http://www.mci.com/SmallBiz/index.html*).

Drinking from the Fire Hose

Brace yourself! There is a lot out there that can be useful to you. There is a torrent of information, and these are just some of best sites to start with. Let's have a closer look at some of the most useful WWW sites, Gophers, and other repositories of business-related information.

CommerceNet

The CommerceNet Consortium (*http://www.commerce.net/information/information.html*) is a not-for-profit 501c(6) mutual benefit corporation that is conducting a large-scale market trial in support of electronic commerce via the Internet. CommerceNet is a place where business people come together to exchange information, conduct joint demonstrations, and share resources in working groups. CommerceNet is also a way to share efforts with regard to Requests for Proposals and news about commerce on the Net. CommerceNet membership allows public and private organizations and individuals to participate at various levels—for example, in working groups on such subjects as public-key encryption certification, Internet security, and technology license agreements. A variety of presentations are available online for members, including an in-depth getting started tutorial.

Commercial Internet eXchange (CIX)

Commercial Internet eXchange (CIX) is a membership organization of public data network service providers, offering unrestricted access to other networks worldwide, concerned with the development and future direction of the Internet. Membership in the Commercial Internet eXchange is open to organizations that offer TCP/IP or OSI public data internetworking services to the general public. CIX offers its members regulatory and legislative analysis, technical and other reports and white papers, a help desk, task forces on various subjects, and hotlinks to "better Web sites" (*http://www.cix.org/CIXhome.html*).

Information Innovation

Based in The Netherlands, with offices in Amsterdam and New York, Information Innovation is a group of companies concentrating on finance and distributed information systems. Their Web page is hosted by EuroNet Internet at *http://www.euro.net/innovation/*. Information Innovation provides a catalog of hotlinks to Web sites useful to business. While some of the services are only available to paying subscribers of their newsletter, The Web Word, other valuable links are available to the public. These free links include a World Wide Web terminology dictionary, the Edupage newsletter, Innovation's electronic book "Guide to Management and Technology," a bibliography of books, articles, and research reports, and a Caribbean newsletter on offshore asset protection.

Access Business Online

Access Business Online, at *http://www.futuris.net/touch/welcome.html*, has a number of options on its opening screen to help you navigate this complex site.The first is made up of industrial classifications and topics/activities and is called Access Business Online. The industrial classifications include manufacturing, technology, telecommunications, government, travel, real estate, retail, and a dozen more. The topics/activities include fast breaking news, locator pages, editorials, and advertisements.

The Economics Gopher

The Economics Gopher at Sam Houston State University (*gopher://Niord. SHSU.edu:70/11gopher_root%3A%5B_DATA.ECONOMICS%5D*) contains a broad variety of business-related material, and includes extensive connections to other business and economics Gophers. With close to a hundred entries under the /*economics* menu, there are items for Federal Reserve information, census, tariffs, and links to other business information sites, including:

```
Economics Resources from NetEc Archive (SHSU mirror)
Economics Working Paper Archive (econwpa.wustl.edu)
Archives of Pol-Econ, FedTax-L, and sci.econ.research
The Cyberchronicle of Political Economy (COPE)
TeX Archive and Related Materials
TEXAS-ONE: Services For Texas Small Businesses
94-budget
Accounting Gopher (ANet.scu.edu.au)
American Political Science Association Gopher
Asia Pacific Business & Marketing Resources
Association for Public Policy Analysis and Management
Bell Atlantic Gopher
Bernan/UNIPUB's Government Publications Network
Bibliographies in Economics (University of Michigan)
Budget of the United States Government, Fiscal Year 1995
Bureau of Labor Statistics, US Dept of Labor (LABSTAT; SHSU mirror)
Business Resources
Business Sources on the Net (SHSU mirror)
Business, Economics, Marketing via U. Missouri, St. Louis
CERRO: the Central European Regional Research Organization
CIA World Factbook (93) Search (Skidmore)
CIA World Factbook -- 1992-present
California Legislative Information
Census Information (various)
Collected Works of Marx-Engels
Congressional Quarterly Gopher Service
Consumer Information Center, Pueblo, CO
Current Business Statistics
Current ECU rates
Daily News - Free Internet Sources
Department of Finance, Graduate School of Business, UTexas
ECONsult international consultancy and forecasting
EForum (csf.colorado.edu)
EGopher archives (Economics Gopher and Information Coordinators)
EconBib (LaTeX/BibTeX style archives for economics; SHSU mirror)
EconData (Economic Data and Analysis Package; SHSU mirror)
Economic Bulletin Board (SHSU mirror of UMichigan)
```

Economic Bulletin Board (U.S. Dept of Commerce via UMichigan)
Economic Conversion Information Exchange (U.S. Dept. of Commerce)
Economic Democracy Information Network (EDIN)
Economic Reports of the President
Economic Research Service (ERS) Reports, USDA
Economic and Social Research Council RAPID (UK)
Economics WWW Page at Dept of Economics, Univ of Michigan
Economics WWW Page at Helsinki
Economics WWW Page at Ohio State University
Economics WWW Page at Trinity College, Dublin
Economics WWW Page from EInet Galaxy
Economics of the Internet WWW Server
Elsevier's ECONbase Economics Electronic
Experimental Stock WWW Server at MIT
FDIC Gopher
FEMECON-L: Feminist Economists Discussion Group Archives
Federal Communications Commission Gopher
Federal Register
Federal Reserve Bank of Boston Data (SHSU mirror)
Federal Reserve Bank of Chicago
Federal Reserve Bank of Philadelphia: Publications & Data (U.Penn)
Federal Reserve Board (at town.hall.org)
FinanceNet (National Performance Review)
Financial Economics Network WWW Server
Florida State University College of Business
Florida State University Population Center
Foreign Exchange Rates (10 am EST)
General Agreement on Tariffs and Trade (GATT)
Gov't Sources -- Bus & Eco Info (T. Austin; K. Tsang) [03-Mar-1994]
Government Information Locator Service (GILS) [11-Nov-1993] DRAFT
Gross State Product Tables; US Bureau of Economic Analysis
H-net: Humanities On-Line
Harvard Business School Publishing Corporation
Hawaii State Legislature Legislative Infomation System
Historic Price Data for UK, US, Canada, Norway, Sweden
Holt's Stock Market Reports
Huang's Weekly Futures Market Report
Human Resources Development Canada
Institute for Advanced Studies, Vienna (IHS)
Institute for East-West Studies European Center-Atlanta
Inter-University Consortium for Political & Social Research
International Institute for Applied Systems Analysis Gopher

Internet Business Journal
Internet Resources for Research on Latin American Economics
Internet Sources of Govt Info (B. Gumprecht) [03-Mar-1994]
Investment Data Collection at Data General
JFK School of Government
Job Openings for Economists (JOE)
Journal of Business and Economics ftp archives
Journal of Statistics Education Information Service
Kiwi Club at University of Texas, Austin
Labor - Institute for Global Communications (IGC)
Law Resources
Law-Related Gophers and Information Servers
Law-Related Resources on the Internet (E.J. Heels) [26-Oct-1994]
Legal Discussion Lists
Legal Information Institute -- Cornell Law School
Links to Political Science Gophers
List of Electronic Pre-Print Archives
Management Archive
MathSource/Mathematica Gopher Server
MathSource: The Electronic Mathematica
NAFTA (North American Free Trade Agreement)
NAFTANET
NBER—National Bureau of Economic Research
NETLIB—Mathematical, engineering and scientific software
NSF Science and Technology Information System
National Consumer Week, U.S. Office of Consumer Affairs
National Health Security Plan (from sunsite)
National Information Infrastructure Information (from sunsite)
National Information Infrastructure Task Force Gopher
National Performance Review (Reinventing Government)
National Trade Data Bank
Nebraska Economic Development Gopher
Network Archive Tools
Networking on the Network
New York University, Stern School of Business
Nobel Laureates in Economics
Norwegian Research Centre in Organization and Management
Numerical Algorithms Group Gopher
OBA/OMB U.S. Budget Gopher
Occupational Outlook Handbooks (1992-present)
Oregon Online
POLITICS and GOVERNMENT menu (from PEG)

Penn World Tables (SHSU mirror)
Personal Fin Resources on Internet (A. Chambers, C. Kummer)
Population Studies Center at University of Pennsylvania
PowerPoint Sample Applications
QuoteCom Financial Market Data Server (WWW)
RISKGopher
Regional Research Institute at West Virginia University
Resources for Economists on the Internet (B. Goffe) (WWW)
Resources for Economists on the Internet (B. Goffe) [05-Apr-1995]
Resources: Internat'l Trade & World Commerce (S. Herro)
[11-Mar-1994]
SEC EDGAR
SMCRO095 -- macros for use with Word4Windows
Science, Research, & Grant Information
Selected USENET newsgroups (sci.econ, etc.; Louisiana Tech)
Social Science Information Gateway (via WWW)
Social Sciences & Humanities Information Facility (ANU)
Solstice (Center for Renewable Energy and Sustainable Technology)
Standard Industrial Codes (SIC)
Stanford Graduate School of Business
Statistics Canada "Talon" service
Statistics, Econometrics, and Computational Economics Collection
TQM Bulletin Board
TQM Collection from USC
Tests
Texas Department of Commerce (TEXIS Marketplace & More)
Texas Department of Information Resources
Texas Legislative Gopher
Texas Secretary of State's Office (via WWW)
The Legal Domain (Chicago-Kent College of Law)
The Political Science List of Lists [17-Feb-1994]
The Scientist - Newsletter
The Texas 500
Trade News
Tucson Economic Development Gopher
U.S. Agency for International Development Gopher
U.S. Census Bureau Gopher
U.S. Commerce Department Gopher
U.S. Consumer Product Safety Commission
U.S. Department of Housing and Urban Development)
U.S. Department of Justice
U.S. Small Business Administration

```
U.S. Small Business Administration, WV District
U.S. Social Security Administration
U.S. Supreme Court Decisions (Project Hermes at CWRU)
U.S.Occupational Safety & Health Gopher (OSHA regulations)
US Bureau of Labor Statistics (LABSTAT)
USDA Economics and Statistics Server at Cornell
United Nations
United States GOVERNMENT Gophers
United States Industrial Outlooks, 1993-1994
University of Michigan Economics Gopher (Hal Varian)
University of Nevada (Economics Collection)
University of Wisconsin-Madison Economics Department
Various Resources, Executive Branch, U.S. Government
Villanova Center for Information Law & Policy
White House Information (President Clinton's Staff; from Texas A&M)
William E. Simon Graduate School of Business Administration
World Bank Public Information Center
```

The Economic Bulletin Board

This resource is reachable at *gopher://una.hh.lib.umich.edu:70/11/ebb*. Maintained by the University of Michigan, this site provides data from the Department of State's Economic Bulletin Board. The *ebb* subdirectory or menu item provides access to many other items:

```
Keyword Search of File Titles
DEPT OF COMMERCE ECONOMIC DATA (UMICH)
AgWorld international ag situation reports
Best Market Reports
Budget of the U.S. Government (STAT-USA)
Current Business Statistics
Defense Conversion Subcommittee (DCS) Info
Eastern Europe trade leads
Economic Indicators
Employment Statistics
Energy statistics
Foreign Assets Control Program
Foreign Trade
General Information Files
Industrial Sector Analysis Reports (ISA)
Industry Statistics
```

```
International Market Insight (IMI) reports
Miscellaneous Economic Files
Miscellaneous Files
Miscellaneous Trade Files
Monetary Statistics
National Export Strategy Files
National Income and Products Accounts
Press releases from the U.S. Trade Representative
Price and Productivity Statistics
Regional Economic Statistics
Software International Articles
Special Studies and Reports
State By State Export Resource Listings
Summaries of current economic conditions
Trade Opportunity Program (TOP)
U.S. Treasury Auction Results
USDA Agricultural leads
United Aid Initiative
```

Files can also be accessed via FTP: *ftp://una.hh.lib.umich.edu/ebb.*

Small Business Information

There are several sites that have information for small businesses. The Company Corporation offers information on incorporation through *http://incorporate.com/tcc/home.html.*

Small business documents are available from the Small Business Administration at *http://www.sbaonline.sba.gov/index.html,* where you can locate a wealth of information under topics such as Starting Your Business, Financing Your Business, and Expanding Your Business.

Entrepreneurs on the Web, *http://sashimi.wwa.com/~notime/eotw/EOTW.html*, is a good place to get small business information and information on WWW issues.

The Internet Advertising Resource Guide at *http://www.missouri.edu/internet-advertising-guide.html* is a useful site consisting mostly of links to sites on how to advertise on the Internet.

The Business Resource Center contains information about starting a new business, managing that business, and marketing products and services: *http://www.KciLink.com:80/sbhc/.*

A rather specialized site, the NAFTAnet Small Business page has good general and specific small business information including information on NAFTA: *http://www.nafta.net/smallbiz.htm*.

Canadian Information

The Internet services of Statistics Canada–Statistique Canada are impressive. Through their Web site, *http://www.statcan.ca*, they offer extensive access to all of their normal reports, and information on their paper publications.

The Canadian Broadcasting Company (CBC) is experimenting with the distribution of radio programming over the Internet. CBC provides lists of its radio programs, lists of transcripts, and sample radio programs in digital audio format (AU). These are available via WWW at *http://www. radio.cbc.ca/*. Progressive Networks has developed a new audio format that will allow the user with a 14.4K baud line to hear CBC audio in real time on the Net.

The Canadian Internet Business Directory (*http://cibd.com/cibd/CIBD Home. html*) is a business directory that lists local sites, but also includes a variety of institutions, government offices, organizations, and educational institutions useful to doing business on the Internet. You can search by company name, province, or type.

Freenets

Freenets are community-based BBS services that generally offer resources local to the system. In most cases, the freenets provide Internet services to urban areas. In some cases, access is still through dial-up or via terminals in public libraries, but increasingly they are available on the Internet through WWW, Telnet, and Gopher. Normally, the freenets are open to guest logins, although sometimes they limit the services that guests are allowed to access. The menus are usually organized by categories named for public services like the library and the courthouse. Table 15.1 shows just a few of the business-related resources that can be found on the freenets. There is a good starting place for reaching the freenets at *http://duke.usask.ca/~scottp/free.html*. It has connections to most of the existing civic nets. See Chapter 8 for a list of freenets and their addresses.

Table 15.1 Freenet business-related sources.

Subject	Freenet
Business & Employment	Michiana and Twin Cities
Business & Industry Park	Youngstown Freenet
Business Abroad-Import/Export	Buffalo
Business, Industry & Tourism	Saskatoon Free Net
Business Information	Eugene Freenet
Buyer's Rights	Denver Freenet
Federal Reserve	Twin Cities Freenet
Foreign Missions	Singapore Citynet
Investing and Taxation	Buffalo Freenet
Jobs	Triangle Freenet
Living & Working	Singapore Citynet
Major Companies	Singapore Citynet
Planning & Zoning	Blacksburg Village
Professional Organizations	Triangle Freenet
SmallbizNet	Michiana
Small Business Development	Buffalo Freenet
Start-up Information	Buffalo Freenet
Transit	Blacksburg Village
Yellow Pages	Triangle Freenet

Los Angeles Free-Net

Los Angeles Free-Net has over a dozen items on its main menu, including community center and local discussion groups; an education center; an emergency network; a government center (including Your Income Tax and the Internal Revenue Code); a health center; Internet resources; library resources; a media center with newspapers, TV, and radio, including hourly CNN updates and Reuters online; Sanford Meisner arts and entertainment center; and weather information. Find it at *telnet://lafn.org* (visitor login: select item 2 at first menu).

Victoria FreeNet—Commerce Building

Although the Victoria FreeNet has a quickly developing Web site, it contains more business resources. The Telnet site includes links to the Bank of Montreal, the Better Business Bureau of Vancouver Island, British

Columbia Business Connection Ltd., a group of business sources on the Net, the Canada/BC Business Service Centre, Canada Net Pages, classifieds, consumer issues, the Greater Victoria Chamber of Commerce, Internet Business Journal, a job market, metal prices, the Vancouver Island Real Estate Exchange, the Victoria Real Estate Board, the Vancouver Stock Exchange, West's Legal Directory, and World Real Estate Listing Service. It can be accessed via *telnet://freenet.victoria.bc.ca* (log in as guest) and *http://freenet.victoria.bc.ca/vifa.html*.

Mobile, Alabama Free-Net Business Center

The Mobile Business Center has local links to an area business directory, the Chamber of Commerce, and a statistical abstract of local information. It also has Internet links to the Small Business Administration (SBA), the AT&T 800 Directory, stocks and commodities pages, business directories, the U.S. Department of Commerce, Mutual Funds Online Magazine, and the Capital PC User Group Investment Page. Its URL is *http://www.maf. mobile.al.us/business/*.

Chebucto (Nova Scotia) Community NetPage: Welcome to Professional Enterprise and Commerce

This freenet's well-constructed business page has links organized in the following categories: local business information (including two daily news sources), other business information, innovative enterprise (including the BARTER NETWORK Regional Atlantic Trading Note Association), professional enterprise, human resources, personal finance, and business support organizations. The local news item called Nova Scotia Monthly Trends in the Economy contains the following current articles: "Employment," "Why has employment stalled?," "Unemployment, Employment Dynamics, Focus on the 65+ Group," "Manufacturing Shipments," "Building Permits," "Housing Starts," "Retail Trade," "Wholesale Trade," "Restaurant Sales," and "Company and Project News." Hit statistics for the page are also available from the page itself. Its located at *http://www.cfn.cs.dal.ca/Commerce.html*.

Akron Regional Free-Net—Business and Commerce Park

The Akron Free-Net has dozens of useful links in its business area. Some of the main menu items are: *Asia Pacific Business & Marketing Resources, Business Publications and Resources, Business Sources on the Net, Economic*

Information from US Dept. of Commerce, Patents Discussion and News, Small Business Admin. (SBA) Industry Profiles, Small Business Admin. (SBA) State Profiles, and *US Commerce Business Daily.* One of the best features of this Gopher menu is that the user is told on each menu item where the information link is from. For example, *Business Sources on the Net [refmac.kent.edu]* indicates that the information under that item comes from Kent State University. The URL is *gopher://gopher.freenet.akron.oh.us: 70/11/Business.*

Internet Wiretap

There is a very useful, if offbeat, site called Internet Wiretap (*gopher:// wiretap.spies.com* or *http:/www.spies.com*) that maintains a large collection of government documents, including GAO publications and other government information. It is a bit of an avant-garde site, offering alternative views of current events. If you are easily offended, use the menus with caution.

Tax Law Information

Villanova University maintains a large database of tax information through the Villanova Tax Law Compendium, *http://www.law.vill.edu/vill. tax.l.compen/* or *gopher://gopher.law.vill.edu:70/11/.taxlaw.* This contains a broad collection of student and faculty tax-related papers. The Villanova Tax Law Society and the Villanova Center for Information Law and Policy jointly sponsor this compendium.

Social Security Administration

The U.S. Social Security Administration is online at *http://www.ssa.gov/,* providing a wide variety of information in both English and Spanish, including benefit information, forms, rulings, a description of their online services, policy information and forum, statistics, legislation, international residents, employer information, and a teacher's kit. They also have a FAQ and a search function.

Cornell Law School

Together, the WWW page and the Gopher at the Cornell University Law School are a gold mine of legal and federal statistical and economic information. The Web site integrates the Gopher-based and the WWW-based offerings of the Legal Information Institute (LII), Cornell Law School. Access is provided to recent Supreme Court decisions (which are distributed on the day of decision under project Hermes), recent decisions of the New York Court of Appeals, the full U.S. Code and more. The site also provides information about Cello, the LII's GUI Web browser.

The site's large collection of links to government information includes links to the U.S. Department Of Commerce, Copyright Office, U.S. Bureau of the Census, Federal Communications Commission, Federal Deposit Insurance Corporation, Federal Reserve Board Data, U.S. Patent Office, and SEC filings (Project EDGAR database).

The LII is on the Web at *http://www.law.cornell.edu/*, or by Gopher at *gopher://gopher.law.cornell.edu:70/*.

RiceInfo

The RiceInfo "Information by Subject Area" page at Rice University has a substantial amount of useful information for businesses (*http://riceinfo. rice.edu/RiceInfo/Subject.html*), and can also be accessed via Gopher (*gopher://riceinfo.rice.edu:70/11/Subject/Economics.*) It has an extensive collection of economics and business resources. There are hundreds of entries of both substantive information and links to other sites. These are the first few entries:

> Accounting Gopher (ANet.scu.edu.au)
> Accounting Historians Database
> Accounting Resources on BUBL
> Arizona State Economic Development Database (3270)
> Asia Pacific Business & Marketing Resources
> Association for Public Policy Analysis and Management
> Automated Trade Library Service at Cal State Fresno (vt100)
> BUBL Economics Section - BH2B2
> Bangkok Post Mid-Year Economic Review 1994
> Banking
> Berkeley Journal of Employment and Labor Law
> Bernan/UNIPUB's Government Publications Network
> Bibliographies in Economics (University of Michigan)
> Bibtex
> British Library for Development Studies (BLDS) Catalogue - link

British Library of Political and Economic Science (LSE)
Brookings Papers on Economic Activity
Budget of the United States Government, Fiscal Year 1995
Bureau of Labor Statistics, US Dept of Labor - Via Sam Houston State U.
Business - Univ of California, Berkeley, Library (InfoLib)
Business Gold: National Technology Transfer Center
Business Information Directory from Tucson, Arizona
Business Journals from CICNet
Business Publications and Newsletters
Business Resources (Babson College)
Business Resources (Nijenrode Univ.)
Business Resources and Services (Mountain Net)
Business Resources on BUBL
Business Sources on the Net

And on...!

UH CBA WWWeb Business Yellow Pages

The University of Houston, College of Business Administration and Information Technology Department, provides this extensive listing of several thousand companies with Web pages at *http://www.cba.uh.edu/ ylowpges/ylowpges.html*. The list was developed at the university by researching publicly available information.

/MouseTracks/

/MouseTracks/, *http://nsns.com/MouseTracks/*, offers numerous links to a variety of resources for the marketing community. Categories of information include:

- Hall of Malls—A listing of virtual malls

- Conference Calls—A listing of conferences

- The List of Marketing Lists—Subscription information for a number of discussion mailing lists with topics of interest to Internet marketers

- Nuts and Bolts—Information on how to market and sell goods and services on the Internet

- New Medium—Information on the Internet as a new way to distribute entertainment and published materials

Online Sources of Business Magazines, Journals, and Serials

The Electronic Newsstand at *http://enews.com/* is an excellent source of access to print publications online. It offers publications under such topics as Business Research Publications, Inc., *Business News and Management, Finance, Real Estate, Investing, Industry, Government and Technology,* and, *International,* with such publications as *Barron's, Business Week, The Economist, Inc. Magazine,* and *Marketing Tools* represented. Usually, there are tables of contents and editorial summaries for the magazines.

Good sources of online access to journals are the RiceInfo page of Rice University's site (*gopher://riceinfo.rice.edu:70/11/Subject/Economics*), and the e-journals project at CICnet (*httpat://ejournals.cic.net/*).

The Harvard Business School Publishing Company (*http://www.hbsp.harvard.edu*) houses a variety of materials including the Harvard Business School catalog, *Harvard Business Review* reprints, Harvard Business School Press book titles, case studies, and MPG (business-related video materials). For most of these, the catalog begins with items from 1989, but classic cases and bestsellers date back to the 1960s. This site also includes access to an online order form.

Internet Discussion Lists and Usenet Groups Related to Business

Table 15.2 shows some useful Internet discussion lists and Usenet newsgroups that can assist you in pursuing business on the Internet.

Kim Bayne maintains a resource called Marketing Lists on the Internet at *http://www.bayne.com/wolfBayne/ htmarcom/mktglist.html*, also available via e-mail from *lists@bayne.com*.

There are a number of Usenet newsgroups that regularly distribute business-related information. Remember that for any particular business and industry, there will be groups on specific subjects as well.

alt.business.misc	All aspects of commerce
alt.business.franchise	All aspects of franchising
alt.business.import-export	Business aspects of international trade
alt.business.multi-level	Multilevel (network) marketing businesses
misc.business.consulting	The business of consulting (moderated)
misc.business.facilitators	Discussions for all types of facilitators

Table 15.2 Selected discussion lists.

List	List Subject
awards-b@vm1.ucc.okstate.edu	Commerce Business Daily—Awards
biz-marketing-consulting@world.std.com	Performing Marketing as a Consultant
carecon@vm1.yorku.ca	Caribbean Economy
china-link@IFCSS.ORG	"China-Link" Newsletter, featuring China Import/Export News
commercial-realestate@syncomm.com	Commercial Real Estate
economy@tecmtyvm.mty.itesm.mx	Economic Problems in Less Developed Countries
edi-l@uccvma.bitnet	Electronic Data Exchange issues list
e-europe@pucc.princeton.edu	Eastern Europe Business Network
finance@vm.temple.edu	The Electronic Journal of Finance
gled@uicvm.uic.edu	Great Lakes Economic Development Research Group
globalmc@tamvm1.tamu.edu	Global Marketing Consortium Discussion List
hep2-l@american.edu	Marketing with Technology (MarTech)
hrd-l@mizzou1.missouri.edu	Human Resource Development Group List
ioobf-l@uga.cc.uga.edu	Industrial Psychology Forum
idforum@vm1.yorku.ca	Industrial Design Forum
Internet-Marketing@popco.com	Discussion of Internet Marketing
mfn-strategy@mailbase.ac.uk (subscribe to mailbase@mailbase. ac.uk with message join mnf-strategy *yourfirstname yourlastname*)	Manufacturing Strategy
nasirn-L@ubvm.cc.buffalo.edu	North American Service Industries Research
quality@pucc.princeton.edu	Total Quality Mangement
pcbr-l@uhccvm.uhcc.Hawaii.Edu	Pacific Business Researchers Forum
ruraldev@ksuvm.ksu.edu	Community and Rural Economic Development

misc.entrepreneurs	Discussions on operating a business
misc.entrepreneurs. moderated	Entrepreneur/business topics (moderated)
sci.op	Operations research/management science
sci.engr.manufacturing	Newsgroup for manufacturing technology

From ClariNet, a commercial news provider, the following may be useful:

clari.biz.economy	Articles of general interest to the business community
clari.biz.market.amex	American Exchange stock information
clari.biz.market.dow	Dow Jones information
clari.biz.market.ny	Information on widely held NYSE stocks
clari.biz.market.otc	Most active OTC stocks
clari.biz.report	Selected mutual fund reports

Career and Employment Resources

There are numerous resources regarding career information and employment opportunities.

CareerMosaic Information Center

CareerMosaic has links to articles and resources on its own server as well as links to several other resources, including the National Business Employment Weekly, Bureau of Labor Statistics, and several professional women's resources. The URL is *http://www.careermosaic.com/cm/cm14.html*.

E-SPAN's Interactive Employment Network

E-SPAN calls itself an Interactive Employment Network. Currently, E-SPAN focuses primarily on the job seeker, but intends to expand its focus to include employers soon. The database of over 3,000 job openings can be searched by keyword, region, industry, and date posted. The Web page includes links to *1995 Salary Guides, Resume Writing Tips*, and *The Occupational Outlook Handbook for 94–95*. The URL is *http://www.espan.com/*.

Best Bets from the Net

This University of Michigan resource lists sources of professional and academic job opportunities by the following categories: *Education & Academe, Humanities & Social Sciences, Science & Technology, Business,* and *Government Jobs.* Each category contains numerous resource links, and each resource link has a thorough description and evaluation of that resource. The URL is *http://asa.ugl.lib.umich.edu/chdocs/employment/*.

Online Career Center

This Internet resource is available via both the World Wide Web and Gopher. Several sources at the Online Career Center may be searched for topics and keywords of interest: *Job Openings, Resumes, Chronicle of Higher Education,* and *MedSearch America.* Other items on the menu include *Career Assistance, College & University Resume Books/Diskettes, Company Sponsors and Profiles, Employment Events, FAQ—Frequently Asked Questions about OCC, How To Enter a Resume,* and *Recruitment; Advertising Agencies.* Find this resource at *http://www.occ.com/occ/* or *gopher://occ.com: 70/11/occ*.

North Carolina State University—Jobs Outside North Carolina

This Web page includes many links to interesting job resources on the Net, including *Career Connections, Job Surfer, Bio Online,* the *National Science Foundation,* the *Academic Position Network, Universities Around the World,* and *Catapult.* (North Carolina State University also provides a linked page for jobs within North Carolina.) The URL is *http://www2.ncsu.edu/ncsu/cals/career/other_jobs.html.*

Employment Opportunities and Job Resources on the Internet

This guide by Margaret Riley is a part of The Clearinghouse for Subject-Oriented Internet Resource Guides, and is the definitive guide. The available files include *How to Internet, Incorporating the Internet into Your Job Search Strategy, Using the Internet in the Career-Planning Process,* and *How to Post Job Listings on the Internet.* Over a dozen major categories of job listing sources on the Internet are also linked. The URL is *http://www.wpi.edu/~mfriley/jobguide.html.*

A Few Other Sites...

Monster Jobs on the Web

http://www.monster.com/home.html

National Association of Colleges and Employers' JobWeb

http://www.jobweb.org/

George Washington University Career Center—Job Search Process

http://www.jobtrak.com/jobsearch_docs/pointers.html

Useful Tidbits: Directory Information—Time, Telephone, and Postal Codes

Did you ever need to know what time it is in Ulan Bator? Check out Local Times Around the World, *http://www.hilink.com.au/times/*.

Information on cities worldwide is available from *http://www.city.net/*.

Are you interested in the new German postal codes? Or phone books? Or an Estonian-English dictionary? Go to the Virtual Reference collection (*http://thorplus.lib.purdue.edu/reference/index.html*) to find:

Dictionaries, Thesauri, Acronyms

Maps & Travel Information

Periodic Tables and Weights & Measures

Phone Books & Area Codes

Selected Indiana Documents

Selected U.S. Documents

Time & Date

ZIP, & International Country Codes

Other Reference Sources

This is a very handy reference collection for figuring out times and postal codes worldwide, useful information for the business traveler.

The International Business Kiosk (*http://www.webcom.com/~one/world/*), sponsored by Web Communications, is a reference page of information for traveling business people of all sorts. It includes hotlinks to information on international travel, airlines, car rentals, conversions of weights and measures, and several other useful topics.

Here are some other handy sites:

Webcom International Business Kiosk Time Around The World
http://www.webcom.com/~one/world/time.html

US Naval Observatory Master Clock
http://tycho.usno.navy.mil/cgi-bin/timer.pl

USPS Address Quality & ZIP Code Lookup
http://www.usps.gov/ncsc/

World Phone Books by Continent—CSO, WHOIS, X,500, etc.
gopher://gopher.nd.edu:70/11/Non-Notre%20Dame%20Information %20Sources/Phone%20Books--Other%20Institutions

World Phone Books by Continent via Austin Hospital—Australia
gopher://gopher.austin.unimelb.edu.au:70/11/phones/otherphone

CommerceNet Complete List of Area Codes
http://www.commerce.net/directories/news/areacode.html

Just a Few Additional Business Resources

Washington and Lee (*http://honor.uc.wlu.edu:1020*) has a large repository of information under the menu item *Commerce, Business and Accounting*, with over 740 entries.

The Dow Jones homepage gives access to information related to investments, economics, business, customized news services, research services, and electronic publications, at *http://bis.dowjones.com/*.

Source Translation & Optimization's Internet Patent Search System homepage provides access for patent searches, and access to information on the patenting process, at *http://sunsite.unc.edu/patents/intropat.html*.

Science and Technology Information System offers National Science Foundation information, grant material, and databases via *http://stis.nsf. gov/*.

Required Reading

It is important while creating an Internet marketing and business presence on the Internet, that you look at what others are doing online. While there is no substitute for mixing it up online, it is a good idea to subscribe to some of the important newsletters and magazines.

There are a growing number of paper-based and electronic periodicals, journals, newsletters, and magazines that can assist you in learning more about creating and maintaining a business presence on the Internet. Many of the paper-based publications also maintain some online full-text versions of their materials. Here are a few of these resources:

The Internet Letter, a paper-based NetWeek publication, focuses on corporate users and information services. It covers networking issues of all kinds, including technical, regulatory, and governmental issues. It also includes tips and techniques, and information on upcoming events. Edited by Jayne Levin, this is one of the first publications to discuss business on the Internet. You can get more information via e-mail to *info@netweek.com*.

Internet Business Report, edited by Rob Hertzberg, provides broad coverage of electronic commerce. It focuses on the commercial opportunities of the network, and includes articles, opinion pieces, and occasionally a bit of satire.

The Internet Business Journal is one of the earliest publications about business on the Internet. It focuses on commercial opportunities of networking. Published in Canada by Strangelove Internet Enterprises, it has articles, resources, opinion pieces, and company profiles. The editor, Aneurin Bosley, can be reached via e-mail: *editor@strangelove. com*.

Internet World is a paper-based magazine published by the Meckler Corporation that covers all facets of the Internet, including how-to articles, reviews, opinions, and issues.

Matrix News is a monthly newsletter about the global matrix of the Internet, including information on demographics, network statistics, reviews, and commentary. *Matrix News* is published by Matrix Information and Directory Services, and is online at *http://www.mids.org/ mids/* or *gopher://gopher.mids.org*.

The Electronic Journal of Virtual Culture is a multidisciplinary electronic journal devoted to issues of computer-mediated human behavior, thought, and interaction. Subscribe using the standard listserv commands, to *listserv@kentvm.kent.edu* with the message **subscribe ejvc-1 yourname**.

Some other publications to consider:

WebMaster—An online supplement to *CIO Magazine*, published by CIO Communications, Lew McCreary, editor: *http://www.cio.com/WebMaster*.

Internet Week—Offers news regarding Internet business opportunities; published by Phillips Business Information, Minda Morgan Caesar, editor: *http://www.phillips.com:3200/*.

Net Commerce International—Published in England, a newsletter treating all angles of electronic commerce; John Lewell, editor: *http://www. lpac.ac.uk/Trel/NCI.html*.

Software Collections

As you proceed with creating your business presence, you will have need for software such as mail readers, TCP/IP, and Gopher. There are some excellent repositories of software readily available on the Internet. (See Appendix C if you are unsure how to FTP to retrieve software files.)

FTP site	Directory Path
North America	
ftp.cica.indiana.edu	/pub/pc/win3
merit.edu	/pub/ppp
sunsite.unc.edu	/pub/micro/pc-stuff/ms-windows
oak.oakland.edu	/SimTel/msdos
wuarchive.wustl.edu	/pub/MSDOS_UPLOADS
Europe	
garbo.uwasa.fi	/pc
	/windows
micros.hensa.ac.uk	/mirrors/cica/win3/winsock
nic.funet.fi	/msdos
	/winnt
	/msdos/windows/winsock
src.doc.ic.ac.uk	/windows3
	/dos
	/mirror
	/simtel-win3

Australia/Asia

baudin.cc.utas.edu.au	/pc/win3
brother.cc.monash.edu.au	/pub/win3
csuvax1.murdoch.edu.au	/pub/pc/windows
ftp.cc.monash.edu.au	/pub/win3
ftp.hk.super.net	/pub/dos /pub/windows

Finding Even More Information

There are two useful sources of online guides to help you dig further for information, located at the University of Michigan and Kent State University.

The University of Michigan maintains a library of subject-related guides to information on the Internet (*http://www.lib.umich.edu/chhome. html*). Currently the business section contains these guides:

Airlines: M. Seidel

Business: T. Diamond

Business: C. Newton-Smith

Business: S. Webber

Business, Accounting, Finance, Marketing: L. Haas

Business & Economics: T. Austin, K. Tsang

Cyberpreneurship: P. Wilkins, S. Schweitzer

EDI, Electronic Data Interchange, Electronic Commerce, Standards: P. Burns

Employment Opportunities & Job Resources: M. Riley

Human Resources, Industrial Psychology: L. Haas

International Trade & World Commerce: S. Herro

Jobs, Employment, Placement Services: D. Kovacs

Job Search & Employment Opportunities: P. Ray, B. Taylor

Personal Finance: A. Chambers, C. Kummer

Personal Finance: A. Chambers/GNN

Transportation, Commercial Aviation, Airlines: G. Werner

Women & Business: K. Schneider

Business Sources on the Net (BSN) is organized by subject. Each section is a separate file available at the Kent State University Gopher *gopher://refmac.kent.edu:70/1D-1%3A2577%3ABusiness*. The following are currently available under Business Sources on the Net:

BSN.ACCOUNTING

BSN.COMPUTER

BSN.ECONOMICS

BSN.ETHICS

BSN.FINANCE

BSN.GENERAL

BSN.GREEN

BSN.INSURANCE

BSN.INTERNATIONAL

BSN.INTRO

BSN.INVESTMENT

BSN.JOBS

BSN.LOCATION

BSN.MANAGEMENT

BSN.MARKETING

BSN.OPERATIONS

BSN.PERSONNEL

BSN.README

BSN.SMALL

Where from Here...

The next chapter provides more Internet resources, categorized by profession and subject area.

CHAPTER 16

Online Resources, Databases, and Libraries of General Interest

The Internet is bristling with resources, databases, and information of all kinds and formats. Much of that information relates to specific subjects or fields, but there are some more general resources available for browsing:

- Libraries
- Electronic texts
- Reference resources
- U.S federal, state, and local government documents and information
- Canadian government information
- International resources

Libraries

Thousands of libraries worldwide are reachable online. In most cases, the catalog and some databases are available for remote searching using Telnet, Gopher, and WWW. There are public libraries, consortiums of libraries, and individual, technical, college, university, and organization libraries.

You can get access to libraries on the Internet in a variety of ways. Some libraries have WWW connections, some have Telnet addresses, some are connected using Gopher, and others are connected through alliances. Many Gophers have gateways to library catalogs, so that once you have reached one library, you can usually network out to others.

Library Alliances

Some libraries have created consortiums or alliances in order to extend and expand their services. In the 1970s and 1980s, they formed these consortiums in order to provide access to services and materials that were not on-site before the Internet really started to grow. Now, alliances such as these are providing their collective services on the Internet:

- Access Colorado Library and Information Network
- Boston Library Consortium
- Colorado Alliance of Research Libraries (CARL)
- C*O*N*N*E*C*T: Libraries in the Greater Hartford Area
- DALNET (Detroit Area Library Network)
- Fenway Libraries Online, Inc.
- Florida State University System
- HELIN (Higher Education Library Information Network)
- Houston Area Library Automated Network (HALAN)
- ILLINET On-line Catalog
- KELLY: Regional Online Catalog for WESTNET
- MARMOT Library Network
- Maryland Interlibrary Consortium
- Nevada Academic Libraries Information System (NALIS)
- OhioLink
- University of Maryland System
- Washington Research Library Consortium

A large library consortium, the Colorado Alliance of Research Libraries (CARL), provides a number of interesting services. CARL can be contacted by way of the Web (*http://www.carl.org/cinfo.html*), and via Telnet (*pac.carl.org* and log in as **PAC**). In addition, CARL is on the menu of numerous other libraries. Using CARL's UnCover database, you can search through and read thousands of magazine and journal abstracts, and using a credit card, order the full text for fax delivery within 24 hours.

University and Research Libraries

There are hundreds of research organization, college, and university libraries that have online catalogs and other services including access to databases and special collections. This is just a sample of those libraries that are currently online:

- Air Force Institute of Technology
- Arizona State University
- Auburn University
- Bates College
- Boston University
- Bowdoin College
- Bowling Green State University
- Brandeis University
- Brookhaven National Laboratory
- Brown University
- Bucknell University
- Cal Polytechnic State University
- California Institute of Technology
- California State University, Long Beach
- Carnegie-Mellon University
- Case Western Reserve University
- Central Michigan University
- City University of New York
- Colby College
- Colgate University
- Colorado School of Mines
- Colorado State Department of Education
- Columbia University
- Connecticut State University
- Cornell University
- Museum of Fine Arts, Boston
- National Center for Atmospheric Research

- Nebraska State Colleges
- New England Conservatory
- New Mexico State University
- New York University
- North Carolina State University
- Rice University
- Rochester Institute of Technology
- Rockefeller University
- Roger Williams University
- Rutgers University
- University of Illinois at Urbana/Champaign
- University of Iowa
- University of Kansas
- University of Maine System

Canadian and European Libraries

Worldwide, there are a large number of libraries online, offering catalogs and databases in English and other languages. A sample of Canadian libraries includes:

- Acadia University
- Canada Centre for Mineral and Energy Technology
- Carleton University
- Concordia University
- Dalhousie University
- Ecole Polytechnique (Montreal)
- Laurentian University
- Laval University
- McGill University
- McMaster University
- Memorial University, Newfoundland
- Nova Scotia College of Art and Design
- Ontario Institute for Studies in Education

- Ottawa Public Library
- Saskatoon Public Library
- St. Boniface General Hospital Library
- University of British Columbia
- University of Calgary
- University of Guelph
- University of King's College
- University of Lethbridge
- University of Manitoba Libraries
- University of New Brunswick
- University of Ottawa
- University of Prince Edward Island
- University of Saskatchewan
- University of Toronto

Libraries from the United Kingdom include:

- Aberdeen University
- Cambridge University
- City of London Polytechnic
- City University
- Cranfield Institute of Technology
- Dundee Institute of Technology
- Durham University
- Edinburgh University
- Edinburgh University Online Information System
- Essex University
- Glasgow University
- London University Central Libertas Consortium
- London University, British Library of Political and Economic Science
- London University, Imperial College
- London University, Kings College
- London University, Queen Mary College

- Manchester University
- National Library of Scotland
- National Library of Wales
- Natural Environment Research Council (NERC)
- North East Wales Institute
- Nottingham University
- Open University
- Oxford Brookes University
- Oxford Polytechnic
- Oxford University
- Oxford Westminster College
- Queens University Belfast
- Reading University
- Royal Greenwich Observatory
- Public Libraries

City and Metropolitan Libraries

There are some public libraries currently accessible using the Internet, with more coming online. The following is a sampling:

- Abilene Public Library
- Atlanta-Fulton Public Library
- Bangor Public Library
- Beaumont Public Library
- Bemis Public Library
- Boulder, Colorado, Public Library System
- Carnegie Library of Pittsburgh
- Cedar Rapids Public Library
- Central and Western Massachusetts Public Libraries
- Cleveland Public Library
- Denver Public Library
- Detroit Public Library
- Estes Park Public Library

- Fort Morgan Public Library
- Harris County Public Library
- Houston Public Library
- Keene Public Library
- Lynchburg Public Library
- New York Public Library
- Pasadena Public Library
- Port Arthur Public Library
- Port Neches Public Library
- Seattle Public Library
- Sonoma County Library
- Sterling Municipal Library
- Sterling Public Library

Some Particularly Useful Libraries

There are some libraries that are particularly useful for the general and business user. These range from a virtual public library to the Library of Congress.

The New York Public Library

The venerable New York Public Library (with the lions Patience and Fortitude now virtually standing guard) has a database of all holdings in all branches, as well as in their special collections. A visit to their homepage (*http://www.nypl.org*) reveals:

```
About the Information Found Through This Web Site
Introduction and History
NYPL Celebrates its Centennial
Exhibitions, Programs and Performances at NYPL
NYPL Multi-media Sampler
The New York Public Library Publications Catalog
Corporate Services
```

The Internet Public Library

The Internet Public Library is an experiment in melding some traditional public library functions with those of the Internet community—exploring the hybrid of librarianship and the Internet. It provides services and information that enhance the value of the Internet, with an eye toward bringing diversity. It also takes on a significant educational function by providing access to MOOs, and a virtual classroom, exhibit hall, and reading room. Its URL is *http://aristotle.sils.umich.edu/*.

The University of Michigan Library in general is a great access point of information. The Michigan Electronic Library, GoMLink, is a joint project between The University of Michigan and the state's public libraries. While its specialty is in information about the state of Michigan, this electronic library of Internet resources covers some subjects in depth, including *Business & Economics*, and *Computers & Technology*; it also offers *News Services & Periodicals*, and a *Reference Desk*. The *Business & Economics* section is divided into 24 subcategories, ranging from *Agribusiness* to *Workplace Safety*. Each subcategory is then represented by several linked resources. Access is at *http://mlink.hh.lib.umich.edu/main-index.html*.

Library of Congress

The Library of Congress contains links to many federal government information sources. It provides access to legislative information through the THOMAS Web server and LOCIS Telnet service. LOCIS includes copyright information and foreign law as well. Two other components are Library of Congress Machine-Assisted Realization of the Virtual Electronic Library, also called LC MARVEL, and the Global Electronic Library. LC MARVEL, which is a Gopher-based information system, provides lists of resources by subject. The Global Electronic Library links to sites with information on local, state, and federal government; library resources; news and government documents; publishing resources; Internet resources; and World Wide Web meta-indices and search tools. All this can be found at *http://lcweb.loc.gov/global/*.

National Library of Canada

The National Library of Canada is currently working on a project that will provide access to World Wide Web sources of Canadian information by subject. The project, called Canadian Information by Subject, has a selection of sites available now, with a comprehensive listing being developed. Canadian Information by Subject already contains these links: *Canada Net Pages, Canada's School Net, Canadian Broadcasting Corporation, Canada and Radio-Canada International, Canadian Kids Home Page, Canadiana, Central*

Index of Canadian WWW Servers, CultureNet, Humanities Canada, National Atlas Information Service, NETLiNkS!, and *Open Government.* The first link, *Canada Net Pages,* includes the following business-related categories: *White Pages, Business Directory, Real Estate, Tourism,* and *Stocks and Funds.* These Web pages are available in French as well as English, at *http://www. nlc-bnc.ca/ehome.htm.*

Portico—The British Library Board

Portico provides a World Wide Web resource list of search tools and guides, as well as a description of each resource. In addition to the search tools, subject trees, and guides, Portico provides links to British libraries, the government of the United Kingdom, the European Union, broadcasting and news services, library organizations, and publishing and bookselling entities. Under broadcasting and news services, listings for the BBC, CNN Interactive, FutureNet World News, and The Electronic Telegraph can be found. The URL is *http://portico.bl.uk.*

National Library of Australia

The National Library of Australia provides a list of guides and directories to help both the novice and the experienced user navigate the Net. This list includes *Starting Points, Arrangements by Subject, Interesting Sites, Searching Tools, Additional Resources, Listserv Guides,* and *Australian Resource lists.* Each of these topics contains several links to online resources. The URL is *http://www.nla.gov.au.*

Electronic Texts

Full-length books and other large documents found on the Internet are called electronic texts. There are several sources of electronic text; primary among them are Project Gutenberg and the Online Book Initiative at World Software Tool & Die. These can be found on the Web, Gopher, and by way of Telnet.

Project Gutenberg

Project Gutenberg is a collection of English texts including literature, religious documents, works by Shakespeare, political documents, and reference works. The documents, which are available for free, can be searched by title or author. All the electronic texts are available in ASCII so that any text editor or word processing program can read them. All the texts can also be searched with almost any search program. URL: *http:// jg.cso.uiuc.edu/PG/welcome.html*.

Alex: A Catalogue of Electronic Texts on the Internet

Alex: A Catalogue of Electronic Texts on the Internet is a resource maintained by Radcliffe Science Library of Oxford University. It has over 1,800 entries on its Gopher server. You can explore Alex by author, date, host, language, subject, and title. As an example, a search for documents with titles that begin with the letter "f" yielded over 70 texts. A searchable Gopher Jughead index is also available. This resource is at *gopher://rsl.ox. ac.uk:70/11/lib-corn/hunter*.

Columbia University: Project Bartleby

Project Bartleby (the scrivener) is an online collection of complete hypertext books of classic literature. The collection currently includes:

```
Bartlett, John. 1901. Familiar Quotations, 9th ed.
Chapman, George, trans. 1857. The Odysseys of Homer.
Dickinson, Emily. 1896. Poems.
Inaugural Addresses of the Presidents of the United States. 1989.
Keats, John. 1884. Poetical Works.
Melville, Herman. 1853. Bartleby, the Scrivener. A Story of
Wall-street.
Shelley, Percy Byshe. 1901. Complete Poetical Works.
Strunk, William, Jr. 1918. The Elements of Style.
Whitman, Walt. 1900. Leaves of Grass.
Wilde, Oscar. 1881. Poems.
Wordsworth, William. 1888. Complete Poetical Works.
```

Project Bartleby provides a search interface to specific works or the entire collection. The URL is *http://www.cc.columbia.edu/acis/bartleby/*.

And a Few Others...

Electronic Books at Wiretap—*gopher://wiretap.Spies.COM:70/11/Books*
Online Book Initiative—*gopher://ftp.std.com/11/obi/book*

Dartmouth University Library—*http://www.dartmouth.edu*; a large collection of the works of Dante in electronic form is offered at *gopher://gopher.dartmouth.edu/1/AnonFTP/pub/Dante*.

Reference Resources

Reference materials are available online at many sites. These include phone books, dictionaries, the CIA Fact Book, news and weather, census information, zip code information, and more.

The Virtual Reference Desk

The Virtual Reference Desk at the University of Massachusetts at Lowell is a rich collection of reference materials under the following headings:

Business Resources
Chemistry Resources
Physics Resources
Government Documents and Resources
Health Resources
On-line Text (etext)
Subject Access
Search Tools
General Reference Tools

This is one of those sites worth repeat business—put it in your bookmarks: *http://libvax.uml.edu/www/VLResources.html*.

The Online Reference Works Page

This page offers an extensive number of links to online reference works. You can use references such as dictionaries, encyclopedias, Internet resources, and place-oriented and geographic references. You can even find a hypertext version of Webster's Dictionary—all at *http://www.cs.cmu.edu/Web/references.html*.

Washington & Lee's Reference Collection

The Washington & Lee Law Library has an outstanding reference section with 90 entries, and a search feature, as seen on their page (*http://honor.uc.wlu.edu:1020*):

```
..Restrict by Subject
..Restrict by Domain
..Restrict by Type (Telnet, Gopher, WWW)
..Sort: Date (for date coded entries) [90 items]
..Sort: Geographic [90 items]

Academic Resources
Answers to Your Computer Questions
Area Code Lookup
Australian Postcodes Database (WAIS db)
Biographical Information
BUBL's Bibliographies & Reviews
BUBL's Directories: Helping you Find the Information You
BUBL's Electronic Mail Discussion Lists (E-mail)
BUBL's Glossaries, Acronymns and Definitions
Catalogue of Projects in Electronic Text (CPET), Georgetown
CIA World Fact Book 1993 (Search)
CIA World Fact Book 1993 (search)
City/Zip Code Lookup
City/Zip Lookup through Geographic Name Server
comparative-literature (Mailbase)
Computer Jargon: the New Hacker's Dictionary
DA - Library Oriented Directories
DB - Internet Oriented Directories
DC - E-mail Directories (see also section DB)
DD - Information Servers/Services Directories
DE - Access to Directory Searching Facilities (World Wide)
Diane Kovacs Electronic Conference List
Dictionaries
Directories: Phone, Place, Time & Weather Information
E-mail and Phone Directories
Electronic Addresses (Email) Directories
Electronic Journal Collections
Electronic Serials
Electronic Text Collections
Emergency and Disaster Information Services
Employment Opportunities
Encyclopedia Britannica (Rice Only, WWW)
English-Spanish Electronics Dictionary (experimental) Johns
Hopkins U.
F01 - UK Mailing Lists
F03 - Non-UK Mailing Lists
```

```
F06 - E-mail Discussion Lists and Related: Lists of Lists
FAQs: Frequently Asked Questions files (via FTP from MIT)
FAQs: Frequently Asked Questions files (via gopher from UNB)
FAQs: Frequently Asked Questions files (via WWW from Ohio State)
FAQs: List of Periodic Informational Postings (FAQ of FAQs)
FAQs: Search Frequently Asked Questions files (via WAIS)
Frequently Asked Questions (FAQs) on Everything [1637]
Global Collection (Internet Resources of Global Scope)
Global Electronic Library (by Subject)
Government & Non-Profit Group Information
Government-Provided Information
Grant and Funding Information Resources
Grant, Foundation & Scholarship Information
GreyNet - Grey Literature Network Service
Hacker's Dictionary (via Tenn. Tech. U.)
International Information
Internet Guides
Internet Guides and Resources
Internet Guides, Policies, and Information Services
Internet Nonprofit Center (Nonprofit Organization Info)
Internet Reference
Konferanser -- World Wide Conference Announcements from Norway
Library Catalogs of the World
Lookup Acronyms (from UK)
Lookup Computer Jargon
Modern-british-fiction (Mailbase)
Museums, Exhibits and Special Collections via Gopher Jewels
National Science Foundation Award Abstracts
National Science Foundation Publications
New and Changed Gophers
News and Weather
On-Line Ready Reference
Phone Books
Phone Books Menu
Reference calendars (P. Riddle, Rice U.)
Reference Collections
Reference Shelf
Resource Guides
Roget's Thesaurus
Search Geographic Name Server by City or ZIP code
Spell Checker (via Mid. East Tech. U, Turkey)
Subject Index to Concepts, Terms and Definitions
```

```
Technical Reports
The Free On-line Dictionary of Computing - Search
Thesauri
Thesauri (ADFA)
U.S. State Department Travel Advisories
U.S. Telephone Area Codes
U.S. Zipcode Search
U.S. Zipcodes Directory (WAIS db)
USENET News
Voice of America and Worldnet Television
Webster's Dictionary (Indiana University) (telnet)
Webster's Dictionary (University of California, San Diego)
..Text copy of links
```

Government Documents and Information

The amount of state and local government information available varies greatly by location. Agencies at the federal level have been directed to provide more public information online, and so there is a broad range available.

The Library of Congress

The mother of U.S. libraries, the Library of Congress, is online with a wealth of information and methods of access to information, as seen on their opening menu (*URL: http://www.loc.gov/*):

```
About the Library and the World Wide Web
        See what's new in September 1995 on this server, access
        usage statistics, and read about the Library of Congress
        and the World Wide Web.

Exhibits and Events
        View major exhibits of the Library of Congress and read
        about other Library events.

Services and Publications
        Read about Library services, visit reading rooms,
        publications, and conferences.

Digital Library Collections
```

```
        Search and view items from digitized historical
        collections (American Memory); read about other special
        Americana  collections held by the Library.

    LC Online Systems
        Search LOCIS (Library of Congress Information System) via
        Telnet or using a new Z39.50 fill-in form, LC MARVEL (the
        Library's Gopher-based Campus-Wide Information System),
        the POW/MIA database, and others.

    Congress and Government
        Search congressional information through THOMAS, and
        access federal and state government information.

Library of Congress Indexes to Other World Wide Web Services
        Find selected information on the Internet by subject or
        genre.
```

FedWorld

The FedWorld Information Network is an information service maintained by the National Technical Information Service (NTIS), part of the U.S. Department of Commerce. FedWorld concentrates on online U.S. government information, with a focus on scientific, technical and business-related information. Hotlinks are organized by NTIS subject categories, and lead to World Wide Web servers, FTP, Gopher, and Telnet sites. The FedWorld FTP site includes information files on business, health and safety, and the Environment. The FedWorld Telnet site is a gateway to other U.S. government computer bulletin boards. Approximately 30 percent of the FedWorld technical and business information is gathered from international sources. The URL is *http://www.fedworld.gov/*.

The Federal Web Locator (The Villanova Center for Information Law and Policy)

The Federal Web Locator is a service provided by the Villanova Center for Information Law and Policy at Villanova University. This is your one-stop shopping place for federal government information on the World Wide Web. Villanova intends the site to be comprehensive, and has adopted the motto "Federal Government information at your fingertips." Over 100 links to all parts of the federal government are already available. Visitors may notice a page dedicated to Friends of VCILP, who have helped provide missing federal government links for the Locator. The URL is *http://www.law.vill.edu/fed-agency/*.

The General Accounting Office (GAO)

The full texts of Government Accounting Office (GAO) reports are available as ASCII electronic files from the Government Printing Office (GPO). You can access this service via a WAIS database—Telnet to *swais.access.gpo.gov* and log in as **gao**, and then do a search for documents you want. E-mail questions can be sent to *documents@gao.gov*, and questions on using the GPO system can be referred to the GPO by e-mail at *help@eids05.eids.gpo.gov* or through their page. Access is at *gopher://dewey.lib.ncsu.edu/11/library/disciplines/government/gao-reports/* and *telnet://swais.access.gpo.gov*.

U.S. Federal Laws from Personal Library Software, Inc.

This is a collection of links to a wide array of federal government information, including the *Federal Register*, the Federalist Papers, GAO reports, GSA publications, House documents, the works of Thomas Jefferson and Thomas Paine, various Presidential documents, reports and rules of the House and Senate, statutes, regulations, and treaties, all at *http://www.pls.com:8001/his/2.htm*.

Town Hall—Government Databases

This page, sponsored by Internet Multicasting Service, has links to several sites containing information on federal entities, resources, and documents, including the Congressional Record, the Joint Economic Committee, SEC EDGAR documents, the U.S. Patent Database, the General Services Administration, and the Federal Reserve Board. The URL is *http://town.hall.org/govt/govt.html*.

The Federal Register

The *Federal Register* is available through a commercially produced system (Counterpoint Publishing) that will allow you to browse or search the daily *Federal Register*. While the system limits the amount and type of information that nonsubscribers can retrieve, it is a useful resource, particularly for its free search of tables of contents. Access is at *gopher://gopher.counterpoint.com:2002/11/*.

Census Data

The Census Bureau maintains a page with access to a great deal of its geographical and populational data, including:

Population and Housing
Economy
Geography
Data Access Tools
About the Census Bureau
Latest News
Ask the Experts
Market Place
Search
Pop Clocks
Data Maps
Genealogy
Radio Broadcasts
Employment Opportunities
Other topics

The data is provided in a number of formats, and searching is available as well:

Archie
HTTP Files
FTP Files
BBS
Excellent Sites

One of their most popular tools is the Population Analysis Spreadsheets (PAS), consisting of 45 spreadsheets to be used with Lotus 1-2-3. The Census Bureau URL is *http://www.census.gov/*.

Other Sites with Government Information

State and Local Governments on the Net
   http://www.webcom.com/ ~piper/state/states.html

Meta-Indexes for State and Local Government Information
   http://www.loc.gov/global/state/stategov.html

Social Security Administration—SSA Home Page
   http://www.ssa.gov/SSA_Home.html

U.S. Department of Labor: Occupational Safety and Health
Administration
http://www.osha.gov/; Bureau of Labor Statistics—*http://stats.bls.gov/*

Congress and Legislation

There is an increasing amount of congressional and legislative information available online, including the powerful THOMAS server.

THOMAS

THOMAS (named for Thomas Jefferson) puts a broad range of legislative information online, including:

- *Full Text of Legislation*—Full text of all versions of House and Senate bills, searchable by keyword or by bill number
- *Full Text of the Congressional Record*—Full text of the daily account of proceedings on the House and Senate Floors, searchable by keyword
- *Hot Legislation*—Major bills receiving floor action in the 104th Congress as selected by legislative analysts in the Congressional Research Service
- *The Constitution of the United States*—The full text of the Constitution and its amendments, searchable by keyword
- *House of Representatives Gopher*
- *House of Representatives Constituent E-Mail* and *U.S. Senate Constituent E-Mail*
- *U.S. House of Representatives Audit*
- *Senate Gopher*
- *C-SPAN (Cable-Satellite Public Affairs Network) Gopher*
- *Library of Congress World Wide Web Home Page*
- *Library of Congress Gopher LC MARVEL*

The URL is *http://thomas.loc.gov/*.

Other Legislative and Executive Access

The U.S. House of Representatives, Senate, and White House have Web pages providing access to many resources. Here are some access points:

U.S. House of Representatives Home Page
http://www.house.gov/

U.S. Senate
gopher://gopher.senate.gov:70/

Congressional E-Mail Addresses
http://www.webcom.com/~leavitt/cong.html

The White House
http://www.whitehouse.gov/

The Catalog of Federal Domestic Assistance

The Catalog of Federal Domestic Assistance provides information on more than 1,000 U.S. government assistance programs, from more than 50 federal agencies. It is keyword searchable at the Gopher at *marvel. loc.gov* under the heading *federal government information* and then using the menus to find information by agency. Access is at *gopher://solar.rtd.utk. edu:70/11/Federal/CFDA*.

State Department Travel Advisories

The State Department makes its travel advisories available through an archive of State Department travel information and advisories. The information is arranged by country. The files include information on medical facilities, crime, drug penalties, registration, current conditions, country descriptions, entry requirements, and embassy and consulate locations. These are at *http://www.stolaf.edu/network/travel-advisories.html*.

Guides to Other Sources of Government Information

A very useful guide to government resources and documents called *Internet Resources: US Federal Government Information*, by Maggie Parhamovich, is available via *gopher://una.hh.lib.umich.edu:70/00/inetdirsstacks/usfedgov% 3Aparhamovich*.

Community/Civic/Rural/Local Info is a list of mailing lists that focus on community, civic, rural, or local issues, people, culture, and governments, compiled by Art McGee. It is an eclectic grouping, but provides a good guide to some interesting mailing lists related to community and government. It is available via *ftp://ftp.netcom.com/pub/am/amcgee/community/ communet.msg*.

Canadian Government Documents

A variety of Canadian government documents and resources are available online from a variety of sources. Federal and provincial information is available in both English and French as a rule.

Statistics Canada—Statistique Canada

Statistics Canada makes the full text of its daily reports available, as well as various press releases, lists of publications, and other information, at *http://www.statcan.ca.*

Welcome to Canada's Parliament

Canada's Parliament server provides access to online nonpartisan information on the role, history, proceedings, and activities of Parliament. Hotlinks are provided to the Senate, the House of Commons, and the Library of Parliament Web pages. Also available are an online tour of Parliament Hill and transcripts of the proceedings of the committees of the House of Commons. (This information can also be accessed in French.) The URL is *http://www.parl.gc.ca/english/.*

Open Government—Gouvernement Ouvert

Information on Industry Canada's server focuses on the main political bodies on Parliament Hill, but eventually it is promised that links to information from all government departments will be provided. This server provides a keyword search tool and Champlain, an information retrieval service. The Champlain Broker allows users to search across most Canadian government information on the Internet. The URL is *http://info.ic.gc.ca/opengov/.*

Investing and Doing Business in Canada

This Web page sponsored by the Department of Foreign Affairs and International Trade attempts to answer many business and international trade questions from the Canadian government's point of view. Some of the issues addressed include Canada's economic strengths, the Free Trade Agreement (FTA), the North American Free Trade Agreement (NAFTA), government policies, government review of investment transactions, special licenses, intellectual property protection, repatriation of foreign investments, Canada's banking system, import and export taxes, the Goods and Services Tax (GST), corporate tax, allowable business entities, anti-dumping laws, and packaging and labeling requirements for goods sold in Canada. There is a FAQ available. The page includes links to missions and consuls abroad, and to international trade centers within Canada. Also on the page are links to some frequently requested Canadian government publications. Enter at *http://www.dfait-maeci.gc.ca/english/invest/menu.htm.*

International Sources

The Internet is by its nature international in scope, and there are many resources that are helpful for locating relevant information.

Worldwide Resources (Information Bank)

The Information Bank server provides links to compilations of information about cities and regions around the world, national home pages, microstates and principalities, a world guide to business, and the U.S. Army's Country Studies/Area Handbooks. Information Bank divides the world into regions, and provides hotlinks of resources for Russia, former Soviet Republics, and Eastern Europe; Asia; Europe and the Middle East; Africa and Latin America; and U.S. states and Canadian provinces. The URL is *http://www.clark.net/pub/global/country.html.*

The NandO Times World

The NandO Times, sponsored by The News and Observer Publishing Co., presents a daily world news summary, with links to the entire text of the major headline stories. The Times also provides links to other sections of news including the United States, sports, politics, business, information technology, and entertainment. The URL is *http://www2.nando.net/nt/world/.*

Time Daily News—Pathfinder from Time Warner

The Time Daily News page is updated continuously throughout the news day. Within articles, hyperlinks are provided to related articles and background information on correspondents. You can also search for additional articles using the Personal Library Software (PLS) search engine, which is preloaded with appropriate search words for many of the articles. Acrobat PDF format is used on some of the supporting documents, and an Acrobat PDF reader can be downloaded from the page. The URL is *http://www.pathfinder.com/@@d6ByfdAbUAEAQAEn/time/daily/time/1995/latest.html*.

United Nations Development Programme

The United Nations Development Programme operates a very eclectic Gopher to share information, announcements, and what's new about what the United Nations is and what it does. It includes current information such as highlights, press releases, and briefings; documents about the General Assembly, Economic and Social Council (ECOSOC), and the Security Council; conferences; United Nations system directories and Telecommunications catalogs and other documents; and United Nations and related Gophers. It also links to related information and to still other Gopher and information servers, and provides access to external public databases. Access is at *gopher://nywork1.undp.org/*.

City.Net

City.Net is a very international guide to communities around the world, providing information on travel, entertainment, local business, government, and community services. Links are organized by geographical regions: Africa, Antarctica, Arctic, Asia, Australia and Oceania, Caribbean, Central America, Europe, Middle East, North America, and South America. Within each region, listings are arranged alphabetically by country name, and there is a searchable alphabetical index that includes countries, territories, and cities of interest. The URL is *http://www.city.net/*.

UT-LANIC Home Page

University of Texas Institute of Latin American Studies supports the Latin American Network Information Center, which provides access to information on and from Latin America. Hotlinks are provided by country or by topic. Countries include Argentina, Barbados, Belize, Bolivia, Brazil, Chile, Colombia, Costa Rica, Cuba, Dominican Republic, Ecuador, El Salvador, Guatemala, Guyana, Haiti, Honduras, Jamaica, Mexico, Nicaragua, Panama, Paraguay, Peru, Surinam, Uruguay, and Venezuela. Topics include art, anthropology, economy, government, health, libraries, maps, networking, news, publications, and travel. The URL is *http://lanic.utexas.edu/*.

The Geneva International Guide

The Geneva Guide provides a comprehensive set of links to international organizations, including the United Nations and U.N. specialized agencies (such as the Economic Commission for Europe, European Free Trade Association, International Labour Office, International Telecommunication Union, United Nations Conference on Trade and Development, United Nations Educational Scientific and Cultural Organization, World Intellectual Property Organization, and the World Meteorological Organization); non–United Nations international organizations (including the General Agreement on Tariffs and Trade and the International Organization for Standardization); nongovernmental organizations (including the European Association of Development Research and Training Institutes, the European Broadcasting Union, and the European Computer Manufacturers Association); and international organizations on the Internet. The URL is *http://www.isoft.ch/GenevaGuide/orgfil/inx/io.html*.

Electronic Newsletters

Now, for a few useful items for keeping up-to-date. Here are some newsletters of general interest:

E-D-U-P-A-G-E

E-D-U-P-A-G-E is an electronic information service, sponsored by Educom, regarding information technology. It provides summaries, primarily of newspaper articles and from other major news sources, on information technology and the media. It is issued three times weekly. Individual articles are short, rarely over two paragraphs, allowing busy professionals to keep up on developments with a minimum of time invested. E-mail subscriptions are also available free as a listproc subscription to **listproc@educom.unc.edu**. This publication is also available in French, Portuguese, Spanish, and Italian. The URL is *http://educom.edu/*.

CompuNotes

CompuNotes is a weekly publication available through an e-mail distribution list and an FTP site. It features reviews, interviews, and commentary concerning the personal computer industry, including news, reviews, a Web site of the week, an FTP file of the week, and an interview with an industry insider. To subscribe to the e-mail version, send a message to *subscribe@supportu.com* with **subscribe** in the message body. The URL is *ftp://ftp.uu.net:/published/compunotes.*

HotWired

HotWired is the San Francisco, California online alter ego of the print *WIRED* magazine. It contains feature articles and regular columns. You can customize your free subscription by selecting from the categories available: Signal, World Beat, Piazza, Renaissance 2.0, Coin, and Wired. While certain features require you to be a HotWired member, joining is free by completing an online information form. Don't forget your password. An Architext search engine will search the full text of the entire site, based on a word or a concept. HotWired is online at *http://www. hotwired.com/.*

Technology Review

Technology Review is Massachusetts Institute of Technology's national magazine of technology and policy. The online magazine contains well-prepared articles in hypertext that link to references and further information. The main links are to the current issue, the past issue archive, a feedback page, an online career center (The Tech Review, brought to you by the alumni and alumnae), an online book catalog, a way to get a free issue of the print magazine, and other features. The URL is *http://web.mit. edu/afs/athena/org/t/techreview/www/tr.html.*

From Here...

For additional Internet resources more specifically oriented to particular professions, continue on to Chapter 17.

Resources for the Professions

This chapter covers a sampling of Internet resources, listed by profession, that provide good starting points for developing your own custom list. They are organized in the following categories:

- Aerospace and Astronomy
- Allied Health and Medicine
- Computer Science and Math
- Education
- Environment, Land Use, Geography, and Natural Resources
- High Technology, Science, and Engineering
- Investing, Stocks, and Economics
- Journalism
- Law
- Psychology and Mental Health
- Social Sciences
- Telecommunications

There are a number of subject-specific guides available from Clearinghouse for Subject-Oriented Internet Resource Guides at the University of Michigan at *http://www.lib.umich.edu/chhome.html*. It is a good starting place for locating information about specific subjects.

It is important to remember that Internet resources can change locations, contents, login procedures, and addresses in the twinkling of an eye. If one of these resources is unavailable, use one of the search tools such as McKinley's Magellan or WebCrawler mentioned in Chapters 11 and 14 to find it.

Aerospace and Astronomy

There are many useful resources in the fields related to space, because of their early use of the network.

NASA

URL: *http://www.nasa.gov/*

NASA's homepage is a compendium of information about NASA, its projects, and all of its various agencies. Here you can find all kinds of information about NASA itself, and links out to its branches, including information on NASA Educational Programs, NASA Online Educational Resources, and NASA Information Sources by Subject. NASA's numerous centers ranging from the Ames Research Center to the Goddard Centers, the Jet Propulsion Laboratory, and the Johnson and Kennedy Space Centers. This site also has gateways to their other resources, personnel information, and more as seen on the main menu:

```
.....Guide to NASA Online Resources (NAIC Ames)
.....NASA On-line Information (Langley)
.....NASA Personnel Lookup [X.500] (Ames)
.....NASA-Wide Programs (e.g., NASA STI, NASIRC)
.....NASA-affiliated Institutes and Organizations
.....NASA Technical Report Server
.....NASA Commercial Technology
.....NASA Procurement (business opportunities, awards, forecasts, etc.)
.....Other Space Agencies
.....Other Aerospace Sources
```

The Smithsonian Astrophysical Observatory

http://sao-www.harvard.edu/sao-home.html

The Smithsonian Astrophysical Observatory maintains this site with news, mail, and documents concerning information relating to the Advanced X-Ray Astrophysics Facility and the ASAF Science Center.

Data Dissemination Network of the European Space Agency

http://www.esrin.esa.it/

This site covers fairly standard information about the agency, members, publications, news information, and programs including earth observations, telecommunications, and launches.

Hubble Space Telescope Center

http://ecf.hq.eso.org/stecf-homepage.html

This site provides an itemized list of the Hubble telescope's activities scheduled and accomplished for each 24-hour period, a newsletter, archives, conferences, announcements, and a rich library of spectacular telescope images. It offers a search feature as well.

Allied Health and Medicine

Allied health resources on the Internet abound. Some of the most interesting are listed here.

HealthNet

http://hpb1.hwc.ca/healthnet/home.html

HealthNet is a very complete site. It is a demonstration project of Health Information Infrastructure Consulting, Canadian federal government partners, and members of the global health community. Its goals are to provide a single point of access to health care resources on the Internet, and to demonstrate the innovative ways in which many health groups are using currently available Internet and communications technologies. It highlights the potential of existing communications technologies that can be applied toward the development of a health information infrastructure for Canada.

At *http://hpb1.hwc.ca/healthnet/lhlist/hancock.html* HealthNet maintains access to one of the best resources for health care: Lee Hancock's guide to health related information on the Internet.

Healthline

http://healthline.umt.edu:700/

The University of Montana Student Health Services site provides information on drug and alcohol addiction, mental health, sexuality, disabilities, and general health and medical information. While maintained at a university clinic, this page provides very broad information and access to resources.

Food and Drug Administration Electronic Bulletin Board

http://www.fda.gov/fdahomepage.html

Topics covered on this page include topics under *Cosmetics, Human Drugs, Foods, FDA News, Animal Drugs, Biologics, Toxicology, Medical Devices, Radiological Health, Inspections and Imports, Current Information on AIDS,* and *Enforcement Report;* and FDA consumer magazine index and selected articles, FDA Federal Register summaries by subject, summaries of FDA information, index of news releases and answers, text of testimony at FDA congressional hearings, veterinary medicine news, and import alerts.

National Institutes of Health

gopher://gopher.nih.gov:70/11/campus/ABSD

The National Institutes of Health have a site (*http://www.nih.gov/*) where they offer general information about affiliated agencies, and access to other Web sites. In addition, they offer access to their scientific directories and bibliographies:

```
About the Scientific Directory and Annual Bibliography
How to Search the Directory and Bibliography
Search Scientific Directory 1994
Search Annual Bibliography 1993
Individual ICD listings for Scientific Directory and Annual
bibliography
```

The Policy Information Exchange Online (PIE)

http://pie.org/

PIE Online is the Web site of the Policy Information Exchange, a nonprofit institution that disseminates U.S. health care policy information to physical and mental health care professionals. There is information and data about current national health policy, health care reform, testimonies before the U.S. Congress, federal legislative schedules, technical assistance materials, policy research library resources, budget and grant information, full-text articles about health care reform from PIE's newsletter, bibliographies, and information on joining PIE as a member.

The Nightingale Gopher

gopher://nightingale.con.utk.edu/

The University of Tennessee maintains a Gopher focused on nursing called Nightingale. The information is arranged from a nurse's point of view, and supplies data, information and links to all sorts of nursing information, including practices, education, research, communications, philosophy, directories, publications, and more.

Computer Science and Math

Because of the history and nature of the Internet, computer resources are some of the most numerous on the Internet. Almost all of the major computer hardware and software companies have a business presence on the Internet.

Center for Information Systems Management—University of Texas

http://cism.bus.utexas.edu/

The homepage of the Center for Information Systems Management contains information and resources for computer science, information science, and MIS professionals. While the focus is on information on academic research related to those disciplines, you will also find numerous useful resources relating to business and professional use of information technology. The MIS collaborative bulletin board is quite popular—it is an area where users can read about issues, and read and post comments.

Cornell Theory Center

http://www.tc.cornell.edu/ctc.html

This site for the Cornell Theory Center is part of a larger site for Supercomputer Research. The site provides access to information on hardware, software, manuals and documentation, parallel computing topics, programming languages and tools, files available via FTP, tutorials, and a search feature. In addition there are links out to other sites and Web resources.

National Center for Supercomputing Applications—NCSA, Home of Mosaic

http://www.ncsa.uiuc.edu/General/NCSAHome.html

NCSA is the site that developed the GUI browser called Mosaic. In addition to access to information about Mosaic and the actual free software, the site provides information about NCSA, events, NCSA FTP and Gopher servers, affiliated groups on allocations, applications, research, parallel computing, communications, consulting, education, science and math, industrial programs, strategic planning, publications, software development, marketing communication, training, and the NCSA virtual environment group.

Mathematical Resources on the Web

http://www.math.ufl.edu/math/math-web.html

This page is a large collection of links organized by topic. It provides access to WWW homepages, Gopher servers, FTP servers, and guides, journals, preprints, news, BBSs, discussion lists, job listings, addresses, bibliographies, biographies, libraries, and conference and lecture announcements all related broadly to mathematics. It also provides links to sites with information on the "cousin subjects" of computer science, physics, statistics, and issues of policy and the future of the Internet. The site also provides eclectic information on software archives and documentation, pedagogy, commercial online services, travelers' aids, reference works, and vendors.

E-Math from the American Mathematical Society

http://e-math.ams.org/ or *gopher://e-math.ams.org* or *ftp://e-math.ams.org*

This site is the American Mathematical Society's vehicle for providing Internet access and delivering electronic products and services to mathematicians. Members are offered a broad range of items, but visitors can read a portion of the material that includes published articles, preprints, job listings and employment information, committee reports, and TeX resources. Currently the WWW access is limited, but the Gopher is quite complete. AMS products include electronic journals on e-MATH, the MathSci database in several electronic formats, books and journals in print, and more.

The Online World Resources Handbook

http://login.eunet.no/~presno/index.html

This is an unusual shareware resource covering all aspects of the online world with a distinctive international flavor. This online version links to a large number of international news sources, broadcast networks, resources for world travel, international affairs, business, search capabilities, the Usenet newsgroups, search engines, and more. If you register your copy of the book, you are placed on the mailing list of a companion newsletter, the Online World Monitor.

Education

One of the earliest users of the Internet was the higher education community. There are resources for all levels of education on the Internet, and some of the most useful are given here.

EdWeb

http://edweb.cnidr.org:90/resource.cntnts.html

This award-winning site created by Andy Carvin is devoted to K–12 educational uses of the Web. It has a broad range of resources including:

```
The K12 Internet Testbed -- sources of technology grants
The Role of WWW in Education -- articles and links
The HTML Crash Course -- help for those wanting to create homepages in
    schools
The Information Highway Debate -- exploration of the various visions of
    the Internet
```

```
Education Reforms for the 21st Century -- school redesign and reform
Computers and Kids: Life on the Front Lines -- what are schools doing
The Educational Resource Guide
The SchoolWeb Exploration Project -- getting schools on the web
The WWWEDU Home Page -- the discussion list
The Corporation for Public Broadcasting Home Page.
The NPR Home Page.
The PBS Home Page.
Child Safety on the Information Superhighway.
Search EdWeb
```

NASA—Quest

http://quest.arc.nasa.gov/

Quest is the online home of the NASA K–12 Internet Initiative. This comprehensive site is designed for teachers seeking to get their classrooms connected and to work on projects promoting science learning. Some of the links for teachers, parents, and students are to current, past, and future projects involving space exploration, atmospheric sciences, and environmental sciences. Other areas are for grants and funding information, Schools on the Net, and teachers' guides to the Internet and to NASA.

AskERIC (Educational Resources Information Center)

http://ericir.syr.edu/

ERIC (Educational Resources Information Center) is one of the premier providers of access to educational materials of all kinds. This site provides a meta-index of searchable information on education-related resources. AskERIC comprises three major components: the AskERIC Q & A Service, the AskERIC Virtual Library, and the AskERIC R&D service. Some of the links include education conferences, indexes of electronic journals, book reviews, and reference tools, various Internet guides and directories, bibliographies, digests, news and announcements, and information on some professional and commercial organizations, education listserver archives, lesson plans, FAQs, and more.

The World Lecture Hall

http://wwwhost.cc.utexas.edu/world/instruction/index.html

The World Lecture Hall page contains links to pages created by faculty who are using the Web to deliver educational information and class materials. Some of the materials include course syllabi, assignments, lecture notes, exams, class calendars, multimedia packages, and textbooks. A sampling of the disciplines covered are:

Communication
Computer Science
Cultural Studies
Economics
Education
Electrical and Computer
Engineering
Engineering Science
English and Technical Writing
Environmental Science
Finance
Geography
Geology
History
Humanities
Journalism
Language
Law
Library and Information Science
Management
Management Information Systems
Marketing
Mathematics
Mechanical Engineering
Medicine

EOS—Educational Online Sources

http://netspace.students.brown.edu/eos/main_plain.html

EOS offers access to bulletins and announcements ranging from Rural Curriculum resources to a Math Learning Forum Online Project. The site also contains FAQs on academic and Internet training, and pointers to Gopher, FTP, and WWW sites in education. This site offers user options for those with a variety of Internet connections.

Academe This Week

http://chronicle.merit.edu/.index.html
gopher://chronicle.merit.edu

The venerable *Chronicle of Higher Education* provides a site with abstracts of articles, some full-text articles, news updates, and job listings.

Some Additional Information Sources

CoSN—the Consortium for School Networking—*http://digital.cosn.org/*—provides support to schools and other educational institutions in facilitating access to the Internet and the National Information Infrastructure.

EdLinks (*http://www.marshall.edu/~jmullens/edlinks.html*) is a huge resource covering all levels of education, including links to commercial services, general links to related information such as the Adolescent Directory Online, access to the Daily Report Card, projects, newsgroups, government sites, organizations, libraries, and networks.

Some useful guides to educational resources on the network can be located at the University of Michigan's subject-oriented guides collections (*http://www.lib.umich.edu/chhome.html*), under education:

```
Adult/Distance Education; J. Ellsworth
Adult Education, Literacy; T. Eland
Africa; A. Dinar
Computer Training & User Support; M. Kovacs
Education; C. Beaumont
Education; C. Woodbury
Education (Alumni, Student Groups); D. Kovacs
Education (CAI, Educational Technology); D. Kovacs
Education (Higher, Adult, Continuing); D. Kovacs
Education (Home, School); P. Yandell
Education (Primary, Secondary, Vocational, Technical);D.Kovacs
Education (Research, Grants, Funding); D. Kovacs
Education (Special, Disabled); D. Kovacs
Education; J. Harris
Educators; P. Smith
Extension Studies; D. Richardson
Home Schools; J. Shemitz
Institutional Research; J. Milam
```

```
Instructional Technology; M. Ryder
K-12 School Libraries; R. Troselius
Math & Science Education; T.C. O'Haver
Physical Education, Recreation, Dance; K. Robinson
```

Environment, Land Use, Geography, and Natural Resources

One of the most popular topics on the Internet is the environment. Geography and land use information is in abundance, and the following are some of the sources of information.

Geographic Name Server

http://wings.buffalo.edu/geogw

In response to a city name or a zip code, this server provides city, county, state, nation, telephone area code, elevation, feature code, latitude/longitude, and population. In addition, because it is a gateway between the Geographic Name Server at *martini.eecs.umich.edu* and the World Wide Web, with links to maps from Xerox Information, it can also provide a map of the area.

US Naval Observatory Automated Data Service

http://tycho.usno.navy.mil/ads.html or *ftp://tycho.usno.navy.mil/*

This Washington, D.C. site provides frequently updated information on the Global Positioning System, LORAN, OMEGA, USNO time service publications, the TRANSIT satellite, astronomical data, and navigational information.

National Center for Earthquake Engineering Research

http://nisee.ce.berkeley.edu/

The National Center for Earthquake Engineering Research (NCEER) provides access to a database of bibliographic information relating to earthquakes, earthquake engineering, and natural hazards mitigation. It has available citations, abstracts, and information on acquiring monographs, journal articles, maps, videotapes, technical reports, and conference papers.

Oceanic—The Ocean Information Center

http://diu.cms.udel.edu/index.html

This is an in-depth service for researchers in the fields of oceanography and marine studies provided by the University of Delaware's College of Marine Studies. Information is available on current research, oceanographic research observations, many research sites, programs and projects, drifters, sea level data, hydrography, time series, and databases of algorithms and standards. There are also schedules of research vessel cruises and a directory of active oceanographers and marine studies researchers. The site covers the World Ocean Circulation Experiment (WOCE) and TOGA Coupled Ocean-Atmosphere Response Experiment (TOGA COARE).

The Earth Resources Observation Systems (EROS) Data Center Distributed Active Archive

http://sun1.cr.usgs.gov/landdaac/landdaac.html

The Earth Resources Observation Systems (EROS) Data Center Distributed Active Archive Center (EDC DAAC) is part of NASA's Earth Observing System Data and Information System (EOSDIS) initiative to promote the interdisciplinary study and understanding of the Earth system. The site provides access to land observation data, including data acquired by satellite and aircraft and stored in the EDC DAAC's archives.

The Weather Information Superhighway

http://thunder.met.fsu.edu/nws/public_html/wxhwy.html

The Weather Information Superhighway is an award-winning site sponsored by the National Weather Service, Tallahassee, Florida. The site contains a comprehensive collection of the meteorological data, information, and image sites around the globe. The links cover a variety of data such as Usenet FAQs; Weather; WWW Virtual Library; Meteorology; Government Weather Information Services; National Weather Service WWW Sites; National Hurricane Center, current bulletins and data on hurricanes in the Atlantic, Caribbean Sea and Gulf of Mexico, NOAA's Hurricane Research Division; NOAA's National Data Buoy Center; NOAA/Atlantic Oceanographic and Meteorological Lab; National Severe Storms Laboratory's current research; Center for the Analysis and Prediction of Storms (CAPS); NOAA Defense Meteorological Satellite Program; NOAA AVHRR Oceans Pathfinder Home Page; National Climatic Data Center (NCDC); NOAA National Geophysical Data Center; Climate Prediction Center Long-Range Forecasts Climate and Long-Range predictions; The Weather Underground: University Weather Services, and more.

Global Land Information System (GLIS)

http://edcwww.cr.usgs.gov/glis/glis.html

This is a site with access to datasets, news, access to remote systems, and ordering information. GLIS is an interactive computer system developed by the U.S. Geological Survey (USGS) for scientists seeking sources of information about the Earth's land surfaces. GLIS contains metadata—that is, descriptive information about data sets.

Advanced Technology Information Network

http://caticsuf.csufresno.edu/

This California Technology Information Network database provides supporting databases for agricultural marketing, international exporting, and the educational community of California.

High Technology, Science, and Engineering

The following sections describe resources for science, high technology, engineering, and related fields.

National Science Foundation

http://stis.nsf.gov/start.htm

The National Science Foundation (NSF) Web page covers a lot of ground, including access to publications, grant and research opportunities, science trends, tip sheets, news releases, program guidelines, applications deadlines, and more. The site also serves as a jumping-off place for many other related agencies.

National Nuclear Data Center (NNDC) Online Data Service

http://datwww.dne.bnl.gov/html/nndc.html;
newsletter: *http://datwww.dne.bnl.gov/nndcnews943.html.*

NNDC, which is located at the Brookhaven National Laboratory in Upton, New York, provides the following databases: NSR, ENSDF, NUDAT, CINDA, CSISRS, ENDF, and XRAY.

Physics Information Network (PINET)

http://www.aip.org/pinet/pinethome.html

This fee-based service and database of the American Institute of Physics has information in the fields of physics and astronomy. Areas covered include jobs in industry and academia, a searchable calendar of meetings and symposia, prepublication advance abstracts of member society journals, abstracts of more than 120 journals going back more than 20 years, news, newsletters, and electronic mail. For information on fees and services, have a look at their homepage.

Internet Chemistry Index

URL: *http://www.chemie.fu-berlin.de/chemistry/index/*

This rather austere site covers numerous chemistry and related sources, information, and databases:

Analytical Chemistry and Chemometrics
Biochemistry
Biographies of Chemists
Chemistry and Development of the Web
Chemistry Databases
Chemistry Indexes
Computational Chemistry
Conferences
Crystallography
General Chemistry
Inorganic Chemistry
Internet Chemistry Sites
Internet Chemistry Sites
Macromolecular Chemistry, Polymers

Mineralogy
Miscellaneous
Molecular Modeling and Visualization
Organic Chemistry
Physical and Theoretical Chemistry
Reprint/Preprint Databases, Electronic Journals
Software
Spectroscopy

National Technology Transfer Center

http://iridium.nttc.edu/nttc.html

NTTC's online system provides information on business opportunities that have resulted from federally funded research and development projects. NTTC is the hub of a national network linking U.S. companies with federally funded technologies, and provides information and networking about how those technologies can be converted into practical, commercially relevant applications.

You can choose from items such as *Self Guided Tour, NTTC Activities, Projects, and Information Gateway; Technology Transfer Gateway, Environmental Technology Gateway—Envirogate, Government Agency Gateway, Links to over 600 Federal Government Home Pages; Health, Assistive, and Rehabilitation Technology Gateway; Technology Information from the Department of Veteran's Affairs, National Institute on Disability and Rehabilitation Research, NIDRR Directory; Law Enforcement Gateway; Licensing and Partnership Opportunities Gateway; Manufacturing Technology Gateway; Solicitations and Opportunities Gateway; Small Business for Innovation Research (SBIR) Solicitations, Small Business for Technology Transfer (STTR) Solicitations, Technical; Financial, and Business Assistance Gateway, Technical and Economic Assistance for Small Businesses; Search NTTC Databases (20 Different Databases), Search All NTTC Non-Database Text Files,* and more.

Investing, Stocks, and Economics

The Internet contains numerous excellent sites for obtaining information on investing, the stock market, and related areas. These are some of the most useful.

Stocks and Stock Reports Page

http://nearnet.gnn.com/gnn/meta/finance/res/invest.stocks.html

This page offers links to a large number of sites with a lot of valuable stock market information including the Market Watch page, which provides a minute-by-minute summary of activity for Dow Jones; Standard & Poor's, and the New York Stock Exchange indices; the Weekly Market Summary, with data on trading, index performance, money rates, earnings announcements, and gold and silver prices; Quote.Com, a commercial stock market information service; the MIT Experimental Stock Market Data charts; recently updated mutual fund charts; Holt's Market Reports; and lots more.

Quote.Com

http://www.quote.com

Quote.Com is a commercial venture that offers some of its services for free, and an expanded set of services for subscribers, through a secure server. It contains a great deal of information about the current and historical performance of the main exchanges, including the New York Stock Exchange, the Sydney Futures Exchange, the Vancouver Stock Exchange, and others. Subscribers can get quotes of particular stocks, charts of historical data, commodities quotes, access to Standard & Poor's Stock Guide database, balance sheet data for over 5,900 domestic common and preferred stocks, and the text of Standard & Poor's MarketScope Alert.

Pawws Financial Network

http://pawws.secapl.com/

Pawws Financial Network is a source for investors that is designed to allow quick access to the large amounts of information necessary for the successful management of a securities portfolio. The page puts together tools for services relating to portfolio accounting, securities, research, and online trading, and is divided into several areas: *Portfolio Accounting*, *Brokerage Services*, *News & Commentary*, *Market Analysis*, *Real-time/Delayed Pricing*, and *Fundamental Data*.

Lombard Real-Time Trading and Research Information

http://www.lombard.com

The Lombard Institutional Brokerage Real-Time Trading and Research Information Center maintains a significant online presence. Their philosophy is: "Through the use of cutting edge technology, we are dedicated to providing our customers in the Internet community with a wide variety of investment options, enhanced investment tools and an unparalleled commitment to customer service." The secure site is easy to navigate, with numerous options.

Data Transfer Group—The Group

http://www.thegroup.net/invest/

This very complete site provides a large collection of links, full-text articles, and information about investments, commodities trading, stocks, commodities histories, technical analysis, and profitable investing techniques. Some of the full-text articles include a late summer stock market outlook, how to try to pick individual stocks, disciplined investing, and how to use your computer to invest. The site connects to numerous quote servers:

```
Investor's Edge
Security APL Quote Server
PC Quote/Spacecom Systems Quote Server
E*TRADE Quotes Page
```

resources for technical data:

```
Investors In Touch
CPCUG's Investment Special Interest Group
MIT Artificial Intelligence Lab Experimental Stock Market Data
```

and resources for fundamental data:

```
Money and Investing Update
FINWeb
Securities and Exchange Commission EDGAR Database
```

Also included are links to Usenet groups of interest, FAQs, and resources dealing with mutual funds, futures, options, and more.

Journalism

Journalists are heavy Internet users, and some of the most interesting resources in journalism and publishing are given here.

The National Press Club

http://town.hall.org/places/npc/

The National Press Club (NPC) offers a very useful collection of Internet resources for journalists; the site was particularly designed for journalists hunting for information from the Internet as deadlines approach. It includes access to the Eric Freidheim Library and the Internet Town Hall, plus information about the press club itself, including its purpose, its history, and geographical information. Lists of the speakers at NPC luncheons are available, as well as audio clips. (Watch out though, these are huge files, some in excess of 30MB!)

A Guide to Resources for Journalists

URL: *http://www.jou.ufl.edu/commres/default.htm*

The Journalism List by John S. Makulowich is a useful guide providing links, reviews, and resources in subjects related to journalism, mass media, and communications:

```
Country Codes - a map of IP domains to country names
Other communications WWW sites
Commercial WWW News Services
The Federal Register
The Virtual Reference Desk at UC Irvine.
Chicago-Kent College of Law
The Journalist's Toolbox - an list of government resources.
The Internet Web Textbook - a list of net and World Wide Web
    resources by John December.
The Media List 3.0 a list of media-related e-mail addresses
    collected and produced by Adam Gaffin
Journalism newsgroup - read the current news from the USENET
    newsgroup alt.journalism
University of Florida's library system - logon as Luis and then
    choose Luis
Federal Communications Law Journal WWW server.
Global Legal Studies Journal from Indiana U.
```

The Journalistic Resources Page

http://www.algonet.se/~nikos/journ.html

The Journalistic Resources pages, compiled by Nikos Markovits, have an international flavor, covering a lot of ground. The main page offers access to numerous resources organized under headings for broadcast media, journalism, and online newspapers:

```
The Broadcasting Link
     European Broadcasting
     Broadcasting - other countries
     Other Broadcasting Resources

Links to Journalism
     Lists and Sites of interest for journalists and others
     members of the Internet community

The Online Edition
     Online Newspapers and Magazines
     Schools of Journalism
     WWW-pages Worldwide
```

The Awesome List

http://www.clark.net/pub/journalism/awesome.html

This is an eclectic page designed by John Makulowich to gather the resources of greatest use to journalists, speakers, and Internet trainers. It was designed to be used online. It was also designed to highlight the value, breadth, and depth of the Internet. It is broken into two sections: the Truly Awesome, which is a short list of the best, and then the rest, which are just Awesome.

Law

The Internet abounds with resources for lawyers and other professionals in need of legal information.

Technology Law Resources

http://www.kuesterlaw.com/

The Technology Law Resources page is a great resource of information related to technology law, intellectual property law, patent law, copyrights, and trademark law. It has a large set of hotlinks out to resources on patents, consumer law, trademarks, full text of intellectual property documents, legal documents, and a variety of other legal resources and law firms.

The Information Law Web

http://starbase.ingress.com/tsw/rcl/infolaw.html

Using the metaphor of loading disks of people, places, and things, The Information Law Web site provides a collection of information, databases, documents, and links, all related to information law, including landmark information law opinions, intellectual property, trademark and copyright sites, statutes, a bibliography, a FAQ, and Supreme court decisions related to intellectual property.

Trade Law Library Internet Sites for Law, Commerce, Finance and Economics

http://ananse.irv.uit.no/trade_law/nav/law_ref.html

This is quite a complete library of information on trade law, commerce, finance, and economics. They have good links to sites such as Yahoo, Galaxy, ITLP International Trade Law Materials, the CTI Law Technology Centre at Warwick University in the U.K., and more.

Canadian Legal Resources

http://www.mbnet.mb.ca/~psim/can_law.html

This site covers information organized by categories such as *Organizations and Other Sources, Courts and Tribunals, Law Reform Commissions, Legislation and Related Materials, Tax and Accounting, Lawyers and Law Firms, Universities and Colleges, Canadian Federal Government, Canadian Provincial Governments, Free Speech and Privacy, Publishers,* and *Commercial Sites.*

EcoNet's Endangered Species Action and Information Guide

http://www.econet.apc.org/endangered/

The EcoNet's Endangered Species Action and Information Guide provides access to references, legal resources, and hotlinks all broadly related to ecology. Some of the topics include endangered species action alerts and news, the EcoNet Endangered Species Gopher, law links to such sites as the U.S. Fish and Wildlife Service, and access to the Endangered Species Protection Law Summaries. The site also provides links to inventories and databases including the *List of Threatened Animals*; Occurrence of Endangered Species in Australia, and the World Conservation Union publications directory.

Nolo Press's Self-Help Law Center

http://gnn.digital.com/gnn/bus/nolo/

Nolo Press specializes in self-help law. The site provides access to a great number of useful documents and links, including information on trademarks, legal briefs, laws that affect you every day, an update service, your legal rights in the workplace if you lose your job, wages and compensation, the text of some of Nolo's books, and software on consumer subjects such as wills, small claims court, divorce and debt problems.

The Wiretap Copyright Gopher

gopher://wiretap.spies.com/11/Gov/Copyright

The Copyright Gopher index at Wiretap provides links to text documents such as the U.S.–Berne Convention, the U.S. copyright law revision of 1976, U.S. Copyright Basics, U.S. Copyright law, the U.S. Depository Library Program, and more.

Psychology and Mental Health

A variety of sources exist for mental health professionals, particularly in psychology and related topics.

Psychiatry On-Line

http://www.cityscape.co.uk/users/ad88/psych.htm

Psychiatry On-Line is a monthly online publication designed for mental health professionals of all kinds. The articles maintained at the Web site cover issues such as depression, dementia, organic brain disorders, resources for mental health, SSRIs and psychotropic medications, religion and psychiatry, and sexual dysfunction. Other resources include case studies, and information on academic programs in psychiatry, psychology, and related disciplines. Since letters are accepted, you will find debates about these topics, too.

Psycoloquy

gopher://gopher.Princeton.EDU:70/1ftp%3Aprinceton.edu@/pub/harnad/ Psycoloquy/Background/

Psycoloquy is an international, interdisciplinary electronic journal covering psychology, neuroscience, behavioral biology, philosophy, linguistics, computing, and behavioral and cognitive sciences. This is one of the earliest and most successful migrations of content to an online environment. It is a refereed journal, and is supported by the American Psychological Association.

PsychNET

http://www.apa.org/
gopher://gopher.apa.org

The American Psychological Association's PsychNET is the official Internet service of the world's largest and oldest psychological organization supporting both WWW and Gopher access. Well organized, it contains extensive links to and information on APA's programs, publications, news releases, job listings, and a few articles from publications. PsychNET takes a broad view, and includes information on the science of psychology, practice, management, education, and more. Information is searchable by keyword.

Social Sciences

There is a lot of information on the Internet relating to the social sciences, as shown here.

Coombsweb—The ANU Social Sciences Server

http://coombs.anu.edu.au/CoombsHome.html

This site is part of the Coombs Unit of the Research Schools of Social Sciences and Pacific & Asian Studies at the Australian National University. It has particular strength in the social sciences, humanities, and Asian studies. In addition to providing the usual hotlinks to related collections, Coombsweb maintains its own large archive of information, accessible by various methods.

Social Science Information Gateway (SOSIG)

http://sosig.esrc.bris.ac.uk/

SOSIG is an index of a broad range of Web resources relating to the social sciences. Well organized, it covers all of the social sciences as well as topics such as feminism, statistics, and more, plus information on job openings and news. It also has a search feature.

The Inter-University Consortium for Political and Social Research (ICPSR) Gopher

gopher://tdis.icpsr.umich.edu/

ICPSR is said to be the world's largest database of computer-based research and instructional data for the social sciences. Areas covered include criminal justice, economics, history, gerontology, political science, public health, law, and sociology. ICPSR is a not-for-profit consortium of universities and colleges, but nonaffiliated individuals can get accounts. This is a Gopher site that provides access to information, data, and services, most of which is are searchable using WAIS and other tools. These include data from the 1990 U.S. census, a database of information useful for surveys, and archives such as the National Archive of Computerized Data on Aging.

Social Science Data Archives (Australia)

http://ssda.anu.edu.au/

Located at the Australian National University, this Web site for the Social Science Data Archives offers information and resources in a broad range of the social sciences including political science, sociology, and economics. Users can access documents on opinion polls, the Australian census, and Australian studies, with hotlinks to the Australian Consortium for Social and Political Research and other useful social science Internet resources.

Social Sciences Data Collection (UCSD)

http://ssdc.ucsd.edu/

The Social Sciences Data Collection at the University of California at San Diego is a large collection of resources related to economics, education, health care, political science and public opinion, and sociology. The collection is organized by title, subject, and some special collections; also provides hotlinks out to related sites.

Telecommunications

Telecommunications is a growth area for information on the Internet; these sites provide information from a variety of perspectives.

Research and Technology Development in Advanced Communications Technologies in Europe (RACE)

http://www.analysys.co.uk/race.htm

The RACE site provides information on Integrated Broadband Communication. The site provides general information on the RACE project, subprojects of RACE, and access to databases of RACE information, cost-benefit analysis, and telecommunications forecasting. There are hotlinks to other European commission servers and other information related broadly to telecommunications.

Telecommunications and Information Infrastructure Assistance Program (TIIAP)

http://www.ntia.doc.gov/tiiap/tiiap.html

The TIIAP program is part of the U.S. Department of Commerce National Telecommunications and Information Administration (NTIA). The program provides funding and matching grants to state and local governments, educational institutions including universities and school districts, health care providers, libraries, social service organizations, public safety services, and other kinds of nonprofit organizations, so that they can access and use new telecommunications technologies. The page provides information on the grants program, application procedures, a FAQ, and agency contact information.

Information Infrastructure Task Force (IITF)

http://iitf.doc.gov/

This page for IITF (which is a division of the National Information Infrastructure) provides a variety of information about IITF's events and activities, including its objectives, fact sheets, press releases, contact lists, committee reports, and minutes from meetings. Access is provided to a collection of online documents, papers and transcripts from the IITF, and the NII archives.

Alliance for Competitive Communications

http://bell.com/

The Alliance for Competitive Communications maintains a site that provides access to the texts of legislation relating to the telecommunications industry, press releases, consumer information, demographics, access issues, and hotlinks to the Alliance's members' pages. The seven Regional Bell Operating Companies (RBOCs) form the alliance.

From Here...

At this point, now that you have reviewed the many resources available on the Internet, continue on to Chapter 18 in order to get going on your business and marketing plan for using the Internet.

PART VII

Your Business Online—
Now and in the Future

CHAPTER 18

Putting Together a Complete Internet Business and Marketing Plan

Getting Down to Brass Tacks

Now that we have discussed why businesses are using the Internet and explained some techniques for creating a business presence, it is time to review, take stock, and prepare to get on the Internet, if you are not there already. There has been a lot information presented up to this point, but to make it valuable to your business it should be analyzed and assimilated into some concrete plans.

As you've seen, businesses are using the Internet, and particularly the Web, for many reasons and business functions, including communications, data transfer, logistics, cost containment, reaching new markets, collaboration, information retrieval, and direct sales. In each case, the Internet is useful in accomplishing these business functions.

Step One: Get on the Internet!

If you are not already on the Internet, get on now—call one of the Internet providers in your area and get an account. You are not wedded to your initial decision regarding an Internet service provider. Review Chapter 3 concerning access providers and use the chart in Figure 18.1 to help you further in deciding which provider has the services that you need.

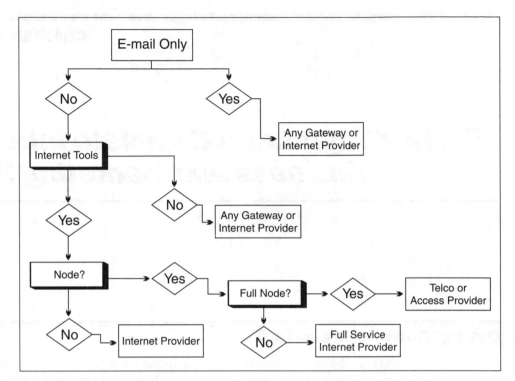

Figure 18.1 Flowchart of Internet provider decisions.

Step Two: Check Out the Competition

The next step is to join a few discussion lists, read some newsgroups, surf the Web, use the Web search tools such as Lycos and WebCrawler, and look around at the various Gophers and information sites. It is important to look around at what is currently going on to gain insight and ideas for planning.

What are your competitors doing? If they are not already using the Internet, you can beat them to the punch; if they are, you can learn from what they are doing, and do a better job. Here are some strategies for locating your competitors and seeing what they might be up to:

- *Use the World Wide Web*. Use the WWW to locate business and product information. It is the fastest growing tool in the Internet right now, and many companies are creating homepages for searching it. Chapter 11 provides good starting points for searching for

WWW information. Analyze other businesses' use of the Web in light of the techniques discussed in Chapter 9.

- *Use the lists.* Join several discussion lists that are related to your industry or products. Review the membership list using the listserver commands outlined in Chapter 13. Look for company domain names and names of familiar people. Read the archives, searching for particular products and companies or individual names. What are they concerned or asking about? What information are they providing?

- *Use the Usenet newsgroups.* Begin regularly reading newsgroups of all kinds that touch upon your interests and industry. What are the hot topics, and who is talking about them? As with the lists, review the postings and .sig files of members. Finger the addresses of the individuals posting interesting information to look at their .plan files.

- *Use Gopher and Veronica.* Don't overlook the power of Gopher and Veronica to search for businesses, products, and subjects. Be creative in your searching—use a broad range of keywords. Chapter 14 can help you in using Gopher and searching with Veronica. (Reminder: Many GUI browsers can be used as client software to get information from Gopher servers.)

- *Observe .sig and .plan files.* As you cruise the Web, lists, newsgroups, and Gophers, look for clues about competitors, their activities, and their interests. Request information through their automated reply e-mail services, look at their Web homepages and their Gophers, and review their FTP sites.

- *Use FTP and Archie.* Do some Archie searches as outlined in Chapter 14 to hunt for files and directories containing keywords of interest such as names of companies and products.

- *Subscribe to Net-happenings. Net-happenings* is a list that sends update information on Internet-related items. It covers new Gophers, FTP sites, services, and more. It's like the hometown newspaper for the Internet. Use the normal majordomo subscription procedure to subscribe: send a message to *majordomo@lists.internic.net* with the body of the message reading subscribe net-happenings.

- *Finally, be an active citizen of the network.* By "mixing it up" you will be able to keep tabs on your competitors and learn about the interactive nature of the Internet.

Step Three: Create the Business Plan

Now is the time to begin your business plan for using the Internet. How will you use the Internet? Most companies do business plans for a variety of reasons that include clarifying the corporate planning process, aiding companywide coordination, or requesting funding.

If you decide to use the Internet in direct marketing and sales, you will need to construct an Internet marketing plan. Which Internet tools and resources will you use? Figure 18.2 shows which Internet tools are recommended to aid in various business functions.

Doing a business needs assessment can help clarify which Internet tools and resources to use, and which to emphasize. What are your particular business's needs? The form below outlines some of the key reasons that companies typically have for using the Internet.

Needs Assessment

__ 1. Communication

    __ Internal—networking

    __ External—vendors, customers, suppliers

__ 2. Data Transfer—between sites, to/from other companies, on-the-road staff

__ 3. Information Retrieval/Research/Utilization—marketing research, new materials, training, professional development

__ 4. Logistics—scheduling, planning, calendars, inventory

__ 5. Cost Containment—alternative communications

    __ Telephone

    __ Mail

    __ Personnel—efficiency of customer support, telecommuting, reduce the need for meetings

    __ Other—announcements, newsletters, etc.

__ 6. Collaboration/Product Development—workgroups

__ 7. Marketing Research—primary and secondary, surveys

__ 8. Direct Marketing/Advertising

__ 9. Sales—product support, distribution channels, information for vendors/customers, online sales

__10. Other _____

_____

	E-mail	.sig	.plan	Lists	Gopher	FTP	Newsletters	Usenet	WWW
Product Announcements	x	x	x	H	x		H	H	H
Product Flyers	x		x	x	x	x	x	x	H
Product Specifications	x		x		x	H	x		H
Pricing Information	x		x		x	H	x	x	H
Catalogs	x		x		H	H	x		H
Events and Demos	x		x	x	L		x	x	H
Free Software					x	H			x
Customer Support	H			H	x	x	x	x	H
Company Contracts	H			L	L	x	x		x
Promotional Notices	x	H	x	H	L	x	x	H	x
Documentation	x				H	H	x		x
Multimedia	L								H
Surveys	H			x	x		x		H
Performance Data	x		L		x	x			x
Service Evaluation	x			x	x	x	x		x
Product Reviews				x	H	H	H	H	x
Customer Service Information	x		L	x	x	L	x	H	H
Job Placement/Recruitment	x			x	x	x	x	x	H
Dialog	H			H	L			H	H
L = Limited Usefulness or Access x = useful H = major source									

Figure 18.2 Analysis of Internet tools.

Using the results of this needs assessment, you can then turn to creating a plan for your Internet business presence.

Your Business Plan

After you have done considerable work on considering how the Internet can be used for business, it is time to develop or revise your business plan. A traditional business plan will often contain much of the following information. The Internet can, as appropriate, be used in all facets of the plan.

The plan starts with a cover sheet, the Executive Summary and a Table of Contents. The Executive Summary hits all the high points of your plan, in a sense previewing the plan in a concise, cogent manner. This is your up-front chance to create a positive impression.

Most business plans then contain the following five sections:

I. Company Organization and Business Description

This would include business name, address, owner, followed by business goals and objectives—why you are or want to be in business.

This section frequently contains:

- Organization, description and chart
- Key personnel and functional overview
- Officers and founders
- Resumes of key personnel—often appended at the end of the plan

The description of the business should also include an industry analysis—be sure to describe the industry as a whole, what opportunities exist, who the big players are, and how they have performed.

In this section you would also include information on any telecommuting personnel, or in the case of a business heavily immersed in using the Internet, a description of your virtual corporation, and any strategic partnerships. Frequently, businesses use consultants and contract personnel that use the Internet to "come" to work.

II. Product/Service Description

This is a very detailed outline of your core business. It explains why you are offering these particular products or services. It should also outline how you are using the Internet for the creation of products, distribution, communication, scheduling, and technical and customer service. You would include a description of operations.

III. Sales and Market Analysis

In this section you describe your markets by size, niche, including pricing and sales terms. It should describe all the channels that you will use for marketing, sales, and advertising, and it is here that you would include information on your various Internet strategies. A formal Marketing Plan would be included, and cover:

- Product market overview
- Analysis of competition
- Pricing
- Product market potential

The market itself would be described in terms of:

- Size of the market

- Analysis of competitor products
    sales by distribution and value
    potential market share

- Potential consumption
    demographics, market share, seasonal, geographical

Also included would be your advertising, sales promotion, and public relations plans, with your plans for using the Internet and the Web, as outlined in Chapters 8 and 9. Start-ups most often also include elaborate timelines and PERT charts of milestones to be achieved.

IV. Revenue Plan

The revenue plan outlines all of the financial information related to the business and includes your operating requirements—equipment, facilities, and personnel needed for your business. This would include both start-up and ongoing costs of any Internet connections and services, and a description of how your business will make use of virtual offices.

If you are approaching outside organizations or venture capitalists for funding, a funding request and justification is needed. This section would also include all facets of financial management and budgets, including:

- Expected profit or return on investment (ROI) for the first year
- Projections of income and balance sheets for 3 years
- Cash flow statement for 12–18 months

Usually, spreadsheets of all statements and balance sheets are included as appendixes.

V. Conclusions

A summative statement is usually added—in a sense "telling them what you have told them."

Marketing with the Internet

In creating a marketing plan, the first activity is to examine your company mission, goals and objectives, and growth strategy. What is your underlying business philosophy, and your major business and marketing goals? What is your current position in the market? The following outline is intended to remind you of considerations important to any marketing plan.

If you are planning to use the Internet for marketing, you will have many of the same market concerns as you would conventionally:

Marketing Process	*New Product*
Identify opportunity	Discover unmet consumer need
Plan action	Create new product to meet needs
Execute plan	Simulate, test market
Evaluate results	Compare test market with plan
Review and revise plan	Look for improvements, recycle

Market Research

Use focus groups, collect and analyze consumer problems and complaints

Test alternatives

Track test results

Identify dissatisfactions

Test revised product

This analysis can yield strategies for marketing existing or new products, and suggest places where the Internet can assist. In developing Internet marketing strategies, use the usual indicators:

- Market potential
- Market forecast
- Sales potential
- Sales forecast
- Market share
- Market size
- Customer and noncustomer needs

The Internet itself can be used for both primary and secondary market research. For market research, use some of the resources noted in Chapters 11, 14, 15, 16, and 17. Companies are also using the Internet to survey both current customers and potential customers. This is especially effective on Web sites using input forms pages.

For example, in order to gain specific demographic information and reading habits about Internet users, one company that provides access to newspapers and magazines ran a contest for those willing to fill out an online survey. The company put out a news release to the *Net-happenings* mailing list, announcing that the information was being made available on its Gopher. Here is the Gopher entry:

```
Sweepstakes -- Win Two Round-trip Air Tickets to Europe!

1. Win Two Roundtrip Tickets to Europe -- READ THIS.
2. Enter the Sweepstakes Online <TEL>


------------------------------------------
Win two round-trip air tickets to Europe!
------------------------------------------


Imagine yourself sipping espresso on the Champs-Elysees or
strolling among the art masterpieces of the Uffizi Gallery in
Florence. Perhaps you have relatives you'd like to visit in
London, or Berlin, or Stockholm?

Here's your chance to win two round-trip air tickets to any
destination in Europe you choose. NO PURCHASE NECESSARY. All
you have to do to enter is send us the following seven pieces
of information about yourself by email to: Sweepstakes
1. Name and address
2. Gender
3. Age
4. Occupation/Profession
5. Level of Educational Attainment, i.e. High School Graduate,
College Graduate, Graduate Degree, etc.
6. Favorite Magazine
7. Household Income Level (Use the corresponding number below.)
     Under $15,000         = 1
     $ 15,000 to $ 24,999 = 2
     $ 25,000 to $ 34,999 - 3
     $ 35,000 to $ 44,999 = 4
     $ 45,000 to $ 54,999 = 5
     $ 55,000 to $ 64,999 = 6
     $ 65,000 to $ 74,999 = 7
     $ 75,000 to $ 84,999 = 8
     $ 85,000 to $ 94,999 = 9
```

```
$ 95,000 to $104,999 = 10
$105,000 to $124,999 = 11
$125,000 and over     = 12
```

This was followed by a disclaimer that the survey was only seeking composite data, and that names and addresses would not be used for solicitation or sold to another vendor.

This kind of survey can also be conducted by announcing it on appropriate lists and groups, and then, in response to requests, sending the survey out via e-mail. And of course, the Web is very effective as a vehicle for surveys using data input forms. Some companies have been sponsoring scavenger hunts to take users out to other pages on the Web too.

As you develop your own ideas, combine your responses to the preceding forms, and use the form below to identify the specific Internet tools that will fit your particular strategy and tactics. You can hone your specifications for creating your Internet presence.

Internet Tools Needed for Strategy #1

__ 1. E-mail

__ 2. Access to discussion lists

__ 3. Your own discussion/mailing lists

__ 4. Use of Telnet

__ 5. Use of file transfer protocol (FTP)

__ 6. Your own FTP archive area

__ 7. Use of Gopher

__ 8. Your own gopherspace

__ 9. Use of World Wide Web (WWW)

__ 10. Your own WWW server

__ 11. Use of GUI such as Netscape/Mosaic

__ 12. Use of Usenet newsgroups

__ 13. Use of WAIS

Use copies of this form for each of your strategies, so you can develop a picture of your Internet needs and implementations.

Web Site Considerations

There are three basic models for creating and maintaining a Web site:

- Create your own documents on a shoestring by learning HTML, and put your pages on the Web server of your local Internet service provider.

- Engage the services of a Web site provider; provide raw information, and let the provider take it from there.

- Create, install, and maintain your own site using both existing and new personnel and equipment.

If you are installing your own node, or putting up your own Web, Gopher, or FTP site, you may need to hire additional personnel. Using one of the commercial providers with rental space will not usually require additional personnel, though it may mean some training costs and personnel time for maintaining and updating the files.

In choosing your particular Internet configuration, consider the human resources implications of your decisions. To have your own local Web or Gopher server, and FTP archive requires that you have your own node—through a full-time SLIP connection via standard phone lines, or via ISDN or leased lines. These are sophisticated hardware and software installations requiring considerable technical expertise, as well as the installation of TCP/IP connections. Most companies considering this level of Internet connectivity either hire personnel to install and maintain the equipment and software, or hire a consultant in the planning and training phases—sometimes both.

Many companies are arranging to "rent" Web, Gopherspace, FTP archiving, and other services through their Internet service provider. These are almost turnkey operations, which have numerous advantages—you do not need any special equipment or technical expertise, you have no extra firewall or security concerns, and you do not need to worry if your node has technical difficulties. Many service providers will assist you in setting up these tools. Your involvement then becomes one of keeping information up-to-date on the server and responding to inquiries.

Getting Up and Running on the Web

Initial costs:

Setup:	High-end	Low-end
Server hardware and software	$15,000 ($6,000–30,000)	$0
Leased Line installation	$2,500 (varies by locale)	$0
Personnel time to set up	$13,200	your time
Account setup		$10–40

Personnel to implement:		
Web site designers	$10,000–40,000	$0
Content preparation	$5,000–10,000	$0
Image preparation	$3,000–8,000	$40

Initial site support:		
Training	$500	your time

Ongoing costs:

	High-end	Low-end
Personnel to maintain and run	$30,000	your time
Leased line	$20,400 (varies widely)	$0
Cost of an account	$0	$20–40

Marketing:		
non-Internet	$9,000 (paper-based)	$20

Hardware/software upgrades and maintenance:		
upgrades	$2,000	$0
service contract	$3,100	$0

Creating an Internet Marketing Plan

If you have made the decision to use the Internet for marketing, the following can help you create or revise your marketing plan. Marketing plans tend to be pretty generic and contain the same information, and an Internet marketing plan is no different.

The plan will describe the scope of the plan, objectives, strategies and tactics, distribution, segmentation, share, demand, trends, customers, sales and sales tactics, and budget, and will include a profit and loss statement.

The four P's of marketing—Place, Product, Price, and Promotion—are all important in an Internet marketing plan:

- Place: In this case, the place is the Internet, and that choice has to make sense as a coordinated channel.

- Product: All kinds of products and services are marketed on the Internet, as you've seen in earlier chapters. Fulfillment can be either off- or online.

- Price: This is similar to offline pricing, but online marketing and selling require less overhead.

- Promotion: This is a primary strength of the Internet—it is a vehicle for advertising, marketing, public relations, customer and technical support, and building goodwill.

Sections of a Typical Marketing Plan

I. Goals and Major Strategies

This introductory section provides the overview for the rest of the Marketing Plan, and can specify how using the Internet will maintain, improve, or give up market shares. It would identify the kind of market (vertical/horizontal, etc.), and any unique features of the plan. It is here that you would present your case for the Internet as a channel.

II. Objectives

This is where you explicitly state your objectives in measurable terms—what specifically you will accomplish with your Internet sales, research, public relations, and methods.

III. Profit and Loss

A typical P&L statement gives a general indication of whether your Internet marketing plan will be a success or not. The usual method is to state your case in terms of volume, share, costs, sales, advertising and promotion, and other costs, and then to project profits before taxes.

IV. Methods

This section covers the ways in which you will meet your goals—what your main messages and positioning are, with what audience, and in what medium. In this case your medium is the Internet, and you should describe how you will use the Web, Gopher, FTP, e-mail, IRC, and so on.

You should project your costs, and try to describe the reach and frequency of the Internet. In addition, this section should include specific plans, including Web layout and copy, promotional events, and strategic partnerships.

V. Marketing Research

Marketing research plans include both the strategy for the research and the details of the research to be carried out. The Internet itself is valuable for the research stage, as mentioned earlier.

VI. Pricing Considerations

This section will outline your pricing position in detail and will include information on your competitive position, strategy for pricing relative to the competition, multiple and discount pricing, and service costs. Many cost reductions can be made using the Internet, which in some cases may give you a competitive pricing advantage.

Step Four: Staged Implementation

Many businesses just beginning to use the Internet find that a staged approach to implementation is useful. The first few months, they simply experiment with using their .sig file and .plan files to begin a billboard type of presence. They use the vast resources of the Internet for market research and get a feel for what is going on.

Depending upon how that works out, they begin to put out informative announcements, and later add a Web and/or FTP presence. It is important to remember that caution is a virtue—breaching netiquette can gain you a bad name in minutes. Take the time to do it right the first time.

For most business users there is a phase-in of activities needed, similar to the strategies outlined earlier for learning about your competition:

1. Get on the Internet, scope out the competition as outlined earlier, and exercise your Internet skills. Subscribe to *Net-happenings* and other appropriate lists and newsletters, and read newsgroups. This usually is a one- or two-month undertaking, of 5–10 hours a week.

2. Consider hiring a consultant for advice on an Internet business plan—many Internet providers and independent consultants are offering this kind of assistance.

3. Take some initial steps to create a business presence on the Internet by creating and updating a .sig and .plan file. Get your name out there. This is a one- or two-month undertaking, with no particular increase in your time investment from the 5–10 hours a week of step 1.

4. Consider the next logical steps. For many businesses, the next step might be to put up a modest Web homepage, or to put your information in one of the cybermalls, which offer a broad range of online visibility from simple product announcements to full-blown storefronts. This is usually a one- or two-month activity, but may require a substantial time investment and some overall increase in the time commitment for Internet-related activities. The good news is that if you are successful, you will have some increase in business.

5. Finally, the last step, if appropriate, is to do a full-court press into doing business on the Internet through a well-designed Web site supported by a Gopher and FTP archive, either rented or on your own node.

Start slowly and build upon your successes.

Step Five: Evaluate the Plan, Assessing Success and Your Position

Once your plan is under way, you should evaluate its progress, checking on its effectiveness and profitability, but do not try to do a "bottom line" assessment too soon. Like all business strategies, Internet plans need to be fine-tuned and to mature; and Internet users need to become aware of your presence.

Here are some indicators of success (depending upon your specific activities):

- An increase in e-mail traffic by 2–10 times (or more).
- Growth across 2–3 months in the number of requests for specific information, or general inquiries.
- Survey returns: If you do any kind of online surveys with customers or potential customers, Internet returns via e-mail usually exceed those through snail mail by 1.5 to 3 times; Web-based surveys are very popular.
- The receipt of flames: Yes, it means people are seeing what you are doing. Read flames, and consider what they have to say, but remember that no matter what you do, there will most likely be a few flames. (Resist the temptation to flame in return.) The number of flames you receive will vary all over the map, but some recent research reveals that the usual ratio is now 1:65 (bad to good) if you are using the correct approach; if it is worse, take the complaints very seriously. Learn from the negative comments as well as the positive.
- Good return on investment: Generally, Internet-related activities take from 6 to 24 months to gain profitability, depending upon the level and cost of the activity. A full-node installation might take two to three years to show profitability, depending upon your savings on telephone, delivery services, equipment and personnel costs, and so on, whereas a simple Web installation could become profitable in a month or two.
- Compare your results: Many Internet business users will share numerical and anecdotal data on discussion lists and in Usenet newsgroups.

One popular way to find out how you are doing is to have friends or employees monitor lists and groups, keeping an ear to the ground. You can also have them mention your business in discussion in a low-key way, and monitor the responses. Has anybody heard of you? What do they think?

Overall, consider these questions in evaluating your plan:

- Have the objectives been accomplished, and to what degree?
- Has the level of achievement justified the level of expenditures?

- To what degree has the strategy enabled you to meet customer needs?
- To what degree has the activity maintained or expanded your market share?
- What has been the net impact of the strategy in terms of both financial reward and improvements in business reputation and goodwill?

Finally, consider what improvements need to be made. Track your results, review your effectiveness, and recycle your plan.

A Reminder—Planning How to Give Something Back to the Internet

A business's image on the Net, as with any venue, is important. There are a couple of rules of thumb about maintaining a good network image: First, do no unsolicited advertising or bulk e-mailing, and second, find a way to give something back to the Internet, both for goodwill and to attract customers.

If your plan for your business involves the use of the Internet, you should be exploring methods for returning something of value to the Internet. This could take the form of:

- Providing free services or products of value
- Providing free original content
- Providing an Archie or Veronica search site
- Providing carefully chosen, thematic lists of links to Web and other resources
- Distributing useful information
- Giving opportunities for interaction
- Supporting discussion lists
- Providing space for nonprofit organizations

Most companies find that this is a natural extension of their charitable and community activities. Precisely what you provide is less important than making it your business to provide something of value. If you are just using the Internet for communication or for data transmission, you only need to be a good Net citizen. If you are going "whole hog" and putting together a coordinated presence with a Web site, Gopher, FTP site, or other high-visibility activity, then the level of information and service provided needs to be higher.

What you provide is also related to the kind of business you are doing. Content-oriented services such as newspapers, magazines, and book publishers naturally provide some content for free. Software companies provide free working demos or small working utilities, while Internet providers give access to services such as Web services, Gophers, and FTP sites, or support for activities such as those of nonprofit or community groups.

How much you contribute to the network depends upon your level of use, visibility, and type of product; but it is, in conjunction with your products, what will determine public opinion about your company, and the number of customers you will attract.

Where from Here...

The next chapter takes a look at the future of the Internet for business.

CHAPTER 19

The Future of Business on the Internet

The Internet is constantly and rapidly changing, and so too will the methods, resources, and services for doing business on the Internet. Participating in this enterprise is important—stay plugged into the lists and Usenet, surf the Web, and observe what others are doing.

Lacking a working crystal ball or a connection to the psychic friends hotline, predicting the future of business on the Internet is hardly an exact science. The following are just some of the trends that can be identified for the short-term future.

- *Growth*—The Internet has grown explosively, and shows no signs of slowing down. The commercial sector particularly is ripe for more growth, with estimates that there will be more than 100 million users on the Internet by the end of this decade. Currently, the Internet is not running up against any substantial technical or other constraints to growth.

  One strong influence on growth is the rise in the availability of easy-to-use, "point-and-click" GUI software for the Internet. This is enticing people who found it too daunting before to try the Net, making business on the Net even more interesting and attractive.

- *New users*—New users are coming online in unprecedented numbers through ISPs and the online commercial services. This trend is likely to continue due to the use in Windows 95 and OS/2 Warp of integrated TCP/IP stacks, which makes software installation, configuration, and connection easier.

The commercial online services such as America Online, CompuServe, Prodigy, and the MicroSoft Network are also bringing new, more diverse users to the Internet, creating a whole new customer base for businesses.

• *Speed*—New compression technologies, if incorporated into browsers, could dramatically speed page transfers, and allow more complex and high resolution graphics to be used.

Increased availability of ISDN and the use of 28,800 baud modems allows for reception of audio broadcasts, Internet voice mail, and interactive telephone calls, as well as some videoconferencing capabilities.

Other technologies hold promise for a few years down the road: One system under development claims to be able to provide a television channel and a phone call at the same time over existing copper phone lines.

• *Protocols and languages*—New Internet protocols will continue to be developed, and existing ones will rapidly improve. There is strong motivation for businesses to develop more powerful Web page display protocols and systems and to make secure transactions a ubiquitous feature of the Internet.

• *HTML and its cousins*—HyperText Markup Language is undergoing changes of many kinds, and it is likely that it will continue to evolve. New kinds of tags and operations, and new capabilities are in the process of development now. Look for increased capabilities to handle formatted text in a variety of formats other than HTML such as Adobe Acrobat; the ability to better interact with and search databases and indexes; and easier feedback to page owners. Java in particular has great potential for interactive multimedia applications which are dynamically upgraded with no effort on the part of the user.

With the latest crop of HTML editors and word processor add-ons, HTML authoring can be done by anyone who can do word processing. The authoring process will no longer be an impediment to getting on the Web and maintaining up-to-date pages. HTML editing is now even included with the Netscape 2.0 Gold browser.

Large business and organization databases should start appearing online in greater numbers, due to the recent availability of software that links proprietary databases to the Web.

The fact that there are altogether, over 30,000 different discussion lists and Usenet newsgroups shows the tremendous popularity of this type of Internet communication. Software has recently been developed that allows a Web site to offer interactive discussion forums through a Web page. Combining the popularity of discussion groups with the ease of use of the Web should make Web-based discussions incredibly popular.

- *Virtual reality*—As Virtual Reality Modeling Language (VRML) becomes more commonplace, all kinds of virtual malls, showrooms, and product demos can become part of the Internet. Customers will be able to look at an object from many angles, walk through a mall, or perhaps even "drive" a car. When better telepresence is delivered, business on the Internet will move from 2D to 3D presentations. Currently there are some experimental forms of teleoperation on the Internet. You can, for example, operate cameras, talk to people, run robots, watch activities in remote locations, and more.

- *Security*—Look for the Internet to become more secure for data and transactions. Secure Multipurpose Internet Mail Extensions (S/MIME) and Privacy Enhanced Mail (PEM) will make business transactions and communications more secure. In addition to enhancing privacy and security of e-mail, this will facilitate the use of the Internet for commerce, banking, and sales. Electronically verifiable signatures will allow the verification of messages and transactions. The challenges right now are to make these security measures standardized, easy to use, convenient, and user-friendly.

Look for a broad variety of approaches to more secure transactions, authentication of messages and identities, enhanced privacy e-mail, and more sophisticated encryption. As the number of options and methods increase, so too will the business possibilities.

- *Multimedia*—It is likely that the audio and video capacity of the Internet will continue to grow, creating many new business opportunities, including videoconferencing, real-time interactions of many kinds, and better integrated audio and video through packages such as CU-SeeMe and I-Phone. Mbone (Multicast Backbone) now facilitates Internet transmissions, and Internet video conferences are in limited use already. Sports and music events are already being broadcast. These multimedia capabilities open a new set of possibilities for online businesses.

- *New products and services*—New products and services are coming online quickly that will enhance business activities and create new opportunities. These include new browsers like Hot Java, Web site tracking software, secure servers, and Internet access through cable television systems. These kinds of products and services will provide opportunities for other businesses to reach much larger and more demographically diverse audiences.

  The search engines and services on the Web are growing in number and complexity. Some of these search tools are headed toward personalized, intelligent agents and "searchbots" (search robots) that will be able to sniff out specifically the information you want. Such programs are designed to increase the quality and accuracy of searches. Some experimental work has been done on shopping agents—they search for bargains on the Internet.

- *Access*—Access to the Internet is changing. New ISPs are springing up everywhere, rural datafication is afoot, ISDN is more available, and cable providers and phone companies want to become Internet providers. Satellite links just might make the Internet available almost anywhere.

A Final Thought

Don't be surprised at being repeatedly surprised by the Internet—this is a network that is not only changing itself, but also changing the world. Remember that business on the Internet is a participation sport—where the Internet goes from here may well be influenced by you and your business.

Bon voyage!

Hardware and Software Considerations for the Newcomer

This appendix is for those who have not previously used communication software and modems to connect to a BBS or other dial-up service, and those who are currently limited to older, or text-only, nongraphical computers. It should give you an idea of what hardware, software, and information you need to get online.

If you have already used communication software, even if you aren't an advanced user, you are probably currently ready to contact an Internet access provider and go online.

Hardware

Despite the tremendous size and high-tech nature of the Internet, the minimum required hardware is quite simple and inexpensive. Of course, specifications can be written for a $250,000 hardware package, but a few hundred dollars can get you started even if you don't have any equipment now.

Computers

The basic requirements for the computer are that communications software is available for it, and that there is some means of connecting a modem. This describes almost any computer built in the last ten years—

from the Commodore 64 to the current Macs and Pentium computers. For e-mail, FTP, Gopher, and the World Wide Web (without graphics), even an old IBM XT will work (though any file processing thereafter would be considered tedious by today's standards). It is not necessary to have the fastest, most sophisticated equipment to use the Internet.

Because you will be downloading large files, lists, and software, you will find that the more disk space you have, the better. It is quite amazing how fast another 10MB of data can come onto your hard drive when you are harvesting the Internet. Files can of course be stored on floppy disk, but that takes extra time, and the data becomes less accessible for searching or using—another cost/time trade-off. Do get the fastest and largest machine that is reasonably affordable, because it will save a lot of time; but don't let anyone tell you that you can't use the Internet if you're not running one of the latest machines.

Modems

This is the one place to spend the money and get the best. A near-state-of-the-art modem for use on standard phone lines runs at the speed of 28,800 baud and has, under the correct conditions of data compression, the ability to send and receive data with the equivalent of 115,200 baud. Such modems are available starting at $175 from mail order houses.

> **Note:**
>
> If you purchase a 28,800 baud modem, be sure that it is compatible with the v.34 standard, or actual flow of data may be under 28,800 baud.

There are cheaper but slower modems available—14,400, 9,600, and 2,400 baud modems. But consider this if you are thinking of the cheaper modem: If a file is being downloaded from your Internet access provider using a 28,000 baud modem and that (rather large) file takes 2 minutes, the same file will take 1 hour and 36 minutes with the 2,400 baud modem. Even if time is not a consideration for you, imagine the difference in long distance charges and the access provider's connect time charges between 2 minutes and 1 hour, 36 minutes! Faster and more expensive may be more economical in the long run.

Don't even *think* of using that old 300 baud modem that someone will give you for free: The same 2-minute download would take 12 hours and 48 minutes on that snail!

Another consideration in buying a modem is whether to get an "internal" or "external" modem. Many computers have a "bus" or other connection system inside, which will allow you to install the modem inside the computer. The advantages are that the modem sold in this form is usually a bit cheaper, and that you have fewer external wires to worry about. The external modem, however, can be moved from computer to computer more easily and is not made to work with just one type and model of computer. It also usually has a set of indicator lights on the front that allow you to keep track of the data transfer (especially helpful when things aren't working correctly).

For IBM PC–Type Computers

Some PCs over a couple of years old have circuits that can't reliably keep up with external modems over 9,600 baud. Replacement internal circuit board and chips are available, but the easiest approach is to get an internal modem—this bypasses the slow circuitry.

The internal modem is installed according to the manufacturer's instructions; you then connect a phone line between it and the phone jack in the wall of your house or office. The manufacturer usually supplies an extra jack on the modem so that you can reconnect the phone directly to the modem instead of to the wall jack.

External modems require three connections: (1) the phone wiring, which is done in the same way as for the internal modem; (2) the power connection, usually a small transformer that plugs into an electrical outlet in the wall, with a thin wire and connector that goes to the matching connector on the back of the modem; (3) the data connection, usually a 9-pin or 25-pin connector. If a data cable didn't come with the modem, you will need to purchase one. This cable connects the data jack on the back of the modem to one of the COM connectors on the back of the computer.

Other Hardware Considerations

A standard monochrome monitor can certainly be used for most text-based Internet resources, but a VGA (or similar color graphics monitor) increases readability and ease of use of the Internet a great deal. It also allows the use of the graphical browsers that display the formatted text and pictures from the World Wide Web. A Super VGA (SVGA) or other high-resolution monitor allows more lines on the screen at one time and therefore improves your ability to quickly scan long menus and documents. Also, the variations in color on a color graphics screen make the status indicators in various programs much easier to see.

Software

There are a number of easy to install SLIPP/PPP based Internet access packages, among them are Spry, GNN, and NetManage's Internet Chameleon. The Internet Business Kit provides instant access using NetManage's Chameleon package and templates for getting a business up and running on the Web. Also see Chapter 4, "Web Browser Basics," for reviews and instruction for several popular browsers.

Spry

http://www.spry.com
1.206.515.2995 ext 6121

Spry offers a one-disk complete Internet package. It is available through a number of sources including Internet in a Box, Mosaic Direct, and CompuServe. It is now being distributed with several Internet magazines as a free disk. To sign up requires a paid registration with an Internet access provider that is made available during the installation process.

To start, just insert the disk and choose **File Run**, and type **A:\setup.exe**. This setup takes you through the installation process.

Spry is a classic Windows application with pull-down menus. The package includes a winsock dialer, a GUI browser called Air Mosaic, and some utilities.

Global Network Navigator

http://www.gnn.com
1.800.819.6112

As a part of AOL's new Internet services, full-featured access to the Internet can be obtained through their GNN service. The software, like many others, includes one-disk installation and setup, combined with online services available through an instant sign up procedure.

As with Spry, just insert the disk and choose **File Run**, and type **A:\setup.exe**. The setup program takes you through the complete installation of a browser, e-mail package, some utilities, a winsock dialer, and the registration process.

GNN contains a full-featured browser called GNNworks, an e-mail and NetNews package called GNNmessenger, and an IRC Chat client, GNNchat.

Chameleon

http://www.netmanage.com
1.408.973.7171

NetManage offers the Internet Chameleon suite of tools which includes the WebSurfer Web browser, Telnet, Gopher, FTP, Finger Whois, and Archie clients. As with Spry and GNN, you choose **File Run**, and type **A:\setup.exe**.

During the installation you will be prompted to sign up with one of the listed Internet Services Providers, and then the software will configure itself for use with that provider.

The Internet Business Kit

http://www.wiley.com/ibk.html
1.800.225.5945

Our Internet Business Kit published by John Wiley & Sons features three books: *The Internet Business Book, Marketing on the Internet,* and a guide to the use of the Chameleon software.

This kit gives you more information about doing business and marketing on the Internet, and some HTML templates to quickly get your business up and running on the Web.

Non-SLIP/PPP Access

If you currently don't have access to a SLIP or PPP account, but do have access to a "shell" account (see Chapter 3 for explanations of SLIP and shell accounts), you can still access many of the Internet resources by using standard terminal emulating software on your PC, and connecting to an Internet service provider's shell account via your modem and the phone lines. Look for terminal software for your computer that has VT100 terminal emulation. While many services will work with other terminal emulations, VT100 is the most popular.

There are hundreds of commercial and shareware communications programs available that are suitable for a shell account on the Internet. They vary in the numbers of terminal emulations they handle, the downloading protocols available, availability of scripts, and dozens of convenience factors.

Communications programs vary greatly not only in features, but in the methods or keys they use to accomplish even the most common communications procedures. The following example uses a popular DOS-based program called Procomm Plus. Check your communications program manual or on-disk documentation for directions in accomplishing similar procedures using your communications software.

Procomm provides a summary of commands on the help screen shown in Figure A.1, listing the key combinations to use to access menus or to send immediate commands to the program. Here's how Procomm is given the information it needs to communicate with an access provider.

1   Hold down the **Alt** key and press the **d** key. The Procomm dialing directory will be displayed.

2. Press the **a** key. A window will open which will allow you to add a new phone number, name, and communications protocols (Figure A.2).

3. Type in the name you want for this phone entry, press Enter, enter the phone number, then press the Enter key again. Now enter the maximum baud rate of your modem and press Enter. Continue in a similar manner with parity (none), data bits (8), stop bits (1), and

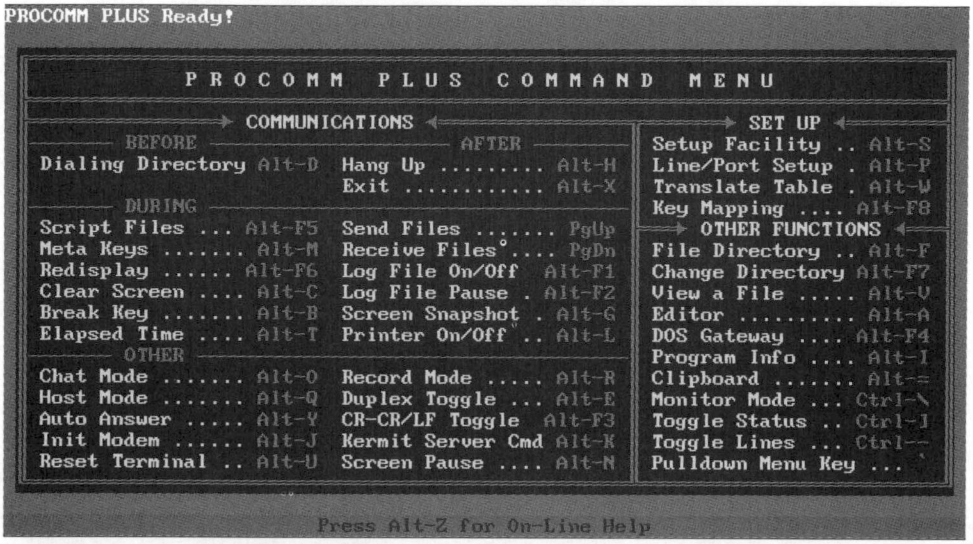

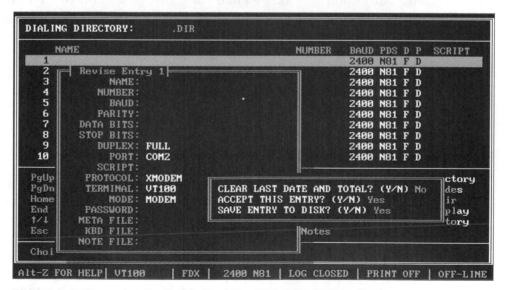

Figure A.1 Procomm's main help screen.

duplex (full). (Some access providers and networks use 7 data bits, even parity, and 1 stop bit—try these settings if you see random characters on the screen when you first connect with an access

Figure A.2 Procomm's dialog box for entering dialing and communications protocols.

provider.) The port you select will depend on how your internal modem was configured (check your modem manual for the default setting), or on which serial port you plugged your external modem into (check the back of the computer and look for a label next to the connector that says COM 1, COM 2, etc.). On all other items, just press Enter to accept the default value.

Determining Which Port Your Modem Uses

If you have trouble determining which port your modem is connected to, set your port number in the communications software to COM 2, then, from the terminal screen type **ATZ** and press Enter. If you don't see "OK" on the line under "ATZ," change the port number and try again.

---

4. With this phone number highlighted on the dialing screen, press Enter to dial the number.

A status box will appear showing which number is being dialed, how long your computer has waited for a response, and other information. Through your modem, you will probably also hear a dial tone, the sounds of dialing and ringing, and then a raucous sound of the other computer's modem. When the second modem sound joins in, your modem will go quiet and you will soon see a "connect" notice on your screen. Now you should see your Internet access provider's login screen and its prompts for your login name and password.

Packages with Communications Software

There are hundreds of other freestanding communications programs. In addition, there are communications programs that are part of integrated packages such as Microsoft Works. These integrated packages include applications such as word processors, spreadsheets, databases, and file-handling utilities, along with the communications program. They all use one common structure and appearance. If you are just getting started in computing, one of these integrated packages may save learning time and therefore make the computer a productive tool more quickly.

Obtaining Hardware and Software—Hints and Tips

While there are many good deals on computers, software, and peripherals at local retail stores and at national retail chains, in some cases purchasing through mail order can provide some extra options and price breaks.

The computer equipment market is volatile, so getting up-to-date price and availability information is important. This information can be found through a variety of magazines and periodicals, such as *Computer Shopper*, *PC Magazine*, *Home Office Computing*, *Byte*, and *Windows Magazine*, which have large sections of mail-order advertisements. There are magazines and guides specifically for laptops, mobile computing, wireless technology, Macintosh, Amiga, and other areas. These magazines and guides offer direct mail-order shopping from some of the major computer vendors, including IBM, Dell, Gateway, and Compaq. A variety of Macintosh products are available via mail order as well. There are also numerous catalogs of supplies, hardware, and software offered through these magazines.

Increasingly, software vendors are offering free disks with demonstrations and working versions of their software. These are useful for trying out software before you buy. (Don't forget that a lot of software is available for free or for purchase via the Internet, too.)

Many people who buy directly order via the telephone, or increasingly, through the Internet itself. When placing a telephone order, be sure to state your understanding of the terms of the sale, such as price, tax, shipping data, return policies, and warranties. Be sure to state all of the specifications such as make and model, size, and included components. Don't assume that a computer shown with a monitor in the advertisement will necessarily come with a monitor. Be sure to find out if a substitute will be sent if your model is unavailable, and let the dealer know if that is acceptable.

Keep notes of your conversation, and always ask for the salesperson's name. Using your credit card to pay will give you some additional legal options if things do not go well with your purchase.

Networking—The Old-Fashioned Way

Sometimes you'll be able to get new hardware and software working with no trouble, but usually there are problems to be worked out. For the computer, modem, and other hardware there are often manufacturer or vendor help lines, and the same goes for commercial software packages. Internet service providers also usually have technical help lines. With these sources and some work with the manuals and documentation, you should be able to solve most problems.

Local computer clubs can also be excellent sources of information. With over 4,000 clubs in the United States, and thousands of other clubs worldwide, there is usually a computer club near you with people very willing to give technical assistance and information.

Some Useful UNIX Commands

The UNIX operating system is ubiquitous on the Internet. Many of the Internet access providers use the UNIX operating system, so you are likely to encounter UNIX face-to-face from time to time on the Internet. If you have a UNIX shell account, you will most certainly have to use at least a few UNIX commands to interact with your account, messages, and files. The following is by no means an exhaustive collection of UNIX information; rather it is a list of items particularly helpful to Internet users.

Files to be aware of (these file names each begin with a dot):

.login   A file that contains configuration information for your particular account that is used by your access provider's computer when you log in.

.plan   A file that is sent out when someone uses the finger program to find out who you are. You can write your own .plan file if you want one. It might contain, for example, information about you and your business.

.signature A small file that contains personal and business information that you can appended to e-mail and Usenet postings (see Chapter 12).

Useful key combinations:

Ctrl-c   Interrupts the current process. This can be used to escape from a program that isn't operating correctly.

Ctrl-s   Suspends the screen scroll. If text is scrolling by the screen too quickly to read, this will stop it.

Ctrl-q   Resumes the screen scroll.

UNIX commands (press the Enter key after typing each command):

Note:

UNIX commands are case sensitive (which means that ls is not the same as LS or Ls).

cat   Displays file contents (scrolls on screen until end of the file).
syntax: **cat** *filename*

more   Displays file contents one page at a time (use the spacebar to advance to the next screen, the **b** key to go back a screen).
syntax: **more** *filename*

pwd   Displays the name of the directory you are currently in.
syntax: **pwd**

cd   Changes directory.
syntax: **cd** *directoryname*
            cd *directoryname/subdirectoryname/* [etc.]

mkdir   Creates a new directory.
syntax: **mkdir** *newdirectoryname*

rmdir   Removes or deletes a directory.
syntax: **rmdir** *directoryname*

ls   Lists the files and subdirectories in the current directory.

ls -l   Lists files and subdirectories in long form, with file size, date, etc.

ls -a   Lists all files, including hidden files.
syntax: **ls**
         ls -l
         ls -a
         ls -a -l

cp   Copies a file; use to duplicate the file under a new name in the same directory, or to copy it to a different directory.
syntax: **cp** *oldname newname*
         cp *oldfilename anotherdirectory/newfilename*

rm   Removes (deletes) a file.
syntax: **rm** *filename*

mv   Moves or renames a file.
syntax: **mv** *oldfilename newdirectory/newfilename*
         mv *oldfilename newfilename* (to rename)

help   On some systems, gets you the help files and/or a list of available commands (you can specify a command with **help**). On other systems you will have to use **man**.
syntax: **help**
         help *topicname*

man   Gets help from the online manual for commands you specify (usually more exhaustive and advanced information than provided by help files).
syntax: **man** (for list of manual contents)
         man *command* (for information on a specific command)

clear   Clears the screen.
syntax: **clear**

logout   Ends your online session. (Some systems also use "exit" or "bye" or "quit.")
syntax: **logout**

whoami   Shows your current finger name information.
syntax: **whoami**

chfn   Changes your finger name (the name that you are known by to the system). You will then be prompted for the new name.
syntax: **chfn**

passwd   Changes your password. (Follow instruction prompts on the screen.)
syntax: **passwd**

kermit   Invokes the Kermit file transfer program.
syntax: **kermit**

sz   Sends a file using the Z-Modem file transfer protocol.
            syntax: **sz -b** (to send a binary file)
                    sz -a (to send an ASCII file)

rz   Receives a file using the Z-Modem file transfer protocol.
            syntax: **rz -b** (to receive a binary file)
                    rz -a (to receive an ASCII file)

Sending and Receiving Files

This is a quick overview of how to upload (send) and download (receive) files. If you have a shell account with an Internet access provider, you will often need to transfer files from your computer to the access provider's computer, and from the access provider's computer to your personal computer. These files might include e-mail messages that you want to save on your personal computer, or files that you want to attach to your e-mail messages. You will also need to transfer files that you obtained while using Gopher, FTP, Usenet, or the World Wide Web. While some of these files can be read and then left on the Internet access provider's computer, others, such as software for your personal computer, obviously need to be *downloaded* to be used.

Some definitions:

Upload—The process of sending a copy of a file that is stored on your local computer or personal PC to a remote computer

Download—The process of getting a copy of a file from a remote computer to your own PC

Downloading

Let's suppose that you have used FTP to get a file called **pricelist.txt** from one of the many FTP sites on the Internet. The file is now located in your account's directory on your Internet service provider's computer. The next step is to bring it to your own personal computer.

The details for downloading a file vary depending on which communications software you use in your PC, your Internet access provider's software, and the downloading protocol you select, but here are some fairly standard procedures:

1. Boot up your computer, and use your communications program to contact your dial-up Internet provider.

2. Log on to your service as usual.

3. Choose your download protocol—this could be Z-Modem, X-Modem, Kermit, or others, depending upon the protocols supported by your service provider and your communications software. Check with user services to get more information, or type **help** and look for information on file transfer.

4. Type **ls** to look at a list of your files to be sure of the correct spelling of the file name.

Then follow the instructions that go with the selected protocol.

Z-Modem Protocol

ASCII Files

5. Initiate the transfer by typing in a command that tells the remote computer to send a file to you. For example, to send an ASCII text file called **pricelist.txt** using Z-Modem, type this at the system prompt:

```
sz -a pricelist.txt
```

6. After you have given the send instructions to the remote computer, you will need to tell your personal computer's communications software to receive the file. Using Procomm, for example, you would press the Page Down key and choose **Z** for **Z-Modem** to initiate the download. (Some communications software is able to detect that the remote computer is attempting to send a file and will automatically go into receive mode.)

Many files on the Internet are stored on systems that allow for very long file names. When these files are downloaded to a system that allows fewer characters for a file name like DOS and Windows 3.1, which allow only eight-character names), some accommodation needs to be made. Some PC software truncates (shortens) the file name by using only the first eight characters. This can cause difficulties if you download several files with the same first characters. Two files **pricelist1.txt** and **pricelist2.txt** would both download as **pricelis.txt**. If your communications software doesn't have a system to renumber such duplicate files, the second file downloaded will overwrite (erase) the first download. If your software doesn't automatically rename these files, rename them yourself before downloading (see Appendix B for appropriate UNIX commands).

Binary Files

5. To download a binary file called **catalog.zip**, type:

```
sz -b catalog.zip
```

6. As before, give the receive command to your local computer.

Kermit Protocol

5. To use Kermit to download an ASCII text file called **pricelist.txt**, type **kermit** at the system prompt to bring up the Kermit program on your Internet access provider's computer, and then at the kermit prompt give it a command to send the file:

```
kermit
Kermit>send pricelist.txt
```

6. As before, you will need to tell your local communications software to receive the file. In Procomm, this means pressing the Page Down key, followed by choosing **K** for Kermit.

7. To download a *binary* file called **catalog.zip** using Kermit, there is an extra step involved:

```
kermit
Kermit>set file type binary
Kermit>send catalog.zip
```

Then, as above, use your communications program to receive the file.

The file is now located on your personal computer, ready for use.

Uploading

Uploading a file to your account works in a similar way—it is the flip side of downloading.

1. You must tell the remote computer to expect an upload. For Z-Modem protocol (ASCII files) this is done by typing **rz -a** *filename*, or for a binary file, **rz -b** *filename*; to use Kermit, type **kermit** and Enter, then type **receive** *filename*, or for a binary file, set the file type to binary as above, then type **receive** *filename*.

2. You then must have your communications software upload the file using whatever command your particular software uses. In the case of Procomm, press the Page Up key and identify the protocol with a **Z** or a **K** as appropriate to match the remote computer's protocol, and then enter the file name when prompted.

After a few seconds (or minutes, depending on the size of the file and modem speed), the process will end. You can then list your account's directory at the remote computer to confirm that the transfer was successful.

Communications software programs will differ in the specific keys to press, but they all have some method for carrying out these functions.

How to Transfer Files Stored at FTP Sites

Thousands of the computers on the Internet have files available free to the public through the use of the File Transfer Protocol (FTP). Many companies maintain large FTP sites of software, software patches, and utilities. These may range from a dozen assorted files available from one location to an in-depth collection of thousands of software programs or business-related files. The FTP system will transfer both ASCII and binary files of almost any size and type: data files from spreadsheets, CAD, word processors, databases, photo images, and desktop publishing, as well as software and plain text files. This FTP system for file transfer is very powerful, but it is a little hard to learn to use.

There are four basic methods for getting these files:

- Using a GUI Web browser
- Using a text-based Web browser
- Using command-line FTP with a shell account
- Via e-mail

These vary greatly in their flexibility, speed, and ease of use:

- Using a GUI Web browser such as Netscape or Mosaic is the easiest, but requires that you have an Internet access provider with a

429

SLIP/PPP connection, or that you have a shell account and TIA (see Chapter 3).

- If you have a shell account that offers Lynx, you can use that text-based browser to FTP.
- If your shell account doesn't have a text-based browser, you can use command-line FTP.
- If you only have an e-mail account you can use the slow, but effective, e-mail procedure to get FTP files.

Retrieving Files with a GUI Browser

Most Web browsers can be used to retrieve files stored at FTP sites. This makes navigation among the FTP sites, directories, and files very easy.

To use FTP with a browser, follow the same procedures that you would for entering a Web site's URL in your browser, but use the FTP form of URL. If the FTP site's address is, for example, **nic.merit.edu**, and the files you are interested in are in the **newsletter** subdirectory, the URL would be:

`ftp://nic.merit.edu/newsletter/`

If you don't know which subdirectory to specify, simply enter:

`ftp://nic.merit.edu`

You can then select a subdirectory from those listed.

If you know the subdirectory and the file name (e.g., **INDEX.news letters**), you can go right to the file of interest (and if it is a text file, read it on your screen):

`ftp://nic.merit.edu/newsletter/INDEX.newsletters`

Figure D.1 shows the Netscape browser displaying the **newsletters** subdirectory of the **nic.merit.edu** FTP site. Note that the directory listing has two types of icons. Netscape uses a sheet-of-paper icon to indicate individual files, and a file folder icon to represent subdirectories.

Click on the file icon, and the browser will display the text of the file, or provide you with a method to download a binary file. Click on the subdirectory icon, and the browser will go down to the subdirectory you

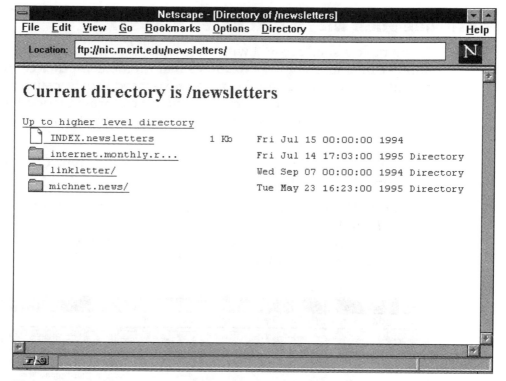

Figure D.1 Netscape, a graphical user interface browser, displaying an FTP site directory.

have selected. To go up to the previous directory, click on the "Up to a higher level directory" link.

Most of the other features of the browser, such as bookmarks, print-outs, and file saving, can also be used with FTP.

> **Note:**
>
> If a file at the FTP site is an HTML document and marked with the appropriate file name extension (.html), some browsers will display it as a fully formatted page with working hotlinks and other features. View and/or save it as you would any other HTML document.

Retrieving Files with a Text-Based Browser

If you have a shell account with an Internet access provider, or access to another business's or organization's mainframe computer connected to the Internet, you may be able to use a text-based browser such as Lynx to get FTP files. To do so, connect with your access provider or other system via your terminal or a terminal program (see Chapter 4, Lynx section). Start the Lynx program as usual.

To view an FTP file or look at an FTP directory, type **G** (**shift-g**) and then type the FTP URL in the input line.

Figure D.2 shows the same subdirectory (newsletter at the nic.merit. edu FTP site) as was displayed by the GUI browser in Figure D.1. The arrow keys are used in the usual Lynx manner to move up and down the file/directory list, and the right arrow is used for displaying or down-

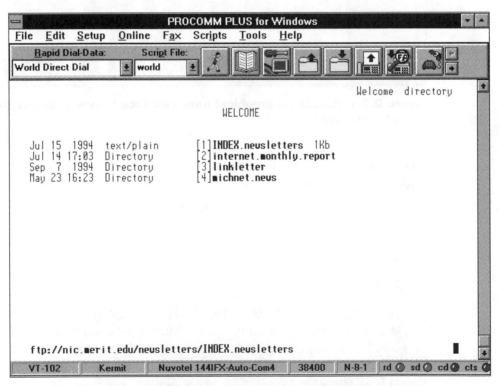

Figure D.2 The Procomm Plus for Windows terminal program with the text-based Lynx browser's display of an FTP site directory.

loading the file. Lynx doesn't display an "Up to a higher level directory" link as the Netscape browser does, but you can go back up the directory tree using the left arrow. Like the GUI browsers, Lynx lets you use most of its features such as bookmarks, downloading, and the history list, at FTP sites.

Retrieving Files with Command-Line FTP

In order to use this transfer system, your Internet service provider's computer must have the FTP software installed. If you are in doubt as to its availability, you can check with your system administrator or your system's documentation and help files. A quick way to find out if your system is FTP-ready is to type **FTP** at your system's main prompt (%, $, etc.). If FTP is installed, you will receive a new prompt: **ftp>** (to get back to your main system prompt, type **quit** and press the Enter key).

FTP is usually used when you already have these three pieces of information:

- The address of the site where the file you are interested in is stored
- The directory (subdirectory) in which the file is stored at that site
- The name of the file

These three pieces of information may be obtained in a variety of ways, for example:

- Using the Archie search tool discussed in Chapter 14
- From messages others have posted to discussion or Usenet groups that you are a member of
- From one of the many lists of FTP sites and files that are maintained in discussion group archives and at FTP sites themselves
- From the README or INDEX files found at most FTP sites, often in the *pub* directory
- From many places throughout this book

A Plain Vanilla File Transfer

Let's assume that you have come across a list mentioning a file for new Internet users that answers commonly asked questions. The list says that the file's name is **fyi_04.txt**, that it is located at **nic.merit.edu**, and that it is in the **documents/fyi** directory. Now you want to find the file and transfer it to your computer so that you can read it. Here's what a typical FTP session seeking that file would look like (in this example, *world%* is the system prompt from the Internet service provider, and the boldface items are typed in from the user's keyboard):

```
world% ftp nic.merit.edu
Connected to nic.merit.edu.
220 nic.merit.edu FTP server (SunOS 4.1) ready.
Name (nic.merit.edu:oakridge): anonymous
331 Guest login ok, send ident as password.
Password:
230 Guest login ok, access restrictions apply.
ftp> cd /documents/fyi
250 CWD command successful.
ftp> get fyi_04.txt
200 PORT command successful.
150 ASCII data connection for fyi_04.txt (192.74.137.5,3672)
(98753 bytes).
226 ASCII Transfer complete.
101220 bytes received in 4.4 seconds (22 Kbytes/s)
ftp> bye
221 Goodbye.
world%
```

Whew! Now, let's break this down into its components and see how that collection of cryptic characters actually can get the file to your computer.

To start the process of retrieving the file, type at your access providers system prompt *ftp* followed by a space the FTP site's address:

```
world% ftp nic.merit.edu
```

> **Note:**
>
> All steps in this FTP process are followed by pressing the Enter key.

You will get the following response from your host computer:

```
Connected to nic.merit.edu.
220 nic.merit.edu FTP server (SunOS 4.1) ready.
Name (nic.merit.edu:oakridge):
```

When All Else Fails

If now or at any other point in the FTP session the system seems to stop working correctly, try holding down the Ctrl key and pressing the **c** key to escape from FTP.

Now, type in the word **anonymous** and the host computer will respond with a request for a password:

```
331 Guest login ok, send ident as password.
Password:
```

The password is your e-mail address—for instance, *oakridge@world. std.com*. As the address is being typed in it will not be echoed back, that is, you will not see what you are typing appear on the screen. When you've typed in your e-mail address as your password and pressed Enter, the host will respond with anything from one line (as shown below) to a full screen of information about that FTP site and its notices, rules, and so on.

```
230 Guest login ok, access restrictions apply.
```

Now the directory information comes into play: type in **cd**, then a space, then a forward slash (/, not \), followed by the full directory path (the directory and subdirectories in which the file is located):

```
ftp> cd /documents/fyi
```

The host computer will respond with the line shown below and another *ftp>* prompt. Now type in the command **get** followed by a space and the file name:

```
250 CWD command successful.
ftp> get fyi_04.txt
```

After you press the Enter key, several transfer status lines like those shown below will appear. If your system has "hash" turned on, you will

> **Note:**
>
> File names are case sensitive at FTP sites; copy the upper- and lowercase letters just as they were shown in your original source of information about this file. *Index*, *index*, and *INDEX* would be considered three different file names.

also see, for each block of data transferred, a "#" character printed to the screen.

```
200 PORT command successful.
150 ASCII data connection for fyi_04.txt (192.74.137.5,3672)
    (98753 bytes).
226 ASCII Transfer complete.
101220 bytes received in 4.4 seconds (22 Kbytes/s)
ftp>
```

When the new *ftp>* prompt appears, you can finish the process by typing in **bye**; being polite, FTP will respond by saying *Goodbye* and returning you to your host system's prompt:

```
221 Goodbye.
world%
```

The file you requested is now in your account's subdirectory on your access service provider's computer (if you changed to another subdirectory before using the FTP command, it will be in that subdirectory). Appendix C explains how to download the file from the host computer to your personal computer.

File Transfers with All the Bells and Whistles

Getting a simple text file may only involve the steps just shown, especially if the site address, directory, and file names were exactly correct. But those who maintain files may update them and change their names, or they may decide to group them differently in different directories. The FTP system has several commands and functions that help deal with these and several other problems.

The following is an FTP session that will get two more files that were in the same directory as the file obtained in the preceding example. Only the steps that are different from those in the preceding example will be discussed. The session begins as before, by making a connection and logging in:

```
world% ftp nic.merit.edu
Connected to nic.merit.edu.
220 nic.merit.edu FTP server (SunOS 4.1) ready.
Name (nic.merit.edu:oakridge): anonymous
331 Guest login ok, send ident as password.
Password:
230 Guest login ok, access restrictions apply.
ftp>
```

At any FTP prompt, the current directory can be listed to your screen. If you do this before using any **cd** (change directory) command, the top directory available to the public will be shown:

```
ftp> dir
200 PORT command successful.
150 ASCII data connection for /bin/ls (192.74.137.5,4847) (0
bytes).
total 58
-rw-r--r--  1 nic       merit      21219 Feb 11 02:30 INDEX
-rw-r--r--  1 nic       merit      16326 Oct 22 23:18 READ.ME
drwxr-sr-x  2 nic       merit        512 Sep 15  1992
acceptable.use.policies
drwxr-sr-x  2 root      system       512 Sep 15  1993 bin
drwxr-sr-x  3 cise      nsf          512 May 12  1993 cise
drwxr-sr-x  4 nic       merit        512 Oct 31 20:59
conference.proceedings
dr-xr-sr-x  2 root      staff        512 Aug  6  1993 dev
drwxr-sr-x  9 nic       merit        512 Nov 30 22:37 documents
drwxr-sr-x  2 root      system       512 Aug  6  1993 etc
drwxr-sr-x 12 nic       merit        512 Jan  7 19:24 internet
drwxr-sr-x  3 nic       merit        512 Nov 30 21:04
internet.tools
drwxr-sr-x  2 nic       merit       1024 Mar 11 12:03
introducing.the.internet
drwxr-sr-x  2 root      staff        512 Aug  6  1993 lib
drwxr-sr-x  2 nic       merit        512 Oct 13 19:26 maps
drwxr-sr-x  9 nic       merit        512 Mar  3 19:25 michnet
drwxr-sr-x  7 nic       merit        512 Oct 14 23:39 newsletters
drwxr-sr-x  7 nic       merit        512 Jan 10 17:53 nren
```

```
drwxr-sr-x 13 nic        merit       512 Oct 13 23:13 nsfnet
drwxr-sr-x  2 omb        omb         512 Sep 10  1993 omb
drwxr-sr-x  5 nic        merit       512 Mar 17  1993 resources
drwxr-sr-x  4 nic        merit       512 Jul 26  1993 statistics
drwxr-sr-x  3 root       system      512 Jun 12  1993 usr
drwxr-sr-x  3 nic        merit       512 Jul 15  1992
working.groups
226 ASCII Transfer complete.
ftp>
```

As you can see, the directory listing looks rather cryptic, but there are several useful pieces of information you can pull out of the alphabet soup:

- A line that begins with the letter *d* is a directory. To move to a directory type *cd* followed by the name of the directory (listed at the right end of the line).

- A line that begins with a dash (-) is a file, and is usually available to you for downloading.

- The number just before the date shows the size of the file in bytes. File transfers on the Internet itself are so fast that file size is rarely a concern in terms of Internet time. But you should be aware of the file size in case your Internet provider has restrictions on how much you can store. Another point to consider is that downloading the file from your access provider's computer to your own computer can consume quite a bit of time and cost a lot in phone charges. A 500,000-byte file downloaded on a 2,400 baud modem using some download protocols would take about an hour and fifteen minutes (though a good quality 28,000 baud modem using other protocols would only take around three minutes). See Appendix A for information on modems.

- At the end of the line is the name of the file or subdirectory. Names may contain no spaces, so characters.like_these-will_be_used_to_link_words_together.

An alternative to **dir** is **ls**. Using **ls** provides a list of just the file and directory names, with no other information. This may be of some value if you are using a slow modem and the directory is very large.

Files intended for the public are often in the directory *pub* (though not in this example). Directories marked *system* (in the column near the middle of the screen), such as *etc* and *bin* in this example, have to do with the remote system's operation, and will generally not contain public files. A file named **ls-lR** in the top directory at some sites lists every file in the system (no descriptions). This is usually a huge file.

In this example, after moving to the *fyi* directory using the **cd** command, the directory can be listed again to see if the file **fyi_04.txt** is there:

```
ftp> cd documents/fyi
250 CWD command successful.
ftp> dir
200 PORT command successful.
150 ASCII data connection for /bin/ls (192.74.137.5,4894) (0
bytes).
total 1640
-rw-r--r--  2 nic      merit        4723 Feb 22 16:24 INDEX.fyi
-rw-r--r--  4 nic      merit        7722 Mar 25  1990 fyi_01.txt
-rw-r--r--  4 nic      merit      308528 Jun 24  1993 fyi_02.txt
-rw-r--r--  5 nic      merit       95238 Aug 19  1990 fyi_03.txt
-rw-r--r--  5 nic      merit       98753 Mar 11 11:49 fyi_04.txt
-rw-r--r--  4 nic      merit       18175 Aug 22  1990 fyi_05.txt
-rw-r--r--  4 nic      merit        3547 Jan 11  1991 fyi_06.txt
-rw-r--r--  4 nic      merit       32829 Feb 28  1991 fyi_07.txt
-rw-r--r--  4 nic      merit      254910 Jul 22  1991 fyi_08.txt
-rw-r--r--  4 nic      merit       92119 May 28  1992 fyi_09.txt
-rw-r--r--  5 nic      merit       71176 Jan 14  1993 fyi_10.txt
-rw-r--r--  4 nic      merit      132147 Jan  3  1992 fyi_11.txt
-rw-r--r--  4 nic      merit       29135 Feb 25  1992 fyi_12.txt
-rw-r--r--  4 nic      merit        9392 Mar 13  1992 fyi_13.txt
-rw-r--r--  4 nic      merit       35694 Mar 13  1992 fyi_14.txt
-rw-r--r--  4 nic      merit        8858 Aug  3  1992 fyi_15.txt
-rw-r--r--  5 nic      merit       53449 Aug 14  1992 fyi_16.txt
-rw-r--r--  4 nic      merit       48199 Oct  7 17:14 fyi_17.txt
-rw-r--r--  5 nic      merit      104624 Jan  7  1993 fyi_18.txt
-rw-r--r--  5 nic      merit        7116 May 27  1993 fyi_19.txt
-rw-r--r--  5 nic      merit       27811 May 27  1993 fyi_20.txt
-rw-r--r--  4 nic      merit       34883 Jul 22  1993 fyi_21.txt
-rw-r--r--  4 nic      merit      113646 Feb 22 16:10 fyi_22.txt
226 ASCII Transfer complete.
```

Before actually getting the file, you might decide to take a look around at what else this site has stored under the *documents* directory. Since the *documents* directory is one step up the directory tree from *fyi* (*documents/fyi*), the command **cd ..** can be used (that's **cd**, followed by one

---

If You Are Lost in the Directories

If you are not sure where you are in the directory tree, type **pwd**
for a full list of directories above the one you are in.

---

space, followed by two periods). To move two steps up the tree, type in
cd ../.. (three steps, **cd ../../..** etc.). After pressing Enter, you can again use
dir to see the directory.

```
ftp> cd ..
250 CWD command successful.
ftp> dir
200 PORT command successful.
150 ASCII data connection for /bin/ls (192.74.137.5,4910) (0
bytes).
total 57
-rw-r--sr-  1 nic    merit    2300 Jul 31  1992 INDEX.documents
drwxr-sr-x  2 nic    merit     512 Mar 11 12:03 fyi
drwxr-sr-x  3 iesg   ietf     2048 Mar 17 08:12 iesg
drwxr-sr-x..4 iesg   ietf     3584 Mar 17 08:13 ietf
drwxr-sr-x  2 iesg   ietf    24576 Mar 17 08:14 internetÄdrafts
drwxr-sr-x  2 nic    merit     512 Jul 15  1992
michnet.tour.guides
drwxr-sr-x  2 nic    merit   19968 Mar 14 15:05 rfc
drwxr-sr-x  2 nic    merit    1536 Mar 14 15:17 std
226 ASCII Transfer complete.
```

You can now go back to the *fyi* directory by typing **cd fyi**. Notice that
the whole directory path statement (*documents/fyi*) is not needed, since
the move is from *documents* down one step to *fyi*, not from the top
directory to *fyi*.

```
ftp> cd fyi
250 CWD command successful.
ftp> dir
200 PORT command successful.
150 ASCII data connection for /bin/ls (192.74.137.5,4929)   -
(0 bytes).
total 1640
-rw-r--r--  2 nic    merit        4723 Feb 22 16:24 INDEX.fyi
-rw-r--r--  4 nic    merit        7722 Mar 25  1990 fyi_01.txt
```

```
-rw-r--r--  4 nic      merit       308528 Jun 24   1993 fyi_02.txt
-rw-r--r--  5 nic      merit        95238 Aug 19   1990 fyi_03.txt
-rw-r--r--  5 nic      merit        98753 Mar 11  11:49 fyi_04.txt
-rw-r--r--  4 nic      merit        18175 Aug 22   1990 fyi_05.txt
-rw-r--r--  4 nic      merit         3547 Jan 11   1991 fyi_06.txt
-rw-r--r--  4 nic      merit        32829 Feb 28   1991 fyi_07.txt
-rw-r--r--  4 nic      merit       254910 Jul 22   1991 fyi_08.txt
-rw-r--r--  4 nic      merit        92119 May 28   1992 fyi_09.txt
-rw-r--r--  5 nic      merit        71176 Jan 14   1993 fyi_10.txt
-rw-r--r--  4 nic      merit       132147 Jan  3   1992 fyi_11.txt
-rw-r--r--  4 nic      merit        29135 Feb 25   1992 fyi_12.txt
-rw-r--r--  4 nic      merit         9392 Mar 13   1992 fyi_13.txt
-rw-r--r--  4 nic      merit        35694 Mar 13   1992 fyi_14.txt
-rw-r--r--  4 nic      merit         8858 Aug  3   1992 fyi_15.txt
-rw-r--r--  5 nic      merit        53449 Aug 14   1992 fyi_16.txt
-rw-r--r--  4 nic      merit        48199 Oct  7  17:14 fyi_17.txt
-rw-r--r--  5 nic      merit       104624 Jan  7   1993 fyi_18.txt
-rw-r--r--  5 nic      merit         7116 May 27   1993 fyi_19.txt
-rw-r--r--  5 nic      merit        27811 May 27   1993 fyi_20.txt
-rw-r--r--  4 nic      merit        34883 Jul 22   1993 fyi_21.txt
-rw-r--r--  4 nic      merit       113646 Feb 22  16:10 fyi_22.txt
```

Often, each directory list will have a file called INDEX, or README, or something similar. It will usually contain information about the other files in the directory. It may briefly describe each file, or may give some background as to the source and nature of the files. Such index files are especially important in figuring out which of dozens of cryptically named files to get. (Note that each of the three directories in this example has an INDEX file.)

You could download the index file just as was done with fyi_04.txt in the plain vanilla example, but then you would need to exit FTP and read the file using your host computer, and then FTP to the site again to get the files you located using the index file. This would be a reasonable solution if the Index file is really large, or if you think it will require a lot of time to figure out which files you want. However, FTP software provides a faster method to look at any text file like INDEX.fyi. This is accomplished by using the ¦**more** (said "pipe more") command in conjunction with the **get** command to print the file, one page at a time, to your screen. After reading each page, press a key, and the next page will be displayed. To use this feature, type **get**, followed by a space, then the file name (copy upper- and lowercase letters exactly), followed by a space and then ¦**more**.

> **Note:**
>
> Some FTP sites use **tt:** instead of ¦**more**.

```
ftp> get INDEX.fyi ¦more
200 PORT command successful.
150 ASCII data connection for INDEX.fyi (192.74.137.5,2444)
(4723 bytes).

<NIC.MERIT.EDU> /internet/documents/fyi/INDEX.fyi   22 July 1995

              Merit Network Information Center Services
                          NIC.MERIT.EDU
                          FTP.MERIT.EDU
                        FTP.MICHNET.NET
                          NIS.NSF.NET
                          (35.1.1.48)


fyi_01.txt    F.Y.I. on F.Y.I.: Introduction to the F.Y.I. Notes
              Malkin, G.S.   (rfc1150.txt)
              227 lines   7722 bytes


fyi_02.txt    FYI on a Network Management Tool Catalog:
              Tools for Monitoring and Debugging TCP/IP
              Internets and Interconnected Devices
              Enger, R., J. Reynolds    (rfc1470.txt)
              10754 lines   308528 bytes


fyi_03.txt    FYI on Where to Start:  A Bibliography
              of Internetworking Information
              Bowers, K.L.   (rfc1175.txt)
              2412 lines   95238 bytes


fyi_04.txt    FYI on Questions and Answers:  Answers to
              Commonly asked "New Internet User" Questions
              Malkin, G.S., A. Marine   (rfc1325.txt)
              1795 lines   71232 bytes
```

```
fyi_05.txt      Choosing a Name for Your Computer
                Libes, D.   (rfc1178.txt)
                451 lines  18175 bytes

fyi_06.txt      FYI on the X Window System
                Scheifler, R.W.   (rfc1198.txt)
                171 lines  3547 bytes

fyi_07.txt      FYI on Questions and Answers:  Answers to
                Commonly asked "Experienced Internet User" Questions
--More--
```

Notice the *--More--* that appears at the bottom of the screen after each page is displayed. This lets you know that there is more to the document which you can read by pressing any key. The number of lines displayed per screen depends on how your account is configured on your Internet access provider's computer, and can be set to match whatever your communications software needs.

FTP can be set to transfer files in binary or ASCII mode. ASCII files are normally plain text files of letters, numbers, and symbols with no special fonts or formatting (except what can be accomplished with carriage returns and blank spaces). They can be read on most word processors and editors. Binary files may be program files, or they may be the data files from particular programs that can only be used by compatible programs: spreadsheets, CAD files, word processing files, configuration files of various types, digitized pictures and sound files, and so on.

Whether a file is ASCII or binary can often be determined by looking at the file name extension, which is the group of letters after the last period in the file name (for example, **txt** in the file name **fyi_04.txt**). Some common ASCII file name extensions are **txt**, **doc**, **asc**, **uu**, **hqx**, and **bsc**. Some common binary file name extensions are **exe**, **com**, **zip**, **bin**, **sit**, **arc**, **tar**, **z**, **arj**, **gif**, **pcx**, and **jpg**; many extensions are assigned to data files by programs, and indicate that the files are designed to work with particular programs. Not all file names have extensions.

While ASCII files will transfer well in both the binary and ASCII modes, binary files must be sent with the FTP software set to binary. Most FTP sites now make their default setting binary, but just to be sure, you can do the setting yourself. At any *ftp>* prompt, type in **binary** and press

Enter. The response will say *Type set to I.* (**I** stands for Image, which is what the FTP program calls this type of file.)

```
ftp> binary
200 Type set to I.
```

To find out which directory on your host computer FTP is going to send the file to, use the **lcd** command. The directory shown will be the place to look for your new files when you finish with the FTP session.

```
ftp> lcd
Local directory now /home/foyer/oakridge
```

The status of some of the settings that the FTP user can change are shown in a report that is available at any *ftp>* prompt just by typing in **status** and pressing Enter. (Note the report *Type: binary*—this is the file type setting that was just done.)

```
ftp> status
Connected to nic.merit.edu.
No proxy connection.
Mode: stream; Type: binary; Form: non-print; Structure: file
Verbose: on; Bell: off; Prompting: on; Globbing: on
Store unique: off; Receive unique: on
Case: off; CR stripping: on
Ntrans: off
Nmap: off
Hash mark printing: off; Use of PORT cmds: on
```

To explore further some of these status report items or to get a list of all of the possible FTP commands, type **help** at the *ftp>* prompt and press Enter.

> **Note:**
>
> There are quite a few different FTP programs, and several different versions of many of these. While these programs are compatible and interact correctly with each other, their user interfaces and features vary somewhat. The **help** command allows you to read the documentation and discover the differences.

```
ftp> help
Commands may be abbreviated. Commands are:
```

!	debug	mget	pwd	status
$	dir	mkdir	quit	struct
account	disconnect	mls	quote	system
append	form	mode	recvs	unique
ascii	get	modtime	reget	tenex
bell	glob	mput	rstatus	trace
binary	hash	newer	rhelp	type
bye	help	nmap	rename	user
case	idle	nlist	reset	umask
cd	image	ntrans	restart	verbose
cdup	lcd	open	rmdir	?
chmod	ls	prompt	runique	
close	macdef	proxy	send	
cr	mdelete	sendport	site	
delete	mdir	put	size	

You can select any item on the screen to get help on, just by typing **help** followed by that item. As an example, help for **runique** is obtained by typing **help**, then a space, then **runique**.

```
ftp> help runique
runique    toggle store unique for local files
```

This says that **runique** can protect files in your home directory from being overwritten with newly downloaded files that happen to have the same name. This feature will rename the new file with most of the original name and a number. The status report above shows that this feature is on. Here is how to turn it on if it isn't on by default at your site:

```
ftp> runique
Receive unique on.
```

In the first example of an FTP session shown in this chapter, the **get** command was used. A similar command, **mget**, allows you to download several files at one time, without having to type in each file name separately. For example, if files **fyi_21.txt** and **fyi_22.txt** are of interest, you could type in **mget**, followed by a space and then **fyi_2*.txt**. The * is a *wild card* standing for any characters, and this command tells FTP to download all files having names starting with **fyi_2** and ending with **.txt**. In this particular case, that would be the last three files in the directory:

fyi_20.txt, **fyi_21.txt**, and **fyi_22.txt**. When each file is ready for transfer, the FTP program prompts you for a **y** or an **n** (Yes or No) as to whether you want that particular file sent. In the example below, I only wanted 21 and 22, so I responded with **n** for 20 and **y** for 21 and 22.

```
ftp> mget fyi_2*.txt
mget fyi_20.txt? n
mget fyi_21.txt? y
200 PORT command successful.
150 Binary data connection for fyi_21.txt    (192.74.137.5,1260)
(34883 bytes).
226 Binary Transfer complete.
34883 bytes received in 2.9 seconds (12 Kbytes/s)
mget fyi_22.txt? y
200 PORT command successful.
150 Binary data connection for fyi_22.txt    (192.74.137.5,1270)
(113646 bytes).
226 Binary Transfer complete.
113646 bytes received in 5.6 seconds (20 Kbytes/s)
```

FTP allows the user to rename a file at the same time it is being retrieved. In this example, the INDEX file displayed during this session showed that the file **fyi_04.txt** had to do with answers to questions that new users have about the Internet. To make it easier to remember the file's contents after it is transferred to your computer, you might rename it **new-user.txt**. To do this, type in the **get** command, followed by a space, followed by the name of the file exactly as shown at the FTP site, followed by another space and the new name for the file. Changing the name is also helpful in reducing the file name to the 8-plus-3-character size of DOS file names, allowing you to provide a file name that is easier to understand than one produced by letting your communications software chop the name down to size.

```
ftp> get fyi_04.txt new-user.txt
200 PORT command successful.
150 Binary data connection for fyi_04.txt    (192.74.137.5,1158)
(98753 bytes).
226 Binary Transfer complete.
98753 bytes received in 3.1 seconds (32 Kbytes/s)
ftp> bye
221 Goodbye.
world%
```

> **Note:**
>
> If you still have an ftp> prompt after FTP has said "Goodbye," type **quit** and press Enter to get back to your system prompt.

For information about how to download these new files from your Internet access provider's computer to your own personal computer, see Appendix B.

Uploads

Many FTP sites also allow uploads of files (usually to a particular directory called something like *in.coming*, where files are checked by system administrators before they are offered to the public). To upload files, use the same logon, change directory, and other repeat procedures as outlined previously, but use the command **put**, followed by the name of the file that you want to send (**mput** with the wild card character * can be used in a manner similar to **mget** for sending multiple files).

FTP can also be used as a private system for transferring files between various sites. For this purpose the FTP software is configured to accept connection only with people who have the correct user names and passwords.

E-mail Access to FTP Files

Several methods have been devised to help those with e-mail access to the Internet, but not FTP access. These methods are not as convenient or as fast as direct FTP, but if your only access to the Internet is through e-mail, they provide an opportunity to use the many millions of files at FTP sites throughout the world.

Instead of linking directly to an FTP site, using FTPmail you can send e-mail messages to a special mail server, which then interprets your message as a script and connects to the FTP site to make your requests. The mail server then gets the information or files you requested and sends them back to you in an ordinary e-mail message.

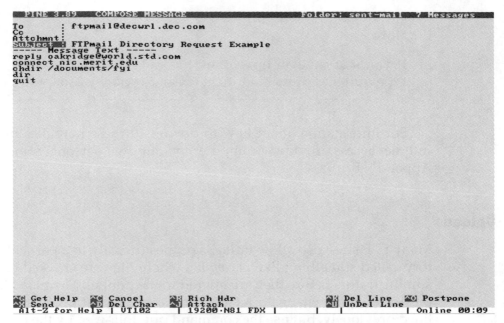

Figure D.3 FTPmail request for a directory listing.

Requesting a Directory Listing from an FTP Site

Suppose, again, that you want to get a copy of the file **fyi_04.txt** via FTP mail. The first step could be to examine the directory that the file is supposed to be in, to see if it is still there and whether it is of a manageable size. Refer to Figure D.3 for each of these steps:

1. First, log on to your host computer and bring up your mailer as usual. (See Chapter 12 for a full explanation of how to send and receive e-mail.)

2. In the *To* field, type **ftpmail@decwrl.dec.com**. This address will always be the same, no matter what site the FTP files are on, since this is the address of the mail server that will *process* your message. (Other FTP mail servers are available from time to time.)

3. In the *Subject* field, type in any name that will remind you of what is being requested. If you have several requests out at one time, this helps keep track of which request is being responded to. The mail server doesn't look at this line.

4. In the body of the message, type **reply**, a space, and then your full e-mail address.

5. On the next line, type **connect**, space, and the name and address of the FTP site where the files you are seeking are stored.

6. On the next line, type **chdir**, space, forward slash (/), and the name of the directory where the files are stored.

7. On the following line, type **dir**. This is a request for the FTPmail to send the directory listing for the current directory.

8. On the last line, type **quit**.

9. Now send the message in the usual manner.

You should get a message back, with the directory listing in the body of the message. This can take anywhere from 1 minute to several days, depending on how busy the mail server is.

Requesting an ASCII File from an FTP Site

Refer to Figure D.4 for each of these steps involved in retrieving a file via FTPmail:

1. Fill out the *To* and *Subject* fields as described previously when requesting the directory listing.

2. In the body of the message, type in the **reply**, **connect**, and **chdir** lines just as before.

3. On the next line, type **ascii**. This forces the FTP site to send in ASCII mode, which is appropriate for this text file. If the FTP site sent the file in the binary mode, the file would be damaged. This is different from a direct connection to an FTP site, in which both binary and ASCII files can be sent in the binary mode.

4. On the following line, type **chunksize**, followed by a space, and then the maximum number of bytes your Internet access provider allows incoming mail messages to be. If you are uncertain, try 32,000, which is acceptable on almost all systems. The **chunksize** command tells the mail server to break down large files into pieces of the size that you specify, and send them to you in a series of messages.

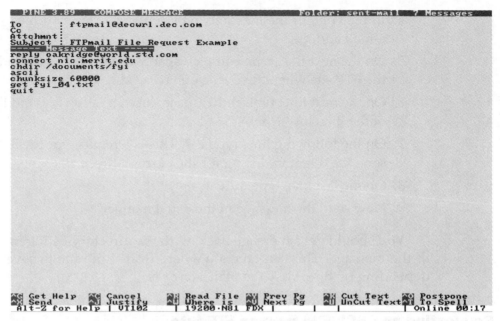

Figure D.4 An e-mail message ready to send as a request for an ASCII (text) file stored at an FTP site.

5. Now, the file can be requested with the **get** command. Type **get**, then a space, and then the full file name.

6. Finish the message with **quit** as the last line.

7. Send this message as a normal e-mail message.

The file will come to you as a normal e-mail message (or messages) with the file's contents as the body of the message.

Requesting a Binary File from an FTP Site

In the following example, a calendar program that is in the compressed file *year.zip* is retrieved from the *systems/msdos/win3/util* directory

---

Note:

FTP file sites, subdirectories, and file names change often. To find (or refind) a file, use Archie (see Chapter 14).

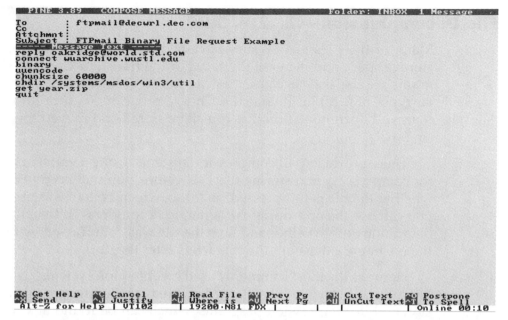

Figure D.5 An e-mail message ready to be sent as a request for a binary file.

at the wuarchive.wustl.edu FTP site. Refer to Figure D.5 for each of the following steps for retrieving a binary file:

1. Fill in the *To* and *Subject* fields in the same way you did previously.

2. Type in the *reply* line with your address as in the preceding examples.

3. Type in **connect**, a space, then the address of the FTP site—in this case, **wuarchive.wustl.edu**.

4. Type **binary** on the next line. This command needs to be followed by a line telling which type of binary-to-ASCII conversion should be applied to the file—either **btoa** or **uuencode**. In this example, **uuencode** is used. See Chapter 12 for information on how to use UUDE-CODE to convert the ASCII back into a binary file.

5. The **chunksize**, **chdir**, **get**, and **quit** lines are used in the same manner as in the ASCII example.

After UUDECODING the file, you may also need to decompress it.

File Decompression—.Z, .ZIP, .ARC

Many of the files at FTP sites have been compressed in order to save storage space and increase the speed of file transfers. Compression programs are also used because they can store a group of files (even dissimilar types of files) inside one file. Thus, a program, its support files, data files, and documentation files can all be stored and moved together as a single file.

There are dozens of compression systems, using a variety of methods for compressing and storing files. Therefore, you will need to determine whether the file is compressed, and if so, which system was used, so that you can use the appropriate program to decompress it. Usually you can determine both whether and how the file was compressed by looking at the file name extension (the characters after the dot).

Here are the most commonly used compression systems, listed alphabetically by file name extension. Also listed are files that contain compression and decompression programs, which can be found at various FTP sites (the search tool Archie discussed in Chapter 10 can be used to locate these files).

* .arc

DOS: The programs ARC and PKARC compress files; ARCE and PKXARC decompress files. Software—pk361.exe, arc602.exe.

UNIX: Software—arc521e.tar.z, arc.tar.Z.

Mac: The program ArcMac compresses, and MacARC decompresses. Software—Stuffit Deluxe and MacARC (commercial packages, not available via FTP).

* .arj

DOS: The program ARJ compresses files and ARN decompresses. Software—arj230ng.exe, arj239f.exe, unarj230.zip.

UNIX: Software—unarj230.tar.Z.

Mac: Software for decompressing—unArjMac.

* .exe

DOS: Software for *making* self-extracting files—pklte115.zip, lzexe91e.zip.

Several compression programs will, in addition to making normal compressed files, make a *self-extracting* file. Such a file will have an extension of .exe or .com. The INDEX or README files at the FTP site may help in determining whether the file you have received is a single program file or a self-extracting file. To use a self-extracting file, move it to a separate subdirectory, and then run it as you would any other program. It will then decompress and separate the file(s) that are stored in it. You will usually see status reports on the screen while it is decompressing.

* .F

UNIX: A relatively new compression program called freeze. Currently only available for UNIX.

* .hpk

DOS: Software—hpack78.zip.

UNIX: Software—hpack78scr.tar.Z.

* .hqx

Mac: A Macintosh format that uses BinHex to decompress.

* .lzh

DOS: Use LHARC to both compress and decompress files. Software—lha213.exe, lha255b.exe.

UNIX: Software—lha-101u.tar.z.

Mac: Both compress and decompress with MacLHa.

* .SHAR

UNIX: A UNIX format that uses unshar for decompressing files.

* .Sit

Mac: A Macintosh format that uses Stuffit for both compression and decompression.

* .sqz

DOS: Software—sqz1083e.exe.

* .tar

DOS: Software—tar4dos.zoo.

UNIX: .tar is primarily a UNIX compression method. Often, after a file is compressed with .tar, it is compressed again with .Z, so you will need to go through at least two steps to get the file(s) you want. Software—standard on UNIX systems.

* .Z

This compression is primarily used on UNIX systems. Note that the compression system denoted by this uppercase Z is not the same as the system denoted by the lowercase z.

DOS: Software—comp430d.zip.

UNIX: Software—standard on UNIX systems.

* .z

DOS: Software—gzip107.zip.

UNIX: Software—gzip-1.0.7.tar, pack (on UNIX systems).

* .zip

By far the most popular compression system; software is available for many types of computers.

DOS: Software—pk204g.exe, unz50p1.exe, zip19p1x.zip.

UNIX: Software—unz50p1.tar.Z, zip19p1.tar.Z.

* .zoo

DOS: Software—booz20.zip, zoo210.exe.

UNIX: Software—booz20.tar.Z, zoo210.tar.Z.

As you can see, there are many compression systems and even more compression programs. Each program has its own unique way of operating which is described in the program's documentation, but there are enough similarities that you can often decompress a file without having to dig too deeply into the instructions. Generally the syntax for decompressing a file looks like this:

```
decompression-program  switches  name-of-file-to-decompress
```

For example, to decompress the file *year.zip* with the pkunzip.exe program, move to the directory where *year.zip* is stored. Assuming that pkunzip.exe is stored in a subdirectory called *compress*, this is how the command to decompress would appear:

```
c:\compress\pkunzip -o  year.zip
```

In this example, the switch **-o** is used so that the program will automatically overwrite existing files of the same name. The list of switches that allow you to change various characteristics of the program can often be displayed to the screen by changing to the directory where the compression program is stored and just typing the program's name. If this doesn't work, type the name followed by a space and one of these: **?** or **/?** or **/h** or **-?** or **-h** or **help**.

Searching for Files

As you can see, FTP works well for getting a specific file when you already have the site address, directory, and file name, but is a slow and hit-or-miss way to search for files of interest. Fortunately, there are several search tools available that will scan Internet-wide file storage sites. For FTP files, Archie is the best. See the Archie section of Chapter 14.

How to Use Telnet (Remote Login)

The Telnet system allows you to command your browser software, or your Internet access provider's computer, to connect to another computer on the Internet. You can then operate that remote computer much as if you were directly connected to it. With the Telnet system you can use BBSs, databases, search tools, services, and files otherwise not available on your host computer. The use of a Telnet site to maintain a business presence on the Internet has declined with the rapid rise in the use of the World Wide Web, but some unique and valuable resources are currently available only through Telnet.

Connecting to Telnet Sites Using a Browser with a SLIP Connection

Using Telnet with a GUI browser like Netscape is easy. First you need to assemble a URL for the site. This is done by taking the prefix **telnet://** and then adding an address of a Telnet site (for example, Marketplace Online Catalog's address **mb.com**). The resulting URL in this example is **telnet:// mb.com**. (See the "Telnet Sites" section later in this appendix for information about Telnet site addresses.)

This URL is typed in to your browser's input line just as Web pages URLs are. With the Netscape browser, for example, click on the **File** menu, select **Open Location**, and then type the URL in the input box that is displayed.

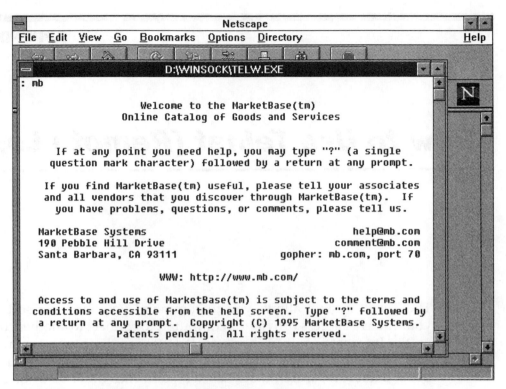

Figure E.1 GUI browser being used for a Telnet session.

The browser will then open a Telnet window on the screen and make contact with the Telnet site (see Figure E.1).

From this point on you are interacting directly with the remote site's computer. Each site is different, but by following the menus, or by typing in requests for help (**help** or **?** are often used), you should be able to

> **Note:**
>
> Many browsers come with an external Telnet program that pops up on the screen, or have internal ways of handling Telnet sites. If your browser does not, you may need to check your browser's documentation to determine how to install and configure a Telnet program (a number of Telnet programs are available on the Internet as shareware).

navigate the remote sites. Many features of your browser will not be operational during a Telnet session.

You can use Telnet URLs with a text-based browser such as Lynx as well. In Lynx, press **g** for Go, and enter the URL as above.

Shell Account Access to Telnet Sites

In order for you to use Telnet, both your service provider's computer and the remote computer that you want to access must have the Telnet software installed. Also, you must have an account with the remote computer, or the remote computer must be set up to allow open access to some portions of its system.

If you are unsure if your Internet access provider offers Telnet service, log in to its computer, and at the main prompt (%, $, etc.) type **telnet** and press the Enter key. If the Telnet software is available, a new prompt will appear looking something like this: *Telnet>*. To return to your system's main command prompt, type **quit** and press the Enter key. (This is a quick way to check, but is not 100 percent accurate, since the software might have been installed on a host computer under another name, or without a full Telnet-compatible connection to the Internet.) If Telnet doesn't seem to be working, check with your computer system's administrators.

There are two pieces of information that you will need to make a Telnet connection: the address of the Telnet site, and the login word (see the Hytelnet section of this chapter for suggestions on where to locate this information).

The Plain Vanilla Telnet Session

The following example will present a Telnet session with the MarketBase Online Catalog of Goods and Services, whose address is mb.com and whose login word is **mb**. To see how this works, follow this example, which simply logs on to MarketBase's computer and then logs off. In the next section of this chapter, Telnet will be explored in more depth.

At your main system prompt (in this example, *world%*), type **telnet** followed by a space and then the address of the site you would like to connect to, then press Enter. The computer will respond with *Trying,* and then you will see the numeric address of the site you are connecting to:

```
world%  telnet mb.com
Trying 198.99.196.10...
```

If a connection is established, a report will be displayed, confirming connection to the address you requested, and displaying what the escape character is (its use will be explained in the next section):

```
Connected to mb.com.
Escape character is '^]'.
```

These lines are followed either by the *login*: prompt or by some announcements from the site itself—in this case, there is a note that **mb** is the login word to use.

```
login: mb
```

At this point, Telnet itself will be in the background, out of sight, shuttling data to and from the remote computer. All of the commands, announcements, menus, and anything else you see displayed will be unique to the site that you are connected to. In this case, MarketBase gives several welcome and information screens and then offers choices on how to access its products.

```
            Welcome to the MarketBase(tm)
            Online Catalog of Goods and Services
```

Each site will have its own commands for leaving; if they aren't obvious, typing a question mark (**?**) or **help** will often result in the display of a list of commands.

```
Enter keyword followed by the return key: ?

            MarketBase(tm) commands:

Note that most commands begin with a colon (':')

?, :h, or :help
Print this screen.

:k or :keyword
Specify a new keyword and execute a new search.

:q or :quit
Terminate this MarketBase(tm) session

:r or :restart
Return this MarketBase(tm) session back to the first screen.
```

```
:t or :terms
View the terms and conditions of use of this system.

Please type one of the commands above when ready to continue,
or hit the return key to go back to the previous non-help
screen: :q
```

Usually, **x**, **exit**, **quit**, or **bye** will end the session. In this case, the command is :**q**.

After you enter the :**q** command, this site sends commands to the Telnet software to disconnect and exit from the Telnet program, resulting in a return to the host computer's main prompt (in this case, *world%*):

```
              Thank you for using MarketBase(tm)

Connection closed by foreign host.
world%
```

A Telnet Session with a Few Bells and Whistles

Most Telnet sessions resemble the plain vanilla example, but at times you will want to use a few Telnet features that can help out in some problem cases. In this next example, the session is with Book Stacks Unlimited, Inc. Its address is books.com and the login is accomplished just by pressing the Enter key one time.

This time a different method of connecting to the remote site will be used, one that is preferred by some. First, type the command **telnet** and press Enter. Your system's response is the *Telnet>* prompt. This indicates that the Telnet program is active and can accept Telnet commands. To connect to the remote site, type **open** followed by a space and then the address. The connection will be made in the same manner as in the plain vanilla example.

```
world% telnet
Telnet> open books.com
Trying 192.148.240.9...
Connected to books.com.
Escape character is '^]'.

Book Stacks Unlimited, Inc.
Cleveland, Ohio  USA
```

```
The On-Line Bookstore

Modem    : (216)861-0469
Internet : Telnet books.com

Enter your FULL Name (e.g SALLY M. SMITH):
```

If, instead of getting connected, nothing happens, or you receive a response such as *host unavailable*, the remote computer or some links may not be working at the moment. Wait a while and try again. If, instead of getting a connection, you receive a response such as *host unknown*, the most likely problem is a misspelled address, although it is possible that the remote computer has been removed from the Internet.

Note:

There are two ways that the address may vary in appearance from those used in these examples:

- The address may be followed by a number—for example, **books.com: 3000**. The number is called a port number. If the port number is shown with the address, it has to be used.
- The address may be in the form of numbers and dots—for example, **192.148.240.9**. You can use this form of address in the same manner as an alphanumeric address.

Sometimes, due to hardware or software problems, you may not be sure if you're connected to the remote computer. You can use the **status** command to check. To use this command, first get back to Telnet's command mode. This is usually accomplished by holding down the Ctrl key and then pressing the right bracket key (]), but the key combination varies from system to system. To know which keys to use for escape, be sure to read the initial connect messages. In this example, the line after *Connected to books.com* tells you that the escape character is ^] (the caret ^ symbol represents the Ctrl key).

In this case, when you hold down the Ctrl key and press], the Telnet prompt will appear. Now you can type the command **status** to see if you are connected to the computer you want to access:

```
Telnet> status
Connected to books.com.
Operating in single character mode
Catching signals locally
Remote character echo
Local flow control
Escape character is '^]'.
```

After each command Telnet returns to the *input mode*—in other words, whatever is typed in now will go directly to the remote computer. To use another Telnet command, use the escape character again. To see which Telnet commands are available, use the escape character and then type in a question mark and hit Enter. Some common Telnet commands are shown in Table E.1.

The **display** command allows you to view all of Telnet's current settings. It is good to know how to view these settings if you are having

Table E.1 Telnet commands.

Command	Meaning
close	Close current connection
logout	Forcibly logout remote user and close the connection
display	Display operating parameters
mode	Try to enter line or character mode ('mode ?' for more)
open	Connect to a site
quit	Exit Telnet
send	Transmit special characters ('send ?' for more)
set	Set operating parameters ('set ?' for more)
unset	Unset operating parameters ('unset ?' for more)
status	Print status information
toggle	Toggle operating parameters ('toggle ?' for more)
slc	Change state of special character ('slc ?' for more)
z	Suspend Telnet
!	Invoke a subshell
environ	Change environment variables ('environ ?' for more)
?	Print help information

a recurring problem with Telnet so that you can explain problems to your computer system administrator, but don't be concerned with deciphering this report now.

If you cannot find the remote site's exit command, you can use Telnet's **close** command. First use the escape character, and then at the *Telnet>* prompt, type **close**. This will disconnect your host computer from the remote computer, but leave you in the Telnet program.

```
Telnet> close
Connection closed.
```

Your host computer will no longer be connected to the remote computer, and a *Telnet>* prompt will appear. The fact that the computers are disconnected can be confirmed with the **status** command:

```
Telnet> status
No connection.
Escape character is '^]'.
```

The **quit** command can be used to leave Telnet and return you to your host computer's prompt. The **quit** command can be used instead of **close** in order to disconnect the computers and leave Telnet in one step:

```
Telnet> quit
world%
```

> **Note:**
>
> Occasionally during Telnet sessions the systems get locked up in such a way that the Telnet escape character will not put Telnet into command mode. In this case sometimes using Ctrl with the **c** key (or whichever key your host system considers its BREAK key) will return you to your system prompt . It is not good practice to force your software to hang up the phone line in this situation, since this may leave the remote computer and your host computer connected for an extended period of time, which is both bad netiquette and may cause extra charges for you if you pay for your access based on connect time. Check with your host system administrators for advice on how to best handle such lock-ups.

Telnet Sites

The Telnet commands and protocols are, as you can see, quite simple and easily learned. The challenging parts of using Telnet are, first, to find out where the sites are, and second, to learn the variety of different commands needed to use the many different services at these remote sites. The following are some examples of Telnet sites.

Hytelnet

Hytelnet provides a database of Telnet sites. It contains address, login, and other information about Telnet-accessible libraries, BBSs, freenets, Gophers, and other resources. It is available as software to run on DOS-based, Macintosh PCs, and on UNIX and VMS systems. A database of Telnet-accessible sites and information about the software is at *http://www.usask.ca/cgi-bin/hytelnet*. (Those using a shell account can use the text-based Lynx browser to view and download this information.)

BBSs

BBS software provides an easy method for offering databases, e-mail, topical conferences, and file distribution. While BBSs are generally thought of as small amateur systems with names like *The Pink Slime-Mold* or *The Dungeon of Demented Wizards*, BBS software can be used for the distribution of business and scholarly material. There are many BBSs available on the Internet via Telnet. Since there are many different BBS programs available and each can be configured in many ways, you will need to read introductory screens and other announcements in order to navigate well within a BBS. Fortunately, most are menu-driven and have a common "look and feel," so after you use several, you'll find it easy to learn others.

There are thousands of BBSs that you can explore throughout the Internet. For a current list of BBSs, check this FTP site:

Address: *wuarchive.wustl.edu*; Directory: *systems/msdos/msdos/bbs*

Read the index file to determine which lists are of interest to you.

Or, check this two-part list at MIT's FTP archive:

rtfm.mit.edu/pub/usenet/news.answers/internet/bbs/list/part1
rtfm.mit.edu/pub/usenet/news.answers/internet/bbs/list/part2

For discussions of new and current BBSs, read the Usenet newsgroups comp.bbs.misc, alt.internet.services, and alt.bbs.internet.

A two-part set of FAQ files is available via FTP from rtfm.mit.edu under these subdirectories and file names:

/pub/usenet/alt.bbs.internet/=_8_95_GUIDE_to_SELECT_BBS_s_ on_ Internet_[1_2]_=
/pub/usenet/alt.bbs.internet/=_8_95_GUIDE_to_SELECT_BBS_s_ on_ Internet_[2_2]_=

Following are a few examples of BBSs available via Telnet.

Business StartUp Information Database

This site, operated by the Michigan Department of Commerce, contains the following choices on its welcome screen:

```
1. Licensing Information for Specific Types of Business
2. Checklist for Starting a Business
3. Information for Employers
4. List of Business Development Centers
5. Business Financing Information
6. Help_How to Use NEWBIZ
```

Address: *hermes.merit.edu*

Login: Respond to *Which Host?* prompt with **mdoc-vax**, and respond to the *Username:* prompt with **NEWBIZ**.

Window on State Government—Texas Comptroller of Public Accounts

This is a state-run BBS with Texas economic data and tax information, and a section on state and federal grants. An additional feature is the dial-out service, which can connect you to state agency BBSs such as those offered by Parks and Wildlife, the Technology Assessment Center, the Employment Commission, and the Ethics Commission. In addition, you can connect to the Texas Marketplace BBS.

Address: *window.texas.gov*

Login: new

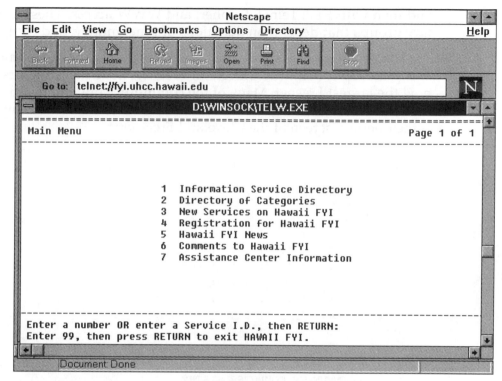

Figure E.2 Hawaii FYI's Telnet directory.

Hawaii FYI

This BBS's information is quite varied, but has one common theme: life in Hawaii. Topics include Hawaii's fishing limits, news from the governor, the Hawaii INC BBS, landlord-tenant code, tax information, septic tank information, and veterans' services. Select *Directory of Categories* from the main menu to get to the *Business and Finance* section.

> **Address:** *fyi.uhcc.hawaii.edu* (see Figure E.2)

> **Login:** Press the Enter key two times.

Freenets and Community Computer Systems

Freenets and Community BBSs often provide free dial-up access to large, local BBSs. Increasingly, these BBSs are getting connected to the Internet—usually first with e-mail connections and access to Usenet News, and then with FTP, Telnet, Gopher, and WWW access. These are voluntary groups that depend on donations of time, money, and equipment.

The bulletin boards with the name "Freenet" share a common style and philosophy with the Cleveland Freenet, which was the first and is now the largest Freenet. Many of the community bulletin boards use the metaphor of a city to organize their services and files. As an example, here is the opening screen of the Cleveland Free-net:

```
                                   /\
        WELCOME TO THE...        _!  !_
                               _!__  __!_
                 __             !       !
              _!  !_            !  !  !  !
             !      !    /\     !  !  !  !
             !      !  !  !     !  !  !  !___
             !      ! !  !  !   !  !  !  !   !
             !      !_!_  !  !  !  !  !  !   !
             !      !  ! !  !   !  !  !  !   !
           _!       !  !_!_  !          !   !_
            !       !     !_!           !     !
          !                                   !
          !         CLEVELAND FREE-NET        !
          !      COMMUNITY COMPUTER SYSTEM    !
          !_____!

                   brought to you by
             Case Western Reserve University
            Community Telecomputing Laboratory
        Are you:
                 1. A registered user
                 2. A visitor
        Please enter 1 or 2: 2


        [[[ CLEVELAND FREE-NET DIRECTORY ]]]

           1 The Administration Building
           2 The Post Office
           3 Public Square
           4 The Courthouse & Government Center
           5 The Arts Building
           6 Science and Technology Center
           7 The Medical Arts Building
```

```
 8 The Schoolhouse
 9 The Community Center & Recreation Area
10 The Business and Industrial Park
11 The Library
12 University Circle
13 The Teleport
14 The Communications Center
15 NPTN/USA TODAY HEADLINE NEWS
------------------------------------------------

How Your Business Can Get Involved:
```

Many of these community sites currently have only a small amount of business-oriented information (though most do have a business section). They are not suitable for any heavy-duty marketing or sales. There are, however, three ways that businesses can get involved:

- Donating time, equipment, and/or expertise to set up a Freenet in your community provides a highly visible way of developing name recognition for your business and a positive public image.

- Sponsoring a community computer system provides a way to continue this high visibility.

- Maintaining information files or databases (especially those connected with the expertise of your business) can provide an ongoing business presence, public goodwill, and recognition of your company's knowledge and skills.

Since a community system can offer whatever services it wants to, a system can be set up by several businesses in an area, with a strong local business component as well as community service features.

Glossary

Address (Network Address)—Internet site addresses come in two forms: as a set of numbers such as *192.74.137.5* and alphanumerics such as *world.std.com* (both of these represent the same address, and either could be used, for example, with Telnet). An individual's e-mail address at this site, for example, Ben Franklin's, might look like this: *bfranklin@world. std.com*. (See Chapter 12.)

Anonymous FTP—The use of the FTP protocol with Internet-connected sites that offer public access to their files without requiring personal IDs or passwords. Usually, after making a connection with the FTP site the user responds to the login prompt with the word **anonymous** and then to the password prompt with his or her full Internet address. (See Appendix D.)

Archie—A service that can be used to search network-wide for FTP-accessible files and directories. (See Chapter 14.)

ASCII (*American Standard Code for Information Interchange*)—Now a world-wide standard in which the numerals, uppercase letters, lowercase letters, some punctuation marks, some symbols, and some control codes have each been assigned a number from 0 to 127. This number can be stored in digital form as a 7-bit binary number. For instance, using ASCII, the letter "a" is always stored as binary number 1000001. Plain text and document files are usually stored in this manner. The Internet e-mail system uses primarily ASCII.

Authentication—Any of several methods used to provide proof that a particular document received electronically is actually from the individual it claims to be from, and is unchanged.

Binary—In its broadest sense, binary has to do with any data stored or transferred in digital form. In more common use, binary refers to data stored with 8 bits (which in decimal number terms provides 256 numbers). Unlike 7-bit ASCII files, binary files have no standard way of being interpreted. Instead, they are used for software and for data files that are only meaningful when used with a compatible program (for example, a word processing data file from WordPerfect is not readable on all other word processor programs).

BBS (Bulletin-Board System)—Usually menu-oriented, this is a remote computer user-interface that may be used to offer a variety of services such as e-mail, ways to post public messages in various topical "discussion groups," ways to offer files to the public and receive files from the public, and increasingly ways to access to other remote computers and services. Access may be via the Internet and/or through direct dial-up. BBS software for PCs is readily available on the Internet.

Bounce—When e-mail is undeliverable it is sent back to you (bounced) so that you will know it was not delivered, and be able to determine if the problem was in your addressing. (See Chapter 12.)

Browser—Any of a number of programs used for retrieving and viewing HTML documents. Mosaic and Netscape are GUI browsers.

Campus-Wide Information Systems (CWIS)—A navigation and information retrieval tool that provides data from a variety of campus sources accessed through one user interface.

Client/Server—A way of distributing information on a network that involves using a small number of server programs to provide data to client programs installed on many computers throughout the network. The server program maintains databases and provides information to the client programs, through the network, when requested. Some server programs also have the ability to collect data and update their database files themselves. The client programs provide a user-friendly and consistent interface. Examples of Internet client/server systems include Gopher, Archie, Veronica, and the World Wide Web.

Command Line—On your PC, and on your Internet access provider's computer, when you are at the system's main prompt you are on its command line (prompts often end in symbols such as $ or % or >). More broadly, any time that you can type in commands to the computer, whether you are at the operating system's prompt, or within a program, you are at the "command line." Command line programs often require you to remember and type in commands. These programs are usually harder to learn to use than programs that offer menus or lists of commands from which to select. (See also *GUI*.)

Communicon (Communication + Icon)—Combinations of letters and symbols used in Internet e-mail and public postings to provide emphasis, perspective, or clarification. These include very loosely standardized "smileys," "emoticons," abbreviated phrases, underlining methods, and parenthetical phrases. (See Chapter 6 for details.)

Communications Software—Usually refers to programs that are run on personal computers to allow the computer to communicate via a modem, and phone lines. These programs also allow the personal computer to "look like" a particular type of terminal to the computer it is connected to through the phone lines.

Cross-Post—Sending the same message to more than one mailing list or discussion group. It is usually discouraged unless the posting is specifically appropriate for each list it is sent to, and there is reasonable expectation that each mailing list has a substantially different audience.

CSO—A widely used system for retrieving data from simple database files such as phone books. Named after the University of Illinois's Computing Services Organization (CSO).

Cybermall—A collection of virtual storefronts offered online by one Web access provider, usually with some similarity in appearance and functions, and usually listed on one top page. In other words, a group of businesses using one Web access provider to do sales online, emulating a shopping mall.

Daemon—A UNIX program that will, among other things, report errors in delivering your e-mail messages.

Domain Name System (*DNS*)—An Internet addressing system using a series of names that are listed with dots (.) between them in the order of the most specific to the most general group. In the United States the top (most general) domains are network categories such as **edu** (education), **com** (commercial), and **gov** (government). In other countries a two-letter abbreviation for the country is used, such as **ca** (Canada) or **au** (Australia). (For more about Internet addresses, see Chapter 12.)

Download—To receive on your local computer a copy of a file that currently exists on some remote computer. Many protocols for doing this have been devised, including Z-Modem, X-Modem, Y-Modem, and Kermit, each with its own commands and syntax. (For more information on uploading and downloading, see Appendix C.)

E-journal (*Electronic Journal*)—A publication distributed on the Internet at regular intervals. Distribution may be by active means such as e-mail mailing lists, or by placing the publication at an FTP site, on a Web page, or at some other public location for people to retrieve. Most e-journals are distributed in standard ASCII text, though some are offered as formatted text with graphics. Some are offshoots of paper-based publications, but most are purely electronic and are distributed for free.

Electronic Mail (*E-mail*)—Private messages delivered via networks to an individual's e-mail account. Used with automatic group mailing list software, e-mail is the basis for discussion groups and many other Internet services. E-mail is used both as a noun and verb. (e.g., I received his e-mail three days after I e-mailed him.) (See Chapter 12.)

Emoticons (emotion + icon)—One group of communicons that include both "smileys" and expressions of surprise, annoyance, sarcasm, etc. (See Chapter 6.)

FAQs (*Frequently Asked Questions*)—Because newcomers are always arriving at Usenet newsgroups and on topical mailing lists, the same questions can be asked repeatedly (to the dismay of more advanced, long-time members of the group). Therefore, volunteers will often assemble a document that presents, in question-and-answer format, the basic facts about the topic and group. This FAQ is revised and posted to the group at regular intervals and is also stored, for access at any time, at a public location such as an FTP site. (See Chapter 13 for listings of some useful FAQs.)

Finger—An Internet system that allows you, if you have someone's e-mail address, to find out who the person is, when he or she last checked in for mail, and several other bits of information. If that person has written a

".plan" or ".project" file, that will also be displayed. For example, to see the account information and .plan file for the address oakridge@world. std.com, just type **finger oakridge@world.std.com** at your access provider's main prompt.

Firewall—A hardware and/or software method used to protect a network from unauthorized use by those outside of a network. Businesses and organizations that have connected their computers to the Internet often install a firewall to protect their data from theft and alteration.

Flame—To send e-mail or make public postings with harsh, provocative tirades. This can result in flame wars and other negative consequences. (See Chapter 6 for cautions and guidelines concerning flaming.)

Freeware—Software available from many locations on the Internet (often via FTP) that is totally free.

FTP (File Transfer Protocol)—A system used to transfer copies of files from one computer to another on the Internet. It includes several features to make this process easier. (See Appendix D.) (See also *Anonymous FTP*.)

Gateway—A computer that connects two or more networks. Especially in the past, before TCP/IP protocols were so widely used, these computers often had to pass data between incompatible network systems.

GIF (Graphics Interchange Format)—A type of picture storage file developed by CompuServe, and now widely used on the Internet. Files in this format have an extension of .gif as in *mars.gif*. GIF files vary greatly in size depending on the image height and width, and the number of colors it uses.

Gopher—A widely used Internet tool for finding and retrieving files of all kinds throughout the Internet. It is a menu-oriented, client/server system, with a top menu at each Gopher site leading to many submenus and files throughout the Internet. (See Chapter 14.)

GUI (Graphical User Interface)—Any of a number of programs and operating systems, such as Windows and Macintosh systems, that are operated by using a mouse input device to move a pointer to various graphics, icons, and menus (versus command-line or other text-based methods).

Host—Your Internet access provider's computer. You may use one of its hardwired terminals if you are at an institution with a mainframe computer connected directly to the Internet, or you may dial up and use a modem to connect with the Internet access provider's host computer. (As computer systems have changed, the term "host" has changed in meaning, so do expect some confusing references to host at times.)

HTML (HyperText Markup Language)—A standardized (but evolving) set of commands and syntax rules used for encoding text files with formatting and document linking information. These documents are encoded for use on the World Wide Web and are viewed with a Web browser.

HTTP (HyperText Transfer Protocol)—A standardized set of rules for transferring and processing HTML and other documents on networks. (See S/HTTP also.)

Hypertext—Text written with special encoding that provides links to other locations within a document, or to other documents. Documents are displayed with some of the words highlighted. These highlighted words represent links to other documents that allow you, with just a few keystrokes or clicks of a mouse, to view these other documents. These other documents may also have links to still other documents.

Inline—Graphics and pictures that are automatically downloaded and displayed when viewing an HTML file are said to be "inline" images. (In contrast, external images are linked to the HTML file, but are only loaded and displayed when their anchor is activated.)

Internet—A digital communications network connecting over 60,000 other, smaller networks from many countries throughout the world. It transfers data using a standardized protocol called TCP/IP.

IRC (Internet Relay Chat)—An Internet system that allows Internet users to "chat" (via keyboard) in real time. Separate channels are available with various options for privacy, filtering out unwanted messages, and one-to-one messages.

ISP (Internet Service Provider)—A business or institution connected to the Internet that provides Internet access to others (usually via phone lines).

JPG—The file name extension used on JPEG (Joint Photographic Experts Group) graphics/picture files (e.g., moon.jpg). This file format can be much more compressed than, for example, GIF, but high compression causes some loss of detail.

Listserv—A program that provides automatic processing of many functions involved with mailing lists (discussion groups). E-mailing appropriate messages to it will automatically subscribe you to a discussion list or unsubscribe you. It will also answer requests for indexes, FAQs, archives of the previous discussions, and other files. (See Chapter 13.)

Log File—In PC communications programs, there is often a feature that allows you to save in a file everything that is displayed to the screen in a log file, thus providing a full recording of the activity for a full or partial online session.

Login—When one computer seeks to establish a connection to another computer, there will be a login process on the remote computer that usually involves some user steps beyond those things taken care of by the computer software. This may be as simple as pressing Enter, or may require a specific login word and a password to be entered. (Usually used interchangeably with "logon.")

Logoff—The process of leaving, or disconnecting from a computer system. Often accomplished by selecting a menu item for disconnecting, or typing **exit**, or **bye**, **quit**, or **logout** at the command line prompt.

Lurk—To read messages from discussion groups or Usenet newsgroups without contributing any.

Mailing lists—Also known as "lists," "discussion lists," or "discussion groups." These are discussions carried on by sending e-mailing messages to an automated remailer, which then sends a copy of each message via e-mail to everyone who has subscribed to the list for that particular discussion group. (See Chapter 13.)

MIME (*Multipurpose Internet Mail Extensions*)—An improvement on the Internet mail system standards that allows binary files to be sent as e-mail through the Internet. Formerly only ASCII files could be sent. This system is not available on all sites yet. (Also see S/MIME.)

Mosaic—A graphical user interface browser program that works as client software for FTP, Gopher, Usenet news, WAIS, and WWW servers. It is available in both commercial and free versions.

Modem (*mo*dulator + *dem*odulator)—An electronic device that converts computer signals into audio (sound) signals so that they can be sent over normal phone lines and received by another modem, which will convert the sound back into computer signals. Virtually all modems combine both the send and receive functions in one unit. (See Appendix A for a discussion of modems.)

Moderator—In discussion lists (groups) that are moderated, the moderator watches the postings as they come in to be sure, for example, that they relate to the topics and goals of the list and that the language and nature of the messages are suitable for public posting. The types and extent of moderating ranges widely, from merely restating the goals and limits occasionally, to actual editing of incoming messages. (See Chapter 13.)

Netiquette (network + etiquette)—Customs and socially accepted behavior for network users.

Netscape—A commercially available World Wide Web GUI browser, somewhat similar to the Mosaic browser.

Network—A group of computers connected together in any way that allows data to be sent among them.

Newbie—Anyone new to the Internet. Due to the rapid growth of the Internet, most people on the Internet are newbies, and therefore this is not considered a particularly negative term.

NIC—Network Information Center. A site designated to provide useful information services to network users.

NSFnet (National Science Foundation + net)—The system of high-speed data transfer links and nodes that used to form the backbone of the Internet in the United States. (See Chapter 1.)

Offline—Anything that happens when your computer is not connected to another computer. For instance, a program may download many messages and files quickly and then allow you to read them offline in order to save on connect charges and long-distance phone charges.

Online—Any activity carried out while your computer is connected to another computer or network.

PGP (Pretty Good Privacy)—A data encryption/deciphering system that uses two digital "keys" (similar to passwords) to protect messages or other information from being read by anyone other than the intended recipient.

Plan file (*.plan*)—A file that you write, telling anything you want about yourself or your business, or any other subject. It is stored in your home directory on your Internet access provider's computer, and a copy of it can be obtained by anyone who uses the finger program to check your e-mail account.

Post—To send an e-mail message to one of the public discussion groups.

Postmaster—The person at each site who is responsible for handling e-mail problems at that site. Send e-mail to the postmaster of a site if you are having some difficulties getting a message through, or need other information about the site. E-mail messages to this person are addressed to *postmaster@(site name)*, for example, *postmaster@world.std.com*.

PPP (Point-to-Point Protocol)—A standardized set of rules describing the procedures for a computer to connect with another and exchange TCP/IP packets. This procedure allows a user of a dial-up connection to an Internet access provider to directly interact with the Internet. (See also SLIP.)

Prompt—What is displayed when a computer system is waiting for some sort of input from you.

Protocol—A formal, standardized set of operating rules governing the format, timing, error control, etc. of data transmissions and other activities on a network.

README files (or *READ.ME*)—A common method used in program documentation and in directories at FTP sites, to direct the newcomer to index files or other useful information about the files in that directory.

RFC (Request for Comments)—Documents relating to the Internet system, protocols, proposals, etc. These documents are stored at FTP sites and are the basis for discussions about evolving Internet standards.

Secure Transactions—Financial or other business transactions carried out using privacy and authentication procedures adequate to the nature and risks of the transaction. In general, on the Internet, this means using Secure HTTP, Secure MIME, encryption, or other procedures to protect privacy and the use of credit card numbers and other personal information.

Shareware—Software available from many locations on the Internet. It is initially free, but the authors expect payment to be sent voluntarily after an initial test period. Quality varies from bad, to better than some commercial software. Prices are usually excellent. Some initial versions are limited in function in some way, with an upgrade available if you pay the fee.

S/HTTP (*Secure HyperText Transfer Protocol*)—An HTTP-compatible protocol that adds security and authentication to Web documents.

SIG (*Signature File*)—A sig is the short message placed at the bottom of an e-mail message or a discussion group posting that identifies the sender and includes items such as phone number, fax number, address, information about the person's occupation or company, and even a philosophical saying or humorous message. (See Chapter 12.)

SLIP (*Serial Line Internet Protocol*)—A standardized set of rules describing the procedures for a computer to connect with another and exchange TCP/IP packets. This procedure allows a user of a dial-up connection to an Internet access provider to directly interact with the Internet.

Smiley—Any of several smiling faces created by various keyboard letters and symbols such as :) and 8-). (See *Communicon* and Chapter 6.)

S/MIME (*Secure Multipurpose Internet Mail Extensions*)—A MIME-compatible protocol that adds security and authentication to documents sent via e-mail. (See also *MIME*.)

Snail Mail—An irreverent reference to standard paper-based postal mail from those on the Internet used to the speed of e-mail.

Sysop (*system operator*)—The individual who does the hands-on work of being sure a computer system, or some portion of it, is operating correctly. Sometimes called "sysgod" in jest.

TCP/IP (*Transmission Control Protocol/Internet Protocol*)—The agreed-on set of computer communications rules and standards that allows communications between different types of computers and networks that are connected to the Internet.

Telnet—(Also called remote login.) A system that allows access to remote computers on the Internet. Many of the features of the remote computer can then be used as if your personal computer or terminal was directly connected to it. (See Appendix E.)

Terminal Emulator—Communications software that can make itself "appear" to another computer as if it were a specific type of terminal. Some common terminals that are emulated are VT100, VT52, and ANSI. (See Appendix A.)

Thread—Within Usenet newsgroups and topical discussion groups, a thread is one of several subdiscussions. For instance, in a forestry discussion group there may be ongoing discussions of old growth forests, the spotted owl, forest fires, etc. Each thread is started with an original posting, which others follow up on using the same subject name preceded by "RE:". (See Chapter 13.)

TN-3270—Telnet software that provides IBM full screen support.

UNIX—An operating system, widely used on the Internet, developed by AT&T Bell Laboratories, that supports multiuser and multitasking operations.

Uploading—File transfers from your local computer to a remote one. (See *Downloading* and Appendix C.)

URL (*Uniform Resource Locator*)—An addressing system that can uniquely name most files found on the Internet. It includes a protocol name (such as *gopher* or *http*), plus a site name (such as *world.std.com*) and subdirectory path (such as */pub/software/msdos/*), and a file name (such as *newsletter.html*) Example: *ftp://ftp.std.com/pub/oakridge/newsletter.txt*.

Usenet Newsgroups (*Netnews*)—Thousands of discussion groups that use newsreader software and servers (different than the listserver e-mail–based discussion group system). (See Chapter 13.)

User Name—A short name (with no spaces allowed), unique to you on your Internet access provider's system. Sometimes it is assigned, sometimes you can select your own. This user name (or ID) followed by your site name becomes your e-mail address. For example, if Ben Franklin had an account at world.std.com, and he chose a user name of bfranklin, his e-mail address would be *bfranklin@world.std.com*.

UUCP (*Unix-to-Unix Copy Program*)—A protocol used for communication between consenting UNIX systems.

VAX—Hardware produced by the Digital Equipment Corporation, in use by some sites on the Internet. The VMS operating system is used on VAX computers.

Veronica—A client/server system that provides a way to search for a particular word of interest in all Gopher menus, at all Gopher sites known to the Veronica server database. (See Chapter 14.)

Virtual Reality—Any of various combinations of user interface features that permit a user to interact with a computer or system in a manner that more closely mimics how humans normally operate in the real world—may include use of speech synthesis, speech recognition, three-dimensional graphics, hand and head position sensors, etc.

Virtual Storefront—An online business presence for online sales. This is usually accomplished through use of Web pages. The pages display information about the products, often including pictures. Information on ordering is also given, and/or an on-screen input form is displayed to take the customer's order.

VRML (Virtual Reality Modeling Language)—A document encoding protocol that provides for robust audio, video, and interactive elements.

VT100—Originally a type of terminal used by DEC (Digital Equipment Corporation). Now, a widely used terminal standard on the Internet that is often emulated by communications software.

WWW (World Wide Web)—Initially created in Switzerland, WWW is a client/server system designed to use hypertext and hypermedia documents via the Internet. It uses the HTTP (hypertext transfer protocol) to exchange documents and images. The documents are formatted in HTML (hypertext markup language). (See Chapter 2 for more information.)

Index